THE ISLAMIC–BYZANTINE BORDER IN HISTORY

THE ISLAMIC–BYZANTINE BORDER IN HISTORY

From the Rise of Islam to the End of the Crusades

Edited by
D. G. Tor and
Alexander D. Beihammer

EDINBURGH
University Press

Edinburgh University Press is one of the leading university presses in the UK. We publish academic books and journals in our selected subject areas across the humanities and social sciences, combining cutting-edge scholarship with high editorial and production values to produce academic works of lasting importance. For more information visit our website: edinburghuniversitypress.com

Edinburgh University Press Ltd
13 Infirmary Street
Edinburgh EH1 1LT

First published in hardback by Edinburgh University Press 2023

Typeset in 11/15 Adobe Garamond by
IDSUK (DataConnection) Ltd

A CIP record for this book is available from the British Library

ISBN 978 1 3995 1302 9 (hardback)
ISBN 978 1 3995 1303 6 (paperback)
ISBN 978 1 3995 1304 3 (webready PDF)
ISBN 978 1 3995 1305 0 (epub)

CONTENTS

List of Illustrations vii
Notes on Contributors ix
Acknowledgements xiii

Introduction 1
D. G. Tor and Alexander D. Beihammer

1 The Historical Significance of the Islamic–Byzantine Border: From the Seventh Century to 1291 11
D. G. Tor

2 The Byzantine–Muslim Frontier from the Arab Conquests to the Arrival of the Seljuk Turks 33
Alexander D. Beihammer

3 The Formation of *al-ʿAwāṣim* 71
Hugh Kennedy

4 Caucasian Elites between Byzantium and the Caliphate in the Early Islamic Period 78
Robert G. Hoyland

5 Byzantine Borders were State Artefacts, not 'Fluid Zones of Interaction' 100
Anthony Kaldellis

6 A Christian Insurgency in Islamic Syria: The Jarājima (Mardaites) between Byzantium and the Caliphate 125
Christian C. Sahner

7 The Character of Umayyad Art: the Mediterranean Tradition 166
Robert Hillenbrand

8 Byzantine Heroes and Saints of the Arab–Byzantine Border (Ninth–Tenth Centuries) 204
Sophie Métivier

9 A Cosmopolitan Frontier State: The Marwānids of Diyār Bakr, 990–1085, and the Performance of Power 226
Carole Hillenbrand

10 Byzantine Population Policy in the Eastern Borderland between Byzantium and the Caliphate from the Seventh to the Twelfth Centuries 243
Ralph-Johannes Lilie

11 The Islamic–Byzantine Frontier in Seljuq Anatolia 265
A. C. S. Peacock

Selected Bibliography 291
Index 311

ILLUSTRATIONS

Maps

4.1	Early Medieval Caucasia	79
4.2	Byzantine, Umayyad and Khazar spheres of control in Caucasia in the mid-eighth century	89

Figures

7.1	Jerusalem, Dome of the Rock, exterior	173
7.2	Jerusalem, Holy Sepulchre, reconstruction of its fourth-century form	174
7.3	Jerusalem, Holy Sepulchre and adjacent basilica, reconstruction	175
7.4	Jerusalem, Ḥaram al-Sharīf, aerial view	175
7.5	ʿAnjar, reconstruction	176
7.6	Timgad, Algeria, aerial view	176
7.7	ʿAnjar, main street	177
7.8	Quṣair ʿAmra, exterior	178
7.9	Leptis Magna, hunting baths	178
7.10	Qaṣr al-Ḥair al-Gharbī, model	182
7.11	Pompeii, villa of the Vettii	183
7.12	Qaṣr al-Ḥair al-Gharbī, gateway	184
7.13	Haghia Sophia, scroll in vault of upper room	185

7.14 Jerusalem, Dome of the Rock, drum 186
7.15 Mshattā, façade 187
7.16 Leptis Magna, triumphal arch of Septimius Severus, reconstruction 188
7.17 Khirbat al-Mafjar, bath hall, portal, reconstruction 189
7.18 Qaṣr al-Ḥair al-Gharbī, floor painting 191
7.19 Qaṣr al-Ḥair al-Gharbī, painted walls 193
7.20 Khirbat al-Mafjar, bath hall, axonometric view 195
7.21 Haghia Sophia, capital with monogram 197
7.22 Al-Muwaqqar, inscribed column and capital 198
7.23 *Dīnār* of ʿAbd al-Malik 199
7.24 Khirbat al-Mafjar, bath hall, central mosaic 201
9.1 Map of the Marwānid territories, 990–1 to 1085–6 228
9.2 Two views of a tower on the walls of Mayyāfāriqīn 233
9.3 Two views of the exterior of the Friday Mosque of Mayyāfāriqīn 234
9.4 Drawing of an inscription in the name of Naṣr al-Dawla at Āmid, 437/1045–6 235

NOTES ON CONTRIBUTORS

Alexander D. Beihammer is Heiden Family College Professor of History at the University of Notre Dame, specialising in Byzantine History. His books include *Byzantium and the Emergence of Muslim–Turkish Anatolia, ca. 1040–1130* (2019); with Maria Parani and Christoph Schabel, *Diplomatics in the Eastern Mediterranean 1000–1500: Aspects of Cross-cultural Communication* (2008); and *Quellenkritische Untersuchungen Zu Den Agyptischen Kapitulationsvertragen Der Jahre 640–646* (2000).

Carole Hillenbrand was educated at the Universities of Cambridge, Oxford and Edinburgh. She was Professor of Islamic History, Edinburgh University, 2000–8, and is now Professor Emerita of Islamic History, Edinburgh since 2008. She was Professorial Fellow (Islamic History), St Andrews University, 2013–21 and is now Honorary Professor there. She has been Visiting Professor at Dartmouth College, New Hampshire, USA, Groningen University, The Netherlands and St Louis University, USA. She was awarded the King Faisal International Prize in Islamic Studies in 2005 (the first non-Muslim and the first woman to receive this prize) and the British Academy/Nayef Al-Rodhan Prize for Transcultural Understanding in 2016. She has published eight single-authored books, four edited books, two translated books, and over seventy articles on Islamic history and thought. She was given the award of Commander of the British Empire (for Encouraging Inter-Faith Relations) by Queen Elizabeth II in 2018, and she received a DLitt (Honorary Doctorate of Letters) at the University of St Andrews in 2022.

Robert Hillenbrand is currently Honorary Professor of Art History at the University of St Andrews and Honorary Professorial Fellow at the University of Edinburgh. Educated at the universities of Cambridge and Oxford (DPhil 1974), he was a chaired Professor of Islamic Art at the University of Edinburgh until his retirement in 2007. Hillenbrand has written numerous books, including *Islamic Art and Architecture*, *Studies in Medieval Islamic Art and Architecture* (2021, 2 vols) and the prize-winning *Islamic Architecture: Form, Function and Meaning* (Edinburgh University Press, 2000, translated into Persian). He has also edited, among many volumes, *The Art of the Saljuqs in Iran and Anatolia* (2022), *Persian Painting from the Mongols to the Qajars* (2001) and *Image and Meaning in Islamic Art* (2005). Hillenbrand has also served on the editorial boards of numerous journals, including *Art History*, *Persica*, *Assaph*, *Bulletin of the Asia Institute* and *Oxford Studies in Islamic Art*. He has also served on the Councils of the British School of Archaeology in Jerusalem, British Research in the Levant, and the British Institute of Persian Studies (Vice-President). He is a Fellow of the British Academy.

Robert G. Hoyland is Professor of the late antique and early Islamic history of the Middle East at New York University's Institute for the Study of the Ancient World. He is the author of a number of publications on the culture, both material and intellectual, of this pivotal region in world history, including *Seeing Islam as Others Saw It* (1997), *Arabia and the Arabs* (2001) and *In God's Path: The Arab Conquests and the Creation of an Islamic Empire* (2014). He has also conducted fieldwork in many countries of the Middle East, and is currently involved in the excavation of a Christian and Muslim settlement in the modern United Arab Emirates that played a long-term role in Indian Ocean trade.

Anthony Kaldellis is Professor of Classics at the University of Chicago. His research explores the history, culture and literature of the east Roman empire – aka 'Byzantium' – from antiquity to the fifteenth century. His research has focused on the reception of ancient Greek and Roman ideas, and he has also translated many Byzantine texts into English. He has just finished a comprehensive history of east Rome from Constantine the Great to Mehmed Fatih, which embeds social, economic, religious and demographic developments within a lively narrative framework.

Hugh Kennedy is Professor of Arabic at SOAS, University of London. From 1997 to 2007, he was Professor of Middle Eastern History at the University of St Andrews. He is a Fellow of the Royal Society of Edinburgh, a Fellow of the British Academy, and a Fellow of the Royal Asiatic Society. His numerous books include *The Early Abbasid Caliphate: A Political History* (2015), *The Prophet and the Age of the Caliphs* (2015), *Muslim Spain and Portugal* (2016), *The Armies of the Caliphs: Military and Society in the Early Islamic State* (2001) and *The Court of the Caliphs* (2005).

Ralph-Johannes Lilie was Professor for Byzantinology at the Free University Berlin and at the Ludwig-Maximilian-University in Munich. Between 1992 and 2013 he also worked at the Academy of Sciences, Berlin, where he directed the research project *Prosopographie der mittelbyzantinischen Zeit (641–1025)* which was published 2013 in print and online. His publications on Byzantine political, economical and cultural history, as well as on Byzantine historiography, include numerous articles and several books including *Die byzantinische Reaktion auf die Ausbreitung der Araber* (1976), *Byzantium and the Crusader States* (1994), *Byzanz. Das zweite Rom* (2003) and *Einführung in die byzantinische Geschichte* (2007).

Sophie Métivier is Professor of Byzantine History at the University of Paris I Panthéon-Sorbonne. She works on the social and political history of the Byzantine empire and on the history of holiness during meso-byzantine times. Published works include two monographs, *La Cappadoce (IV–VIe siècle): Une histoire provinciale de l'empire d'Orient* (2005) and *Aristocratie et sainteté à Byzance (VIIIe–XIe siècle)* (2019).

A. C. S. Peacock is Professor of Middle Eastern and Islamic History at the University of St Andrews and is a Fellow of the British Academy. Recent publications include *Islam, Literature and Society in Mongol Anatolia* (2019) and *The Great*

Seljuk Empire (Edinburgh University Press, 2015). His research interests include the impact of nomadic peoples upon the Islamic world and Islamic manuscripts.

Christian C. Sahner (PhD, Princeton University, 2015) is an associate professor of Islamic history at the University of Oxford and a fellow of St Cross College. His recent publications include *Christian Martyrs under Islam* (2018) and *Conversion to Islam in the Pre-Modern Age* (2020, co-editor). He is currently working on the history of religious and political movements in the mountains of the medieval Islamic world, as well as the history of early medieval Zoroastrianism and its relationship with Islam.

D. G. Tor is Associate Professor of History at the University of Notre Dame, specialising in the history of the pre-thirteenth century medieval Middle East and Central Asia. Tor's publications include the books *Violent Order: Religious Warfare, Chivalry, and the ʿAyyār Phenomenon in the Medieval Islamic World* (2007); *The ʿAbbasid and Carolingian Empires: Studies in Civilizational Formation* (2017); together with A. C. S. Peacock, *Medieval Central Asia and the Persianate World: Iranian Tradition and Islamic Civilisation* (2015) and, with Minoru Inaba, *The History and Culture of Iran and Central Asia: From the Pre-Islamic to the Islamic Period* (2022). Tor has won numerous major research grants and awards, including fellowships from the National Endowment for the Humanities; the Institute for Advanced Study, Princeton; the American Council of Learned Societies; the American Institute of Afghanistan Studies; the Israel Institute for Advanced Studies; and Harvard University. Tor is also the Medieval History editor of the journal *Iranian Studies.*

ACKNOWLEDGEMENTS

The germ of this volume was a conference held at the University of Notre Dame in April 2019. The authors are grateful to the Institute for Scholarship in the Liberal Arts; The Medieval Institute and its director, Thomas Burman; and The Program in Byzantine Studies, for their generous funding of that gathering.

Additionally, the lion's share of the work on this book was undertaken while D. G. Tor was on research leave as a year-long Fellow at the Israel Institute for Advanced Studies, Jerusalem, whose essential support is gratefully acknowledged.

INTRODUCTION

D. G. Tor and Alexander D. Beihammer

The academic study of borders and borderlands, especially the historical study of the subject, has been a well-tilled field in recent decades, resulting in a plethora of conferences and studies. To a certain degree, of course, anyone studying an empire with the history and geopolitical situation of Byzantium, or one with the expansionist drive and history of the Islamic oecumene, has always of necessity to some degree treated the relevant empire's borders and their historical significance and influence. But the historical study of borderlands in recent years – and certainly collaborative efforts in volumes such as the one you are now reading – has tended to take one of two forms: either the overly atomised, divorced from a larger historical context and the tradition in which it was embedded, or the overly generalised and amorphous.

The study of borderlands today has also seen its task as something different from that of traditional frontier history; this intellectual trend is given voice in the following passage, written in the context of American history:

> If frontiers were the places where we once told our master . . . narratives, then borderlands are the places where those narratives come unraveled. They are ambiguous and often-unstable realms where boundaries are also crossroads, peripheries are also central places, homelands are also passing-through places,

> and the end points of empire are also forks in the road. If frontiers are spaces of narrative closure, then borderlands are places where stories take unpredictable turns and rarely end as expected.[1]

One might say that whereas the study of borderlands in the past often involved seeing only the forest at the expense of the trees, today's practice of borderland history runs the danger of committing the opposite error: of failing to see any forest at all, and of focusing only on isolated trees and groves. Obviously, a careful historian should, ideally, not only examine minutely the individual grove within the forest, but also not lose sight of the greater context of the forest, and even the larger region in which the grove finds itself.

Alongside this modern-day tendency to study a borderland in isolation from the civilisation of which it formed a part, an opposite tendency has also manifested itself in attempts to arrive at overarching theoretical constructs deemed to be valid in all places and times, in all borderlands – what one might call a Newtonian Law of borderlands. Such attempts are invariably predicated, though, upon certain modern Western ideological suppositions, especially the norm of the modern, centralised nation state.[2] The irrelevance of such assumptions should be patently clear to the historian of pre-modern times, when not only were there no nation states, but there was no 'state' at all in the centralised, highly bureaucratised, modern sense of the term, and the values, priorities, outlooks, and assumptions of the people living in those times and places differed so markedly from those of the present day.

Among the plethora of conferences and studies devoted to the subject of borderlands, moreover, there have been surprisingly few attempts among scholars of the medieval world to employ standard historical methodology by focusing on one specific border over time, and studying the significance of that border in depth, within the historical context and cultural tradition to

[1] Pekka Hämäläinen and Samuel Truett, 'On Borderlands', *Journal of American History* 98 (2011), 338.

[2] A representative nation-state-centric study of this type is Michiel Baud and Willem van Schendel, 'Toward a Comparative History of Borderlands', *Journal of World History* 8 (1997), 211–42.

which it belonged; and the editors of the present volume can recall no previous such attempt at all with regard to the Islamic–Byzantine border in the pre-Ottoman period, on anything greater than the scale of an individual article. Yet this particular border, and the confrontation and interaction between two world civilisations which took place upon it, was, quite simply, one of the most formative areas and periods in both Mediterranean history and in the history of Muslim–Christian relations.

This book, in short, undertakes something never before essayed: a collaborative volume, including contributions from both Byzantinist and Islamicist scholars, dedicated solely to the examination of the Islamic–Byzantine border and borderlands, and covering the large span of time stretching from the rise of Islam in the seventh century until the fall of the last Crusader principality in the Levant shortly before the year AD 1300, with the aim of elucidating some of the most significant ramifications the history of this specific border had upon the course of both internal and trans-civilisational religious and cultural development. This volume should therefore be viewed as a pioneering effort, rather than the final word on the subject; while it ranges far and wide in time, space, and theme, there remain of course innumerable areas for further exploration and explication, not least because our primary concern was answering the research question of how the existence of the Islamic–Byzantine border influenced above all the internal developments of each of the two respective civilisations or cultural worlds which shared it.

The first two chapters, **D. G. Tor**'s 'The Historical Significance of the Islamic–Byzantine Border: From the Seventh Century to 1291' and **Alexander Beihammer**'s 'The Byzantine–Muslim Frontier from the Arab Conquests to the Arrival of the Seljuk Turks', provide civilisationally specific overviews of the history of the Islamic–Byzantine border and the major relevant historiography. Tor's article then delivers an overview of the cultural importance and influence of that border within Islamic civilisation over the centuries treated in this volume, while Beihammer's contains a critical discussion of the historiographical discourse and future directions for research.

Hugh Kennedy's chapter on 'The Formation of *al-ʿAwāṣim*' examines one of the two terms that appear constantly in early Islamic sources regarding the Islamic–Byzantine border and its special organisation and status within the early caliphate: the border hinterlands known as '*al-ʿAwāṣim*', an administrative concept created under Hārūn al-Rashīd, the caliph most famously preoccupied with jihad on the Islamic–Byzantine border, as recorded in ninth- and tenth-century sources. The chapter elucidates clearly, for the first time, the actual meaning of the term, demonstrating that it refers to reserved or protected property, and showing that the *ʿAwāṣim* of Syria had, not a military role, but rather a fiscal and administrative one: the Barmakids set aside the revenues of the *ʿAwāṣim* in order to fund and finance the strengthening (through e.g. the building and repair of fortifications) of the actual border areas, the *thughūr*. The later works which constitute our earliest sources on this institution, which claim that the term *ʿAwāṣim* refers to a defensive hinterland which served as a refuge and defensive retreat for Muslim armies at the border, had clearly forgotten the original meaning of the term, and seem to have provided what seemed to them a likely explanation, thereby inventing the unhistorical trope of *ʿAwāṣim* as a military area, rather than understanding them as what they were: administrative tax zones whose revenues financed the fortifications and military needs of the actual border zones, the *thughūr*.

Robert Hoyland's chapter, 'Caucasian Elites between Byzantium and the Caliphate in the Early Islamic Period', deals with the Caucasian borderland situated between the Byzantine and Islamic empires in the East Caucasus, referred to by modern scholars as Caucasian Albania and called Arrān in the Arabic sources. It first supplies an overview of the history of the area prior to the rise of Islam, and then focuses on the struggle for the Caucasus between Byzantium and Islam. After giving an exposition of the history of the region in Umayyad times, the chapter traces the growing Muslim incorporation of the Caucasus within the Islamic empire beginning in the mid-eighth century; the settlement of Arabs in the area; the lordship of Caucasian Albania in the ninth century; and the complex history of the area and its political fragmentation from the mid-tenth through mid-eleventh centuries. Throughout, it traces the continuing role of Christian elites, even under Muslim rulers.

The article demonstrates that the loss of status of the late Roman elites of Syria in the early Islamic period is not true of the Caucasus, where the deeds and dicta of their princes, lords, and nobles fill the pages of our historical texts concerning this region. In part, this is because of its distance from the imperial centres in Syria and Iraq and its mountainous topography, and in part because of its proximity to the empires of the Byzantines and Khazars, whom the local chiefs could call upon for support, or play divide and rule between them and the agents of the Caliphate. On the downside, this meant that imperial actors would meddle in the affairs of Caucasian leaders or force them to support the imperial actors against their enemies, which frequently placed these local potentates in a difficult position between the dominant powers.

Anthony Kaldellis's chapter, 'Byzantine Borders were State Artefacts, not "Fluid Zones of Interaction"', addresses a historiographical trend of recent decades, in which certain claims have been advanced about the Roman and early Byzantine imperial borders: namely, that the empire had no clear or fixed borders – or even no concept of a border to begin with; that there was no expectation that the borders could or should be defended, and no actual ability to do so; that there was no concept of territorial integrity; that the border was always permeable, porous, and fluid; that there was no imperial strategy for the defence of the empire; and that features of the natural terrain were not used or even imagined as borders or as marking the border. Not all of these theses have been advanced in the same publications, but as a coherent constellation they have given rise to a revolutionary understanding of the imperial borders that is often encapsulated in the catchphrase 'fluid zones of interaction'.

This chapter shows, on the contrary, from primary source evidence, that borders were not zones of fluid contact: they were zones of state-regulated contact, which could be more open or more closed depending on policy. There was, of course, a great deal of movement of peoples, goods, and ideas across them; but this by itself does not refute the existence of borders or make them fluid. Borders exist if and only if a state authority has the ability to intervene and regulate or restrict that movement. That is what a border is, and there is every indication that the Roman-Byzantine state had the infrastructural capability to turn that spigot one way or the other.

Christian Sahner's chapter, 'A Christian Insurgency in Islamic Syria: The Jarājima (Mardaites) between Byzantium and the Caliphate', examines the group of mountain Christians, known as Jarājima in Arabic and as Mardaites in Greek, composed largely of bandits and mercenaries, who helped the Byzantines reestablish control over the coastal highlands between Antioch and Jerusalem at the end of the seventh century. Although their success was short-lived, the Jarājima managed to create a Christian guerilla zone on the doorstep of the Umayyads' most important province. In the process, they terrified caliphs, gave hope to emperors, and left a deep impression on the historical record of the period.

This chapter, first, establishes a clear chronology for the Jarājima from the time they first appear in the historical record during the Arab conquest of the 630s, to their last gasp as a militarised movement during the little-studied revolt of Theodore in 759–60. Second, it explores the afterlife of the Jarājima until the tenth century, when for all intents and purposes they disappear from the historical radar. Third, the chapter answers some of the outstanding questions about the Jarājima, showing that they were probably Chalcedonian, Aramaic-speaking locals from Syria's coastal mountains, without a strong ideological programme. Fourth, the chapter places the Jarājima within their wider historical context beyond Syria and the Byzantine frontier, examining, for instance, the rarity of post-Conquest Byzantine revivalism with the ubiquity of Sasanian revivalism; nativist unrest throughout the young Islamic Empire during this period; and the reasons underlying the rarity of Christian insurgencies versus those of other denominations. Finally, the chapter shows how, and the manner in which, the border location of the Jarājima played a critical role in their success.

Robert Hillenbrand's 'The Character of Umayyad Art: The Mediterranean Tradition', is an attempt to explain what happened when Umayyad art came to grips with the pictorial heritage of Byzantium and, further back, of the Graeco-Roman classical world. The period when this encounter took place is short – AD 661–750 – but the pace of change was extraordinarily rapid and intense. During this period, Greater Syria was transformed by glamorous religious buildings such as the Dome of the Rock in Jerusalem and the Great Mosque of Damascus, and by massive investment in the countryside in the form of hydraulic installations, villas, hunting lodges and luxurious 'desert palaces'. In all of this work the classical heritage, embodied by Byzantium itself as the principal remaining rival of the Umayyad state, forms the most important constituent element.

The bulk of this chapter is an attempt to identify the underlying processes which shaped Umayyad art. Three stages emerge with some clarity: imitation, adaptation, and transformation. Each stage is explored in some detail, and illustrated with examples taken from a remarkable variety of media: architecture, with its sister arts of painting, sculpture and mosaic; but also textiles, coins, manuscripts, and metalwork. Iconography also plays a major role. The art of this century takes the Graeco-Roman, early Christian and Byzantine heritage down many unexpected paths, with its time-honoured conventions variously copied, adapted and thoroughly reworked in accordance with a constantly evolving aesthetic. That aesthetic used not only Graeco-Roman art but also the various subsets of Byzantine art – Italian, Balkan, Syrian and Egyptian among them – in unprecedented ways. The chapter concludes by showing how Umayyad art, while rooted in the Mediterranean world, and thus using visual idioms instinctively familiar to a Western observer, nevertheless found its own distinctive voice by 750, creating a foundation on which all later Islamic art rests.

Sophie Métivier's contribution, 'Byzantine Heroes and Saints of the Arab–Byzantine Border (Ninth–Tenth Centuries)', shows that much of the modern scholarly conception of the Islamic–Byzantine borderland as a bilingual, even bicultural, frontier society, a separate cultural space of its own between two civilisations, is actually predicated upon the heroic romance of the border warrior *Digenis Akritas* and similar compositions and their respective heroes, especially in their chronologically later forms, many of which were produced in Constantinople. Many previous scholars have therefore concluded that the heroic border epic was merely a Constantinopolitan production, a vehicle used to legitimise and justify the ascension of aristocratic families in the capital city who were descendants of the commanders glorified in these border epics.

This chapter analyses the development of the heroic border epic tradition in the ninth and tenth centuries, especially those connected with hagiographic lives of militant saints, such as Antony the Younger, in order to show that this consensus is certainly wrong, at least regarding the border epics of this period, which are demonstrably not Constantinopolitan fabrications, confected to honour an aristocratic progenitor. Rather, the development of these heroes takes place within the context of the territorial expansion of the Byzantine empire; the heroes portrayed in these stories are heroes of the conquests/reconquests, not resistance fighters.

Carole Hillenbrand's chapter, 'A Cosmopolitan Frontier State: The Marwānids of Diyār Bakr, 990–1085, and the Performance of Power', constitutes a detailed examination of the Marwanid Dynasty of Diyar Bakr, one of a number of small dynasties that appeared in northern Syria, Diyar Bakr and Armenia, territories which lay near or on the eastern borders of the Byzantine empire or the fringes of the Fatimid empire, in the wake of the dissolution and fragmentation of Abbasid power in the tenth and eleventh centuries. The Marwanid polity, like the other small states which appeared in these border areas, was ethnically diverse; its peoples spoke Arabic, Armenian, Kurdish, Persian or Turkish. The Marwanid Dynasty which forms the subject of this chapter, is intriguing to the historian: first, because it relied on Kurdish nomadic groups for its power; and, furthermore, because it is uniquely well-chronicled in the neglected history *Taʾīkh Mayyāfāriqīn wa-Āmid* of Ibn al-Azraq al-Fāriqī (d. after 1176–7), which focuses especially upon the statecraft of the ruler Nāṣir al-Dawla (r. 1079–85), and how he was able to cultivate a small oasis of prosperity amidst the larger imperial geopolitics of the time.

The next chapter, **Ralph-Johannes Lilie**'s 'Byzantine Population Policy in the Eastern Borderland between Byzantium and the Caliphate from the Seventh through the Twelfth Centuries', focuses on the problem the Byzantines had controlling their border with the Islamic world, and the measures they took to remedy the problem. The chapter identifies four strategies that the Byzantines employed in their border with the Islamic world, and the drawbacks each entailed: (1) Garrisoning the border with additional troops, strengthening existing fortifications and building new ones. This strategy of course did not offer a plan for what to do when the enemy broke through the fortified line and began ravaging the hinterland. (2) Devastating the border region, transforming it into a kind of no-man's-land that would make it more difficult for the enemy to cross the area. The drawback of this method is that this region would be lost for any military or economic utilisation, and its erstwhile population would be dislocated. (3) Strengthening the region's economics, infrastructure and population by creating or supporting small buffer states or semi-independent local forces on both sides of the border. Obviously, this would create a problem of its own, as the Byzantine authorities might find it difficult to control independently-minded minor local powers, especially in times of need. (4) The final, extreme option was to abandon the whole region and to retreat into the interior provinces. This option of retreat did not really solve the problem of border defence, since the former hinterland would become the new border region, with the same problems as before.

Over the centuries the Byzantines tried each of these options, either individually or in tandem. This chapter analyses the methods and effects of each particular policy at the Islamic–Byzantine border, from the rise of Islam through the thirteenth century, showing that policy towards populations at the border was in constant flux, and depended more upon conditions in Constantinople than on events at the border.

Finally, **A. C. S. Peacock**'s chapter, 'The Islamic–Byzantine Frontier in Seljuq Anatolia', addresses the nature of the Islamic–Byzantine frontier in the thirteenth century – the post-Abbasid period before the Ottomans – with the aim, not of describing the frontier, but rather of considering how it was perceived from the Seljuq point of view, particularly regarding the role the Byzantine frontier played in the mental worlds of the educated populations of places such as Konya, the Seljuq capital. Muslim Anatolia in the thirteenth century makes an important case study, not only because it was a period of relative stability on the frontier between Byzantium and the Muslims, but also because it is the earliest period to be adequately attested in the Arabic and Persian sources from Anatolia, which barely exist for the first century of Turkish domination. The thirteenth century also represents the zenith of the territorial extent of the Seljuq state in Anatolia, although after their defeat at Kösedağ in 1243, the sultanate survived only as a vassal of the Mongols, until its final disappearance in 1307.

The chapter examines the concept of the frontier, as well as accounts of frontier warfare, in Seljuq literary texts, concluding that, on the whole, the evidence presented suggests that, contrary to expectations, at least from the beginning of the thirteenth century, the Islamic–Byzantine frontier was of relatively limited importance to the Islamic side. The relative lack of military activity on the Seljuq–Byzantine frontier is indicative of the fact that the Seljuqs stood to gain little from battling Byzantium over the Anatolian countryside: they were already a well-established principality, and had no need to establish their legitimacy anymore; rather, they saw themselves as a major Islamic power, whose prestige was to be enhanced by asserting suzerainty over the Muslim-ruled lands of the Jazira and even Syria. It was not until the rise of Ottoman power in the fourteenth century that the Islamic frontier with Byzantium would again assume major political and ideological importance.

As can be seen from the above summary, this book explores a very broad range of the manifold facets of the Islamic–Byzantine border during the historically important period that began with the Early Islamic Conquests and drew to a close with the end of the Crusading era, and endeavours to elucidate the border's significance, shifting and fluctuating over the course of time, within the religious, cultural, military, political, and economic life of both the Byzantine and Islamic worlds. There remain, of course, a virtually unlimited number of areas and issues awaiting elucidation; it is our hope that this volume will provide not only a useful shedding of light upon this particular border, and its importance during these centuries, but also an impetus for further research and discussion.

D. G. Tor
Alexander Beihammer
The University of Notre Dame
Notre Dame, Indiana

1

THE HISTORICAL SIGNIFICANCE OF THE ISLAMIC–BYZANTINE BORDER: FROM THE SEVENTH CENTURY TO 1291

D. G. Tor

Few borders throughout human history have possessed such significance, over the course of so many centuries, as that which lay between the Islamic and Eastern Roman (Byzantine) worlds – or, viewed through the religious eyes of the Middle Ages, the Muslim oecumene and Christendom. This border first formed with the rise of Islam in the mid-seventh century, and vanished only in 1453, at the final resolution of the long struggle with the victory of the Islamic side in the Muslim conquest of Constantinople and the end of the Eastern Roman Empire. But it is neither temporal perdurance nor symbolism alone that imparts significance to this particular border; for one of the more salient and original features of this border was its long-lasting import, not merely in its political or military aspects, and its dimension of inter-civilisational struggle, but also in its religious and cultural effect upon the development of the internal life of both civilisations. It captured the imagination and the attention of the cultures on either side of the border in a way that, for instance, the contemporaneous Islamic border with the sub-Saharan African world did not.

As with all such borders, moreover, the Islamic–Byzantine frontier not only divided the two rival civilisations, but also brought them into contact with each other, to their mutual enrichment. One of the more neglected aspects of the history of the Islamic–Byzantine border is the ways in which it influenced unique internal developments within each of the surrounding civilisations, in the period from the inception of the Islamic–Byzantine border in the seventh century through to the end of the age of the Crusades, with the fall of the last Crusader polity in the Levant shortly before the year AD 1300.

Historical Overview

The era of Late Antiquity which preceded the rise of the Islamic Empire and the Islamic–Byzantine border was formed by three elements: (1) Diocletian's administrative division of the Roman Empire in the third century into Eastern and Western empires, and the rise of the Sasanian Empire in the Middle East;[1] (2) the Christianisation of the Roman Empire in the fourth century, and the hammering out over the course of the succeeding centuries, through religious controversies and councils, of the major Christian doctrines, both Orthodox and dissenting;[2] and (3) the centuries-long war,

[1] On which see, for the division of the Empire, among the relevant sea of works, Gillian Clark, *Late Antiquity: A Very Short Introduction* (Oxford: Oxford University Press, 2019); Averil Cameron, *The Mediterranean World in Late Antiquity, AD 395–600* (London: Routledge, 1993), 1–12, 30–46; Peter Brown, *The World of Late Antiquity AD 150–750* (New York: W. W. Norton and Company, 1971), 11–27, who attributes the changes in Rome to a 'military revolution' which saved it (p. 24). For the rise of the Sasanians, see Touraj Daryaee, *Sasanian Persia: The Rise and Fall of an Empire* (London: I. B. Tauris, 2010), 1–39; Richard Frye, 'The Political History of Iran under the Sasanians', in Ehsan Yarshater (ed.), *The Cambridge History of Iran. Volume 3 (1): The Seleucid, Parthian, and Sasanian Periods* (Cambridge: Cambridge University Press, 1983), 116–80.

[2] On the Christianisation of the Empire, and its doctrinal developments, see Cameron, *The Later Roman Empire AD 284–430* (Cambridge, MA: Harvard University Press, 1993), 47–84; A. H. M. Jones, *Constantine and the Conversion of Europe* (Toronto: University of Toronto Press and The Medieval Academy of America, 1978); Cameron, *Mediterranean World*, 57–75; Henry Chadwick, *The Early Church* (New York: Penguin, 1993), 54–236, is especially good for a summary of the major theological disputes, on which see also Pauline Allen, 'The Definition and Enforcement of Orthodoxy', in A. Cameron *et al.* (eds), *The Cambridge Ancient History. Volume XIV: Late Antiquity: Empire and Successors, A.D. 425–600* (Cambridge: Cambridge University Press, 2000), 811–34; and Henry Chadwick, *East and West: The Making of a Rift in the Church* (Oxford: Oxford University Press, 1993), 2–63.

ongoing between the Hellenistic and Near Eastern worlds since Antiquity, and instantiated in Late Antiquity in the virtually continual war between the Eastern Roman Empire and the Sasanian or Persian Empire–a precursor and foreshadowing, in some respects, of the succeeding Byzantine–Islamic struggle.[3]

The areas which eventually formed the Islamic–Byzantine borderlands – first Syria, and then later Anatolia – were the ancient cultural heartlands of the Eastern Roman Empire. Christianity, of course, arose in Syria, and two of the five bishoprics of the Pentarchy that held primacy in the Church – namely, Jerusalem and Antioch – were located in Syria. Antioch, in fact, was until the Islamic Conquest one of the great cities of the Eastern Roman Empire, second in importance only to Constantinople.[4] It is therefore unsurprising that the Byzantines, up until the eleventh century, never accepted the Muslim conquest of this city as permanent. After the initial Islamic conquests, the Byzantines launched numerous counter-offensives to regain their lost lands, the most successful of which culminated by 969 in the regaining of Tarsus (which had become the leading centre of Muslim border warfare), Cyprus, Aleppo, and Antioch itself; indeed, by 975 the Byzantine *reconquista*

[3] See Mark Whittow, 'The late Roman/early Byzantine Near East', in Chase Robinson (ed.), *The New Cambridge History of Islam. Volume 1: The Formation of the Islamic World, Sixth to Eleventh Centuries* (Cambridge: Cambridge University Press, 2010), 81–93; Josef Wiesehöfer, 'The late Sasanian Near East', in ibid., 139–50.

[4] For a good overview of Antioch and its role in Late Antiquity, see the relevant chapters in the classic work, Glanville Downey, *Ancient Antioch* (Princeton: Princeton University Press, 1963), 200–78; on the situation of Antioch immediately prior to the Muslim invasion, and especially on the possible influence of the Justinianic plague in Antioch and its environs, see Hugh Kennedy and J. H. W. G. Liebeschuetz, 'Antioch and the Villages of Northern Syria in the Fifth and Sixth Centuries A.D.: Trend and Problem', *Nottingham Medieval Studies* 32 (1988), 65–90 – although Peregrine Horden ('Mediterranean Plague in the Age of Justinian', in Michael Maas (ed.), *The Cambridge Companion to the Age of Justinian* (Cambridge: Cambridge University Press, 2006), 134–60) rightly takes issue with the term itself, and prefers instead the name 'Early Medieval Pandemic'. Muslim authors were well aware of the religious importance of the Patriarchate of Antioch to Christianity, if for no other reason, due to Arabic-language Christian writing on the subject; see, for instance, Yaḥyā b. Saʿīd b. Yaḥyā al-Anṭākī, *Taʾīkh al-Anṭākī, al-maʿrūf bi-ṣilat taʾrīkh Awtīkhā* (Tripoli: Jarrūs Press, 1999), 18.

reached all the way to Mount Tabor, well into southern Syria, and the scenes of Judeo-Christian salvation history.[5]

Until the eleventh century, therefore, northern Syria and the Taurus mountains formed the primary battleground between the two adversaries.[6] These particular borderlands, out of all the frontiers between the Islamic and infidel worlds, even received a special designation in the early Islamic polity, *thughūr*, and were awarded special taxation status and legal status.[7] The Islamic writers considered this Byzantine border area to be fulfilling a special religious function as well, as will be discussed below; and during the Byzantine reconquest era in the tenth century, entire works were composed to

[5] On the Byzantine reaction to the initial conquests, see Ralph-Johannes Lilie, *Die Byzantinische Reaktion auf der Ausbreitung der Araber: Studien zur Strukturwandlung des byzantinischen Staates im 7. Und 8. Jahrhundert* (Munich: Institut für Byzantinistik und Neugriechische Philologie der Universität München, 1976) and John F. Haldon and Hugh Kennedy, 'The Arab–Byzantine Frontier in the Eighth and Ninth Centuries: Military Organization and Society in the Borderlands', *Zbornik radova Vizantološkog instituta* 19 (1980), 79–116; reprinted in 2006 in Hugh Kennedy, *The Byzantine and Early Islamic Near East* (Ashgate: Variorum), article VIII; on the Byzantine advances of the tenth century, and especially the retaking of Tarsus, which had become an important religious centre of jihad, see C. E. Bosworth, 'The City of Tarsus and the Arab–Byzantine Frontiers in Early and Middle ʿAbbāsid Times', *Oriens* 33 (1992), 268–86.

[6] Although the Caucasus were an active battleground as well, of great secondary importance after Syria; this frontier has been relatively neglected until recently (see Alison Vacca, *Non-Muslim Provinces under Early Islam: Islamic Rule and Iranian Legitimacy in Armenia and Caucasian Albania* (Cambridge: Cambridge University Press, 2017); Johannes Preiser-Kapeller, 'Aristocrats, Mercenaries, Clergymen and Refugees: Deliberate and Forced Mobility of Armenians in the Early Medieval Mediterranean (6th to 11th century A.D.)', in Johannes Preiser-Kapeller *et al.* (eds), *Migration Histories of the Medieval Afroeurasian Transition Zone: Aspects of Mobility between Africa, Asia and Europe, 300–1500 C.E.* (Leiden: Brill, 2020), 327–86), and is addressed in the present volume.

[7] Bosworth, 'The City of Tarsus', 270–1; Haldon and Kennedy, 'The Arab–Byzantine Frontier', 106–14; D. G. Tor, *Violent Order: Religious Warfare, Chivalry, and the ʿAyyar Phenomenon in the Medieval Islamic World*, Istanbuler Texte und Studien der Deutschen Morgenländischen Gesellschaft, Band 11 (Würzburg: Ergon Verlag, 2007), 39–76; Michael Bonner, *Aristocratic Violence and Holy War: Studies in the Jihad and the Arab–Byzantine Frontier* (New Haven, CT: American Oriental Society, 1996); and, for a description of the archeological evidence relating to the *thughūr*, Asa Eger, *The Islamic–Byzantine Frontier: Interaction and Exchange Among Muslim and Christian Communities* (New York: I. B. Tauris, 2015), 23–181.

memorialise areas such as Malatya/Melitene and Tarsus, which had returned to Byzantine control.[8]

The geopolitical situation again changed radically in the late eleventh century, however: first with the breaking of the Byzantine *limes* protecting their heartland in Anatolia after the devastating battle of Manzikert in AD 1071, and then in the ensuing Latin Christian reaction released by the desperate Byzantine appeal to the Pope, which resulted in the two-hundred-year-long movement of the Crusades in Greater Syria.[9] This far-reaching change came about due to the arrival of an immensely powerful new force in the Muslim world: The arrival of the Seljuq dynasty at the head of an Oghuz Turkish confederation, in the first wave of what was to be a nine-hundred-year-long Turco-Mongol domination of the Middle East.[10] Not only did this dynasty reunite the Middle East heartlands into one polity again, and recapture Syria,

[8] For example, Abū ʿAmr ʿUthmān b. ʿAbdallāh al-Ṭarsusī, *Siyar al-thughūr*, a fragment of which survives in Iḥsān ʿAbbās (ed.), *Shadharāt min kutub mafqūda fī'l-ta'rikh* (Beirut: Dār al-Gharb al-Islāmī, 1408/1988), 37–48. Another example is Ibn Ḥawqal's treatment – almost an elegy – of areas that were no longer under Islamic control; see Abū'l-Qāsim b. Ḥawqāl al-Naṣībī, *Kitāb Ṣūrat al-arḍ* (Beirut: Manshūrāt Dār Maktabat al-Ḥayāt, no date), 166–72.

[9] On Manzikert itself, see Carole Hillenbrand, *Turkish Myth and Muslim Symbol: The Battle of Manzikert* (Edinburgh: Edinburgh University Press, 2007); for the developments within the Byzantine world leading up to Manzikert, and the consequences of the battle, see Speros Vryonis, *The Decline of Medieval Hellenism in Asia Minor and the Process of Islamization from the Eleventh through the Fifteenth Century* (Berkeley: University of California Press, 1971); for the famous appeal to Latin Christendom that resulted in the Crusades, some of the standard works include Jean Richard, *The Crusades, c. 1071–c. 1291*, trans. Jean Birrell (Cambridge: Cambridge University Press, 1999); Hans Eberhard Mayer, *The Crusades*, 2nd edn, trans. John Gillingham (Oxford: Oxford University Press, 1998); Jonathan Riley-Smith, *The First Crusade and the Idea of Crusading* (Philadelphia: University of Pennsylvania Press, 2009); and Peter Frankopian, *The First Crusade: The Call from the East* (Cambridge, MA: Harvard University Press, 2012).

[10] The most comprehensive political history of the Great Seljuq Dynasty remains that of C. E. Bosworth, 'The Political and Dynastic History of the Iranian World (A.D. 1000–1217)', in J. A Boyle (ed.), *The Cambridge History of Iran. Volume 5: The Seljuq and Mongol Periods* (Cambridge: Cambridge University Press, 1968), 1–202; a briefer overview of Seljuq political history can be found in A. C. S. Peacock, *The Great Seljuk Empire* (Edinburgh: Edinburgh University Press, 2015), chapters 1 and 2 (pp. 20–123). For a history of the Seljuqs of Anatolia, the classic work remains Claude Cahen, *La Turquie pré-ottomane* (Istanbul: Institut Français des Études Anatoliennes, 1988).

but their crushing defeat of Byzantium at Manzikert in 1071, together with the subsequent confirmation of its effects at Myriokephalon in 1176, inaugurated a new phase in the history of the Islamic–Byzantine border. It shifted the borderland from northern Syria, well into Anatolia itself, the Byzantine heartland; this was a major turning point, which inaugurated the long-drawn-out endgame over the very existence of Byzantium, although the Crusades did help to defer the final end.[11]

The Crusading era also witnessed an increase in the complexity of relations between Byzantium and the Muslim world, with the introduction of Latin Christendom as a central political factor, as well as a plethora of Latin Christian polities, orders, and rulers, as a further element affecting those relations; most notably, in forcing Byzantium to try to balance the Latin Christian and the Muslim threats simultaneously. This Latin Christian element became once again more ancillary, however, after the final elimination of the Crusading polities, and the cessation of Crusading movements, in the Levant after 1291.[12]

It should be noted that there has been a recent trend in Western scholarship to emphasise almost exclusively the always present commercial, personal, and cultural contacts, cooperation, and exchanges between Byzantium and the Muslim world;[13] while the effort itself to draw a more highly nuanced picture of the border during these centuries is laudable, sometimes this interpretation

[11] On the battle of Manzikert, see Hillenbrand, *Turkish Myth*, *passim*; as for the Battle of Myriokephalon, Vryonis (*Decline of Medieval Hellenism*, 125) characterises it as 'the single most significant event to transpire on Anatolian soil since Manzikert . . . it meant the end of Byzantine plans to reconquer Asia Minor'. The classic article on the battle is Ralph-Johannes Lilie, 'Die Schlacht von Myriokephalon (1176): Auswirkungen auf das byzantinische Reich im ausgehenden 12. Jahrhundert', *Revue des études Byzantines* 35 (1977), 257–75. For an overview of the historical context of both see also D. A. Korobeinikov, 'Raiders and Neighbours: The Turks', in Jonathan Shepherd (ed.), *The Cambridge History of the Byzantine Empire, c. 500–1492* (Cambridge: Cambridge University Press, 2009), 692–728.

[12] The most useful overviews on the subject remain Ralph-Johannes Lilie, *Byzantium and the Crusader States, 1096–1204*, trans. J. C. Morris and Jean Riding (Oxford: Oxford University Press, 1994); and P. M. Holt, *The Crusader States and their Neighbours, 1098–1291* (London: Routledge, 2004).

[13] For example, Michael Köhler, *Alliances and Treaties between Frankish and Muslim Rulers in the Middle East: Cross-cultural Diplomacy in the Period of the Crusades*, trans. P. Holt, rev. K. Hirschler (Leiden: Brill, 2013); as Morton notes, though, human beings have multiple

crosses the line of anachronism and becomes an attempt to deny that there ever really was any religiously driven underlying conflict or vital religious issue at stake in that far-removed time and place – let alone that it was a motivating factor or desideratum.[14] However, neither the fact that tactical alliances and personal cross-confessional friendships were formed during this era between Byzantium and the Muslims, nor the ever-present commercial and cultural exchange, should obscure the Muslim vision and long-term strategic goal of the time, preserved in the most authoritative hadith: to conquer 'Rome', both Old and New ('New Rome' being Constantinople).[15]

The end of the period examined herein, circa 1300, marks the beginning of the final stage of the realisation of that vision, which had begun with the very rise of Islam in the seventh century, and found its first fulfillment in the conquest of Constantinople in 1453. In other words, together with the ongoing cooperation, trade, and cultural interaction and mutual enrichment between the Islamic and the Byzantine Christian worlds of these centuries, there was nevertheless also an underlying but inexorable zero-sum physical struggle which ended in the actual obliteration of one of the parties; Byzantium and its civilisation were in the end violently conquered, although that final consummation lies outside the scope of the present work.

Cultural Significance of the Islamic–Byzanine Border in the Islamic World

The influence of the Islamic–Byzantine border upon the internal development of Muslim civilisation in the first few centuries of Islam can hardly be overstated. The primary duty of Islamic government, from its inception during

motivations for their actions, and even the same people at different times will be more or less self-interested, impelled by one factor versus another, and so forth; but a good historian does not therefore deny the existence of cultural and religious values and expectations (Nicholas Morton, *The Crusader States and their Neighbours: A Military History, 1099–1187* (Oxford: Oxford University Press, 2020), 203–10).

[14] The reader will certainly be able to call to mind works of this nature without the present author's uncharitably naming them. Ironically, such works revive or echo medieval Latin Christian propaganda accusing the Byzantines of aiding and abetting the Muslims, thus justifying the events of 1204; on this latter subject, see e.g. the insightful analysis of Savvas Neocleous, 'Byzantine–Muslim Conspiracies Against the Crusades: History and Myth', *Journal of Medieval History* 36: 3 (2010), 253–74.

[15] Discussed below.

the Prophet's day, was establishing God's rule on earth and administering his rule through the agency of his vicegerent, or caliph.[16] This fundamental coercive duty of divinely sanctioned rulership had two components: 'Commanding right and wrong' within the Islamic oecumene (*Dār al-Islām*)[17] – that is, ensuring that God's ordinances were followed and the world was ordered according to Islamic religious law and precepts – and the Qur'anically ordained jihad (military 'striving in the path of God') against the *Dār al-Ḥarb* (literally, 'the Abode of War'), the infidel world in which God's rule was not yet established, in order to bring that benighted territory under God's rule.[18]

This divinely ordained warfare was the motive force behind the immense Islamic empire that was established within the first hundred years of Islamic history, on all the lands formerly constituting the Sasanian Empire, which

[16] Patricia Crone, *God's Rule: Government and Islam, Six Centuries of Medieval Islamic Political Thought* (New York: Columbia University Press, 2004), 3–23, 362–73.

[17] On which duty, see Michael Cook, *Commanding Right and Forbidding Wrong in Islamic Thought* (Cambridge: Cambridge University Press, 2000).

[18] For example, Qur'an 4: 74: 'Let those fight in the path of Allāh who sell the life of this world for the hereafter; and whoever fights in the path of Allāh, whether his killed or triumphs, we shall give him a great reward'; Qur'an 9: 110: 'Allāh has bought from the believers their lives and their wealth in return for Paradise; they fight in the way of Allāh, kill and get killed. That is a true promise from Him . . . and who fulfills His promise better than Allāh?', etc. (translations by Majid Fakhry, *The Qur'an: A Modern English Version* (Reading: Garnet Press, 1997)). For a fuller exposition, see Tor, *Violent Order*, Chapter 2; on the post-caliphal use of jihad as a legitimising ideology, see both further chapters in the same volume, as well as D. G. Tor, 'The Islamization of Central Asia in the Sāmānid Era and the Reshaping of the Muslim World', *Bulletin of the School of Oriental and African Studies*, 72: 2 (2009), 272–99. The Ottoman polity, like every preceding non-caliphal dynasty, established its legitimacy by ostentatiously fulfilling this twofold duty of rulership, especially by touting its jihad activities – in the Ottoman case, making use of the jihad against the Byzantines as a legitimising ideology; this was recognised by Wittek in the nineteenth century (Paul Wittek, *The Rise of the Ottoman Empire: Studies in the History of Turkey, Thirteenth–Fifteenth Centuries*, trans. Colin Heywood, Rudi Paul Lindner and Oliver Welsh (reprinted London: Routledge, 2012)). It should be noted that most of the Ottomanists who subsequently attacked this thesis never placed it in its larger Islamic historical tradition and context – the long line of autonomous Sunni dynasties extending from the Ṣaffārids and Sāmanids through the Ghaznavids and, most importantly, the Seljuqs, whose successors the Ottomans claimed to be.

was eradicated, and all eastern and southern territories of the Byzantine empire. From thence, the armies of the caliphate continued their expansion: in the East, into the Sogdian and Bactrian territories of Central Asia, and the lands of the Indian sub-continent; and, in the West, into the post-Roman, Vandal, and Visigothic territories of North Africa and the Iberian Peninsula, continuing into present-day France. But Anatolia, the Byzantine heartland, remained obstinately unconquered, a bar to Muslim expansion to the northwest of the caliphal centre, first in Syria, then, from the second half of the eighth century, in Iraq.

Thus, the Byzantine empire, alone among the powers of Late Antiquity, remained a barrier to the spreading of God's rule, wielded on earth by the caliphate. Worse, it offered an alternative, and rival, religious polity and vision to Islam, in a way that the political entities and beliefs of the Shamanistic/Tengristic, Buddhist, and Hindu peoples of Central Asia and the Indian subcontinent did not. Perhaps this explains why, while different Islamic borderlands held varying levels of importance at various times in pre-Ottoman Islamic history,[19] the religious and cultural significance of the Islamic–Byzantine border was by far the most profound and enduring. The two major periods of this particular border's greatest influence upon the internal life and developments of Muslim civilisation in the period covered by this volume were from the rise of Islam until the late ninth/early tenth century; and then again, albeit to a far lesser degree, from the Seljuq period in the mid-eleventh century to the Mongol conquests in the thirteenth century.[20]

Regarding this first era of its significance, the Muslim–Byzantine border shaped some of the most important Islamic religious and political developments. First, religiously, there was a deep theological aspect to the Byzantine role in the Muslim religious imagination in early Islamic times: as the major military opponent, and only religio-ideological challenger of Islam during the

[19] For example, the Central Asian border during the Sāmanid period, and the Indian border during the Ghaznavid period; see Tor, 'The Islamization of Central Asia'; and, on Maḥmūd of Ghazna as *ghāzī*, Ali Anooshahr, *The Ghazi Sultans and the Frontiers of Islam* (London: Routledge, 2008), chap. 3.

[20] On the Mongol conquest of the Seljuqs of Rum, see Osman Turan, *Selçuklular Târihi ve Türk-Islâm Mediniyeti* (Ankara: Ötüken, 2004), 294–301.

seventh through ninth centuries, the Christian world, including the Islamic–Byzantine border, occupies an outsized place in what one might call the 'Theology of the Enemy' at this time. Thus, in hadith, one finds Abū Dāʾūd al-Sijistānī entitling one of the chapters in his Jihād section, 'In praise of fighting the Byzantines above all other nations', even pagan ones;[21] hadith in al-Bukhārī's Jihād section of his collection relating specifically to 'al-Rūm';[22] and holy warriors on this border writing the first books of jihad in Islam.[23] Supposedly, when the great border warrior ʿAbdallāh Ibn al-Mubārak was asked by a fellow *jihādī* why he, a Khurāsānī, had to go all the way to the Byzantine border to engage in jihad, when there were plenty of Turkish infidels at hand on the eastern border, Ibn al-Mubārak responded that whereas the Turks were only fighting about worldly power, the Byzantines were battling the Muslims over their faith – 'so which is the more worthy of defense: our world or our faith?'[24]

The place occupied by the Islamic–Byzantine border in the Muslim apocalyptic tradition was even greater. As the territorial focal point of the Abrahamic tradition in which Islam was rooted, the Holy Land was the primary apocalyptic scene in which early Muslim eschatology was set.[25] But on a more concrete level, as David Cook and Stephen Shoemaker have shown, the most important theme in early Muslim apocalyptic thought was the struggle itself against the Byzantine Christian empire, including 'a vision among early Muslim groups of totally supplanting Christianity in one fell swoop by conquering all five of its holy cities'.[26] Major Muslim apocalyptic works from the early Islamic

[21] Abū Dāʾūd Sulaymān b. al-Ashʿath al-Sijistānī, *Kitāb al-Sunan: Sunan Abī Dāʾūd*, ed. Muḥammad ʿAwāmma (Beirut: Muʾassasat al-Rayyān, 1998), 3: 204–5, #2480.

[22] Abū ʿAbd Allāh Muḥammad b/ Ismāʿīl b. Ibrāhīm al-Bukhārī, *Ṣaḥīḥ al-Bukhārī* (Beirut: Dār al-Fikr, 1411/1991), 3: 3–5, #2924.

[23] ʿAbdallāh Ibn al-Mubarak, *Kitāb al-Jihād* (Beirut: Sharikat Abnāʾ Sharīf al-Anṣārī, 1409/1988).

[24] Translated by David Cook, 'Muslim Apocalyptic and *Jihād*', *Jerusalem Studies in Arabic and Islam* 20 (1996), 98, from Ibn al-ʿAdīm's *Bughyat al-ṭalab fī taʾrīkh Ḥalab*.

[25] See Ofer Livne-Kafri, 'Jerusalem in Early Islam: The Eschatological Aspect', *Arabica* 53: 3 (2006), 382–403.

[26] Jerusalem, Alexandria, Antioch, Constantinople, and Rome. In the event, throughout the period under consideration in this volume, only three of those had been conquered; the

period, still in print and widely available today, include visions of the conquest of Constantinople,[27] or, alternatively, simply the wholesale conversion of 'The Romans' –and 'the Slavs' (*saqāliba*) – to Islam.[28]

This theological/ideological background helps explain the most far-reaching significance of the Islamic–Byzantine border: the influence it had on internal religio-historical developments in early Islamic times. The very earliest decades of Islamic history, especially in the seventh century prior to the reign of ʿAbd al-Malik (r. AD 685–705), are a much-contested era among scholars, due both to the peculiar absence of contemporaneous Muslim literary sources and to the fact that the extant non-Muslim sources in many respects contradict the later Muslim tradition; but there can be no doubt that the conquest of Byzantine Syria, with its most sacred sites of the Jewish and Christian religions, not only constituted a major religious goal, but also a major turning point in the formation of Islam, even though there is vehement disagreement regarding the precise nature of the influence, and exactly what the state and development of Islam were at that time.[29]

fourth was to fall only in 1453, and the last, Rome, remains as of this writing as yet unconquered. David Cook, *Studies in Muslim Apocalyptic* (Princeton: Darwin Press, 2002), 35; see also Cook, 'Muslim Apocalyptic and *Jihād*', 83. There are also the historical apocalypse cycles Cook identifies which were connected to the war with Byzantium: e.g. the Aʿmāq cycle (*Studies*, 49–80), one of the messianic cycles (ibid., 166–8), and so forth; and Stephen Shoemaker, *The Apocalypse of Empire: Imperial Eschatology in Late Antiquity and Early Islam* (Philadelphia: University of Pennsylvania Press, 2019).

[27] For example, Nuʿaym b. Ḥammād b. Muʿawiya b. al-Ḥārith al-Khuzāʿī al-Marwazī, *al-Fitan* (Beirut: Dār al-Kutub al-ʿIlmiyya, 1418/1997), 295–301; Abū'l-Ḥusayn Aḥmad b. Jaʿfar b. al-Munādī, *Malāḥim*, ed. ʿAbd al-Karīm al-ʿUqaylī (Qumm: Dār al-Sīra, 1418/1998), 145–8, 210.

[28] Ibn al-Munādī, *Malāḥim*, 105, 242.

[29] Among the widely differing interpretations, one should note e.g. Patricia Crone and Michael Cook, *Hagarism: The Making of the Islamic World* (Cambridge: Cambridge University Press, 1977), especially 3–28; Fred Donner, *Muhammad and the Believers: At the Origins of Islam* (Cambridge, MA: Harvard University Press, 2010); Stephen J. Shoemaker, *The Death of a Prophet: The End of Muhammad's Life and the Beginnings of Islam* (Philadelphia: University of Pennsylvania Press, 2012); Shoemaker, *Apocalypse of Empire*, 116–84; and the extremely revisionist essays in Karl-Heinz Ohlig and Gerd-R. Puin (eds), *Die dunklen Anfänge: Neue Forschungen zue Entstehung und frühen Geschichte des Islams* (Berlin: Verlag Hans Schiler, 2005).

From the mid-eighth century, however, the historian is on much firmer historical ground, and here the Islamic–Byzantine border played a key role in some of the most important developments in internal Islamic history and religion, most of which the present author has expatiated upon at some length in previous writings, and all of which were interconnected, including the following: the privatising of jihad, from a massive state-directed endeavour to a smaller-scale, autonomous, and voluntary effort, and the attendant undermining of the religious stature of the caliphate and converse meteoric rise of religious stature this won for the jihadi supererogators, assisted by their practice of a new and very stringent form of ascetism (*zuhd*); the concomitant formation and championing of proto-Sunnism by these same supererogators; and, within a few decades, as a result of the reputation for piety and fervour which their devotion and asceticism had won them, the triumphal proto-Sunni arrogation of religious authority in Islam from the caliphate to the new class of hadith scholars, which reached its tipping point during the reign of Hārūn al-Rashīd, who was, not accidentally, more preoccupied than any other caliph with jihad on the Islamic–Byzantine border, and with trying to propitiate the most prominent of these ascetic border warriors.[30]

In many key respects, this proto-Sunni reformation of Islam resembles the radical wing of the Protestant reformation: its uncompromising championing of individual conscience and individual interpretation of Scripture, rather than reliance upon fallible human precedent; its denial of the theological authority of the head of the religious congregation, who claimed to be God's representative on earth, and denunciation of his luxuriousness and worldliness;[31]

[30] See, in addition to the aforementioned Tor, *Violent Order*, chapters 2–5, Tor, 'Privatized Jihad and Public Order in the Pre-Saljūq Period: The Role of the Mutaṭawwiʿa', *Iranian Studies* 38: 4 (2005), 555–73; and Tor, 'God's Cleric: Fuḍayl b. ʿIyāḍ and the Transition from Caliphal to Prophetic Sunna', in *Islamic Cultures, Islamic Contexts: Essays in Honor of Professor Patricia Crone*, eds Behnam Sadeghi, Asad Q. Ahmed, Adam Silverstein and Robert Hoyland (Leiden: Brill, 2014), 195–228.

[31] Encapsulated in the unforgettable alleged dialogue between the Caliph Hārūn al-Rashīd and the proto-Sunni al-Fuḍayl b. ʿIyāḍ; upon Hārūn's exclaiming to al-Fuḍayl 'What an ascetic [lit., "renunciant"] you are!', the latter replied that Hārūn was far more of one, 'Because I renounce pleasure in this world [only], whereas you renounce pleasure in the Next World; this world is transitory, whereas the Next World is eternal.' See, e.g. Abū

its renunciation of pomp and power, and advocating of a plain and austere life; and a deep-rooted fear of sin, eternal damnation, and one's personal unworthiness of salvation.[32] In these last elements, however, one can perceive another resemblance, and probable direct influence: the Christian ascetics of the Syrian wilderness.[33]

Essentially, the proto-Sunnis stepped into the vacuum they saw being left by the Caliphal failure to fulfil his twin duties mentioned above: 'Commanding right and forbidding wrong' – that is, establishing and upholding God's rule within the Islamic polity, through living an exemplary pious life, ensuring that all Muslims did so as well, and upholding the public and private ordinances of Islamic law; and the complementary duty of establishing God's rule over those parts of the world not yet under it, through jihad. These duties naturally flowed into one another, they were two sides of the same coin, and proto-Sunnism arose because the pious ascetics viewed the caliphs, over a long period of time, as having failed woefully in both. Rather than let Islam simply wither away, they stepped in to fill the breach, much as the later Protestant reformers of

Ḥayyān al-Tawḥīdī, *al-Baṣāʾir waʾl-dhakhṣʾir*, ed. Wadād al-Qāḍī (Beirut: Dār Ṣadr, 1988), 2: 172; Sirāj al-Dīn Abū Ḥafṣ ʿUmar Ibn al-Mulaqqin, *Ṭabaqāt al-awliyāʾ*, ed. Muṣṭafā ʿAtā (Beirut: Dār al-Kutub al-ʿIlmiyya, 1988), 206; Abū ʾl-ʿAbbās Aḥmad b. Muḥammad Ibn Khallikān, *Wafayāt al-aʿyān wa-anbāʾ abnāʾ al-zamān*, ed. Y. ʿA. Ṭawīl (Beirut: Dār al-Kutub al-ʿIlmiyya, 1419/1998), 3: 482.

32 Some of the many statements on this subject which convey the general tenor of the proto-Sunni attitude include 'Blessed is the one who . . . loves the company of his Lord, and weeps over his sins' (Abū ʿAbd al-Raḥmān Muḥammad b. al-Ḥusayn al-Sulamī, *Ṭabaqāt al-ṣūfiyya*, ed. M. ʿAṭā (Beirut: Dār al-Kutub al-ʿIlmiyya, 1419/1998), 27); 'All grief dwindles but the grief of the penitent' (Aḥmad b. ʿAbdallāh Abū Nuʿaym al-Iṣbahānī, *Ḥilyat al-awliyāʾ wa -ṭabaqāt al-asfiyāʾ*, ed. M. ʿAṭā (Beirut: Dār al-Kutub al-ʿIlmiyya, 1418/1997), 8: 104); and the averral that it would have been better to have been born a dog in order not to have to undergo the Day of Judgment (e.g. Abū Nuʿaym, *Ḥilyat al-awliyāʾ*, 8: 87; and Abūʾl-Faraj ʿAbd al-Raḥmān Ibn al-Jawzī, *Ṣifat al-ṣafwa*, ed. A. Bin ʿAlī (Cairo: Dār al-Ḥadīth, 1421/2000), 1: 429). See Tor, 'God's Cleric', and on fear of sin and the Day of Judgment, Christopher Melchert, 'Exaggerated Fear in the Early Islamic Renunciant Tradition', *Journal of the Royal Asiatic Society* 21 (2011), 283–300.

33 Tor Andrae's tracing of this has never been bettered; see Tor Andrae, *In the Garden of Myrtles: Studies in Early Islamic Mysticism*, trans. Birgitte Sharpe (Albany: State University of New York Press, 1987), especially pp. 7–54.

Christendom did when faced with what they viewed as a corrupt and venal papacy and Church establishment.

What concerns us for present purposes, though, is the relationship between the eighth- and ninth-century proto-Sunnis and the Islamic–Byzantine border. All of the great proto-Sunni figures, without exception, practised border warfare on the Byzantine frontier.[34] Indeed, the proto-Sunni movement was born on this frontier, the result of extremely pious men's bitter disappointment with the apparent abandonment by the caliphs, after the failed siege of Constantinople in 717, of full-scale war by the caliphal army against Byzantine Christendom, the apparent relinquishing of an immediate conquest of the Byzantine empire, and the subsiding thereafter of the expansionist campaigns on the Byzantine front into the smaller-scale state-sanctioned raids known as *ghazawāt*, and in particular the summer raids, or *ṣawā ʾif*, both of which had been in existence since early Islamic times.[35] Indeed, even this limited expansionist policy of campaigning by the caliphal government collapsed in the 740s–760s, due to the chaos and struggles of, first, the Third Fitna, and then the Abbasid Revolution and the need of the first caliphs of that dynasty to put down the numerous revolts of the early post-revolutionary years, consolidate their power, and securely establish their rule.[36] The caliphal abandonment of this half of the caliph's essential duties,

[34] Bonner's so-called 'scholar-saints' of the frontier (Bonner, *Aristocratic Violence*, 107–30). For an examination of the nexus between these militant *muḥaddithūn* and their religio-political effect, see Tor, *Violent Order*, 39–81.

[35] The Prophet himself conducted raids (see Khalīfa b. Khayyāṭ al-ʿUṣfurī, *Taʾrīkh Khalīfa b. Khayyāṭ*, ed. Muṣṭafā Fawwāz *et al.* (Beirut: Dār al-Fikr, 1415/1995), e.g. 38, 60), as did the representatives of the Rāshidūn caliphs – e.g. Abū Mūsā al-Ashʿarī's *ghazw* during ʿUthmān's caliphate (ibid., 113). In fact, ʿUthmān is the first caliph for whom we have a list of the commanders whom he appointed for the *ṣāʾifa* raids upon Byzantium (ibid., 134–5). The tradition of sending princes of the blood on summer raids was an Umayyad policy, later revived under the Abbasids; some instances include Muḥammad b. Marwān's leading of the *ṣāʾifa* in the Hijrī years 75, 83 (Khalīfa, *Taʾrīkh*, 209, 256; in this latter case, it is also mentioned that al-ʿAbbas b. al-Walid raided), and 114, one raid of which was led by Muʿawiya b. Hishām, and which joined up with the forces of the legendary ghazi ʿAbdallāh al-Baṭṭāl, and the other of which was commanded by Sulaymān b. Hishām (ibid., 271).

[36] On this change in caliphal policy, see Khalid Yahya Blankenship, *The End of the Jihād State: The Reign of Hishām b. ʿAbd al-Malik and the Collapse of the Umayyads* (Albany: State

and the resultant Byzantine counteroffensive that ensued, was a major part of the impetus that gave rise to the new socio-religious proto-Sunni movement, and found expression in the proto-Sunni 'wildcat' Byzantine border warriors, the *mutaṭawwiʿa* or *muṭṭawwiʿa*. They represented a departure from previous practice in that they regarded the jihad as a personal religious obligation incumbent upon all Muslims, rather than a collective communal duty under caliphal leadership and central government control.

In the face of caliphal abdication of his twin functions aimed at upholding God's rule on Earth, the proto-Sunni militants formed a faith based on a disguised, oddly Emersonian-like idea of self-reliance: although they claimed that, in the absence of a real imam worthy of the name, the only true religious guidance one had to fall back upon was the Prophet himself, he was of course long since unavailable, having died, according to Islamic tradition, over a century previously. The proto-Sunnis, however, developed the belief that this precious Prophetic guidance and example could be retrieved through the collection of the scattered, faint memories, real or imagined, preserved in stories told among the descendants of those who had known the Prophet (hadith), as well as through the Qur'an; what this really meant in practice, was of course that the proto-Sunni, alone with his Qur'an and his memorised traditions of what the Prophet had supposedly said and done, recalled at third-, fourth- or fifth-hand over a century after the fact, was free to interpret everything *sola scriptura*, without reference to living caliphal religious authority.

This was the great Sunni revolution in Islam, and the Islamic–Byzantine border was an integral part of it, in providing a stage for like-minded proto-Sunni ascetic men to gather and elaborate these ideas together with one another, and to acquire the fame and religious prestige, through their authenticity and dedication, which strengthened their position throughout the second

University of New York Press, 1994); in Treadgold's words: 'Fortunately for the Byzantines, the caliphs no longer showed much interest in trying to conquer the whole empire' (Warren Treadgold, *The Byzantine Revival 780–842* (Stanford: Stanford University Press, 1988), 18). As Bosworth noted, it was not until al-Manṣūr had in the 760s 'achieved a greater degree of internal stability . . . [that] a more activist policy along the frontier . . . was pursued' (C. E. Bosworth, 'Byzantium and the Syrian frontier in the early Abbasid period', reprinted in C. E. Bosworth, *The Arabs, Byzantium, and Iran: Studies in Early Islamic History and Culture* (London: Routledge, 2016), XII: 58).

half of the eighth century, and ultimately resulted in their winning the showdown with the caliphate over religious authority, which came to a head in the ninth-century *miḥna*, or religious testing. And, in the wake of the religious hollowing out of the caliphate caused by the Sunni victory, the caliphate's political collapse followed as well. Thus, one can draw a direct line between the theological developments in which the Islamic–Byzantine border played such an important role, and the political collapse of the Islamic oecumene and the diminution of the caliphate in the following century.[37]

Wholly apart from leading to far-reaching developments in Islamic political and religious institution, the lands of the Islamic–Byzantine border, the *thughūr*, as a special place for acquiring religious merit through performing the religious obligation of jihad, also became a major centre of Islamic devotion and religious expression throughout the eighth and ninth centuries – a position it regained to a degree during the Crusading era. Thus, the tenth-century geographer Ibn Ḥawqal, writing shortly after the fall of Tarsus to the Byzantines in the year 354/965, describes the city as it was in his memory: a centre for religiously inspired border warfare, to which *ghāzīs* would flock from every city and town of the Islamic world, each of which had a building there for the housing of its warriors, from which they could sally forth on their raids:

> [Each town] had for its people in [Ṭarsūs] an abode [*dār*] and *ribāṭ* [border warrior fortress], in which would dwell the *ghāzīs* from this town, and they would station themselves for border raids in them [*yurābiṭūna bi-hā*] when they arrived in [Ṭarsūs], and they would receive by means of it rations and the prayers . . . And *mutaṭawwiʿīn* [supererogators in religious warfare] would pass through it . . .[38]

In short, the Islamic–Byzantine *thughūr* of the early Islamic centuries became in the Muslim religious imagination a holy landscape, a place sanctified by

[37] On the *miḥna*, see D. Sourdel, 'The Religious Policy of the ʿAbbāsid Caliph al-Maʾmūn', in E. Kohlberg (ed.), *Shiʿism* (Aldershot: Ashgate, 2003), 333–53; and on its relationship to the challenge of the proto-Sunnis and the collapse of the caliphate, D. G. Tor, 'Privatized Jihad and Public Order', 555–73.

[38] Ibn Ḥawqāl, *Ṣūrat al-arḍ*, 168–9.

ascetics and self-sacrificing warriors for God, people who 'devoted themselves entirely to the *ghazw* and the Jihād, stationed themselves in the borderlands [*rābaṭū fī 'l-thughūr*], and supererogated in the *ghazw*, and sought the *ghazw* in the lands of the infidel when it was not incumbent upon them'.[39] One of the frequently overlooked aspects of the importance of the Islamic–Byzantine border, therefore, is the emotional depth and fervour with which it enriched and inspired Muslim religious life; this emotional resonance carried over into literature as well, in all three of the major Muslim languages, for centuries.[40]

The second era in which the Islamic–Byzantine border rose to prominence once again was from the eleventh century through to the end of the Crusading period in Anatolia and Syria. The coming of the Seljuq dynasty was a pivotal moment in Islamic history; the Seljuqs themselves were the most politically significant dynasty that arose on the politically fragmented ruins of the once unitary caliphate, the first to reunite all the core Middle East Islamic heartlands, from the Oxus River to the Mediterranean, into one realm again.[41] As with all Sunni dynasties that established themselves in the wake of the caliphal collapse, they legitimised their position by conspicuously assuming and executing the two Islamically prescribed duties of caliphal rulership, which was the only rulership recognised in early Islamic theology: 'Commanding right and forbidding wrong', and jihad.[42]

39 ʿAbd al-Karīm b. Muḥammad al-Samʿānī, *Kitāb al-ansāb*, ed. ʿAbd al-Qādir ʿAṭā (Beirut: Dār al-Kutub al-ʿIlmiyya, 1419/1998), 5: 213.

40 For example, the epic cycle of the legend of the great warrior ʿAbdallāh al-Baṭṭāl, active in the eighth century; see e.g. Marius Canard, 'Les principaux personnages du roman de chevalerie arabe *Ḏāt al-himma wa'l-Baṭṭāl*', *Arabica* 8 (1961), 158–73; during the revival of the importance of the Islamic–Byzantine borderlands during the Seljuq era and the Crusades, an entire Turkish epic tradition established around this figure; see e.g. Anon., *Battal-nâme: eski Türkiye türkçesi*, ed. Necati Demir and Mehmet Dursun Erdem (Ankara: Hece Yayınları, 2006).

41 See D. G. Tor, 'Seljuqs (1055–1194)', in Gerhard Böwering *et al.* (eds), *The Princeton Encyclopedia of Islamic Political Thought* (Princeton, NJ: Princeton University Press, 2012), 490–1.

42 On the dual nature of this obligation, see Tor, 'Privatized Jihad', 555–73. Although their advent precipitated a renewed development of Islamic political theology, including theories of a division between religious and political authority; see Crone, *God's Rule*, 234–7; and Carole Hillenbrand, 'Islamic Orthodoxy or Realpolitik? Al-Ghazālī's Views on Government', *Iran* 26 (1988), 81–94.

Although Seljuq jihad of course took place on all frontiers where infidels or heretics lurked, it was on the Islamic–Byzantine border that it had the most far-reaching consequences. For the Seljuqs managed, at the battle of Manzikert, to achieve a breakthrough that had not been dreamt of since the eighth century: at Manzikert, they broke the Byzantine *limes* system completely, and were able to begin the systematic overrunning of Asia Minor, the core Byzantine heartland, beginning its transformation into what would eventually become Muslim Turkey.[43] Thus, the border itself was moved from Syria into Anatolia, and the final endgame of Byzantium commenced. In Carole Hillenbrand's words: 'Historians from the time of Gibbon onwards have traditionally seen this battle as the pivotal moment after which Byzantine Asia Minor was gradually to become Muslim Anatolia.'[44]

The second significance of this Seljuq victory at the Islamic–Byzantine border was that it gave Islamic legitimacy to what was by any measure an alien wave of invaders into the Middle East, the Turco-Mongols, and who would remain as ruling colonisers over the autochthonous peoples of the area for the next nine hundred years– possibly the longest colonial period in recorded history. Once again, it is Hillenbrand who articulates the key role the Islamic–Byzantine border played in this respect – namely, winning acceptance for the alien invaders:

> Medieval chroniclers, Muslim and Byzantine alike, correctly perceived this battle as a pivotal event in the perennial conflict between Christianity and Islam. This awe-inspiring context of salvation history lent an extra charge of, so to speak, eternal significance to the Turkish role in this seminal victory, a victory which delivered Anatolia into the 'House of Islam.' Much could be forgiven the architects of that victory and so, despite the depredations and alien ways of the Turks as invading nomads, Manzikert became the instrument for their rehabilitation – and even glorification – in the Arab and Persian consciousness.[45]

Another major development produced by the Islamic–Byzantine border in the eleventh century was the Crusades, which had various internal Islamic

[43] See Vryonis, *Decline*, 69–285; and Frankopian, 'The Collapse of Asia Minor', *The First Crusade*, 57–70.

[44] Hillenbrand, *Turkish Myth and Muslim Symbol*, 3.

[45] Ibid., 226.

implications. The powder train which ignited the Crusading movement was the Byzantine appeal, after decades of being overrun by marauding Turkmen Muslim warriors in the wake of Manzikert, for Latin Christian assistance in re-establishing the Byzantine bulwark against the Islamic world, in the terms in which the astute Byzantine appeal to Latin Christendom's self-interest as well as its religious fervour couched this request.[46] The arrival of the Crusaders in Asia Minor and Syria accomplished several things in the internal development of the Muslim world: first and foremost, the greater awareness, and engagement, of the Islamic with the Latin Christian world. Western scholars have, understandably, been focused more on what internal Latin Christian changes this greater intercourse between the two civilisations produced; but it was also something that led to internal Muslim developments as well. To take one example for which there is at least convincing circumstantial evidence, the Caliph al-Nāṣir's re-envisioning of *futuwwa* as an actual chivalric order, with homage and fealty owed to the caliph at its apex, strikes the observer as likely based upon the Western model which was serving so well in helping the French kings to regain their political and territorial control throughout this period.[47]

[46] On the Byzantine appeal for aid, and on how this meshed with other social and religious trends in Latin Christendom at the time, see Mayer, *The Crusades*, 7–14; Richard, *The Crusades*, 1–22; Riley-Smith, *The First Crusade*, 13–25; Frankopian, *The First Crusade*, 87–100.

[47] See Angelika Hartmann, *an-Nāṣir li-Dīn Allāh (1180–1225)* (Berlin: De Gruyter, 1975), 93–107; however, while Hartmann (p. 106) notes that al-Nāṣir aspired to reconstitute a united religious and political Muslim order under the caliphate ('eine Widervereinigung oder doch zumindest eine neue Hinwendung aller Muslime an das Chalifat als den allein verbindlichen religiösen sowie weltlichen Mittelpunkt an'), she never poses the question of whether or not the caliphs had a model for this. Taeschner similarly overlooks this aspect, seeing this odd new use of *futuwwa* instead as primarily a way to combat ʿAlid pretences (e.g. Franz Taeschner, 'Die Islamischen Futuwwabünde: Das Problem ihrer Entsteihung und die Grundlinien ihrer Geschichte', *Zeitschrift der Deitschen Morgenländischen Gesellschaft* 87 (1933), 32–3). Taeschner also focuses purely on Sufism and the religious side of *futuwwa*, without ever considering the political aspect of the revenant Abbasid caliphate and its ambitions. This holds true throughout his other writings on the subject as well, although he just misses touching upon the subject in 'Das Futuwwa-Rittertums des islamischen Mittelalters', in R. Hartmann and H. Scheel (eds), *Beiträge zur Arabistik, Semitistik und Islamwissenschaften* (Leipzig: Harrassowitz Verlag, 1944), 357; indeed, on the following page, although he is struck by its resemblance to a Western order ('Da durch näherte such

The Abbasid caliphs had never reconciled themselves to the loss of their actual political power, although they had never been shorn of their theoretical authority, despite having come perilously close to this under the Seljuqs.[48] The history of the Abbasid caliphate in the eleventh and twelfth centuries is therefore the unfolding of one long struggle, first to free themselves from the control of various amirs and sultans, and then to reassert their prerogatives as ultimate supreme rulers of Islam.[49] It is in this context – of the attempt at the restoration of caliphal political power – that one must view al-Nāṣir's intriguing attempt to remake *futuwwa* after the fashion of a European knightly or chivalric order, of the kind that was so obviously present among Latin Christians in the Levant during the twelfth century. After freeing themselves of outside control by 1157,[50] the Abbasids found themselves in much the same situation as, for instance, Louis VI of France had been in several generations earlier: 'He could claim royal powers over the church and over the princes and other great nobles of France which in theory could not be denied, but which were in practice often ignored . . .'[51]

By the time of al-Nāṣir's accession in 1180, the caliphs, although according to Islamic law by right the sole political authority throughout the Muslim world, were de facto only the rulers of Iraq. Al-Nāṣir's attempt to transform *futuwwa* into a kind of feudal order, with Muslim rulers swearing fealty to him and under his headship, is something wholly novel in Islamic history;

das Futuwwaritterum in etwa dem Typus des abendländischen geistliche "Ritteorden"'), he never extends his analysis past the '*geistliche*', to ask whether there might not have been a political aim and import as well.

48 See e.g. Hillenbrand, 'Islamic Orthodoxy or Realpolitik?', 81–94; and Crone, 'God's Rule', 234–7.

49 See e.g. George Makdisi, 'Les Rapports entre Calife et Sultan à l'époque Saljuqide', *International Journal of Middle East Studies* 6 (1975), 228–36; D. G. Tor, 'A Tale of Two Murders: Power Relations Between Caliph and Sultan in the Twelfth Century', *Zeitschrift der Deutschen Morgenländischen Gesellschaft (ZDMG)* 159 (2009), 279–97; and D. G. Tor, 'The Political Revival of the ʿAbbāsid Caliphate: Al-Muqtafī and the Seljuqs', *Journal of the American Oriental Society* 137: 2 (2017), 301–14.

50 Tor, 'The Political Revival', 308–12.

51 Elizabeth M. Hallam, *Capetian France 987–1328* (London: Longman, 1996), 111.

this was something very different from the classical *bayʿa*.[52] Rather, it was a method of reasserting the caliph's theoretical rights and extending his power, in much the same fashion as European rulers had been successfully doing throughout the twelfth century. Thomas Bisson has described this European leveraging of homage and fealty into actual political power as follows:

> The lord-kings profited from two cultural facets of power reserved to them. First, their ritual consecrations virtually enacted for witnessing masses . . . the regal mediation of God's power . . . not so much a tenancy of God's lordship as an execution of it. It follows, secondly, that royal lordship reached out for its own customary sanction in affective expression and pretence. In greater or lesser measure the lord-kings of Leon, Catalonia, Aragon, France, England, Germany and Sicily claimed to dominate tenants in homage and fealty . . . feudal-vassalic lordship lent itself to claims of precedence and hierarchy.[53]

This whole subject of Abbasid re-establishment has, however, been thoroughly understudied, and still awaits further elucidation.

Other important internal effects – almost ongoing domino effects spreading from Manzikert and the Crusades – have been far better studied and expounded. These include the religious promotion of the importance of Jerusalem in Islam;[54] and, paradoxically, an increasingly greater estrangement between the Latin Christian and Orthodox worlds over the course of the Crusades.[55] While the Crusades may have temporarily halted and pushed back the Muslim encroachment in Asia Minor, by leading to the very deep

[52] On which, see Andrew Marsham, *Rituals of Islamic Monarchy: Accession and Succession in the First Muslim Empire* (Edinburgh: Edinburgh University Press, 2009).

[53] Thomas N. Bisson, *The Crisis of the Twelfth Century* (Princeton, NJ: Princeton University Press, 2009), 295.

[54] A. A. Duri, 'Bait al-Maqdis in Islam', *Studies in the History and Archeology of Jordan* 1, ed. A. Hadidi (Amman: Jordan Department of Antiquities, 1982), 355; Carole Hillenbrand, *The Crusades: Islamic Perspectives* (Edinburgh: University of Edinburgh Press, 1999), 141–50.

[55] For example, Ralph-Johannes Lilie, *Byzantium and the Crusader States 1096–1204*, trans. J. C. Morris and Jean Ridings (Oxford: The Clarendon Press, 1993); see also the relevant chapters in Nicolas Drocourt and Sebastian Kolditz, *A Companion to Byzantium and the West, 900–1204* (Leiden: Brill, 2021).

alienation between Latin Christendom and Orthodoxy – made almost irreconcilable by the Fourth Crusade – the Crusades essentially sealed the fate of the Byzantine Empire, facilitating the eventual Muslim conquest. Finally – and this is perhaps the best-known consequence of all – the great changes wrought in the Islamic–Byzantine border from the Battle of Manzikert up until the end of the thirteenth century, provided the conditions for the long-term flourishing of the border beyliks that were to give rise around the turn of the fourteenth century to the Ottoman dynasty, which established the last of the great Turco-Mongol Islamic empires in the Middle East until the present, and extended the reach of Islamic armies to the walls of Vienna.

In sum, while the unfolding of the political events on the Islamic–Byzantine border during these centuries are well-known, the greater significance and consequences of those events, especially in relation to the internal developments these events set in motion within each of the two civilisations, in the pre-Manzikert period in particular, await further elucidation; the present volume is one step in that undertaking.

2

THE BYZANTINE–MUSLIM FRONTIER FROM THE ARAB CONQUESTS TO THE ARRIVAL OF THE SELJUK TURKS

Alexander D. Beihammer

Byzantium's relations with the Muslim world constitute a key feature in the politico-military, socio-economic, and cultural evolution of the medieval Mediterranean and thus attracted a lot of scholarly attention ever since Byzantine studies had emerged as a modern academic discipline in the early twentieth century. In this context, scholars primarily focused on the vicissitudes of war and peace in Asia Minor in the time from the Muslim conquests in the 630s through the eastward expansion of the Byzantine empire in the tenth and early eleventh centuries up to the collapse of Byzantine dominion in central and eastern Asia Minor caused by the Seljuk conquests and the First Crusade in the later eleventh century. Over time, the scope of scholarly debates increasingly widened and reaches now far beyond the initial core areas of political history, diplomacy, and administrative–military structures. Research interests gravitate towards matters of demographic and social change, settlement patterns, living conditions, economic activities, trade networks, the cultural idiosyncrasy of borderland populations, as well as forms of acculturation and mutual influence. The following survey attempts to outline some key aspects of the scholarly work on the Byzantine–Muslim borderland from the viewpoint of Byzantine studies and to present a brief chronological overview of major developments in the region under discussion. The focus of the first part rests on concepts and methodological approaches that dominate the historiographical discourse, as well as on questions as to how they shape our understanding and perception of this frontier, what shortcomings and pitfalls we should be aware of, and what the desiderata for future investigation are. The chronological section distinguishes between the three distinct stages, namely the formation period, the Byzantine eastward expansion, and the reconfiguration of the political and cultural landscape of Asia Minor in the wake of the Seljuk conquests.

Historiographical Concepts

The pioneer studies on Byzantine–Muslim relations produced the narrative of a heroic life-and-death struggle, which after centuries of brave and tenacious resistance transformed the Eastern Roman Empire's cultural vigour and military prowess into a powerful expansionist thrust ousting the Arabs from large swathes of land stretching from Cilicia to the Armenian highlands.[1] The notion of a Christian bulwark against the infidel foes goes hand-in-hand with that of a Byzantine epic of survival and re-conquest. In his classical cultural-historical study on the 'empire of the new center' published in 1965, Herbert Hunger aptly epitomised this view as follows: 'So bildete die Ostgrenze stets die eigentliche Schicksalsgrenze dieses Staates, und der Kampf mit den hier anstürmenden Feinden wurde mehr als einmal zum Existenzkampf.'[2] The

[1] Gustave Schlumberger, *Un empereur byzantin au dixième siècle Nicéphore Phocas* (Paris: Librairie de Firmin-Didot, 1890); Gustave Schlumberger, *L'épopée byzantine à la fin du dixième siècle, Jean Tzimiscès, les jeunes années de Basile II le tueur de Bulgares (969–989)* (Paris: Hachette, 1896); Gustave Schlumberger, *L'épopée byzantine à la fin du dixième siècle, seconde partie, Basile II le tueur de Bulgares* (Paris: Hachette, 1900); Gustave Schlumberger, *L'épopée byzantine à la fin du dixième siècle, troisième partie, les Porphyrogénètes Zoe et Theodora (1025–1057)* (Paris: Hachette, 1905); Alexander Vasiliev, *Byzance et les arabes, vol. 1: La dynastie d'Amorium (820–867)*, French edn Henri Grégoire and Marius Canard (Brussels: Éditions de l'Institut de Philologie et d'Histoire Orientales, 1959); Alexander Vasiliev, *Byzance et les arabes, vol. 2/1: Les relations politiques de Byzance et des arabes à l'époque de la dynastie Macédonienne, première période de 867 à 959* (Brussels: Fondation byzantine, 1968); Alexander Vasiliev, *Byzance et les arabes, vol. 2/2: La dynastie Macédonienne (867–959), extraits des sources arabes*, French edn Henri Grégoire and Marius Canard (Brussels: Éditions de l'Institut de Philologie de d'Histoire Orientales et Slaves, 1950).

[2] Herbert Hunger, *Das Reich der neuen Mitte: Der christliche Geist der byzantinischen Kultur* (Graz: Styria, 1965), 317.

eastern border is perceived as a profound ethnic-cultural divide between two opposed spheres, which afforded protection to the Christian-Roman world against deadly external threats. Ernst Honigmann, who in 1935 published the first, and partly still valuable, historical-geographical study of the eastern border, makes an eloquent statement to this effect: 'Erst am Tauroswall fand der islamische Ansturm einen stärkeren Widerstand; denn hier fiel ein natürlicher Grenzwall nahezu mit der ethnologischen Scheidelinie zusammen, die schon früher die semitische Welt von den Völkern Kleinasiens getrennt hatte . . .'[3]

These visions of the Byzantine–Muslim frontier had a strong impact on modern imaginations, which portray the region in question as a remote and highly militarised wilderness studded with well-defended strongholds and dominated by Christian marcher lords and Muslim champions of Holy War. The communities living there are frequently depicted as a warlike border society embroiled in constant strife and detached from the cultural attitudes, ideologies, and allegiances of the imperial centres and ruling elites. Theirs was a rather hybrid cross-cultural identity, which despite all internecine feuding over time had developed a set of commonalities and affinities on both sides of the border. The Byzantine epic of Digenis Akritas, as well as Arabic and Turkish heroic tales of Dhāt al-Himma, Sayyid Baṭṭāl Ghāzī, and Dānishmend give us vivid descriptions of their mentalities and symbolic universe.[4] While the echo of these views can still be traced in numerous textbooks and works of general interest, specialised studies published since the 1960s sought to develop more adequate tools of analysis for the administrative, social, economic, and political realities of frontier life in the Byzantine–Muslim contact and conflict zone. Especially noteworthy

[3] Ernst Honigmann, *Die Ostgrenze des byzantinischen Reiches von 363 bis 1071 nach griechischen, arabischen, syrischen und armenischen Quellen* (Brussels: Librairie Orientale & Américaine, 1935), 39.

[4] Henri Grégoire, 'Études sur l'épopée byzantine', *Revue des études grecques* 46 (1933), 29–69; Marius Canard, 'Delhemma, épopée arabe des guerres arabo-byzantines', *Byzantion* 10 (1935), 283–300; Irène Mélikoff, *La Geste de Melik Dāniṣmend, étude critique du Dāniṣmendnāme*, vol. 1: *Introduction et traduction* (Paris: Librairie Adrien Maisonneuve, 1960), 41–170; Yağmur Say, *Türk-İslam Tarihinde ve Geleneğinde Seyyid Battal Gazi ve Battalname* (Ankara: Sistem Ofset Matbaacılık, 2009), 7–31.

in this respect are two articles by Hélène Ahrweiler (1962, 1974) on the eastern frontier and the Arab invasions, Nicolas Oikonomides' discussion (1974) of the administrative organisation in the tenth and eleventh centuries, Ralph-Johannes Lilie's monograph (1976) on the Byzantine reaction to the Arab expansion, and a study by John Haldon and Hugh Kennedy (1980) on the military organisation and society in the Byzantine–Arab frontier.[5] The last article is one of the very few attempts to discuss the eastern borderland from both a Byzantine and an Arab perspective by outlining military, structural, and socio-economic characteristics of frontier life on both sides.

In the more recent bibliography, there is a strong trend to split the subject area up into various subtopics and thus to concentrate on specific social, ethnic, or religious communities, such as the Syriac Christians, the Armenians, and Muslim local dynasties, or to single out specific regions.[6] These studies

5 Hélène Ahrweiler, 'L'Asie Mineure et les invasions arabes (VIIe–IXe siècles)', *Revue historique* 227 (1962), 1–32; Hélène Ahrweiler, 'La frontière et les frontières de Byzance en Orient', in Mihai Berza and Eugen Stănescu (eds), *Actes du XIVe congrès international des études byzantines, Bucarest, 6–12 Septembre, 1971* (Bucarest: Editura Academiei Republicii Socialiste Romania, 1974), 209–30; Nicolas Oikonomidès, 'L'organisation de la frontière orientale de Byzance aux Xe–XIe siècles et le Taktikon de L'Escorial', in ibid., 285–302; Ralf-Johannes Lilie, *Die byzantinische Reaktion auf die Ausbreitung der Araber, Studien zur Strukturwandlung des byzantinischen Staates im 7. und 8. Jhd.* (Munich: Institut für Byzantinistik und Neugriechische Philologie, 1976); John Haldon and Hugh Kennedy, 'The Arab–Byzantine Frontier in the Eighth and Ninth Centuries: Military Organisation and Society in the Borderlands', *Recueil des travaux de l'Institut d'études byzantines* 19 (1980), 79–116.

6 Gilbert Dagron, 'Minorités ethniques et religieuses dans l'orient byzantine à la fin du Xe et au XIe siècle: l'immigration syrienne', *Travaux et Mémoires* 6 (1976), 177–216; Wolfgang Felix, *Byzanz und die islamische Welt im frühen 11. Jahrhundert* (Vienna: Verlag der Österreichischen Akademie der Wissenschaften, 1981); Gérard Dédéyan, *Les arméniens entre grecs, musulmans et croisés: études sure les pouvoirs arméniens dans le Proche-Orient méditerranéen (1068–1150)* (Lisbon: Fundação Calouste Gulbenkian, 2003); Wassam Farag, 'The Aleppo-Question: A Byzantine–Fatimid Conflict of Interests in Northern Syria in the Later Tenth Century A.D.', *Byzantine and Modern Greek Studies* 14 (1990), 44–61; Klaus-Peter Todt, *Dukat und griechisch-orthodoxes Patriarchat von Antiocheia in mittelbyzantinischer Zeit (969–1084)*, Mainzer Veröffentlichungen zur Byzantinistik 14 (Wiesbaden: Harrassowitz Verlag, 2018); Bernd Andreas Vest, *Geschichte der Stadt Melitene und der umliegenden Gebiete: Vom Vorabend der arabischen bis zum Abschluss der türkischen Eroberung (um 600–1124)* (Hamburg: Verlag Dr. Kovač, 2007); Thomas Ripper, *Die Marwāniden von Diyār Bakr: Eine kurdische Dynastie im islamischen Mittelalter*, 2nd edn (Würzburg: Ergon, 2009).

significantly deepen our understanding of the complex socio-ethnic and religious mosaic of borderland populations and the numerous regional particularities in this vast zone, but they rarely factor in the broader political, cultural, and societal context framing the historical developments of all these groups and geographical units. There is only a small number of more comprehensive monographs discussing long-term evolutionary patterns and/or the eastern borderland in its entirety. Significant progress has been made regarding our understanding of the prosopography, the social networks, and the political function of the Byzantine aristocracy in Asia Minor in both regional structures and centre–periphery relations.[7] In this respect, one should also mention the work of Georgios Leveniotis, who presented a very detailed analysis of the administrative structures of the entire eastern borderland in the final phase of its existence in the second half of the eleventh century prior to the arrival of the Seljuk Turks.[8]

As regards the Islamic borderland with its two sections of fortified garrison towns stretching from the Cilician plain to the Pyramos/Jayḥān valley around Germanikeia/Marʿash (*al-thughūr al-Shāmiyya*) and from the Upper Euphrates around Melitene/Malaṭya to the Tigris river (*al-thughūr al-Jazariyya*), Michael Bonner examined the local Muslim military and religious elites in the early Abbasid period and their ways of instrumentalising the jihad ideology for military and economic purposes.[9] Recently, Asa Eger presented the first systematic analysis of settlement patterns in the borderlands by distinguishing between different types of inhabitation, communication, and agrarian activity, such as towns, villages, canal and river sites, upland sites, routes, and way stations. His primary evidence consists of literary sources and material remains documented by various types of archaeological surveys. While his primary

7 For a useful survey, see Jean-Claude Cheynet, 'The Byzantine aristocracy (8th–13th centuries)', in Cheynet, *The Byzantine Aristocracy and its Military Function*, Variorum collected studies 859 (Aldershot: Ashgate, 2006), no. I; the most recent monograph on the subject is Luisa Andriollo, *Constantinople et les provinces d'Asie Mineure, IXe–XIe siècle: administration impériale, sociétés locales et rôle de l'aristocratie*, Centre de recherche d'histoire et civilization de Byzance, Monographies 52 (Leuven: Peeters, 2017).

8 Georgios Leveniotis, Η πολιτική κατάρρευση του Βυζαντίου στην Ανατολή, το ανατολικό σύνορο και η κεντρική Μικρά Ασία κατά το β' ήμισυ του 11ου αι. (Thessalonica: Byzantine Research Center, 2007).

9 Michael Bonner, *Aristocratic Violence and Holy War: Studies in the Jihad and Arab–Byzantine Frontier* (New Haven, CT: American Oriental Society, 1996).

focus is on the Muslim-held regions of the borderland, there is also a useful chapter on Byzantine settlement patterns in Cappadocia.[10]

A recent surge of scholarly interest in the question of Byzantine identity resulted in some sophisticated interpretations of how the Byzantines perceived themselves and defined their relations with the world around them. It remains controversial whether we should imagine Byzantine provincial society as a homogeneous ethnic entity steeped in shared Christian-Roman identity features or as a loosely knit multi-ethnic mosaic held together by the coercive power and elite culture of the Constantinopolitan ruling class.[11] In all likelihood, there were differences in time and space, and it is hardly possible to give a definitive answer to this question. What seems to be helpful in this respect is to draw a distinction between different levels of provincial realities and living conditions. This is precisely what Hélène Ahrweiler did by distinguishing between several co-existing notions of frontier.[12] In particular, she singles out five categories: the empire's ideological frontiers rest upon the old binary opposition between the civilised and the barbarian world and coincide with the perimeter of the cultural and religious sphere of Byzantine Christianity. Political frontiers mark the limits of imperial authority and the central government's influence in dependent buffer states. Administrative frontiers delimit the imperial territories with their provincial organisation, institutions, and officials. Fiscal frontiers include not only the taxable subject population but also tributary people living beyond the political boundaries. Military frontiers designate the empire's defensive structures along a well-defended borderline supported by natural barriers and strategically well-situated strongholds in the hinterland.

All these levels of frontier realities, in one way or another, came to bear in the centuries-long history of the Byzantine–Muslim borderland. Diachronic developments were closely linked with social and economic changes in the interior of the empire, altering centre–periphery relations, the living conditions

[10] Alexander Asa Eger, *The Islamic–Byzantine Frontier: Interaction and Exchange among Muslim and Christian Communities* (London: I. B. Tauris, 2015), 246–63.

[11] For a fresh discussion with an argumentation in favour of the former view, see Anthony Kaldellis, *Romanland: Ethnicity and Empire in Byzantium* (Cambridge, MA: Belknap Press, 2019).

[12] Ahrweiler, 'Frontière', 209–13, 215–18.

of frontier societies, and the political constellations at the interface between Byzantium and the caliphate. What makes the eastern frontier unique and pivotal in comparison to other borderland areas in the Balkan Peninsula, Italy, or the Black Sea region, is the fact that it constituted the contact zone between two rival empires with mutually exclusive claims to universal rule, religious truth, and supremacy.[13] This is to say that the overall situation was dominated by a more or less constant state of war and other forms of political antagonism, although both sides were also keen to maintain lines of communication and to reach temporary agreements through a variety of tools and channels of diplomacy.[14] The emergence of independent regional powers in northern Iraq, Syria, and Egypt from the second half of the ninth century onwards, the Byzantine eastward expansion in the tenth century, and the penetration of large parts of Asia Minor by the Seljuk Turks in the eleventh century certainly caused major shifts in the balance of power between the two sides and had a huge impact on the aforementioned levels of ideological, political, administrative, fiscal, and military frontier life. Yet these developments did not radically alter the underlying attitudes and concepts of antagonism between Byzantines and Muslims. Even after the total collapse of Byzantine rule and the extinction of an eastern frontier in Asia Minor during the fourteenth century there still were ideological traditions and behavioral patterns linking the Ottoman sultans and their armies with the Byzantine–Muslim frontier of the classical age, as is aptly illustrated by Paul Wittek's gazi thesis and the scholarly debates it has sparked in recent decades.[15]

A crucial factor that determines our perception and understanding of the Byzantine–Muslim borderland is the nature and quality of information provided by the available literary sources. These include a broad range

[13] Ahrweiler, 'Frontière', 224–6.

[14] Hugh Kennedy, 'Byzantine–Arab Diplomacy in the Near East from the Islamic Conquests to the Mid-Eleventh Century', in Jonathan Shepard and Simon Franklin (eds), *Byzantine Diplomacy: Papers from the Twenty-fourth Spring Symposium of Byzantine Studies, Cambridge, March 1990* (Aldershot: Ashgate, 1992), 133–43.

[15] Paul Wittek, *The Rise of the Ottoman Empire: Studies in the History of Turkey, Thirteenth-Fifteenth Centuries*, ed. Colin Heywood with an Introduction and Afterword (Oxford: Routledge, 2012).

of reports in Byzantine, Syriac, Armenian, and Arab chronicles, occasional references in saint's lives, miracle accounts, and letters, Byzantine military treatises, and Arab geographical manuals referring to the provinces of Asia Minor. Taken together, these texts offer a rich set of data regarding military activities, administrative and defensive measures, the course of action, size, and nature of individual military units, the itineraries and targets of campaigns, battles, spoils of war, and the consequences for the local population. As such, they constitute the backbone for the reconstruction of historical facts concerning political and military developments. Nevertheless, historians have to bear in mind that these snippets of information form part of specific narrative frameworks, ideological discourses, rhetorical strategies, and authorial intentions. They may contain a kernel of truth and their chronological and factual accuracy can sometimes be corroborated by other sources. Yet it is frequently impossible to appraise the reliability and trustworthiness of the written record when it comes to specific details about the sequence of events, individual behaviours, numerical figures for the size of towns and troops, a region's prosperity, or devastations caused by incursions and related acts of war. The boundaries between historical facts, actual experiences, and literary set-pieces are blurred and there are no clear criteria to make a neat distinction. Additional evidence can be drawn from lead seals documenting Byzantine officials and administrative structures in the frontier regions, but due to the dearth of narrative sources providing further historical context the interpretation of the pertinent data is often subject to guesswork.[16]

Living Conditions and Socio-economic Structures

Modern misconceptions, interpretive pitfalls, and the overall scarcity of written and material evidence inevitably distort or obfuscate our knowledge of the

[16] For the wealth of information provided by sigillographic evidence, see, for instance, Jean-Claude Cheynet, 'Thathoul, archonte des archontes', *Revue des études byzantines* 48 (1990), 233–42; Jean-Claude Cheynet, 'La résistence aux Turcs en Asie Mineure entre Mantzikert et la Première Croisade', in *Εὐψυχία, Mélanges offerts à Helène Ahrweiler*, Byzantina Sorbonensia 16 (Paris: Publications de la Sorbonne, 1998), 1: 131–47; Stefan Heidemann and Claudia Sode, 'Christlich-orientalische Bleisiegel im Orientalischen Münzkabinett Jena', *ARAM* 11/12 (1999/2000), 535–95; Stefan Heidemann and Claudia Sode, 'Ihtiyār ad-Dīn al-Hasan ibn Gafras, ein Rūm-seldschukischer Usurpator aus byzantinischem Adel im Jahr 588/1192', *Der Islam* 95 (2018), 450–78.

living conditions, socio-economic structures, and demographic patterns in the Byzantine–Muslim borderland. It will always be impossible to reconstruct a coherent and accurate picture, but we may still try to sharpen our awareness of pertinent problems and thus refine our tools of analysis. The predominant narrative of the Byzantine life-and-death struggle and the subsequent counterattack on the Muslim caliphate conjures up notions of incessant warfare, belligerent warrior elites, and an uncivilised wilderness amidst bleak and desolate landscapes.[17] While it can be safely assumed that fierce fighting, acts of unrestrained violence, and ransacking were recurring phenomena in the unsecure conditions of heavily contested frontier regions, it is also self-evident that such events did not occur at all times and everywhere with the same regularity and intensity.[18] The available evidence demonstrates that the movements of military units and the radius of action of raiding hosts followed certain patterns, which were determined by strategic and logistic considerations, geographic and climatic conditions, existing road networks, the permeability of defensive structures, and the accessibility of promising targets.[19] This is to say that the most devastating effects of warfare were limited to specific periods and regions. Many areas, after being exposed to raids and hostilities, experienced phases of tranquility and economic recovery while more remote sections of the borderland may have remained undisturbed over longer time periods. After the campaigns of the early 780s, which stood under the direct command of members of the Abbasid ruling elite,[20] Muslim large-scale invasions of Byzantine territory became a relatively rare phenomenon. The territorial gains during the Byzantine eastward expansion were in most cases preceded by a decisive weakening of the Muslim defensive position. The annexation of the newly acquired territories thus met only minor resistance and could often be achieved during a single campaign. There certainly is a bias in the literary sources, which place much emphasis on

[17] For a recent discussion of these perceptions, see Eger, *Islamic–Byzantine Frontier*, 1–12.

[18] Eger, *Islamic–Byzantine Frontier*, 2–3, aptly points to the frequent use of the Arabic key term *'imāra* ('rebuild, cultivate') to designate the restoration of settlements and agricultural activities in previously devastated frontier zones.

[19] Ahrweiler, 'L'Asie Mineure', 7–10; for a detailed documentation, see the extensive analysis in Lilie, *Reaktion*, 60–83, 112–33, 143–55, 169–78, 183–200.

[20] Lilie, *Reaktion*, 172–6.

exceptional disruptive events and military matters. But if we put these events into their chronological and geographical context, it becomes clear that the vision of a highly militarised and conflict-ridden frontier was only one aspect within the entire range of living conditions in the borderland. It remains problematic that the available information is all too often insufficient to shed more light on the everyday life of social strata and population groups living in the towns, rural areas, and strongholds of these regions.

This gap can partly be filled by new findings and methodological advancements in the fields of archaeological and environmental-paleoclimatic research. In the past few decades, both areas have developed into vibrant and thriving disciplines, which produce a constant stream of fresh data preserved in buildings and material remains, on the one hand, and biological and geological climate archives, on the other.[21] Making use of such data in the context of historical interpretations, especially if done by non-specialists without the support of interdisciplinary collaboration, always runs the risk to be compromised by methodologically unsound approaches and thus to result in misleading conclusions.[22] Historians are not always aware of the pitfalls of data gained from archaeological surveys, which are biased by differing methods, sampling strategies, and geographical coverage. Linking socio-economic phenomena with environmental impacts and climatic phenomena can lead to over-deterministic explanatory models, over-simplified causal connections, or false generalisations of data obtained from microregional case studies. Yet, recent studies by John Haldon, Michael Decker, Asa Eger, and others have demonstrated that a careful use of material and environmental data in many ways helps illuminate certain trends and phenomena recognisable in the written evidence or modify the conclusions resulting from the latter, especially with respect to long-term evolutionary patterns, as well as large-scale disruptions and continuities that left their traces in archaeological remains and the archives

[21] For recent surveys, see John Haldon *et al.*, 'The Climate and Environment of Byzantine Anatolia: Integrating Science, History, and Archaeology', *Journal of Interdisciplinary History* 45 (2014), 113–61; Philipp Niewöhner (ed.), *The Archaeology of Byzantine Anatolia: From the End of Late Antiquity until the Coming of the Turks* (Oxford: Oxford University Press, 2017).

[22] Haldon *et al.*, 'Climate and Environment', 115–20.

of nature.[23] For all the progress in interdisciplinary research endeavours, however, it remains a tricky task to extract conclusions from microregional findings and to harmonise them with long-term developments and general trends in the Byzantine–Muslim borderland as a whole.

The urban and rural settlement patterns in the eastern borderland form part of the broader evolutionary trends in Anatolian towns and villages between the seventh and the eleventh centuries. Despite all gaps in our knowledge and the controversial debates on methodological and terminological issues, scholars managed to reconstruct a persuasive picture of Anatolian urbanism from the seventh century onwards with respect to demographic changes, settlement patterns, economic and social structures, administrative matters, and the relations with the central government.[24] As John Haldon put it, cities ceased to be 'centers of self-governing administrative regions' and therefore lost their significance as centres of investment, commercial activities, and patronage for the local landowning elite.[25] Instead, they turned into 'seats of administrative establishments', military strongholds within regional defensive structures, and places of refuge affording protection to the rural population living in their vicinity.[26] The urban economy rested primarily upon a subsistence agriculture with the majority of the townspeople owning or working on landed estates in the surrounding rural areas and living from local produce.[27] This is to say that there was very little room for forms of market economy based on surplus investments and trade in luxury goods. Transfers and circulations of coinages were

[23] Haldon *et al.*, 'Climate and Environment', 120–38; Michael Decker, 'Settlement and Economy in the Byzantine East', *Dumbarton Oaks Papers* 61 (2007), 217–67; Asa Eger, 'Ḥiṣn al-Tīnāt on the Islamic–Byzantine Frontier: Synthesis and the 2005–2008 Survey and Excavation on the Cilician Plain (Turkey)', *Bulletin of the American Schools of Oriental Research* 357 (2010), 19–76; Eger, *Islamic–Byzantine Frontier*, 12–21.

[24] The fundamental study on the topic remains Wolfram Brandes, *Die Städte Kleinasiens im 7. und 8. Jahrhundert*, Berliner Byzantinistische Arbeiten 56 (Berlin: Akademie-Verlag, 1989); for brief outlines of recent archaeological research on cities and fortifications, see Philipp Niewöhner, 'Urbanism', in Niewöhner (ed.), *Archaeology of Byzantine Anatolia*, 39–59, and James Crow, 'Fortifications', in ibid., 90–108.

[25] Haldon and Kennedy, 'Arab–Byzantine Frontier', 92.

[26] Haldon and Kennedy, 'Arab–Byzantine Frontier', 92–4.

[27] Haldon and Kennedy, 'Arab–Byzantine Frontier', 90–1.

closely linked with state-controlled activities whereas the local elite invested its wealth in titles and offices granted by the central government.[28] Provincial cities thus stood out as seats of military commanders and tax officials.

As regards developments in the urban morphology of Anatolian cities, it remains problematic that the bulk of the surviving archaeological and material evidence stems from the relatively large and well-researched sites of western Asia Minor and a few better-known sites in the interior, such as Aizanoi, Ankyra, Amorion, and Euchaita.[29] It is hard to say whether and to what extent the findings resulting from these sites can be used for the interpretation of smaller settlements in the less urbanised areas of the frontier region. Another serious obstacle in reconstructing diachronic developments in the time of the Arab invasions results from the fact that most of the datable material pertains either to the late antique period or later phases from the Comnenian era onwards.[30] Recent research in the intervening period between the seventh and the eleventh centuries has produced some remarkable results, but once again they are primarily based on sites in western and central Anatolia. Both written and archaeological evidence makes plain that the reigns of the emperors Anastasius (491–518) and Justinian (527–65) were marked by a boom of fortification works in Anatolia.[31] The imperial government made strong efforts to repair and renew the walls of important provincial centres (Caesarea), places of worship and pilgrimage (Euchaita), and exposed border cities (Theodosioupolis, Amida, Dara), and to protect key arteries in the east–west communications between the interior of Asia Minor and the *limes* of the Orient, such as the road between Sebasteia and Satala (Sadak).[32] There were different types of fortification layouts that made their appearance from the fifth/sixth century onwards and shaped the further development of urban spaces. There was a widely attested tendency to rebuild walls in a smaller, but better defended, circuit. This tendency coincided with the emergence of a new pattern of

[28] Haldon and Kennedy, 'Arab–Byzantine Frontier', 90–1 with the discussion in n. 39.

[29] Niewöhner, 'Urbanism', 42–6.

[30] Crow, 'Fortifications', 92–4, 102–4, 106–7.

[31] Crow, 'Fortifications', pp. 92–4.

[32] Crow, 'Fortifications', 91 (Amida), 92 (Caesarea, Sebasteia, Satala), 93 (Theodosioupolis, Euchaita), 98 (Amida, Dara, Theodosioupolis); for Satala, see T. B. Mitford, 'The Inscriptions of Satala (Armenia Minor)', *Zeitschrift für Papyrologie und Epigraphik* 115 (1997), 137–67.

spatial arrangement, which consisted of a fortress and an extensive circuit surrounding the pre-existing ancient settlement, as can be seen, for instance, in Koloneia (Şebinkarahisar).[33] The examples of Ankyra and Amorion demonstrate that some places in central Anatolia maintained the entire circuit of the ancient walls until they endured heavy attacks in the ninth century and concentrated their defences on the acropolis fortresses (*kastra*).[34] Recent studies on coastal sites in western and southern Asia Minor, such as Miletus, Ephesus, Magnesia, Patara, and Side, demonstrate that there was a phase of refortifications after the turn of the seventh century in response to the exposure of these cities to seaborne raids and other military threats. Philipp Niewöhner has identified a number of 'exclusive circuits', which exclude a significant part of the ancient townscape and create a new well-defended core of urban settlement.[35] The Cappadocian metropolis of Mokissos (Viranşehir/Helvadere) exemplifies fortresses which were relocated to more defensible positions and took the shape of fortified enclosures on acropolis hills serving as military outposts and hilltop defences.[36] Even larger villages could have their own defences, as is attested by the site of Şerefiye Kalesi.[37] Overall, the surviving archaeological remains suggest that the Arab raids rarely entailed a total collapse of pre-existing settlement traditions. The repair and erection of new walls and other centrally sponsored building activities show that cities both at the frontier and in the interior maintained their significance as 'primary nodes of political control', as Michael Decker put it.[38] Characteristic features of ancient urbanism, such as the regular layout and the street grid, were abandoned and there were alterations in their spatial constellations and settlement patterns. The erection of church buildings within and outside walled cities point to some degree of local wealth and prosperity.[39]

[33] Crow, 'Fortifications', 93.

[34] Niewöhner, 'Urbanism', 52–3; Crow, 'Fortifications', 98–9 (in the case of Amorium the outer wall was abandoned after the attack of 838).

[35] Niewöhner, 'Urbanism', 51–2; Crow, 'Fortifications', 95–6.

[36] Crow, 'Fortifications', 92.

[37] Crow, 'Fortifications', 94.

[38] Decker, 'Frontier Settlement', 220.

[39] Niewöhner, 'Urbanism', 52–3.

Some sites in Cappadocia, which are documented by both written sources and archaeological remains, aptly illustrate cases of continuity, disruption, and decay in the borderland during the time of the Arab attacks. Caesarea (Kayseri) stood out as metropolitan see of Cappadocia I, a hub of communications, and a military camp.[40] Despite two Arab conquests in 646 and 726, the city maintained its significance as a well-defended regional centre. There are hardly any remains of late antique or Byzantine monuments within the medieval settlement area, but it can be assumed that sections of the Justinianic fortification were integrated into the Seljuk citadel walls and some adjacent sections of the city walls. This points to a strong continuity in the urban layout between the sixth and the twelfth century. The demographic and economic boom that began with the Byzantine eastward expansion is reflected in a number of church buildings in the rural area around Caesarea dating to the ninth and tenth centuries.[41] Tyana, another metropolis and capital of Cappadocia II, was situated in a fertile and well-watered region, where important road connections coming from Constantinople and the Black Sea region converged.[42] The city endured heavy attacks in the eighth century and seems to have been totally destroyed and abandoned when the caliphs Hārūn al-Rashīd and al-Maʾmūn sought to rebuild and repopulate the place. Despite an extensive irrigation system, the place never recovered and after its final destruction in 833 gave way to the rise of the nearby city of Nakida (Niğde) as new centre in southern Cappadocia.[43] Just as in Caesarea, the Byzantine foundations of the citadel walls are still recognisable but cannot be dated. Mokissos (Viranşehir) was rebuilt by Emperor Justinian in the form of a hill town with an acropolis fort and churches and thus assumed the name of Ioustinianoupolis.[44] In 536 the city first appeared as metropolis of a new ecclesiastical province in Cappadocia II. The modern site which has

[40] Friedrich Hild and Marcell Restle, *Kappadokien (Kappadokia, Charsianon, Sebasteia und Lykandos)*, Tabula Imperii Byzantini 2 (Vienna: Verlag der Österreichischen Akademie der Wissenschaften, 1981), 193–6 (s. v. Kaisareia); Decker, 'Frontier Settlement', 240–2.

[41] Decker, 'Frontier Settlement', 241–2.

[42] Hild and Restle, *Kappadokien*, 298–9 (s. v. Tyana); Decker, 'Frontier Settlement', 242.

[43] Hild and Restle, *Kappadokien*, 243–4 (s. v. Nakīdā).

[44] Hild and Restle, *Kappadokien*, 238–9 (s. v. Mōki(s)sos); Decker, 'Frontier Settlement', 243–5.

been identified with Mokissos is an area of formidable size with numerous archaeological traces including remnants of houses indicating a later abandonment of the Justinianic settlement, streets, and substructures of churches which can partly be dated to the time after 600. In sum, the settlement of Mokissos underwent a profound change from its Justinianic layout to a spacious area extending to the surrounding hills of the Helvadere valley but was never entirely abandoned or destroyed.

Other places are documented by the written sources as episcopal sees of suffragan bishoprics and military strongholds, but the surviving archaeological evidence is rather poor, and thus we can hardly arrive at any safe conclusions regarding their size, urban layout, population, and functional diversification. Kiskisos (Yaylacık) was a bishopric of Cappadocia I and was situated on a pass road running across the Taurus to Adana.[45] Until the early twentieth century there seem to have been visible remnants of church buildings in the village and its surroundings, but nothing has been preserved. Rodandos was situated close to the Cilician Gates on the street to Adana in the valley of the Zamantı Irmağı.[46] Literary sources attest to an extension of the city in 778/9 by an imperial official. Remains of a fortress are still visible but not dated. Podandos was a place of great strategic and military significance in the time of the Arab incursions.[47] It is mentioned as rallying point of troops, a place for prisoner exchanges and for diplomatic contacts in the eighth and ninth centuries, but there are no archaeological remains. All these places apparently played a significant role in the defensive system of the frontier zone separating Muslim-held Cilicia from Cappadocia, and the Byzantines were at pains to fortify and maintain them as advanced outposts. In the absence of sufficient archaeological evidence, it is hard to say what other functions these places might have fulfilled apart from their military tasks. Their existence demonstrates, however, that there was some population even in the immediate vicinity of the Muslim territories and one of the major invasion routes, something that contradicts the widespread notion of a devastated no-man's land. Admittedly, nothing can be said about the living

45 Hild and Restle, *Kappadokien*, 206 (s. v. Kiskisos).

46 Hild and Restle, *Kappadokien*, 266–7 (s. v. Rodandos).

47 Hild and Restle, *Kappadokien*, 261–262 (s. v. Podandos).

conditions in these places and there is no way of knowing whether they were able to develop into larger settlements supported by a local agrarian economy.

The available archaeological evidence roughly corroborates the descriptions provided by the tenth-century military treatise on *Skirmishing*, which was written at the behest of Emperor Nikephoros II Phokas (963–9) and constitutes our main source for the military strategy and the defensive structures in the borderland.[48] The text's repeated references to differing zones of security corresponds with the picture of a multilayered defensive structure which comprised new forms of urban fortresses, regional centres, watchtowers, and village defences, which were scattered over various parts of the frontier and made their gradual appearance in the eighth and ninth centuries.[49] John Skylitzes' famous account of a chain of fire beacons linking the hill-top fortress of Loulon (Çanakçı/Gedelli Kale) situated on the Taurus frontier between Tyana and the Cilician Gates with the imperial capital fits well into this picture.[50] The terminological variety in the primary sources referring to towns and fortresses in the borderland, such as *chora* ('district of a city'), *kastron* ('castle, fortress'), *ochyroma* ('fortified place, fortress'), *polis* ('city'), *phrourion* ('fortress'), and so forth, is also reflective of this complex situation.[51] The

[48] *Skirmishing/Περὶ Παραδρομῆς*, in George T. Dennis (ed. and trans.), *Three Byzantine Military Treatises*, Corpus Fontium Historiae Byzantinae 25 (Washington, DC: Dumbarton Oaks Library and Collection, 1985), 137–239.

[49] *Skirmishing*, ed. Dennis, 150–1 (sentries [βιγλάτορες] are to be stationed in watch posts [βίγλαι] on high and rugged mountains, which are three to four miles apart), 152–3 (watch posts on roads [καμινοβίγλια]), 162–3 ([τραπεζῖται ἤτοι τὰ τασινάκια] and scouts [κατάσκοποι] are to be sent out in the time before the Arab summer raids in September), 182–3 (infantry troops are to occupy secure locations near fortresses), 218–23 (when the *kastron Mistheias* was besieged by Arabs from Cilicia, two generals defended the fortress while another unit attacked the region of Adana; when Sayf al-Dawla attacked Byzantine territory, the commander of Lykandos attacked the region around Aleppo and Antioch), 230–1 (infantry forces are to be dispatched to mountain passes).

[50] John Skylitzes, *Ioannis Scylitzae Synopsis Historiarum, editio princeps*, ed. Johannes Thurn, Corpus Fontium Historiae Byzantinae 5 (Berlin: Walter de Gruyter, 1973), 108; Hild and Restle, *Kappadokien*, 223 (s. v. Lulon).

[51] Skylitzes, *Synopsis*, 108: φρούριόν τι τῇ Ταρσῷ ἀγχίθυρον (i.e. Loulon), 185: πλησιάζοντα τῇ Τεφρικῇ φρούρια ἐκπορθήσας, τὴν Ἄβαραν, τὸν Κοπτόν, τὴν Σπάθην καὶ ἄλλα πολλά, 224: καὶ πλεῖστα φρούρια καὶ ὀχυρώματα καὶ πόλεις βαρβαρικὰς καθελών,

sources defy any unequivocal categorisation or hierarchisation in semantic nuances, but there are some recurring tendencies. The terms *polis* and *chora* usually designate larger provincial centres of administrative and military significance and their hinterland. Smaller fortresses which are situated in the vicinity of a *polis* and form a defensive network with the latter are frequently called *phrouria* or *ochyromata*. The term *kastron* may designate both a city and a well-defended stronghold in a strategic location of the borderland.

It would go beyond the scope of this introductory chapter to discuss the frequently complex and conjectural correlations between altering climatic conditions, human activity, modes of land use, and related societal and economic developments. Establishing over-simplifying links between climate/environment and large-scale political and socio-economic phenomena, such as the rise and fall of political powers, population movements, or the prevalence of certain military forces can hardly stand up to scrutiny. With respect to shifting weather regimes in central Europe, the Balkans, and the Eastern Mediterranean, paleoclimatic studies agree that in central and western Anatolia there was an overall trend towards more humid weather conditions in the seventh and eighth century.[52] For all uncertainties resulting from gaps in the documentation or the inaccurate dating and locating of specific phenomena, this climatic trend seems to correspond with the historical data in that the written sources record considerably more droughts and famines prior to than after 560.[53] Of course, scholars have to factor in numerous regional particularities, which are related to the impact of different large-scale circulation systems and a high degree of geographic differentiation between lowlands, upland plains, mountains, steppes, and so on. In recent years, specialists made great strides in using palynological data gained from pollen in natural deposits for the purpose of interpreting developments in vegetation patterns and land use.[54] These and other methods allow us to view distinct phases of

ἔφθασε καὶ μέχρι τῆς περιβοήτου Μελιτηνῆς. *Skirmishing*, ed. Dennis, 182, line 6: εἰ τύχῃ καὶ πλήσιον κάστρον, 218, line 23: κατὰ τῆς χώρας Ἀδάνης, 218, line 25: ἀπὸ μιλίων δύο τῆς πόλεως αὐτῶν (i.e. Adana).

[52] Haldon *et al.*, 'Climate and Environment', 122–3.

[53] Haldon *et al.*, 'Climate and Environment', 126–7.

[54] Haldon *et al.*, 'Climate and Environment', 132–45.

anthropogenic activity in conjunction with paleoclimatic and historical data, reach a better understanding of the environmental and ecological conditions of socio-economic developments, and make more accurate assumptions about the causal effects and reciprocities that may have been at work.

Large parts of Anatolia up to about 700/800 are defined by palynologists as showing the characteristics of the Beyşehir Occupation Phase, which was 'marked by the cultivation of olive and nut trees, cereal growing, and pastoralism'.[55] Thereafter, the available data point to an expansion of natural vegetation, which, in turn, indicates that forms of intensive exploitation along with pre-existing urban and agricultural customs receded and the demographic development took a downward trend while 'cereal production and livestock raising began to dominate'.[56] In the later ninth and tenth centuries, there seems to have been a new shift, an expansion of large-scale pastoral farming along with the reappearance of cultivars, cereals, vines, olives, and fruits.[57] This indicates a revival of the agrarian economy and new population growth. Changes in the prevailing climatic conditions certainly had an impact on these developments, but the question as to what this meant in specific regions during a given period and how exactly causal effects should be understood is open to much speculation.

As for the Byzantine–Arab borderland, there is a unique site providing outstandingly rich and precisely datable paleoenvironmental evidence: the sediments of Narlıgöl Crater Lake near the village of Gösterli in the modern province of Niğde in southern Cappadocia.[58] The high-resolution record deriving from the pollen analysis of these sediments not only documents the diachronic vegetation patterns of the entire surrounding district along with possible impacts of climatic and anthropogenic factors but also allows a chronologically accurate reconstruction of phases of intensive agriculture up to 670

55 Haldon *et al.*, 'Climate and Environment', 132.

56 Haldon *et al.*, 'Climate and Environment', 138–9 (quotation on 139).

57 Haldon *et al.*, 'Climate and Environment', 140.

58 John Haldon, '"Cappadocia will be given over to ruin and become a desert", Environmental Evidence for Historically-Attested Events in the 7th–10th Centuries', in Klaus Belke, Ewald Kislinger, Andreas Külzer, Maria A. Stassinopoulou (eds), *Byzantina Mediterranea: Festschrift für Johannes Koder zum 65. Geburtstag* (Vienna: Böhlau Verlag, 2007), 215–30, esp. 219–20.

and between c. 950 and 1100, which were interrupted by a sudden collapse of agricultural activities, causing protracted periods of woodland regrowth.[59] As pollen can be aerially transferred over longer distances, the data in question reflect larger regional, rather than local, trends.[60] Moreover, there are no records documenting greater climatic fluctuations or other catastrophic events in Cappadocia during the aforementioned years. Therefore, the watershed of 670 can in all likelihood be ascribed to human-induced phenomena and has most probably to do with the devastations caused by the Arab raids.[61] It is open to debate whether it is permissible or not to draw analogous conclusions with respect to the subsequent changes.[62] In the 950s, Cappadocia was no longer the main stage of Byzantine–Arab warfare, but Cilicia remained in Muslim hands up to 965, and the conflicts with the Ḥamdānids of Aleppo, as well as the civil strife between the Macedonian regime and the great aristocratic chiefs Basil Skleros and Basil Phokas in the years 976–89 must have had some negative impact on Cappadocia as well.[63] Hence, from a political-military viewpoint the second half of the tenth century can hardly be characterised as a period of tranquility. If there was a significant revival of the local agrarian economy, as palynological data from Lake Nar seem to indicate, we may certainly think of profitable activities and investments of wealthy Anatolian aristocratic families with respect to the large and productive landed estates of the region.[64] Yet there must have been other factors stimulating agricultural productivity in a period which was still relatively unstable.

The available documentary evidence for landownership and agrarian economy in the tenth and eleventh century is mostly limited to monastic centres

[59] Haldon, 'Cappadocia', 220–4.

[60] Haldon, 'Cappadocia', 224.

[61] Haldon, 'Cappadocia', 227–9.

[62] Haldon, 'Cappadocia', 230, establishes a very specific causal link with the 'fertile imperial *episkepsis* (estate) of Drizion' in the Melendiz Ovası south of Lake Nar in the 960s and the occupation of the region by the Seljuks in about 1100.

[63] Marius Canard, *Histoire de la dynastie des H'amdanides de Jazîra et de Syrie*, Publications de la Faculté des Lettres d'Alger, IIe Série, 21 (Paris: Presses Universitaires de France, 1952), 735–827; Jean-Claude Cheynet, *Pouvoir et contestation à Byzance (963–1210)*, Byzantina Sorbonensia 9 (Paris: Publications de la Sorbonne, 1996), 27–34, 329–36.

[64] For their political significance and social networks, see Cheynet, *Contestation*, 321–36.

on Mount Athos and some Aegean islands whereas Asia Minor remains in the dark.[65] This dearth of evidence recently induced Anthony Kaldellis to question the notion of landownership as the backbone of aristocratic power altogether. In his view, the aristocratic families kept vying for titles and offices granted by the imperial court as the main source of wealth and influence.[66] He is certainly right in that the contemporary sources place much emphasis on this competition for controlling the imperial court and its sources of revenue. However, there is no reason to assume that the landowning magnates in Anatolia, who on account of their predominant economic and social position had privileged access to landed estates and other sources of provincial wealth, would not have pursued the same strategies of surplus acquisition and land exploitation as their monastic peers in other parts of the empire. Actually, the relative weakness of the Macedonian central government in the period 959–89 and the increasing influence of the Phokades, the Skleroi, and other aristocratic clans strengthened the political and economic autonomy of these families, which in turn may have contributed to a further increase in the agricultural productivity of their estates. This trend held on even after Basil II's victory in 989 and was also supported by the Byzantine 'protectorate' in northern Syria, on account of which the ducate of Antioch loomed large in imperial politics in the East and the economic networks between Syria, Upper Mesopotamia, and the core regions of Byzantine Anatolia.

The Early Formation and Stabilisation of the Borderland

Let us now turn to a chronologically structured survey of major developments in Byzantium's eastern frontier. The traditional narrative singles out two pivotal moments, namely the withdrawal of the troops of the *magistri militum per Armeniam* and *per Orientem* from Syria and Upper Mesopotamia to the territories beyond the Taurus mountains in about 640, which marked the irreversible end of the Roman *limes Orientis*, and the battle of Manzikert in 1071, which signalled the beginning of the Turkification and Islamisation

[65] Nicolas Oikonomidès, *Fiscalité et exemption fiscal à Byzance (IXe–XIe s.)*, Institut de Recherches byzantines, monographies 2 (Athens: Institut de Recherches byzantines, 1996).

[66] Anthony Kaldellis, *Streams of Gold, Rivers of Blood: The Rise and Fall of Byzantium, 955 A. D. to the First Crusade* (Oxford: Oxford University Press, 2017).

of central and eastern Anatolia.[67] However, considering the manifold political-military, territorial, administrative, and demographic changes that occurred over time in the eastern borderlands, it seems appropriate to further subdivide this long period into three distinct stages. The stage of formation (c. 640s–770s/780s) is characterised by Byzantium's endeavours to seek efficient administrative and military responses to the Arab conquests. Eventually, the Abbasid dynasty's switch to a policy of frontier consolidation coincided with a stabilisation of the Byzantine defensive structures. The following stage of equilibrium (770s/780s–870s) experienced only minor territorial changes but was characterised by a further expansion of the thematic system, an increase of centralising control in the interior of Asia Minor, and a simultaneous decay of Abbasid military power in the frontier regions of Syria and Mesopotamia. The protracted third stage of Byzantine expansionism (870s–1070s) brought about considerable territorial gains, the influx of new population groups, among them Syriac Christians and Armenian elites, and the creation of a network of Muslim vassal emirates in the east. The breakdown of the Byzantine administration in the eastern borderland should not be viewed as the immediate outcome of the defeat of 1071. Rather, it should be seen as a gradual infiltration process dominated by Turkish warrior groups of various origins and backgrounds, which began in the 1050s and culminated on the eve of the First Crusade in the 1090s.

The formation of the eastern borderland was closely linked with the repositioning of the Byzantine armed forces in the wake of the Muslim advance and the ensuing crystallisation of the so-called themes, i.e. 'groupings of provinces' for the placement of military units, which initially existed side by side with the late antique provincial organisation.[68] The early-ninth century chronicle of Theophanes the Confessor first mentions the themes of the *Armeniakōn* and *Anatolikōn* units under the years AM 6159 (= 667) and AM 6161 (= 669) respectively. This seems to indicate that the new formations

[67] Walter E. Kaegi, *Byzantium and the Early Islamic Conquests* (Cambridge: Cambridge University Press, 1992), 147–80; Carole Hillenbrand, *Turkish Myth and Muslim Symbol: The Battle of Manzikert* (Edinburgh: Edinburgh University Press, 2007).

[68] John Haldon, *The Palgrave Atlas of Byzantine History* (Basingstoke: Palgrave Macmillan, 2005), 68.

began to take shape during the reign of Emperor Constans (641–69). By 730 they were identified with a specific geographic area.[69] During this period the Byzantine–Arab power struggle in Asia Minor went through its most aggressive phase in which the Umayyad caliphate pursued a strategy of conquering parts of Asia Minor and pushing towards the Byzantine capital. There were long-distance raiding attacks and large-scale invasions reaching numerous regions in central and western Asia Minor and even the walls of Constantinople in the years 660–78 and 695–718. The Byzantine troops responded to this deadly threat with a guerilla-like defensive strategy avoiding pitched battles and focusing on the protection of key cities and strongholds.[70] The death of Caliph Muʿāwiya (680) and the ensuing civil war in the caliphate allowed the Byzantines to increase their pressure in the exposed conflict zones and thus force the Arabs to make territorial concessions, to share tax revenues from population groups living in certain sections of the frontier region, such as Iberia, Armenia, and the island of Cyprus, and to pay annual tributes to the imperial treasury.[71] After an Umayyad army had failed a second time to take Constantinople by force, the Arab raiding activities lost much of their thrust, and advances into the interior of Asia Minor became rarer. While the Khazars in the Black Sea region exerted considerable influence on Transcaucasia, the Byzantine military units stiffened their resistance especially at sea and in the western coastland and began to take the offensive, achieving some important victories, as happened in the battle of Akroinon in 740.[72] With the rise of the

[69] Theophanes, *Chronographia*, vol. 1: *textum Graecum continens*, ed. Carl de Boor (Leipzig: Teubner, 1883; reprint Hildesheim: Georg Olms, 1980), 348 (AM 6159): ὁ τῶν Ἀρμενιάκων στρατηγὸς Σαβώριος Περσογενὴς ἐστασίασε κατὰ Κώνστα τοῦ βασιλέως . . .; 352 (AM 6161): οἱ δὲ τοῦ θέματος τῶν ἀνατολικῶν ἦλθον ἐν Χρυσοπόλει . . . English translation: *The Chronicle of Theophanes Confessor: Byzantine and Near Eastern History AD 284–813*, trans. with Introduction and Commentary by Cyril Mango and Roger Scott (Oxford: Clarendon Press, 1997), 488, 491; Haldon, *Palgrave Atlas*, 68 ('a clear geographical identity').

[70] Lilie, *Reaktion*, 89–96; for a new dating of the first siege of Constantinople to the period 667–8 rather than the traditional 674–8, see Marek Jankowiak, 'The First Arab Siege of Constantinople', *Travaux et Mémoires* 17 (2013), 237–320.

[71] Lilie, *Reaktion*, 99–112, 133–7.

[72] Lilie, *Reaktion*, 122–33, 137–42 (second siege of Constantinople), 143–62 (Arab invasions into Asia Minor, 720–50).

Abbasid dynasty, Arab raiding activities decreased for some time whereas the Byzantines continued their policy of securing the borderland by temporarily occupying exposed strongholds, deporting the local population, and creating stripes of devasted no-man's land. By the 780s, the Abbasid caliphate had largely abandoned the previous conquest strategy and concentrated instead on fortifying its own frontier districts while, at times, launching large-scale raiding campaigns in the name of Muslim jihad. Caliph Hārūn al-Rashīd led his troops in person into the Byzantine borderland in 803–4, and Caliph al-Maʾmūn did so in the years 830–3, but apart from the caliphs' personal involvement in military affairs and diplomatic contacts with the emperor, these expeditions did not go beyond the customary scope of small-scale skirmishes in the Cappadocian frontier.[73] An exceptional, but isolated, event was Caliph al-Muʿtaṣim's famous and well-documented 838 campaign, which culminated in the conquest of the provincial centre of Amorion. For all the extraordinary character of this attack, it had no lasting impact on the military situation in Asia Minor.[74] Overall, the balance of power between the two sides had become more evenly matched.[75]

The Byzantines had certainly suffered some serious setbacks. They had lost the Cilician plain and their positions in the Amanos mountains from which their Mardaite allies had been able to exert pressure on northern Syria.[76] Despite some successful counterattacks, the Arabs had taken hold of some important outposts in the Cilician and Cappadocian frontier zone.[77] By the late eighth century, the borderland had become more stable but was still highly permeable. While it is not possible to identify a veritable borderline, we may imagine a thinly populated stripe of no-man's land, at the fringes of which both sides maintained some degree of military presence in the form of garrisons, fortified strongholds, and observation posts. The southernmost edge can be located at the Mediterranean coast east of Seleucia (Silifke).

[73] Warren Treadgold, *The Byzantine Revival, 780–842* (Stanford: Stanford University Press, 1988), 133–5; Vasiliev, *Byzance et les Arabes*, 1: 98–124.

[74] Vasiliev, *Byzance et les Arabes*, 1: 144–77.

[75] Lilie, *Reaktion*, 162–72, 178–82.

[76] Lilie, *Reaktion*, 102–11, 119–20, 137–8, 163, 167–8.

[77] Lilie, *Reaktion*, 169–78.

Thence, the border zone stretched along the main crest of the Cilician Taurus range and then in a northeasterly direction through Cappadocia, running parallel to the mountain chains near the left bank of the Halys (Kızıl Irmak) river. At some point east of Tephrike (Divriği) the boundary followed the uppermost course of the Euphrates as far as the region west of Theodosioupolis (Erzurum). Thence it continued in a northerly direction across the Pontic Alps, reaching the Akampsis (Çoruh) river at the city of Sper (İspir). The Byzantines gradually strengthened their control over the entire river valley as far as its estuary on the Black Sea coast.[78]

According to the terminology of the Roman provincial administration, the Byzantine–Muslim borderland comprised the easternmost districts of the provinces of Isauria, Cappadocia, Armenia minor, and Pontus.[79] The structural and organisational changes in the Anatolikon and Armeniakon themes, in which these territories from the seventh century onwards came to be integrated, brought about the emergence of well-defended military districts (*kleisourai*, *kleisourarchiai*) in the vicinity of important junctures and passes in the borderland, the separation of thematic subunits (*tourmai*) along with their development into new autonomous themes centred around local key points, and the establishment of new units in newly acquired territories.[80]

The *kleisoura* of Seleucia abutted the Arab territory of the Cilician plain at the Lamos (Limonlu) river (west of modern Mersin) and became a separate theme at an astonishingly late date under Emperor Romanos I (920–44). The region was of crucial significance for the defence of the southern coastland and the organisation of prisoner exchanges, which in the ninth and tenth centuries developed into a regular form of Byzantine–Arab diplomacy with temporary truces and ritualised exchange procedures at a bridge across the Lamos river.[81] The last exchange of this kind took place in the year 946

[78] Honigmann, *Ostgrenze*, 43–55; Haldon and Kennedy, 'Arab–Byzantine Frontier', 85–6; Haldon, *Palgrave Atlas*, 58–9 (maps 5.1 and 5.2).

[79] Haldon, *Palgrave Atlas*, 34 (map 3.1 showing the slightly different system of the Justinianic period).

[80] Haldon and Kennedy, 'Arab–Byzantine frontier', 85–6, 101–4.

[81] Honigmann, *Ostgrenze*, 44, 81–2; Haldon and Kennedy, 'Arab–Byzantine frontier', 85–6; for the prisoner exchanges of the ninth and tenth centuries, see Maria Campagnolo-Pothitou, 'Les échanges de prisonniers entre Byzance et l'islam aux IXe et Xe siècles', *Journal of Oriental and African Studies* 7 (1995), 1–56.

following negotiations with the Ikhshīdid rulers of Egypt and Syria, as well as the Ḥamdānid emir Sayf al-Dawla.[82] The *kleisoura* of Lesser Cappadocia, originally a *tourma* of the Anatolikon theme, became a theme before 863 and was crucial for fending off incursions coming through the Cilician Gates.[83] The fortress of Charsianon, which most probably has to be located at the plateau between Caesarea and the Halys river, was first attacked by the Arabs in 730, appeared as a *kleisoura* after 793/94 and as an independent theme from 872 onwards.[84] The *kleisourai* of Sebasteia (Sivas) and Koloneia (Şebinkarahisar) were at least until the 840s districts of the Armeniakon theme. The earliest mention of a *strategos* of Koloneia dates to 863. The theme of Sebasteia included the strongholds of Larissa (Mancınık) and Abara (near Mutmur) near the Euphrates bench north of Melitene (Malatya).[85] A key stronghold in the Koloneia district was Kamakha, which was frequently attacked and seized by Arab forces but never permanently occupied.[86] From these border districts the Byzantines managed especially after 837 to build up increasing pressure on Melitene, one of the most exposed Muslim strongholds in the Jazira frontier.[87] The northernmost *kleisoura* of Chaldia had Trebizond as its metropolis and comprised seven bishoprics in the tenth century.[88]

The Byzantine Eastward Expansion

The Byzantine eastward expansion was a complex long-lasting process which stretched over a period of almost two centuries. It began with a number of campaigns headed by Emperor Basil I in the years following the final defeat of the Paulicians in 872 and came to a halt with the annexation of the Armenian kingdom of Kars in 1064.[89] By that time considerable portions of the borderland in northern Syria, Mesopotamia, and Armenia were already exposed to the attacks of the Seljuk Turks. Almost all available

82 Campagnolo-Pothitou, 'Échanges', 45–6.

83 Honigmann, *Ostgrenze*, 44–9.

84 Honigmann, *Ostgrenze*, 49–52; Hild and Restle, *Kappadokien*, 163–5.

85 Honigmann, *Ostgrenze*, 51; Hild and Restle, *Kappadokien*, 274–6.

86 Honigmann, *Ostgrenze*, 56–8.

87 Honigmann, *Ostgrenze*, 58–60.

88 Honigmann, *Ostgrenze*, 53–4.

89 Honigmann, *Ostgrenze*, 55–63, 188–9.

descriptions of this period project the narrative of a heroic age of forceful conquests and imperial restoration. Warlike representatives of the Macedonian dynasty, capable generals belonging to the most powerful lineages of the Anatolian aristocracy, and the so-called military emperors Nikephoros II Phokas (963–9) and John I Tzimiskes (969–76) accomplished unprecedented feats of valour in the wars against the Arabs, regained vast swathes of territory, and annexed a large number of Armenian and Georgian vassal principalities. Nevertheless, this idealised image should not inveigle us into adopting outdated notions of a grand strategy of reconquest pursued by an ethnically-religiously unified and politically-economically reinvigorated Christian-Roman empire. An appropriate understanding of this process requires a parallel analysis of measures taken by the Constantinopolitan central government and of peripheral constellations in the eastern borderlands. Campaigns, expansionist movements, and the ensuing implementation of new administrative and defensive structures have to be studied in conjunction with developments among the leading aristocratic factions and regional population groups in the eastern provinces, be they Orthodox Greeks, Monophysite or Melkite Syrian Christians, or Armenians, and the changing fate of the Arab and Kurdish emirates on the Muslim side of the border. It is in this period that Byzantine–Arab coalitions and cross-border relations, be it on a personal or collective level and in the form of personal networks, intermarriages, and formal treaties and alliances, began to make their appearance on a large scale and became a basic characteristic of political and social life in the borderland.

In the diachronic development of the administrative organisation which the imperial government implemented with the creation of new military districts there was a first expansionist thrust directed towards the Upper Euphrates region stretching from Melitene and the juncture with the Arsanias river (Murat Nehri) as far as Theodosioupolis (Erzurum). Two decades after the establishment of the theme of Lykandos in the waterheads region of the Pyramos/Jayḥān river (914), Byzantine forces managed to seize Melitene (934).[90] As a result, the imperial

[90] Honigmann, *Ostgrenze*, 66–9, 72–5; Hild and Restle, *Kappadokien*, 224–6 (Lykandos), 233–5 (Melitene).

administration solidified its presence in the wider region by installing the theme of Mesopotamia comprising the Armenian districts of Tekēs, Kamakha, and Keltzēnē, the *kleisoura* of Romanoupolis, the theme of Charpezikion around Charpete (Harput) and, some years later, the themes of Chozanon (c. 950) and Asmosaton/Shimshāṭ (938–52).[91] It was most probably also in about 934/35 that the Byzantine troops conquered Theodosioupolis and founded a theme there, which included districts south of the Araxes river (Aras Nehri), such as Awnik.[92]

As the foundation of the theme of Lykandos suggests, another key zone of military control and expansion during the 940s and 950s was the region stretching from the upper course of the Jayḥān river with its passes and frontier strongholds, such as Germanikeia/Marʿash and Adatā/al-Ḥadath, as far as the Euphrates fortresses situated opposite the Arab territories of Diyār Muḍar and Diyār Bakr, such as Samosata (Samsat; 958) and Kayshūn (Keyşun).[93] All these conquests prepared the ground for major territorial acquisitions that were accomplished under the leadership of Nikephoros II Phokas. In particular, he seized the cities of the Cilician plain (965), the Armenian province of Taron (966/7) stretching along the Arsanias valley west of Lake Van, and, on 28 October 969, the city of Antioch and its hinterland, which a few months later led to the conclusion of a treaty with the Ḥamdānid rulers of the emirate of Aleppo.[94] This agreement is one of the very few surviving texts describing a well-defined borderline between the Byzantine and the Muslim territories in the region along the Orontes river and includes a number of clauses stipulating the payment of tribute and substantial Byzantine influence in the internal affairs of the emirate.[95] The modern scholarly literature usually talks about a Byzantine protectorate over Aleppo in the decades following this treaty, which despite a number of serious military clashes with

[91] Honigmann, *Ostgrenze*, 70–2, 75–9.

[92] Honigmann, *Ostgrenze*, 79–80.

[93] Honigmann, *Ostgrenze*, 82–7.

[94] Honigmann, *Ostgrenze*, 93–7, 147–9.

[95] Franz Dölger, *Regesten der Kaiserurkunden des oströmischen Reiches von 565–1453*, vol. 1/2: *Regesten von 867–1025*, 2nd rev. edn Andreas E. Müller with Alexander Beihammer (Munich: C. H. Beck, 2003), no. 728a.

the Fatimid caliphate and extended periods of turmoil in Aleppo lasted until the Seljuk takeover.[96] In 968/69, the time in which the imperial government was about to annex the Antioch region, a Byzantine detachment headed by Bardas Phokas attacked and destroyed the stronghold of Manzikert.[97] This event signalled the increase of Byzantine influence from the land of Taron to the Lake Van region and the beginning of a power struggle with the Kurdish lord Bād and his successors, who ruled in the cities north of Lake Van, such as Manzikert, Chleat/Akhlāṭ, Arčesh/Arjīsh, and Perkri/Barkirī, as well as the province of Apahunikʿ/Bājunays.[98] Although the civil wars with the Skleroi and Phokades and their supporters in the years 976–89 put a temporary halt to Byzantine expansionist plans and reduced the influence of the imperial government in many parts of Asia Minor,[99] Basil II, after his victory over his internal opponents, resumed this policy of territorial annexations in the Armenian and Georgian kingdoms of Transcaucasia.

The Byzantine prevalence over the Ḥamdānids of Aleppo and some other minor emirates sealed the definite end of Muslim incursions into Byzantine territories, and the centuries-old practice of Muslim jihad in the borderland was interrupted until the arrival of the Seljuk Turks in the 1040s. Hence, the Byzantine administration was facing a new situation in which the constant threat of Muslim raids no longer persisted. The defensive priorities of the preceding period gave way to objectives of military predominance and economic exploitation of local population groups and resources. As innovative features in the administrative organisation of this period one may single out the creation of *doukata* as overarching administrative units comprising clusters of small size *themata* in the most exposed frontier districts and the forging of alliances with Muslim vassal lords, who received Byzantine court titles and stipends in exchange for personal loyalty and military services. In this way, the imperial government implemented a centrally controlled network of command structures and allegiances, which surrounded the core

[96] Farag, 'Aleppo Question', 44–61.

[97] Honigmann, *Ostgrenze*, 149.

[98] Ripper, *Marwāniden*, 109–41; Catherine Holmes, *Basil II and the Governance of Empire (976–1025)* (Oxford: Oxford University Press, 2005), 309.

[99] Holmes, *Basil II*, 240–98, esp. 255–68.

provinces on the Anatolian plateau with an inner shield of marcher districts and an outer zone of buffer principalities mediating between Byzantium and the supra-regional powers in the Muslim world. On the basis of the so-called *Escorial Taktikon*, the composition of which can be dated to the years 971–5, Nicolas Oikonomides argued that this array of *themata* in newly conquered provinces in the frontier region was the result of a reorganisation carried out by the emperors Nikephoros II Phokas and John Tzimiskes.[100] Initially, there were three larger administrative units placed under the command of a *doux* or *katepano*. The ducate of Chaldia stretched from the Black Sea shores to the districts of Keltzēnē and Derzēnē in the region of the Euphrates headwaters.[101] The ducate of Mesopotamia comprised districts in the central section of the borderland from Kamakha and the province of Daranlis in the Upper Euphrates valley to the Anti-Taurus range.[102] Both ducates came into being through upgrading and expanding older *themata* founded in the first half of the ninth century. Over time, the land of Taron, the so-called *Armenika themata*, and the region of Melitene developed into separate units headed by their own commanders and local officials.[103] The southeastern section of the borderland was dominated by the ducate of Antioch, which straddled the lands east of the Jayḥān river with key points like Germanikeia/Marʿash and Telouch/Dulūk, the Amanos mountains, and the northern coastland as far as Tripoli.[104]

The last phase of territorial expansion into the Armenian and Georgian lands of Transcaucasia and the region of Edessa/al-Ruhā took place in the period 1000–65. It is noteworthy that the last two decades of this time span also witnessed the arrival of the Seljuk Turks, a number of major campaigns led by Seljuk sultans and their subaltern commanders, and the incursions of Turkmen warrior groups in Armenia, northern Iraq, Syria, and the adjacent

100 Oikonomidès, 'L'organisation de la frontière orientale', 285–302; for an edition of the *taktikon*, see *Les listes de préséance byzantines des IXe et Xe siècles*, ed. and trans. Nicolas Oikonomidès (Paris: Centre Nationale de la recherche scientifique, 1972), 255–77.

101 Holmes, *Basil II*, 313–22.

102 Holmes, *Basil II*, 322–30.

103 Oikonomidès, 'Organisation', 290 and n. 31 (Melitene as imperial *kouratoreia* governed by a *basilikos*); Holmes, *Basil II*, 326–7, 330.

104 Holmes, *Basil II*, 330–60.

Byzantine provinces. Hence, while the imperial government was still able to think about expanding its territories and spheres of influence in certain areas, it was already facing new hostile forces, which partially undermined the network of Muslim buffer states in the borderland and wrought havoc to certain areas within the Byzantine realm. In 1000/1, Basil II incorporated the territories of the Georgian ruler David of Tao east of the Akampsis river.[105] This acquisition formed the springboard for further annexations that followed suit, namely the Artsruni principality of Vaspurakan in 1019 or 1021/2 and a part of the Bagratid kingdom of Iberia in 1022/3. The imperial government organised these newly acquired provinces as ducates of Vaspurakan and Iberia.[106] The final acts of Byzantine expansionism were the acquisition of the kingdoms of Shirak/Ani in 1045 and of Vanand/Kars in 1064/5.[107] The conquest of Edessa by the Byzantine general George Maniakes in October 1031 was an isolated incident, which resulted from power struggles of the local Muslim elite and led to the establishment of another ducate comprising the Euphrates region, the Harran plain, and the Balīkh river valley.[108]

The network of Muslim emirates entertaining relations of vassalage with Constantinople in the period 970–1070 extended from Transcaucasia and Azerbaijan to the Syrian desert. According to the highly fragmented character of the political structures in the regions in question, this cluster of allies was very disparate and evinced various degrees of dependencies, ranging from loose and sporadic contacts to close personal links with the Byzantine officials in the borderland and the bestowal of high ranks in the Byzantine court hierarchy. Moreover, the imperial government was facing the competition of Muslim rival powers, which were at pains to keep the emirs in the borderland within their own sphere of influence by granting honorifics and having the rulers' name mentioned in the Friday prayer and inscribed on coins. Before the death of the Great Emir ʿAḍud al-Dawla on 26 March 983, the Buwayhids of Baghdad exerted a strong influence over Upper Mesopotamia.[109] The Fatimids,

[105] Holmes, *Basil II*, 320–1.

[106] Holmes, *Basil II*, 360–7.

[107] Leveniotis, *Πολιτική κατάρρευση*, 74–9, 116–17.

[108] Felix, *Byzanz und die islamische Welt*, 143–4.

[109] John J. Donohue, *The Buwayhid Dynasty in Iraq 334H./945 to 403H./1012: Shaping Institutions for the Future*, Islamic History and Civilization 44 (Leiden: Brill, 2003), 70–85.

who since 973 resided in their newly founded capital of Cairo and maintained a predominant position in Palestine and southern and central Syria, vied with the Byzantines for control over northern Syria and the emirate of Aleppo.[110] The peace treaty which Constantinople reached with Caliph al-Ḥākim in the year 1000 put an end to a period of open conflicts and set mutual relations on more amicable terms, but the antagonism continued to swelter and resurfaced with every incident of internal turmoil in Aleppo.[111]

The Shaddādids of Ganja and Dvin were especially powerful in the 1030s–50s. While making obeisance to Sultan Ṭughril Beg in 1054, they also had treaties with the imperial government of Constantine IX Monomachos (1042–55) and thus were eager to maintain relations with both sides.[112] The Kurdish Marwānid dynasty, which after Bād's death extended its rule over the Diyār Bakr province and the lands and cities north of Lake Van, had an especially close relation with the imperial government under the reign of Mumahhid al-Dawla (997–1011), who was appointed *doux tēs anatolēs*, that is, 'commander of the east', and was granted the title of *magistros*.[113] The ʿUqaylid dynasty held sway over the northern Jazira between Mosul and Jazīrat b. ʿUmar and Niṣībīn. They were too far off to be fully integrated into the Byzantine network of allies, but the sources attest to some diplomatic contacts and interest in friendly relations. When Muslim b. Quraysh in 1079 took possession of Aleppo, Byzantine influence in the region had already collapsed.[114] The Numayr Arabs in the Diyār Muḍar district loomed large as allies and opponents of Byzantium, especially in the time following Maniakes' conquest of Edessa in 1031.[115] Among the Arab tribes in central Syria and Palestine especially important for Byzantium was the Jarrāḥ clan, which belonged to the Ṭayyiʾ Arabs. They had a long tradition of seditious

110 Thierry Bianquis, *Damas et la Syrie sous la domination Fatimide (359–468/969–1076), essai d'interprétation de chroniques arabes médiévales* (Damascus: Institut Français de Damas, 1986–9); Holmes, *Basil II*, pp. 346–51.

111 Dölger, *Regesten*, 789e, 792b, 792c.

112 Alexander D. Beihammer, *Byzantium and the Emergence of Muslim–Turkish Anatolia, ca. 1040–1130* (London: Routledge, 2017), 58.

113 Holmes, *Basil II*, 321; Beihammer, *Muslim–Turkish Anatolia*, 58.

114 Beihammer, *Muslim–Turkish Anatolia*, 58–9.

115 Beihammer, *Muslim–Turkish Anatolia*, 59.

behaviour against the Fatimids, and their chief Ḥassān b. al-Mufarrij formed an anti-Fatimid alliance with Byzantium in the 1030s.[116]

The most important Arab allies of Byzantium in northern Syria were the Mirdāsids of Aleppo, whose leader Ṣāliḥ b. Mirdās established his rule over the city in 1025.[117] Emperor Romanos III's 1030 campaign against Aleppo was a failure in terms of military achievements but initiated a new phase of close cooperation and diplomatic relations between Aleppo and Constantinople, which was to last until the ousting of the last Mirdāsid emir in 1079. In their frequent contacts and negotiations, the emirs obtained increasingly higher court titles, including *magistros*, *vestarches*, *patrikios*, and eventually even *proedros*.[118] Although Byzantines, Fatimids, and the regional powers engaged in a number of fierce military conflicts, warfare in this period differed quite sharply from the annual incursions and large-scale attacks of earlier centuries or the clashes with the Ḥamdānid forces of Sayf al-Dawla and his relatives. There was no immediate threat to the Byzantine core areas and their economic structures in Asia Minor, and Byzantium was fighting from a position of strength, focusing on extending its sphere of influence in northern Syria, Upper Mesopotamia, and the Armenian highlands. This period is also characterised by an especially sophisticated network of diplomatic contacts, which was dominated by axes of communication with Cairo and Aleppo and had regular exchanges with numerous other local rulers. The tasks and challenges of cross-border diplomacy had become more complicated. Instead of short-time truces and prisoner exchanges, the focus lay with terms of mutual recognition, amicable relations, and stability. The *status quo* had to be upheld and after expirations or times of friction treaties had to be carefully renegotiated.

The Turkish Expansion and the New Frontier in Western Asia Minor

As for the new decay of agricultural productivity, which according to the pollen data of Lake Nar can be dated to the time around 1100, it is hardly convincing to ascribe this economic and structural change exclusively to the

[116] Beihammer, *Muslim–Turkish Anatolia*, 60–1.

[117] Dölger, *Regesten*, no. 817b, 817c.

[118] Beihammer, *Muslim–Turkish Anatolia*, 59–60.

influx of Turkish nomadic groups into central Anatolia in the wake of the breakdown of Byzantine dominion in the eastern provinces. The displacement of the Byzantine provincial elites by newcomers of Turkish, Armenian, or Frankish origin certainly constituted a disruptive event with respect to the pre-existing structures, but this process was rather complicated and stretched over a period of several decades. The raids and military activities of the Seljuk Turks began to spread from the Armenian highlands and the Euphrates region to various parts of central Anatolia as early as the 1050s and 1060s, while the situation was further exacerbated by civil wars ravaging the eastern provinces in the 1050s and 1070s.[119] During the 1070s Turkish chiefs, among them Sulaymān b. Qutlumush and his brothers, a junior branch of the Seljuk dynasty, became increasingly involved in the internecine feuding of hostile factions within the Byzantine aristocracy. Inevitably, these events led to devastations and displacements of population groups in the target areas of the Turkish raids and the conflict zones of the Byzantine civil strife. Moreover, certain regions were heavily affected by the breakdown of the Byzantine provincial organisation. The vacuum of power accruing therefrom was filled by local commanders, disaffected units of the Byzantine army, Norman mercenaries, and Armenian magnates.[120] The emancipation of Armenian commanders from the Byzantine central government and the simultaneous influx of Armenian aristocrats and their followers from the Armenian highlands and Cappadocia into Cilicia, the Jayḥān valley, and the Upper Euphrates region led to the establishment of a range of semi-independent

119 For different approaches to and interpretations of the transformation of Byzantine Asia Minor in the wake of the arrival of the Seljuk Turks, see, for instance, Speros Vryonis, *The Decline of Medieval Hellenism in Asia Minor and the Process of Islamization from the Eleventh through the Fifteenth Century* (Berkeley: University of California Press, 1971), 69–142; Claude Cahen, *The Formation of Turkey, The Seljukid Sultanate of Rūm: Eleventh to Fourteenth Century*, trans. and ed. Peter M. Holt (Harlow: Pearson Education, 2001), 7–20; Osman Turan, *Selçuklular Zamanında Türkiye, Siyasî Tarih Alp Arslan'dan Osman Gâzi'ye (1071–1318)*, 18th edn (Istanbul: Ötüken, 2004), 45–111; Andrew C. S. Peacock, *Early Seljūq History, a New Interpretation* (London: Routledge, 2010), 128–63; Beihammer, *Muslim–Turkish Anatolia*, 92–168, 198–231.

120 Turan, *Selçuklular Zamanında Türkiye*, 75–111; Beihammer, *Muslim–Turkish Anatolia*, 171–243.

local lordships covering the entire southern section of the old Byzantine–Muslim borderland.[121]

During the three campaigns of Emperor Romanos IV Diogenes in the years 1068–71, large army units with a constant need for fodder, water, and food supplies moved, fought, and camped in various parts of Anatolia. Much more pressing than the emperor's defeat against the Seljuk Sultan Alp Arslan in the battle of Manzikert north of Lake Van must have been the consumption of food reserves and the exhaustion of agricultural zones caused by the protracted presence of these troops in Cappadocia, the Upper Euphrates region between Melitene and Theodosioupolis, the Armenian provinces of Taron and Vaspurakan, and in northern Syria between Antioch and Manbij.[122] Even more destructive was the crossing of Anatolia by the hosts of the First Crusade in 1097–8, which was paralleled by a simultaneous large-scale campaign of Emperor Alexios I in western Asia Minor.[123] In addition to the immediate consequences of warfare and supply needs, there was a new wave of displacements with Turkish groups pursuing a scorched earth policy and retreating from the western coastland to the Anatolian plateau. The final outcome was the gradual formation of a new frontier some 500–600 miles to the west of the old borderland. This new divide ran from the Sangarios valley through Bithynia and western Phrygia to the fringe areas of the Anatolian plateau east of the headwaters of the Hermos (Gediz), the Kaystros (Küçük Menderes), and the Maeander (Menderes) rivers. It proved no less resilient than the old borderland. From early on Turkish nomads intruded into the Maeander valley and the mountainous hinterland of Caria, and in the early thirteenth century the Seljuk sultanate of Konya extended its sway over the coastland of Pamphylia and Lycia, as well as the port of Attaleia. Despite

[121] For a very detailed analysis of the Armenian lordships, see Dédéyan, *Les Arméniens entre Grecs, Musulmans et Croisés*), 1: 32–73, 77–178, 183–280, 287–355, 365–517; for Byzantine–Armenian relations in the time of the First Crusade, see John H. Pryor and Michael J. Jeffreys, 'Alexios, Bohemond, and Byzantium's Euphrates Frontier: A Tale of the Two Cretans', *Crusades* 11 (2012), 31–86.

[122] John Haldon *et al.*, 'Marching across Anatolia: Medieval Logistics and Modeling the Mantzikert Campaign', *Dumbarton Oaks Papers* 65–6 (2011–2012), 209–35.

[123] John France, *Victory in the East: A Military History of the First Crusade* (Cambridge: Cambridge University Press, 1994), 122–96; Jason T. Roche, 'In the Wake of Mantzikert: The First Crusade and the Alexian Reconquest of Western Anatolia', *History* 94 (2009), 135–53.

these encroachments, however, the western Anatolian frontier remained by and large intact up to the late thirteenth century.[124]

All these events and developments, in one way or another, impacted the pre-existing social and economic structures in the eastern provinces and frontier regions of Asia Minor. The collapse of Byzantine imperial rule elicited a general trend towards a fragmentation and regionalisation of political structures. It was not before the mid-twelfth century that the nascent Seljuk sultanate of Rūm began to develop into a new centralising power based on its capital in Konya and several local urban centres, which partly rested upon Byzantine traditions and partly emerged from newly established communications and trade networks with the Muslim heartlands in the east.[125] Other parts of Anatolia came to be dominated by small-size regional lordships of Byzantine, Armenian, Frankish, or Turkish identity, which maintained varying bonds of political allegiance and cultural-religious affinity with Constantinople, Konya, or the Crusader states. Greek and non-Greek population groups from the pre-conquest period came to live under the dominion of newly arrived foreign elites, which exerted their authority by combining pre-existing structures and administrative practices with their own traditions, institutions, and ideological concepts. Political constellations and social structures were characterised by a high degree of cross-border mobility and close interactions between various ethnic groups, religious communities, and political formations. Members of the Byzantine ruling elite sought refuge and began new careers at the Seljuk court of Konya, and Turkish noblemen became part of the imperial court hierarchy.[126]

[124] Speros Vryonis, 'Nomadization and Islamization in Asia Minor', *Dumbarton Oaks Papers* 29 (1975), 41–71, esp. 43–57.

[125] Turan, *Selçuklular zamanında Türkiye*, 223–90.

[126] For various aspects of cross-cultural encounter and exchange in Pre-Ottoman Anatolia, see the contributions in Andrew C. S. Peacock and Sara Nur Yıldız (eds), *The Seljuks of Anatolia: Court and Society in the Medieval Middle East* (London: I. B. Tauris, 2013); Andrew C. S. Peacock, Bruno De Nicola and Sara Nur Yıldız (eds), *Islam and Christianity in Medieval Anatolia* (London: Routledge, 2015); for Turkish population groups and cultural and linguistic influences in Byzantium, see Rustam Shukurov, *The Byzantine Turks, 1204–1461*, The Medieval Mediterranean 105 (Leiden: Brill, 2016); for apostasy and defection among Byzantine and Turkish elite circles, see Alexander Beihammer, 'Defection across the Border of Islam and Christianity: Apostasy and Cross-Cultural Interaction in Byzantine–Seljuk Relations', *Speculum* 86 (2011), 597–651.

In the framework of a highly volatile political environment, both elite members and common people frequently experienced unexpected twists of fate and sudden displacements and had to adapt to new constellations and overlords. Political procedures in the Armenian and Turkish small-size principalities rested upon frequently changing networks of local alliances, which went across religious and ethnic boundaries.[127] Another important factor was the presence of Turkish nomadic groups, who followed a lifestyle of transhumant pastoralism and dominated remote mountainous regions and the fringe areas between Byzantium and the Seljuk sultanate. There is an ongoing debate about the nature of their relationship with the central authorities in Konya and the sedentary population in the towns and villages of the borderland. Traditional views of a conflict-ridden antagonism give way to new interpretations, which stress mutual economic dependencies and cultural influences.[128] Be that as it may, Anatolia in the early twelfth century differed quite sharply from Byzantine Asia Minor in 1000. It had turned into a politically fragmented and culturally-religiously diverse landscape, which was characterised by multiple elites, migrating nomads, and an ethnically mixed population, which was exposed to a broad range of cultural, religious, and ideological influences. This was to be the hallmark of Anatolian landscapes up to the early twentieth century.

Conclusion

To sum up, studies on the Byzantine–Muslim frontier over the past decades have significantly expanded their scope and diversified their concepts and methods. The notion of Byzantium's role as an ethno-religious bulwark, as

[127] For twelfth-century developments in the various branches of the Seljuk sultanate of Konya and the Dānishmendid emirate in Cappadocia, see Turan, *Türkiye Selçukluları zamanında*, 175–260, and the brief survey in Cahen, *Formation of Turkey*, 18–33, 38–49. For the Dānishmendid emirate, see now Muharrem Kesik, *Dânişmendliler (1085–1178): Orta Anadolu'nun Fatihleri* (Istanbul: Bilge Kültür Sanat, 2017). For the eastern Anatolian emirates of the Saltukids, Mengücekids, Ahlat-Şâhs, and Artukids, see Osman Turan, *Doğu Anadolu Türk Devletleri Tarihi*, 6th edn (Istanbul: Ötüken, 2001); Muharrem Kesik, *Anadolu Türk Beylikleri* (Istanbul: Bilge Kültür Sanat, 2018), 37–156.

[128] Apart from the classical study by Vryonis, 'Nomadization and Islamization', cited above, note 124, see Andrew Peacock, 'The Seljuk Sultanate of Rūm and the Turkmen of the Byzantine Frontier, 1206–1279', *Al-Masaq: Journal of the Medieval Mediterranean* 26 (2014), 267–87.

articulated in the statements by Herbert Hunger and Ernst Honigmann quoted at the beginning of this chapter, is still alive in popular perceptions and the national historiographies of Southeast Europe. What seems to matter more for modern scholarship is to perceive and interpret this region as a multilayered zone of conflict, contact, interaction, and exchange in the shadow of empires. In this framework, the Byzantine–Muslim frontier developed its own cultural characteristics, institutions, and socio-economic structures, which often defy modern categorisations of ethnicity and identity and contravene the artificial delineations of academic disciplines. Over time, the region underwent various stages of transformation, which were in tune with and resulted from broader historical developments in the Eastern Mediterranean and Eurasia. While scholarly debates in traditional subject areas continue to put older opinions under scrutiny and produce new insights and reinterpretations, there are still many dark spots and understudied aspects when it comes to settlement patterns, living conditions, and economic structures in the eastern borderland. These topics require a comprehensive evaluation of both written and material evidence. Hence, historians and archaeologists are called to exchange their results and support each other's interpretive endeavours. As of yet, we are only at the beginning of unravelling the relations between agrarian production, pastoralism, local markets, and cross-border trade networks linking the borderland with the ports of the Mediterranean and the trade routes of the Muslim world.[129] The environmental and ecological history of Byzantine Asia Minor is also still in its infancy.[130] Nevertheless, recent innovative studies have already begun to uncover causes and factors that contributed to the survival and reinvigoration of Byzantium in the centuries following the Islamic conquests.[131] Finally, the Byzantine–Muslim borderland needs to be compared more thoroughly and systematically with

[129] Asa Eger (ed.), *The Archaeology of Medieval Islamic Frontiers: From the Mediterranean to the Caspian Sea* (Louisville: University Press of Colorado, 2019), see especially Ian Randall, 'Conceptualizing the Islamic–Byzantine Maritime Frontier', pp. 80–102.

[130] Adam Izdebski and Michael Mulryan (eds), *Environment and Society in the Late Long Antiquity* (Leiden: Brill, 2019).

[131] John Haldon, *The Empire that Would not Die: The Paradox of Eastern Roman Survival, 640–740* (Cambridge, MA: Harvard University Press, 2016).

other frontier regions of medieval Europe and Eurasia.[132] In what respect is the region in question a case of its own? Where do we see parallels and commonalities with other borderlands? What conclusions can we extract from Byzantium's eastern frontier regarding pre-modern borderland societies in general? It remains to be seen how coming generations of scholars will respond to these and other questions.

[132] Daniel Power and Naomi Standen (eds), *Frontiers in Question: Eurasian Borderlands, 700–1700* (Basingstoke: Macmillan Press, 1999); David Abulafia and Nora Berend (eds), *Medieval Frontiers: Concepts and Practices* (Aldershot: Ashgate, 2002); Florin Curta (ed.), *Borders, Barriers, and Ethnogenesis: Frontiers in Late Antiquity and the Middle Ages* (Turnhout: Brepols, 2005); in this volume, see especially the contribution by Ralph-Johannes Lilie, 'The Byzantine–Arab Borderland from the Seventh to the Ninth Century', 243–64.

3

THE FORMATION OF *AL-ʿAWĀṢIM*

Hugh Kennedy

The history of the *ʿAwāṣim* is a widely known and accepted part of the history of the Byzantine–Islamic frontier and of Abbasid administrative systems more generally.[1] The usual account of the origins and history of this administrative area, as summed up in Marius Canard's article in the second edition of the *Encyclopaedia of Islam*, shows the area, previously part of the *jund* of Qinnasrīn, being made into a separate entity by Caliph Hārūn al-Rashīd in the year 170/786. The word itself is, conventionally but rather strangely, translated as 'protectoresses', plural of *ʿāṣima*. The purpose of this change, we are told, was to create a sort of back-up area of fortification to support the advanced outposts in the *Thughūr* and to province refuge for Muslims when they needed to retreat from the more advanced outposts.[2]

More recently, the great historian of the Arab–Byzantine frontier, Michael Bonner, returned to the question.[3] He accepts without question that the *ʿAwāṣim* were a series of strongholds, 'the "protectoresses", so-called because the warriors could seek refuge with them after their raids or when under attack'. After a discussion of the earlier administrative geography of the

[1] For a clear account of the generally accepted view, see M. Canard, 'al-ʿAwāṣim', in Peri Bearman *et al.* (eds), *Encyclopaedia of Islam, 2nd edn*, 13 vols (Leiden: Brill, 1954–2009) (*EI*^{2}).

[2] Al-Ṭabarī, Abū Jaʿfar Muḥammad b. Jarīr, *Taʾrikh al-rusul waʾl-mulūk*, ed. M. J. de Goeje *et al.*, 3 parts (Leiden: Brill, 1879–1901), iii, 604.

[3] M. Bonner, 'The Naming of the Frontier: ʿAwāṣim, Thughūr and the Arab Geographers', *Bulletin of the School of Oriental and African Studies* 57 (1994), 17–24.

Thughūr he goes on to argue that Hārūn had two aims: 'first to break up the old conglomeration of the Umayyad North, thereby limiting the great barons' potential for mischief: and secondly, to associate Hārūn's person with the frontier and with the *jihād* generally'.[4] While the second of these aims is supported by other indications of Hārūn's policy on the holy war at this time, there seems to be no firm evidence for the first at all and none of the texts support it directly. At no point does Bonner provide any evidence that this area was the scene of any military activity.

In an attempt to arrive at some more precision about the origins of the *ʿAwāṣim* and the meaning of the word, we must turn to the written sources of the Abbasid period. There are two important textual traditions about the formation of the *ʿAwāṣim*: the *taʾrīkh* narratives and the writings of the geographers.

The clearest and most important historical narrative is found in al-Ṭabarī's history. It records the decision of Hārūn al-Rashīd to give the *ʿAwāṣim* a separate administrative identity. 'In that year (170) al-Rashīd took away all the *Thughūr* from al-Jazīra and Qinnasrīn and made them into one *ḥayyiz* which was called *al-ʿAwāṣim*.' This is a stand-alone entry in the *Taʾrīkh* and no further details are given. Al-Ṭabarī mentions the *ʿAwāṣim* on a small number of occasions later in his chronicle but never in the context of wars against the Byzantines. The most significant of these relates to the year 187/803, when al-Rashīd sent his son al-Qāsim, who was being groomed for the third position in the succession arrangements the caliph was then devising, to lead the summer raid against the Byzantines, at the same time putting him in charge of the *ʿAwāṣim*,[5] suggesting that there was at this time a link between the area and the warfare on the frontier, but not necessarily a military one. In 235/849–50 it is mentioned along with the Syrian and Jaziran *Thughūr* and Qinnasrīn as one of the areas given by al-Mutawwakil to his heir apparent al-Muntaṣir.[6] In 271/884 we hear that the *ʿAwāṣim*, along with Raqqa and the *Thughūr*, were governed by one Ibn Daʿbāṣh on behalf of the ruler

[4] Bonner, 'The Naming of the Frontier', 19.

[5] Al-Ṭabarī, *Taʾrīkh*, iii, 688.

[6] Al-Ṭabarī, *Taʾrīkh*, iii, 1395.

of Egypt, Ibn Ṭulūn, while Ibn Kundāj controlled Mosul for the Abbasids.[7] Finally, in 296/899 Qinnasrīn and *al-ʿAwāṣim* were handed over to Abbasid control by the men of the young ruler of Egypt, Hārūn b. Khumārawayh.[8] It is clear that by this stage if not before, the *ʿAwāṣim* were simply an administrative area like any other and any special or separate status they may have had had long since disappeared.

In his *Taʾrīkh*, al-Yaʿqūbī mentions the *ʿAwāṣim* on a number of occasions, but always in an administrative context, never as fortresses in frontier warfare or as performing any other military role. Apparently anachronistically, he mentions the tax yield of Qinnasrīn and *al-ʿAwāṣim* under Muʿāwiya[9] and the local lords of Qinnasrīn and *al-ʿAwāṣim* during the disturbed conditions at the beginning of the reign of ʿAbd al-Malik.[10] After the coming of the Abbasids he notes that Qinnasrīn and *al-ʿAwāṣim* were controlled by the Abbasid Ṣāliḥ b. ʿAlī for the caliph al-Manṣūr[11] and later by his son ʿAbd al-Malik b. Ṣāliḥ,[12] and finally as an administrative appointment along with Qinnasrīn at the beginning of the reign of al-Muʿtaṣim (218/833).[13] He does not mention the separation of the area by Hārūn al-Rashīd as described by al-Ṭabarī, but treats it as if it was part of an administrative arrangement which went back to the earliest days of Muslim rule in Syria.

The second textual tradition is the explanation which derives from al-Balādhurī's *Futūḥ al-Buldān*, composed in approximately 865 CE. It can be found in al-Balādhurī's original text, which is put in a slightly wider context by Yāqūt writing around 1220 CE, who preserves the text of the *Futūh* as we have it verbatim:

> ʿAwāṣim is the plural of *ʿāṣim*, which means the defender (*mānīʿ*), as the Highest says in his words: 'There is no protector from the will of God except

[7] Al-Ṭabarī, *Taʾrīkh*, iii, 2105.

[8] Al-Ṭabarī, *Taʾrīkh*, iii, 2187–8.

[9] Al-Yaʿqūbī, *Taʾrīkh*, ii, 278.

[10] Al-Yaʿqūbī, *Taʾrīkh*, ii, 304.

[11] Al-Yaʿqūbī, *Taʾrīkh*, ii, 461.

[12] Al-Yaʿqūbī, *Taʾrīkh*, ii, 526.

[13] Al-Yaʿqūbī, *Taʾrīkh*, ii, 575.

> mercy'. It is an active participle which is why it has the alīf. The ʿAwāṣim: The protecting fortresses and the province (*wilāya*) which surrounds them between Aleppo and Antioch and its capital (*qaṣaba*) is at Antioch. Some people built them to take refuge there from the enemy. Most of it is in the mountains and it named because of that. Sometimes al-Maṣṣīssa and Ṭarsūs and those areas are included in it. Some claim that Aleppo is not part of it and others that it is, and the truth (*dalīl*) is that it is not. They agree that it was part of the province (*ʿaʿmāl*) of Qinnasrīn and they speak of 'Qinnasrīn and al-ʿAwāṣim' and not an independent unit. This is the truth and God knows best.[14]

Balādhurī's text also provides historical background:

> Aḥmad b. Yaḥyā b. Jābir (al-Balādhurī) said: Qinnasrīn and its district (*kūra*) continued to be attached to Homs until the reign of Yazīd b. Muʿāwiya. He made Qinnasrīn, Antioch and Manbij and their dependencies into a separate jund. When the Commander of the Faithful Hārūn b. al-Mahdī (al-Rashīd) became caliph he detached Qinnasrīn and its *kuwar* (districts) and made it into a separate jund. He also detached Manbij, Dulūk, Raʿbān, Qūrus, Antioch and Tīzīn and called them al-ʿAwāṣim, because the Muslims *yaʿtaṣimūna ilayhā*, and they provide them with protection and refuge when they return from their expeditions and come out of the *thaghr*. He made Manbij their *madīna*. ʿAbd al-Malik b. Ṣāliḥ b. ʿAlī b. ʿAbd Allāh settled there in 173/790–1 and built famous buildings.[15]

Later, in a chapter heading, he distinguishes between 'the *jund* of Qinnasrīn and the cities which are called al-ʿAwāṣim'.[16]

Later geographers' accounts are largely derivative from al-Balādhurī's account, but it should be noted that both Ibn Khurradādhbih[17] and Qudāma b. Jaʿfar[18] in their records of taxation list Qinnaṣrīn and *al-ʿAwāṣim* together

[14] Yāqūt al-Ḥamawī, *Muʿjam al-buldān* sv., i–vi, ed. F. Wüstenfeld (Leipzig, 1866–73/1924).

[15] Aḥmad b. Yaḥyā Al-Balādhurī, *Futūḥ al-Buldān*, ed. M. J. de Goeje (Leiden: Brill, 1866), 132.

[16] Al-Balādhurī, *Futūḥ al-Buldān*, 144.

[17] Ibn Khurradādhbih, *Al-Masālik waʾl-mamālik*, 75.

[18] Qudāma b. Jaʿfar, *Kitāb al-kharāj*, ed. M. J. de Goeje (Leiden: Brill, 1889), 246.

as a fiscal unit separate from the *Thughūr*. Ibn Khurradhādhbih adds the towns of al-Jūma, Būqā, Bālis and Ruṣāfat Hishām, ancient Sergiopolis, far away in the Syrian desert, to the list; and Ibn Ḥawqal includes Bālis, Sanja, Sumayṣāṭ and Jisr Manbij.[19] By the end of the tenth century and the collapse of the Abbasid administration, these divisions became irrelevant for practical purposes , though they were still remembered by later scholars like Ibn Sahddāḍ, and the poet al-Mutanabbī also refers to the *ʿAwāṣim* in his great panegyric on Sayf al-Dawla, quoted by Yāqūt in his article on the *ʿAwāṣim*, but he adds no further details. As Bonner neatly puts it, 'The original meaning of *ʿawāṣim* became lost in the geographical literature which appeared in the next few generations, though the word itself remained.'[20] The textual evidence, then, presents a simple picture of a secondary line of military defence and fortification to support the outposts on the *Thughūr*, a function which became redundant with the passing of time.

There are, however, some reasons to doubt this simple picture. The first is philological. The word *ʿawāṣim* comes from the root *ʿaṣama*, which implies preservation and protection; *ḥayyiz*, used by al-Ṭabarī to describe the area, derives from *ḥāza*, and the second form *ḥayyaza* means a thing which is one's property and is guarded or protected. *Ufridat* has the implication of being set aside or separated. The *ʿAwāṣim* are never described as a *jund* or a *kūra*, the two words commonly used for a province in the administrative vocabulary of Abbasid Syria, nor does the area ever seem to have its own *wālī* or *ʿāmil* apart from al-Qāsim b. al-Rashīd's brief tenure. There are many words in the Arabic of the time for fortifications: *ḥiṣn*, *maʿqil*, *qalʿa*, *maslaḥa* are some of the ones commonly used. *ʿAwāṣim* is, however, not one of them.

The second reason is historical and military. Apart from Antioch, the small towns mentioned, Manbij, Dulūk, Raʿbān, Qūrus and Tīzīn, are not recorded in either the geographical literature or in the archaeological evidence as having any fortifications at all, which is strange if they were places of refuge for the Abbasid army. It is also in clear contrast with settlements on

19 Abūʾl-Qāṣsm al-Naṣībī Ibn Ḥawqal, *Kitān ṣūrat al-arḍ*, ed. J. H. Kramers (Leiden: Brill, 1939), 187.

20 Bonner, 'The Naming of the Frontier', 21.

the *Thughūr* – like al-Ḥadath, Tarsūs and Malatiya for example, for which the building and rebuilding of fortifications is well-recorded – that there are no details given of the building of military structures or the establishment of garrisons in the towns of the *ʿAwāṣim*. The archaeological record is admittedly scanty, but there is no evidence of fortifications from the early Islamic period at any of these sites.[21] The campaigns of the Muslim armies on the frontier are also well-noticed in the historical records and, while the sources describe the triumphs of Muslim arms with some enthusiasm, they do not gloss over setbacks and defeats. Yet never once in this extensive record is there any mention of Muslim armies retreating to or taking refuge in the *ʿAwāṣim*. In short, the accepted explanation for the creation and existence of the *ʿAwāṣim* seems to make little sense. What then is going on?

To explain the creation and administration of the *ʿAwāṣim*, we should look not to the military history of the period, but to the fiscal and administrative developments. Much of the land in the *Thughūr* was held as *ʿushr* land, that is to say it paid a tithe rather than the full *kharāj* taken from other agricultural lands.[22] This was largely because it was held as *qaṭāʾiʿ* (essentially privately owned properties), which were given to encourage settlement in these exposed frontier areas. These tax breaks meant that the *Thughūr* produced little if any financial surplus and were in fact a drain on the treasury.[23] The defences of the frontier would have required regular subsidies from the caliphal administration

However, from the reign of al-Mahdī, the Barmakid family, notably Yaḥyā b. Khālid, and their allies among the bureaucrats pressed a policy of fiscal centralisation, that is to say that any surpluses from a province after the payment of the local *jund* (if there was one), were to be forwarded to the *bayt al-māl* in Baghdad rather than distributed locally by the governor. This policy, strictly interpreted, would have effectively prevented this sort of cross-subsidy.

From the time when he had led expeditions against the Byzantines during his father's reign, though, Hārūn had been determined to develop and publicise

[21] For the very slight archaeological evidence for the sites named as cities in the *ʿAwāṣim*, see Asa Eger, *Islamic Byzantine Frontier* (London: I. B. Tauris, 2015), 96–101.

[22] Al-Balādhurī, *Futūh al-Buldan*, 265.

[23] As confirmed in al-Balādhurī, *Futūḥ al-Buldān*, 171.

the role of the caliph as leader of the *jihād* and the struggle of the Muslims against the ancient enemy. The formation of the *ʿAwāṣim* looks like a device to 'protect' the revenues of the area from the demands of the *bayt al-māl* in Baghdad so that they could be separated off and used to sustain the troops and fortifications of the frontier itself. The revenues from these areas were in fact to be preserved, ring-fenced if you will, to support frontier warfare. The 'protectoresses' protected not the Muslim armies from enemy attack, but the financial resources needed for campaign and fortification.

Why then did al-Balādhurī provide this very clear indication of the putative military function of these towns in the *ʿAwāṣim*? After Hārūn's death and the civil war which followed, these fiscal structures collapsed, and by the time al-Balādhurī was writing in the 860s the term was simply a geographical one; the original purpose, and the meaning of the name, had been forgotten. Al-Balāḍhurī in fact seems to have tried to supply an etymology for the name, as he did for other unusual names, and came up with the idea of 'protectoresses' to explain a designation whose original force and meaning had long since been lost. It is al-Balādhuri's imaginative reconstruction which informed later geographers and historians down to and beyond Marius Canard but which, I would tentatively suggest, should now be understood for what it is, an imaginative but unhistorical trope.

4

CAUCASIAN ELITES BETWEEN BYZANTIUM AND THE CALIPHATE IN THE EARLY ISLAMIC PERIOD

Robert G. Hoyland

Introduction

Caucasia is something of an in-between zone, with the Anatolian plateau and Black Sea to the west and the Caspian Sea to the east, and the western Central Asian steppe to the north and the ancient Mesopotamia-Zagros region to the south (see Map 1).[1] In the millennium before the rise of Islam, it found itself between the Roman and Persian empires, each vying to pull the Caucasian powers over to their side. This tug-of-war intensified in the third–sixth centuries CE, as the Sasanian dynasty that assumed control of the Persian Empire in 224 pursued a more centralising and expansionist

[1] Regarding the term 'Caucasia', see Cyril Toumanoff, 'Introduction to Christian Caucasian History: The Formative Centuries (IV–VIIth c.)', *Traditio* 15 (1959), 6: 'The word "Caucasia", as used here, designates the cis-Caucasian, northeasternmost region of the Mediterranean world that is distinct from the adjacent lands of Anatolia, Syria, Mesopotamia, and Iran. This distinctness is first of all historical; but, geographically too, Caucasia can be regarded as a distinct unity.' This idea is echoed by Stephen H. Rapp, 'Caucasia and the First Byzantine Commonwealth: Christianization in the context of regional coherence', *NCEEER* working paper, 2012, 2: 'Since at least the Iron Age . . . Caucasia has been a cohesive yet diverse zone of cross-cultural encounter and shared historical experience.'

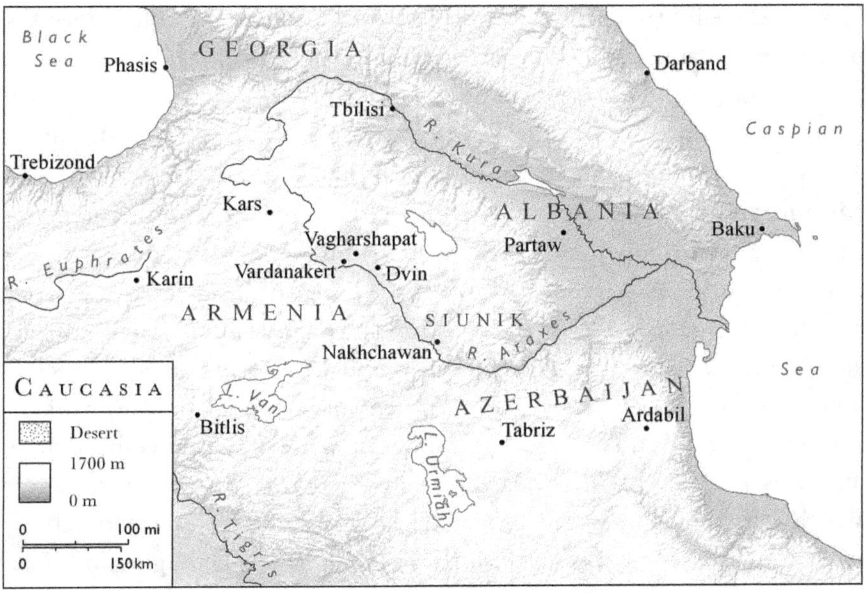

Map 4.1 Early Medieval Caucasia.
© Robert G. Hoyland.

policy than its Parthian predecessor.[2] The success of the Muslim conquests in the seventh century meant that the Caliphate (Islamic Empire) replaced the Persian Empire as the principal adversary of the Roman Empire (or Byzantine Empire, as I will henceforth call the Roman Empire of the seventh–fifteenth centuries CE, following usual practice). Although the Caliphate was the dominant actor in this region, it is the contention of this paper that the Byzantine Empire, and to a lesser extent the Khazar Empire, which had emerged in the eighth century in the northern part of Caucasia, were still major players in this struggle for influence over Caucasia.[3] It is also argued that this struggle

[2] Cyril Toumanoff, 'Christian Caucasia between Byzantium and Iran', *Traditio* 10 (1954), 109–89.

[3] Good overviews are given by Cyril Toumanoff, 'Caucasia and Byzantium', *Traditio* 27 (1971), 111–58; Tim Greenwood, 'Armenian Neighbours (600–1045)', in J. Shepard (ed.), *The Cambridge History of the Byzantium Empire c. 500–1492* (Cambridge: Cambridge University Press, 2009), 333–64; Irina Shingiray, *On the Path through the Shadow Empire:*

hampered the integration of Caucasia into the Caliphate and constrained the processes of Islamicisation and Arabicisation.

The modern Caucasian nations of Armenia, Georgia[4] and Azerbaijan are sometimes assumed to correspond loosely to the polities of Armīniyya, Jurzān and Arrān[5] that are known to medieval Muslim authors. However, these three geographical entities should not in any way be thought of as states or nations. They certainly possessed a degree of distinctiveness, which had been given greater substance by the emergence of an ecclesiastical hierarchy upon their conversion to Christianity in Late Antiquity and by the use of a distinctive language for church literature – Armenian, Georgian and Albanian.[6] However, their borders were very fluid and subject to change over time, and this is reflected in the frequent disagreement in our sources over which settlements belonged to which region. Thus Tiflīs (modern Tblisi) is accounted by some medieval Muslim geographers as belonging to Jurzān and by others as part of Arrān.[7] Furthermore, in none of them was there a single person or group in overall control in the early Islamic period. Rather, there were many different actors, in particular heads of local elite families, who were vying for power amongst themselves as well as with or

The Khazar Nomads at the Northwest Frontier of Iran and the Islamic Caliphate, PhD thesis, Boston University, 2011, chs 3–5.

4 The modern republic of Georgia combines the ancient kingdom of Kartli/Iberia, centred on Mtskheta, with minor kingdoms such as Egrisi/Colchis to the west and Kakheti to the east.

5 This Arabic term (written *al-Rān*) derives from Middle Persian '*Ran*'. Greek, Latin and Armenian sources speak of the land of the 'Albanians' (*Albanoi, Albani, Ałuan-k*ʿ – the kʿ is the plural ending), and this has given rise to the modern term '(Caucasian) Albania'. The similarity of these forms may mean that they all derive ultimately from an indigenous name. Note that I use polities in the loosest possible sense here.

6 See the studies in Werner Seibt, *Die Christianisierung des Kaukasus: Armenia, Georgia, Albania* (Vienna: Österreichische Akademie der Wissenschaften, 2002). On the (Caucasian) Albanian language and its relationship to modern Udi, see Wolfgang Schulze, 'From Caucasian Albanian to Udi', *Iran and Caucasia* 19 (2015), 149–77.

7 Alison Vacca, '*Buldān al-Rān*: The many definitions of Caucasian Albania in the early Abbasid period', in Robert G. Hoyland (ed.), *From Albania to Arrān: The East Caucasus between Antiquity and Medieval Islam* (Piscataway: Gorgias Press, 2020), 52–5.

against outsiders and seeking to extend their spheres of influence. This is an inevitable consequence of the diverse topography and climate of the land, which varies from low-lying coastal plains to high mountain ridges, from fertile river valleys to arid steppes, and which exhibits a corresponding linguistic diversity.[8] Given this diversity, it is impossible to do justice to this region in a short paper, and I shall chiefly focus on Armenia and Arrān and on the period 650–950.[9]

The Struggle for Caucasia between the Caliphate and Byzantium

The arrival of Muslim armies on the scene in the seventh century did not initially change the situation that much, since the Muslims were stretched thin and the Caucasus mountains proved daunting. So, they mostly left local Caucasian rulers to their own devices, offering them autonomy or tax exemption in return for non-aggression pacts or promises to provide military service. One example concerns a certain Shahrbarāz, of a Persian noble family, who was commander of the Sasanian garrison at Darband (*Bāb al-abwāb*), the border town on the Caspian Sea that had guarded entry into Sasanian territory from the steppe lands to the north. The agreement, granted by the Muslim general Surāqa ibn ʿAmr to Shahrbarāz, covered the garrison and residents of Darband and its environs:

> He (Surāqa) grants them security for their persons, possessions and their religion, that they will not be harmed nor impaired. It is required of the people of Darband, newcomers and natives, and their neighbors, that they participate in any military expedition and carry out any task, actual or potential, that

[8] This diversity impeded any conscious sense of pan-Caucasian identity; insiders thought chiefly of their own local territories, and only outsiders applied a single term for the whole region: Greek-speakers used *Kaukasia*, Muslim sources employed either 'the North' (*al-jarbī*) or *al-Armīniyya*, using the name of part for the whole. Two classic studies on early medieval Caucasia are Toumanoff, 'Introduction to Christian Caucasian History', and N. Garsoïan and B. Hisard, 'Unité et diversité de la Caucasie médiévale (IV–XIth s.)', *Settimane di studio* 43 (1996), 275–347.

[9] For the elites on the territory of modern Georgia in the seventh–eleventh centuries, see Rapp, 'Caucasia and the Second Byzantine Commonwealth', 1–31; and Sandro Nikolaishvili, 'Byzantium and the Georgian World c. 900–1210: Ideology of Kingship and Rhetoric in the Byzantine Periphery', PhD thesis, Central European University Budapest, 2019.

> the governor considers to be for the good. Those who agree to this will be exempted from taxation; military service shall substitute for their tribute.[10]

Particularly valuable, since it is preserved for us by a contemporary writer, is the copy of a treaty concluded between Caliph Muʿāwiya (661–80) and the prince of Armenia,[11] Theodore Rshtuni, in 652, which is effectively a vassalage agreement:

> Let this be the pact of my treaty between me and you for as many years as you may wish. I shall not take tribute from you for a three-year period. Then you will pay [tribute] with an oath, as much as you may wish. You will keep in your country 15,000 cavalry, and provide sustenance from your country; and I shall reckon it in the royal tax. I shall not request the cavalry for Syria; but wherever else I command they shall be ready for duty. I shall not send emirs to your fortresses, nor a Muslim army – neither many, nor even down to a single cavalryman. An enemy shall not enter Armenia; and if the Romans attack you I shall send you troops in support, as many as you may wish. I swear by the great God that I shall not be false.[12]

Theodore was something of a reluctant ally and perceived by his peers as a traitor for making a deal with the Muslims. When he died in 655, he was succeeded as prince of Armenia by his son-in-law Hamazasp Mamikonean. The outbreak of civil war among the Muslims in 656 emboldened Hamazasp, who sought to live up to 'the valiant character of his ancestral house',[13] to abandon submission to the Muslims and resume ties once more with the Byzantine Empire.

[10] Muḥammad b. Jarīr al-Ṭabarī, *Taʾrīkh al-rusul wa-l-mulūk*, ed. M. J. de Goeje *et al.* (Leiden: Brill, 1879–1901), 1: 2665.

[11] Armenian (henceforth Arm.): *išxan Hayocʿ*, referring to the prince chosen by the imperial power (Byzantium or the Caliphate) from the noble families of Armenia to maintain order in their realm and to supply military manpower. The institution had pre-Islamic origins and a similar system obtained in Georgia and Arrān. See Alison Vacca, *Non-Muslim Provinces under Early Islam* (Cambridge: Cambridge University Press, 2017), 124–33.

[12] Sebēos, *Patmutʿiwn*, trans. Robert Thomson as *The Armenian History Attributed to Sebeos*, Part I (Liverpool: Liverpool University Press, 1999), 164.

[13] Ibid., 174.

This change of allegiance was warmly welcomed by the Byzantine emperor Constans II (641–68), who gave him silver cushions and formally recognised him as his official representative in Armenia.[14] Most Caucasian leaders followed suit with the Armenians and pledged allegiance to Constans. This meant that there was a Christian pro-Byzantine coalition across Caucasia, and Constans took full advantage of the respite granted him by the Muslim civil war to try to strengthen this bulwark against the Muslims. In his nineteenth regnal year (659–60) he set off on a grand procession through the region, meeting local lords and handing out gifts and titles, as is described in our one historical text on Arrān compiled by the tenth-century author Movsēs Dasxuranc'i.[15] Juanshēr, prince of Arrān (637–80), came to meet him and pledge his allegiance. By 661, however, the Muslim civil war was at an end and Mu'āwiya was reasserting his authority over the conquered lands. Juanshēr observed how the emperor of Byzantium had been rendered powerless and weak by the Muslims, 'who had consumed the former's populous markets and cities like a flame', and he became worried that they might do the same to his lands. He therefore determined to switch sides and join the Muslims. In the year 664 he prepared magnificent presents and took them 'to salute the conqueror of the world'.[16] Mu'āwiya received him with great pomp and ceremony and set his seal to a treaty of sincere and perpetual friendship between them. On his return, Juanshēr met with a number of Armenian nobles who apparently received him with honor, suggesting that they had made a similar decision and that Byzantium's Caucasian bulwark had already crumbled and southern Caucasia at least had once more submitted to the Muslims.

This changed again, however, with the advent of the second Muslim civil war, which began with the accession of Mu'āwiya's son Yazīd in 680, a move towards dynastic succession for the Caliphate that many Muslims opposed, and the fighting only ended with the victory of 'Abd al-Malik (685–705) over all challengers in 692. During this long period of turmoil in the ranks of the

[14] Ibid., 175.

[15] Movsēs Dasxuranc'i, *Patmut'iwn Ałuanic' ašxarhi*, trans. C. J. F. Dowsett as *The History of the Caucasian Albanians* (London: Oxford University Press, 1961), 2: 22.

[16] Ibid., 2: 27.

Muslim rulers, many peoples that they had conquered took the opportunity to pull away. In Caucasia 'the Armenians, the Georgians and the Arrānians ceased to pay tribute to the Muslims, having been subject to them for thirty years',[17] which, if we take this as a reference to the treaty made between Theodore Rshtuni and Muʿāwiya in 652, would place their secession around 682. This rebellion lasted for three years, at which point its leaders were forced to turn their attention northwards, as they faced a major invasion in 685 by the Khazars. The latter had also spotted an opportunity in the Muslims' internal strife and entered southern Caucasia from their territory in the steppe lands north of the Caucasus mountain range, raiding right across the region and killing 'many of the nobles and princes of the Georgians and the Arrānians',[18] who bore the brunt of the attack. Shortly thereafter, Emperor Justinian II (685–95, 705–11) 'sent the general Leontius with a Roman army to Armenia . . . and subjugated it to the Romans'.[19] According to a mid-eighth-century source, this was part of a peace deal struck between Justinian and Caliph ʿAbd al-Malik whereby 'Armenia was not to be divided; rather each one (Justinian and ʿAbd al-Malik) would send word to their respective governors over it that they should contest it (in battle), and whichever side was victorious would get Armenia and the vanquished would get nothing'.[20] However, the general Leontius did not stop at Armenia, but also subjugated 'Iberia, Arrān, Mūqān (Mughan) and Media, and, after imposing taxes on those countries, sent a great sum of money to the emperor'.[21] Furthermore, so we are told by an Armenian author, Justinian himself went to Armenia in his fourth year (688–9) and met with the princes of Armenia, Georgia and Arrān, giving them presents and troops. He accorded the title

[17] Łewond, *Patmutʿiwn*, trans. Z. Arzoumanian as the *History of Łewond the Eminent Vardapet of the Armenians* (Philadelphia: Scholars Press, 1982), §4.

[18] Ibid., §4.

[19] Theophanes, *Chronicle*, ed. C. de Boor (Leipzig, 1883–5), and trans. C. Mango and R. Scott (Oxford: Clarendon Press, 1997), 363.

[20] Agapius, *Chronicle*, trans. in Robert G. Hoyland, *Theophilus of Edessa's Chronicle and the Circulation of Historical Knowledge in Late Antiquity and Early Islam* (Liverpool: Liverpool University Press, 2011), 181.

[21] Theophanes, *Chronicle*, 363.

patrikios exarchos to the Arrānian prince Varazdat, nephew of Juanshēr, apparently trying to create a third exarchate, in addition to those in North Africa and Italy, tasked with organising local defence against the Muslims.[22]

Yet once ʿAbd al-Malik had defeated all opponents of his rule, he immediately acted to assert his authority. Using Justinian's move to evacuate a substantial portion of the residents of Cyprus as a pretext, he dispatched to Anatolia his brother and governor of Mesopotamia, Muḥammad ibn Marwān, who inflicted a major defeat on a Byzantine army at Sebastopolis in northern Cappadocia in 692.[23] This show of strength by ʿAbd al-Malik prompted Smbat Bagratuni, prince of Armenia, to switch allegiance from Byzantium to the Caliphate, and Smbat also killed Leo, the Byzantine governor of Armenia, delivering his corpse to Muḥammad ibn Marwān, now governor of Caucasia.[24] However, only a decade later, the Armenians, angry at an attempt by Muḥammad to impose direct rule over Caucasia, 'made contact with (Emperor) Apsimarus and brought the Romans into their country'.[25] They initially inflicted a crushing defeat on the Muslims at the Battle of Vardanakert in 703, but this provoked a severe response from Muḥammad ibn Marwān, who 'crushed the Romans who had come to Armenia and also killed many Armenians', and, as a grisly warning against a repeat of such conduct, he had a number of Armenian nobles burned alive in a church in Nakhchavan.[26]

The Caliphate Ascendant

This shocking event, which reverberated across the region and is reported in Muslim and Christian sources,[27] seemed to end Caucasian autonomy and to

[22] Stepʿanos Tarōnecʿi, *Universal History*, trans. Tim Greenwood (Oxford: Oxford University Press, 2017), 1.2. An *exarchos* is like a governor of a province, but with augmented political and military authority; *patrikios* is an honorific title for high-ranking imperial personnel.

[23] Reported by a number of sources translated in Hoyland, *Theophilus*, 185–7.

[24] Ibid., 187–8.

[25] Theophanes, *Chronicle*, 372.

[26] Hoyland, *Theophilus*, 195–6.

[27] Alison Vacca, 'The Fires of Naxčawan: In Search of Intercultural Transmission in Arabic, Armenian, Greek and Syriac', *Le Muséon* 129 (2016), 323–62.

bring the region firmly into the Caliphate's sphere of influence. However, the total failure of the Muslim siege of Constantinople in 717 encouraged and emboldened many peoples on the frontiers of the Caliphate to break free. In Caucasia it was the Khazars who once again seized this chance, conducting regular raids right across the region. In 730 they reached as far as Azerbaijan and even sacked its capital, Ardabil, and killed its governor.[28] This impressed the Byzantine emperor Leo III (717–41), who betrothed his son Constantine to the Khazar ruler's daughter, who converted to Christianity, taking the name Irene.[29] This marriage between the future emperor and empress consolidated the alliance that had been developing since the late seventh century and presented a united front in Caucasia against the Caliphate. Their abject failure in Ardabil and the Byzantine–Khazar alliance made the Muslims realise that they needed to integrate within their empire those northern regions that could be pacified and to establish a buffer zone that would keep these pacified regions secure against those areas and peoples that could not be tamed. Accordingly, in the 730s two very senior Muslim generals, Maslama ibn ʿAbd al-Malik and Marwān, son of the aforementioned Muḥammad ibn Marwān, both of the Umayyad family, led a number of campaigns to push back the Khazars. They then instigated, whether knowingly or not, the same three policies that the Sasanians had carried out before them in order to create a more secure border zone: strengthening physical fortifications, concluding agreements with local leaders and settling loyal groups and military personnel in the region.[30] Thus Maslama ibn ʿAbd al-Malik restored the fortifications of Darband and garrisoned there 24,000 Syrians with stipends, and in 737 Marwan marched through Caucasia with a large army to make a show of strength to the Khazars and to the local lords in these borderlands, receiving the submission of the kings of al-Sarīr, Zirikirān, the Lakz (modern Lezgians in Dagestan), Sindān, Ṭabarsarān and Sharwān.[31]

[28] Robert G. Hoyland, *In God's Path: The Arab Conquests and the Creation of an Islamic Empire* (New York: Oxford University Press, 2015), 188–9.

[29] Theophanes, *Chronicle*, 409–10.

[30] Hoyland, *In God's Path*, 189–90; Shingiray, *On the Path*, 290–302.

[31] Aḥmad b. Yaḥyā al-Balādhurī, *Kitāb futūḥ al-buldān*, ed. M. J. de Goeje (Leiden: Brill, 1866), 207–9; cf. Ibn Aʿtham al-Kūfī, *Kitāb al-futūḥ* (Beirut: Dār al-aḍwāʾ, 1991), 8: 263–6.

From this point on, then, the machinery of Muslim government – tax-collectors, governors and state officials – is ever more prominent in Caucasia, especially in the southern part, and the region became increasingly assimilated within the Islamic Empire. Yet the difficult terrain and the distance from major centres of Muslim population meant that native elites still retained a fair degree of power over their locales. As one Muslim historian tells us in reference to the early Abbasid period, the princes (*baṭāriqa*)[32] of Caucasia jealously guarded their territories, and when a tax-collector (*ʿāmil*) came to the frontier zone (*thaghr*), they would check him out, and 'if he was honest, stern and powerfully armed, they would obediently submit to him, but if not they would disparage and scorn him'.[33] A good example of this independence of mind is provided by their treatment of Yūsuf ibn Muḥammad. When he assumed the governorship of Caucasia in 849, he packed off one of the princes of the Armenian Bagratuni family to Samarra and ransacked a famous monastery in southern Armenia. This greatly angered 'the princes, the freeborn and the powerful' (*al-baṭāriqa wa-l-aḥrār wa-l-mutaghalliba*), who hired some local toughs to kill Yūsuf.[34]

Another influential group in Caucasia, besides the native elites, were the Muslim newcomers who settled there, whether they were obliged to do so by the Muslim government or did so voluntarily, seeking new opportunities. Members of the Umayyad family or those close to them had already acquired lands in this region in the first half of the eighth century; thus Marwān ibn Muḥammad took charge of Warthān on the border between Azerbaijan and Arrān: 'He revived its land, fortified it and it became an estate (*ḍayʿa*) for him'.[35] But it was only in the wake of the Abbasid revolution of 750 that colonisation began in earnest; in particular, a wave of Yemeni Muslims relocated

[32] *Baṭrīq*, pl. *baṭāriqa*, from Greek *patrikios* (see note 22 above), is used in Arabic to designate a wide array of elite persons. In accounts about Caucasia, it is often applied to members of noble houses, and hence my translation of 'prince'; note the statement of Ṭabarī, *Taʾrīkh*, 2: 1232, that Sahl ibn Sunbāṭ was given *tāj al-baṭraqa*.

[33] Balādhurī, *Kitāb*, 210–11.

[34] Ibid., 211. This episode is recounted also by Tʿovma Arcruni, *Patmutʿiwn tann Arcruneacʿ*, trans. Robert Thomson as *History of the House of the Arcrunikʿ* (Detroit: Wayne State University Press, 1985), 2: 5–7.

[35] Balādhurī, *Kitāb*, 329.

from Basra to what is now northwest Iran and southern Caucasia. When they arrived, 'everyone grabbed what they could (*ghalaba kullu qawmin ʿalā mā amkanahum*); some of them bought land from the local non-Muslim residents (*al-ʿajam*) and villages were placed under their protection (*uljiʾat ilayhim al-qurā li-l-khafāra*), its inhabitants becoming farmers (*muzāriʿīn*) for the settlers'.[36] A well-known example is al-Rawwād ibn al-Muthannā, who acquired estates from 'Tabrīz (northwards) to Badhdh', and his sons expanded his holdings and played a part in regional politics, so establishing a sort of dynasty, which, through intermarriage and interaction with Kurds and Persians, gained a strong local colouring.[37] Further north the settlement was more particularly directed at defence. Thus, in response to a severe defeat inflicted by the Khazars on his governor of Caucasia, Caliph al-Manṣūr (754–75) dispatched a large number of fighters with labourers and masons, who would then build towns so that the fighters could settle there and be a permanent 'bulwark for the Muslims' (*ridʾan li-l-muslimīn*) against the enemy.[38]

Lords of Caucasia in the Mid-ninth Century

Standard maps showing the extent of Muslim rule in the early Abbasid period convey the idea of a cohesive Muslim province of Caucasia (e.g. see Map 4.2), but this masks the reality of the politics of this province, in which a medley of local potentates vied for control of territory and formed alliances with the major powers of Byzantium and the Caliphate and amongst themselves that would, however, shift according to circumstance. This is more in evidence in the ninth century, when a civil war between the sons of Caliph Hārūn al-Rashīd (d. 809) and the advent of Turkish militias destabilised the Caliphate and allowed a number of strong men and powerful groups to win a measure of autonomy for their followers and in some cases establish dynasties that enjoyed a moderate degree of independence.

[36] Ibid., 329. Cf. ibid., 330: the inhabitants of Marāgha 'placed it (their town) under the protection of Marwān who rebuilt it' (*aljaʾūhā ilā Marwān fa-ibtanāhā*). Surrendering ownership of their land in return for protection and presumably rights to a proportion of the produce seems in some cases to be a survival strategy for the local rural population.

[37] Aḥmad b. Wāḍiḥ al-Yaʿqūbī, *Taʾrīkh*, ed. M. T. Houtsma (Leiden: Brill, 1883), 2: 446, 540.

[38] Ibid., 2: 446–7.

Map. 4.2 Byzantine, Umayyad and Khazar spheres of control in Caucasia in the mid-eighth century.

A good example of this phenomenon in Caucasia is provided by the career of a certain Sahl ibn Sunbāṭ (Arm. Smbat), the lord of Shakkī (modern Sheki) in the north of Arrān. He had taken the opportunity upon the death of Varaz-Tirdat in 822, the last of the Parthian Mihrānid kings of Arrān, to claim suzerainty of this land.[39] He backed up his claim by presenting himself as a descendant of the native Arrān-shāhs, who ruled before the advent of the Mihrānids in the sixth century, and by showing that he could defend his dominion against Muslim predations, successfully rescuing some 1000 men seized by a band of Muslim raiders. And around 835 he managed to prevent the entry of the newly appointed governor Muḥammad ibn Sulaymān

[39] Ibid., 2: 579; Movsēs Dasxuranc'i, *Patmut'iwn*, 3: 19.

al-Samarqandī into Arrān.[40] Sahl was aided in his insurrection by the fact that at this time a lot of the caliph's military resources for this region went into combatting the major rebellion of Bābak, a native of the Ardabil countryside who became leader of a Zoroastrian cult and instigated guerrilla attacks against Muslim colonists for two decades (817–37) from his mountain base at Badhdh, on the border between Azerbaijan and Arrān.[41] After numerous failures, Caliph al-Muʿtaṣim (833–42) finally sent one of his most senior generals, al-Afshīn, who, after two years of pursuing the rebel, finally captured his fortress. Bābak escaped and sought sanctuary with Sahl, who handed him over to the Muslim authorities, presumably because he realised that, with Bābak defeated, he would face the full force of al-Afshīn's wrath directly. Instead, Sahl was now handsomely rewarded, receiving a robe, a crown and a horse and the right to levy tribute, as well as a payment of one million dirhams.[42] He is even said to have received from the caliph 'sovereignty over Armenia, Georgia and Arrān to rule authoritatively and regally over all'.[43] This has been described as an 'obvious exaggeration', but one should note that Arabic sources say something similar, namely that Caliph al-Muʿtaṣim made Sahl his most senior representative in the region (*baṭraqahu ʿalā jamīʿ baṭāriqatih*).[44]

However, even if Sahl was regarded by al-Muʿtaṣim as the chief indigenous potentate in Caucasia, this was almost certainly not the case from the perspective of other local notables. The quantity and variety of powerbrokers in this region is clear from accounts of the general Bughā's efforts to pacify this northern province in the early 850s.[45] He had been dispatched there in response to the assassination of the aforementioned Yūsuf ibn Muḥammad

[40] Ibid., 3: 19; Yaʿqūbī, *Taʾrīkh*, 2: 579.

[41] Patricia Crone, *The Nativist Prophets of Early Islamic Iran: Rural Revolt and Local Zoroastrianism* (New York: Cambridge University Press, 2012), 46–76.

[42] Ṭabarī, *Taʾrīkh*, 3: 1272.

[43] Movsēs Dasxurancʿi, *Patmutʿiwn*, 3: 20.

[44] Vladimir Minorsky, 'Caucasica IV', *Bulletin of the School of Oriental and African Studies* 3 (1953), 510; Ibn Aʿtham, *Kitāb al-futūḥ*, 8: 438.

[45] See in particular Alison Vacca, 'Conflict and Community in the Medieval Caucasus', *al-ʿUṣūr al-Wusṭā* 25 (2017), 66–112, who emphasises the complexity of the allegiances and relations between the Caucasian elites.

and the ensuing turbulence, when many of the local leaders 'agitated and took control of their own areas' (*taḥarraka bi-hā jamāʿatun min al-baṭāriqa wa-ghayruhum wa-taghallabū ʿalā nawāḥīhim*).[46] Bughā marched right across Caucasia, from west to east, demanding submission and fighting all those that refused. At the end of his campaign, he deported to the caliphal court in Samarra a number of local notables, who were perhaps singled out for the strength of the influence that they wielded and so the potential challenge to the Muslim authorities that they represented. Both Armenian and Muslim historians record these deportations, and even though their accounts do not exactly correspond, the following figures feature in both: (1) Qiṭrīj (Arm. Ktrič), prince (*baṭrīq*) of Gardman; (2) ʿĪsā ibn Yūsuf, nephew of Iṣṭifānūs (in Armenian sources: Esayi Apumusē), in the district of Baylaqān; (3) (Muʿāwiya son of) Sahl ibn Sunbāṭ, prince (*baṭrīq*) of Arrān; (4) Smbat son of Ashot (Bagratuni), nicknamed Abū l-ʿAbbās al-Wāthī, commander-in-chief (*sparapet*) of Armenia; (5) Adharnarsī (Arm. Atrnerseh) ibn Isḥāq, 'prince of Albania', of Khāshīn (Arm. Khachen).[47]

Although numbers 1–3 and 5 on this list resided within the region that Muslim geographers referred to as Arrān, there is no clear sense that any one of them was an overall leader. Armenian sources say of ʿĪsā Apumusē that he ruled the land of Arrān and that he was 'prince of Arrān', they also refer to Atrnerseh as 'the great prince', possibly implying that he was considered more powerful than ʿĪsā Apumusē.[48] However, Muslim sources pay more attention to Sahl ibn Sunbāṭ, calling him 'prince of Arrān', though this seems to have been a reward for handing over the arch-rebel Bābak rather than an ancestral title. Besides this dispersal of power, a further complicating factor

[46] Yaʿqūbī, *Taʾrīkh*, 2: 598.

[47] Ṭabarī, *Taʾrīkh*, 3: 1416; Tʿovma Arcruni, *Patmutʿiwn*, 3: 11 (who adds: Grigor, lord of the Mamikoneans; Grigor, lord of Siunik; Vasak, lord of Vajoc-jor; Philip, prince of Siunik; Nerseh, prince of Garicʿayank; he also says that Sahl was deported whereas Ṭabarī says it was his son Muʿāwiya); Yovhannēs Drasxanakertcʿi, *Hayocʿ Patmutʿiwn*, trans. K. Maksoudian as *History of Armenia* (Atlanta: Scholars Press, 1987), 26.9.18 (who adds: Stepʿannos of Uti). Ṭabarī, *Taʾrīkh*, 2: 1232, calls ʿĪsā ibn Yūsuf 'ruler (*malik*) of Baylaqān'.

[48] Tʿovma Arcruni, *Patmutʿiwn*, 3: 10 ('he ruled over the extensive territory of the Ałuank'); Yovhannēs Drasxanakertcʿi, *Hayocʿ*, 26.9.14 ('Esayi prince of Albania'), 26.9.11 ('the great prince Atrnerseh').

for the Caliphate was that these local lords might appeal to outside powers for help, as when Bughā marched against the Tsanar people (Ṣanāriyya) in the Caucasian foothills, who then wrote to the rulers of the Byzantines, Khazars and Ṣaqāliba and obtained their support.[49]

Lords of Caucasia in the Mid-tenth Century

As the Caliphate further fragmented in the late ninth and early tenth century, the politics of the Caucasian borderlands became even more complex and conflicted. We happen to have two documents from circa 950 that nicely illustrate this entangled world. The first is embedded in a comprehensive work sponsored by Emperor Constantine Porphyrogenitus (905–59) on court ceremonial and on bureaucratic and military organisation, which bears the title *Ekthesis tou basileou taxeōs* (usually translated as 'The Book of Ceremonies') and was completed in the mid-940s. Chapter 48 of this work contains a list of the address formulae and seals that are to be used in letters sent from the Byzantine emperor to external powers.[50] After pre-eminent authorities, like the pope and the caliph, the text moves eastwards towards Caucasia, beginning with Armenia and Iberia, then Alania and Abkhazia – all frequent allies of Byzantium – before proceeding to Arrān. As regards the latter, there is no mention of a single ruler, but rather of chiefs or princes (*archōns*). The same goes for the next items on the list, which concern entities even further to the east, either statelets bordering on the Caspian Sea (Sharwān, Mūqān, Barzand and Khurṣān) or peoples like the Tsanars, Didoi and Az (Ossetians). The usual protocol was that the emperor would employ the set formulae in addressing a decree (κέλευσις) to the rulers of these countries, which means that they recognised, at least from the perspective of the Byzantine chancellery, his authority. But this had not been the case in the East Caucasus since the reign of Constans II (641–68), so what explains the presence of these East Caucasian polities in the list – is it just an archaism or a new reality?

[49] Yaʿqūbī, *Taʾrīkh*, 2: 598.

[50] It is thoroughly discussed by B. Martin-Hisard, 'Constantinople et les archontes du monde caucasien dans le Livre des cérémonies, II, 48', *Travaux et Mémoires* 13 (2000), 359–530, and Constantin Zuckerman, 'A propos du Livre des cérémonies, II, 48', *Travaux et Mémoires* 13 (2000), 531–94 (translated into English in Hoyland, *From Albania*, 149–90).

A work composed under the auspices of Constantine Porphyrogenitus, *De administrando imperio*, refers in its forty-fourth chapter to a new power emerging in northwest Iran and southern Caucasia, which it calls *Persis*. It uses this term also for the Samanid Empire in northeast Iran and Transcaucasia, but the western *Persis* is clearly different. It first appears in Byzantine sources around the 890s and evidently refers to the short-lived dynasty principally constituted by Muḥammad b. Abī l-Sāj Dīwdād (889–901) and his brother Yūsuf (901–28), whose power bases were in Marāgha, Bardhaʿa and Ardabil. Muḥammad had been appointed governor of Azerbaijan by the caliph al-Muʿtaḍid (892–902), but he had seized power for himself around 895 (probably meaning that he stopped sending taxes to the caliph and proclaiming allegiance to him on official media), and at that time received an embassy bearing gifts from the Byzantine emperor.[51] He had re-established relations with the caliph in 898, but seems to have enjoyed a high degree of autonomy, and his brother Yūsuf further extended this until his death in 928. Around this time, the Byzantine chief of staff (*domestikos*, rendered in Arabic as *dumustuq*), John Kourkouas (*Qarqāsh*), launched a series of attacks across the borderlands between Azerbaijan and Byzantine territory. In 927, employing siege engines, catapults and flame-throwers, he besieged Dvin and was able to enter it, but was repelled by the Muslim garrison based there.[52] The next year, Kourkouas had more success and captured Khilāṭ (Akhlāṭ), on the north shore of Lake Van, casting out the pulpit from the central mosque and replacing it with a cross.[53] For a period of about four years he campaigned in these border regions, from Raʾs al-ʿAyn in the east to Malatya and Samosata in the west, achieving some victories, though also many reverses. Nevertheless, these campaigns ignited some hope in the Byzantine leadership that they might retake these areas, and, as it would seem from the list in 'The Book of

[51] Ṭabarī, *Taʾrīkh*, 3: 2185; Zuckerman, 'A propos', 537. W. Madelung, 'The Minor Dynasties of Northern Iran', in Peter Avery (ed.), *The Cambridge History of Iran, Volume 4* (Cambridge: Cambridge University Press, 1975), 226–43, gives a useful survey of the dynasties that try to control Azerbaijan and Eastern Caucasia at this time.

[52] Ibn al-Athīr, *al-Kāmil fī l-taʾrīkh*, ed. ʿUmar ʿA.-S. Tadmurī (Beirut: Dār al-Kutub, 1997), 6: 716.

[53] Ibid., 6: 734.

Ceremonies', these hopes were reflected in diplomatic practice as well as military action. Certainly, in the aftermath of the demise of the Sājids in 929, it is likely that at least some of the regions in the list were able to establish a degree of autonomy, predisposing them to overtures and promises of support from the Byzantine emperor.

From around 942, however, a Daylamī by the name of Marzubān ibn Muḥammad ibn Musāfir al-Sallār (founder of a minor dynasty known as the Musāfirids or the Sallārids) gradually asserted control over the Sājid lands, establishing a hold over the three key cities of Ardabil, Bardhaʿa and Dvin.[54] In his section on Caucasia in his geographical work, Ibn Ḥawqal (d. c. 980s) decided to add a lot of new material to the earlier text of his main source, Iṣṭakhrī (d. 957), including our second document: a list of the vassals of Marzubān and the amount of tribute that they agreed to pay to him, which Ibn Ḥawqal says that he drew from 'the receipts of the year 344' (955 CE).[55] He emphasises that in this mountainous region there are many 'kings and lords' (*mulūk wa-aṣḥāb*), who have their own estates, forts, cavalry, clients and servants, and in general enjoy a high degree of autonomy and wealth. Nevertheless, they were tributary rulers and not independent monarchs: 'All of the masters of these districts, who are kings of the marches (*al-aṭrāf*), obey the ruler of Azerbaijan, Armenia and the two Arrāns.'[56] They owed not just obedience, but also taxes. And whereas Ibn Abī l-Sāj had made few fiscal demands, contenting himself with light tribute and otherwise taking his due in the form of gifts, Marzubān ibn Muḥammad 'instituted revenue offices (*dawāwīn*), surveys (*qawānīn*) and supplementary levies (*lawāzim*)'.[57]

Ibn Ḥawqal clarifies that there is an Inner and an Outer Armenia, the former belonging fully to the Muslims and the latter self-governing but paying tribute to the Muslims. These two entities correspond in Ibn Ḥawqal's list of tributaries to 'the sons of Sunbāṭ' (Arm. Smbat) and 'the sons of al-Dayrānī'

54 Madelung, 'Minor Dynasties', 232–5.

55 Ibn Ḥawqal, *Kitāb al-masālik wa-l-mamālik*, ed. M. J. de Goeje (Leiden: Brill, 1873), 254. See the discussion of this document in Minorsky, 'Caucasica IV', 514–29, and Zuckerman, 'A propos', 578–81.

56 Ibn Ḥawqal, *Kitāb*, 249–50. For the expression 'two Arrāns' see below.

57 Ibid., 250.

(Arm. Derenik). These refer to the Bagratuni and Arcruni families respectively, who had both managed to take advantage of the weakness of the Caliphate in the later ninth and early tenth century to extend their influence beyond their core territories of Kars-Dvin (either side of the modern Turkey–Armenia border) and Vaspurakan (around Lake Van). This meant walking a tightrope between the Byzantine and Muslim authorities. Gagik, son of Grigor-Derenik Arcruni, at different times served both sides, allying himself circa 908 with Yūsuf ibn Abī l-Sāj, who 'gave him a royal crown, as well as honors and gifts befitting royalty', and receiving in the 920s the title of chief prince (*archōn tōn archontōn*) from the Byzantine emperor.[58] In cases of disagreement it was likely that both parties would have to pick a side; thus, in their dispute over the leadership of the Bagratuni polity, Ashot II (914–29) son of Smbat and his cousin Ashot son of Shapuh turned for backing to the Byzantine empress Zoe Karbonopsina and to Yūsuf ibn Abī l-Sāj respectively.[59] Ashot II finally won out against his rival in 920 and kept the Muslim forces at bay right up until his death in 929. The following decades were prosperous ones for the Bagratuni regime, as is suggested by their huge payment of two million dirhams to Marzubān, which is double the second largest payment in Ibn Ḥawqal's list.

Out of the ten vassals on this list a number are from Arrān, the two most important being Ishkhānik, lord of Shakkī, and Sanḥārib ibn Sawāda, who is characterised by Movses Daskhuranc'i as the one 'through whom God restored the long extinct kingdom' (3: 22/23). These two families, one based north of the River Kura and one south of it, seem to have enjoyed a degree of pre-eminence in Arrān; they descended from the indigenous rulers of Arrān (Arrān-shāhs) and the Parthian Mihrānid rulers of Arrān respectively, or at least claimed to do so in order to give themselves some degree of antiquity

58 Yovhannēs Drasxanakertc'i, *Hayoc'*, 43.3a. A lengthy account of their meeting is given by T'ovma Arcruni, *Patmut'iwn*, 4: 3, which is very flattering to Gagik; T'ovma also says that Caliph al-Muqtadir sent Gagik a crown. Constantine Porphyrogenitus, *The Book of Ceremonies*, trans. Ann Moffatt and Maxeme Tall (with Greek edition of CSHB) (Canberra: Byzantina Australiensia, 2012), 2: 48.

59 Yovhannēs Drasxanakertc'i, *Hayoc'*, preface; he tells of the struggle between the two Ashots at length in chapters 56–8.

and legitimacy. It is tempting to equate their two realms with the 'two Arrāns' mentioned by Ibn Ḥawqal above, though this is not made clear in our sources.

A comparison of the two aforementioned lists of local Caucasian elites, from the 850s and the 950s, shows that they enjoyed a fair degree of continuity across this time. For example, Ashot III Bagratuni, who pays tribute to Marzubān in 955, is the great-great-grandson of the Smbat son of Ashot in the list of the 850s. Another tribute-payer in 955, Ishkhāniq, 'lord of Shakki', is the son of 'Atrnerseh son of Hamam, lord of Shakki', whom Muslim sources record as the king of the Christian population of Shakkī and its environs, as well as of the substantial number of Muslims who lived among them.[60] This Hamam is said to have 'revived the fallen kingship of the house of Arrān' in the late ninth century, and he is connected to Sahl ibn Sunbāṭ and his son Muʿāwiya, who feature in the list of the 850s as 'lord of Shakkī' and '*baṭrīq* of Arrān'.[61] Arguments have been advanced for identifying other enduring family connections between these two lists, though frequent recurrence of the same list makes them a little uncertain.[62]

Conclusion

From a study of the late Roman elites of Syria and their fate in the early Islamic period, Hugh Kennedy concluded that 'they lost their status and identity, either by death in battle, emigration or by merging themselves in the new order'.[63] This is certainly not true of Caucasia, where the deeds and dicta of their princes, lords and nobles fills the pages of our historical texts concerning this region. In part, this is because of its distance from the imperial centres in Syria and Iraq and its mountainous topography, and in part because of its proximity to the empires of the Byzantines and Khazars, whom

[60] ʿAlī b. al-Ḥusayn al-Masʿūdī, *Murūj al-dhahab/Les prairies d'or*, ed. and trans. C. Barbier de Meynard and Pavet de Courteille (Paris: Imprimerie impériale, 1861–77), 2: 75.

[61] Movsēs Dasxurancʿi, *Patmutʿiwn*, 3: 21/22: Hamam (his exact relationship to Sahl/Muʿāwiya is unclear); Tʿovma Arcruni, *Patmutʿiwn*, 3: 11 (Sahl son of Smbat, lord of Shakkī), and Ṭabarī, *Taʾrīkh*, 3: 1416 (Sahl ibn Sunbāṭ, *baṭrīq* Arrān).

[62] Minorsky, 'Caucasica IV', 521–6, tries to make more connections between the persons on the two lists; Zuckerman, 'A propos', 578–81, makes some corrections and additional suggestions.

[63] 'Syrian Elites from Byzantium to Islam: Survival or Extinction?', in J. Haldon (ed.), *Money, Power and Politics in Early Islamic Syria* (Farnham: Ashgate Publishing, 2010), 198.

the local chiefs could call upon for support or play divide and rule between them and the agents of the Caliphate. On the downside, this meant that imperial actors would meddle in the affairs of Caucasian leaders or force them to provide support against their enemies, which frequently placed these local potentates in a difficult position between the dominant powers. In addition, they had to show to their subjects that they were not the mere playthings of the imperial authorities, but rather possessed a degree of independence. This delicate balancing act is nicely illustrated by the career of Sahl ibn Sunbāṭ, lord of Shakkī, who defeats a band of Muslim marauders and blocks entry of a Muslim governor into his land to bolster his local standing, but then hands over the rebel Bābak to the general al-Afshīn in order to avert any reprisals for his actions and to win the caliph's endorsement of his claim to suzerainty over all of Arrān.

The fragmentation of the Caliphate in the tenth century added an extra layer of complexity and increased risk for these Caucasian elites, since the establishment of local Muslim dynasties meant that they were no longer dealing with a single remote centre of power, the agents of which they might be able to do bargains with or even repel; rather they had to contend with much nearer centres of power – smaller to be sure, but right on their doorstep. A good example of this hazardous state of affairs is offered by the shifting alliances between the caliph, Yūsuf ibn Abī l-Sāj and various Caucasian rulers. When Yūsuf was in open defiance of the caliph, the latter encouraged King Smbat I Bagratuni to oppose Yūsuf. When the latter regularised his relationship with the caliph, he sought revenge against Smbat, and found an ally in Gagik, the Arcruni prince, who was in dispute with Smbat over the city of Nakhchavan. Though Gagik and Smbat were fellow Christians, Gagik willingly became a vassal of Yūsuf so as to take advantage of the latter's military strength to win his argument with Smbat. Evidently, it was not confessional allegiance which necessarily determined loyalties, but, very commonly, realpolitik and personal interests and alliances.[64]

Alison Vacca has argued that Caucasia, after a short period of vassalage in the immediate aftermath of the Muslim conquests, became a full caliphal province and so should be regarded as an integral part of the Islamic

[64] These machinations are narrated at length by Yovhannēs Drasxanakertcʿi, *Hayocʿ*, chapters 42–3.

Empire.[65] It is certainly true that 'Caucasia was not simply a strategic periphery where the tensions between Byzantium, on the one hand, and the Iranian and Islamic worlds, on the other, were played out'.[66] Yet it does have a distinctive place within the Islamic Empire and a different trajectory to other provinces of the Empire. It was able to resist Arabisation/Arabicisation and to substantially impede Islamicisation. Iran and Transoxania did not come to adopt Arabic as their principal language, but they did become majority Muslim; most of the population of Andalus did not convert to Islam, but Arabic did become increasingly dominant there among non-Muslims as well as Muslims from the ninth to the twelfth centuries. However, Arabic never gained a foothold in Caucasia, and Islam only came to predominate in the early modern period, and then only in East Caucasia, which was occupied by Turkish, Mongolian and then Persian powers, whereas Christianity remained dominant in the west of the region.

The mountainous terrain of parts of Caucasia and the survival of elites were contributing factors, but they do not suffice as an explanation, given that they are a facet of other provinces of the Islamic world that did become majority Muslim and/or Arabic-speaking. More important, in my opinion, was the point I made at the beginning of this chapter: that Caucasia was, if not a border region, at least an in-between zone, experiencing centripetal pull not just from the Islamic imperial centre, but also from the Byzantine and Khazar Empires. This meant two things. First, different languages, cultures, commodities and so on circulated freely, for these were not closed borders. Thus, Ibn Ḥawqal tells us that the cities of Qālīqalā (Karin/Erzerum) and Trebizond were frontier towns (*thaghr*), 'in which merchants from Islamic lands might assemble and pass through into Byzantine territory for the purpose of trade'.[67] Second, the native elites could exploit the proximity of these

[65] In her excellent and thought-provoking study *Non-Muslim Provinces;* ibid., 208, states that 'Armenia and Albania, following the Marwānid Reforms, became caliphal provinces', referring to the changes enacted by Caliph ʿAbd al-Malik in the 690s.

[66] Rapp, 'Caucasia and the First Byzantine Commonwealth', 1.

[67] Ibn Ḥawqal, *Kitāb*, 245. *Thaghr* literally means 'gap', so we are talking about access points which people can pass through, not barriers. See Asa Eger, 'Ḥiṣn, Ribaṭ, Thaghr, or Qaṣr? The semantics of frontier forts in the Early Islamic Period', in Paul Cobb (ed.), *The Lineaments of Islam: Studies in Honor of Fred McGraw Donner* (Leiden: Brill, 2012), 437–40, and more

external powers in a number of different ways. If they got into trouble with one side they might seek support from the other, as in the case of Bābak's successor, Nasr, who, upon the arrest of his master, fled with his closest followers to Byzantium, where he was received with honour and allowed to serve in their own unit in the Byzantine army.[68] Some successfully changed allegiances without having to forfeit their home base, as with the aforementioned Sahl ibn Sunbāṭ and Gagik Arcruni, and sometimes different members of the same noble house might serve on either side of the frontier, forming what have been called 'trans-local families'.[69] By these and other survival strategies Caucasian elites strove to maintain their power and status in the face of fluctuating political conditions. Of course, it was a high stakes game that could bring its own new set of problems. Serving different masters could pit family members against one another, as when the Bagratuni house experienced a mini civil war because Ashot II (914–29) son of Smbat and his cousin Ashot son of Shapuh were impelled by their Byzantine and Muslim backers to fight each other for control of the family domains. And recourse to external powers could have unintended consequences, as when, in the early modern era, the Armenians and Georgians invited in the Russians to offset pressure from the Ottomans and Safavids, but then the invitees decided to stay.

generally his *The Islamic–Byzantine Frontier: Interaction and Exchange among Muslim and Christian Communities* (London: I. B. Tauris, 2015), 277–310.

[68] Juan Signes Codoñer, *The Emperor Theophilos and the East, 829–842* (Farnham: Burlington, 2014), 145–72.

[69] Johannes Preiser-Kapeller, 'Central Peripheries: Empires and Elites across Byzantine and Muslim Frontiers in Comparison (700–900 CE)', in Wolfram Drews (ed.), *Die Interaktion von Herrschern und Eliten in imperialen Ordnungen des Mittelalters* (Berlin: De Gruyter, 2018), 93. See also Johannes Preiser-Kapeller, 'Aristocrats, Mercenaries, Clergymen and Refugees: Deliberate and Forced Mobility of Armenians in the Early Medieval Mediterranean (6th to 11th Century A.D.)', in Preiser-Kapeller *et al.* (eds), *Migration Histories of the Medieval Afroeurasian Transition Zone: Aspects of Mobility between Africa, Asia and Europe, 300–1500 C.E.* (Leiden: Brill, 2020), 333–9, on the mobility of Armenian elites across the Byzantine–Islamic border.

5

BYZANTINE BORDERS WERE STATE ARTEFACTS, NOT 'FLUID ZONES OF INTERACTION'

Anthony Kaldellis

In recent decades, a number of remarkable and counter-intuitive claims have been advanced about the Roman and early Byzantine imperial borders. We have been told that the empire had no clear or fixed borders or even no concept of a border to begin with; that there was no expectation that the borders could or should be defended and no actual ability to do so; that there was no imperial strategy for the defence of the empire; that there was no conception of the territorial integrity of the Roman state; that the border was always permeable, porous, and fluid; and that features of the terrain were not used as borders or imagined as marking the border. Not all of these theses have been advanced in the same publications, but as a coherent constellation they have given rise to a revolutionary understanding of the imperial borders that is often encapsulated in the catchphrase 'fluid zones of interaction'.[1]

[1] The publications that advance this thesis are conveniently cited by Geoffrey Greatrex, 'Roman Frontiers and Foreign Policy in the East', in Richard Alston and Samuel Lieu (eds), *Aspects of the Roman East: Papers in Honour of Professor Fergus Millar FBA* (Turnhout: Brepols, 2007), 103–73. Countless references can now be provided to scholars of middle Byzantium referring to 'porous' or 'fluid' frontiers; a few are cited below.

Geoffrey Greatrex has effectively refuted most of the claims made above, with special reference to the borders of the late eastern Roman state (also known as early Byzantium), and many other historians have signalled their doubt regarding this picture or key components of it.[2] In this chapter, I will first present some of the conceptual weaknesses of the idea that borders were 'fluid zones of interaction', a phrase that is now routinely applied by many scholars to Byzantine borders of all periods. In the second part, I will focus on the borders of the middle Byzantine period and argue that, even if they were sometimes porous and fluid, that was not what defined them as borders. All places are porous and fluid absent a force of constraint, therefore borders are better defined as sites of potential intervention by the state to preclude movement. Borders were created, maintained, and regulated by specific state institutions, and any fluidity or interaction that took place across them was usually by their sufferance, indifference, or failure, and not because they did not exist or were completely ineffectual. Premodern state institutions were not as impotent as many think. This means that borders must be defined primarily in terms of institutional practices, and their porousness evaluated against the success or failure of policy goals. We need to understand those goals in their ideological context, and not intone formulas that resonate with modern ideological priorities.

I will be using the term *border* rather than the more usual *frontier* because its connotations are more appropriate for this discussion. The two words are often synonymous, but 'frontier' in English often denotes the current limit in a process of ongoing expansion (as in 'the frontiers of knowledge') or a 'Wild West' scenario where the presence of state institutions is sometimes only nominal or hazy. There were exceptional times and places when Romanía (the real name

[2] Greatrex, 'Roman Frontiers'; other sceptics include (but are not limited to) Mark W. Graham, *News and Frontier Consciousness in the Late Roman Empire* (Ann Arbor: University of Michigan Press, 2006); Peter Heather, *Empires and Barbarians: Migration, Development and the Birth of Europe* (London: Pan Books, 2009), 657, n. 49; Noel Lenski, 'Captivity and Slavery among the Saracens in Late Antiquity (ca. 250–630)', *Antiquité tardive* 19 (2011), 237–66; Andrei Gândilă, *Cultural Encounters on Byzantium's Northern Frontier, c. AD 500–700: Coins, Artifacts and History* (Cambridge: Cambridge University Press, 2018), 2, 6, and chapter 1 *passim*.

of what we call 'Byzantium') was marked more by frontiers than borders, such as during the reabsorption of Greece in the eighth-ninth centuries, and those processes require a different model from the one presented here.[3]

'Fluid Zones of Interaction'

'Fluid zones of interaction' is the most commonly used formula to signal the new paradigm about Roman and Byzantine borders. It is activated whenever scholars who adhere to that school of thought find that people, ideas, and goods crossed the border. I will begin this contribution by offering five reasons why we should not be using this formula or any equivalent of it.

First, it has become an unthinking reflex and mantra. It is recycled and repeated by historians who have done no primary research on borders but who have picked it up as the latest trendy thing to say.[4] It now contains all the dangers of group think, that is of rhetorically compelling formulas that circulate separately from whatever empirical evidence they were once based on. As the formula is no longer in touch with reality, it can take us deep into fantasy and error, for example to the belief that Byzantine borders were 'porous' because 'the efforts made by the Roman empire to establish defended borders were not continued in the Byzantine period'.[5] Scholars have a responsibility to not repeat the formulas of group think. We must always try to explain things in our own language, based on our own individual wrestling with the primary evidence. 'Avoid pronouncing the phrases everyone else does. Think up your own way of speaking, even if only to convey that thing you think everyone is saying.'[6] When we see scholars recycling formulas, our intellectual defences should be activated.

Second, the formula ironically presents itself as a categorical truth while dissembling its own fluid epistemology, which makes it useless for the purposes of actual research and analysis. What do I mean? Clearly, some borders

[3] Anthony Kaldellis, *Romanland: Ethnicity and Empire in Byzantium* (Cambridge, MA: Harvard University Press, 2019), 218–22.

[4] Averil Cameron, *The Byzantines* (Malden, MA: Wiley Blackwell, 2006), 11, 188.

[5] Averil Cameron, *Byzantine Matters* (Princeton, NJ: Princeton University Press, 2014), 29.

[6] Timothy Snyder, *On Tyranny: Twenty Lessons from the Twentieth Century* (New York: Tim Duggan Books, 2017), 59.

were more fluid than others; the same border was more fluid at one time rather than another; the density of interaction varied by circumstance and policy; and 'zone' is a term that encompasses an impossibly wide variety of physical and institutional settings. By what standard are we to decide where on the spectrum to place a particular border? The formula gives us no tools to do this: it has never produced a workable theory of 'fluid mechanics' that goes beyond the mantra. Fluid like water or fluid like tar? What is the viscosity? Faced with a demand for a concrete methodology and granular analysis, we realise that 'fluidity' was always just a vague metaphor that was never intended to produce scholarly rigour. It merely signals conformity to the new group think, but in practice is useless for detailed research. In all the years of its existence and (now) hegemony, I have not come across any attempts, based on evidence, to document just *how* fluid or porous the border was at any time or place. Borders are always supposed to be simply porous and fluid. These words do not solve problems that were previously intractable but are just what we are now expected to say when the topic of borders comes up.

Third, absent any epistemological criteria 'fluid zones of interaction' fails to explain how borders were different from any other kind of place. All places are potentially fluid zones of interaction and porous, for we can describe all human relationships that way if we want to. But were the borders a more fluid zone of interaction than, say, Constantinople or the provinces? The formula gives us no way to measure this. Put differently, if all places are fluid zones of interaction, then the concept is unfalsifiable, making it useless for analysis. It is like calling someone 'a man of his times'. Unless we provide examples of people who were *not*, along with criteria by which to decide between the two options, the statement is literally meaningless. Moreover, if all places are fluid zones of interaction, then it makes no sense to define borders that way because that could not have been what made them borders as opposed to something else. This chapter will argue that borders were specific places or regions where the state deployed institutions that could, if it so chose, intervene to block contact and exchange between areas that were under its control and those that were not. What made borders different from other places is that the state invested resources in them to block fluidity, or significantly reduce it. We have been focusing on the wrong end of the equation.

Fourth, the paradigm of fluidity has enabled historians to arrive at a more sophisticated understanding of Byzantine military strategy along the border and of client-management along the frontier, one which does not depend on crude notions of 'holding the line'.[7] But much of the time the dominant formula of porousness and fluidity is presented as a revolutionary break from a 'traditional' position that never existed in the first place, and so is effectively a straw man. I am aware of no previous scholarship of note which argued that *no* people, armies, information, or ideas ever moved across the Byzantine borders, or that the latter were static and 'impenetrable', so that we should now celebrate the discovery that goods, people, and ideas did move across the borders.[8] This was no discovery or paradigm shift. The difference is only that past historians did not actively fetishise 'contacts' and 'fluidity', because their ideological context did not require or incentivise them to do so.

Some current efforts to highlight porousness in the face of this alleged older view tend instead to point, in spite of themselves, to the opposite thesis that I will present below. For example, one study of the Cilician frontier in the ninth–tenth centuries wants to see it 'as a permeable zone' and to find 'extremely diverse movements of people', but what it does find, because it is rigorously based on the evidence, are armies, prisoners, diplomats, deserters, merchants, and pilgrims, all groups whose movements were regulated, if not controlled, by state institutions.[9] What it does not find is a *free* or even 'fluid' flow of peoples, goods, and ideas, unconstrained by the state.

7 For example, Catherine Holmes, 'Byzantium's Eastern Frontier in the Tenth and Eleventh Centuries', in David Abulafia and Norah Berend (eds), *Medieval Frontiers: Concepts and Practices* (Aldershot: Ashgate, 2002), 83–104.

8 'Impenetrable', etc.: A. D. Lee, *Information and Frontiers: Roman Foreign Relations in Late Antiquity* (Cambridge: Cambridge University Press, 1993), 5, 66.

9 Koray Durak, 'Traffic across the Cilician Frontier in the Ninth and Tenth Centuries: Movement of People between Byzantium and the Islamic Near East in the Early Middle Ages', in Apostolos Kralides and Andreas Gkoutzioukostas (eds), *Βυζάντιο και Αραβικός κόσμος: Συνάντηση Πολιτισμών* (Thessalonike: Aristotle University of Thessalonike, 2013), 141–54; for the regulation of trade, see below and also Youval Rotman, 'Byzantium and the International Slave Trade in the Central Middle Ages', in Paul Magdalino and Nevra Necipoğlu (eds), *Trade in Byzantium* (Istanbul: Anamed, 2016), 129–42, here 137–41.

Fifth and finally, historians should stop pretending that the current formula is new, or that it is a brave underdog struggling against some (allegedly) dominant view of impenetrable borders. The formula of frontiers as zones of interactions is at least seventy years old even within Byzantine Studies, and that field usually lags behind others in picking up new catchphrases.[10] Fluidity has long been a dominant formula, though it always likes to pose as a perpetual underdog.

Some scholars take porousness so far that they make the border effectively disappear. These approaches play into the rhetoric of fluidity, 'hybridization', 'transmission', 'receptiveness', 'interaction', 'exchange', and 'multivalent, pluralistic layers', code words that are assumed to deliver 'a more complex vision of the frontier than traditional historical views'. A. Asa Eger's first-rate survey of the archaeological data in *The Islamic–Byzantine Frontier* is one such study.[11] He looks at the shared ecologies on either side of the border on such a granular level that he has little use for the state in his analysis. But by explicitly 'dispensing' with the state, he finds that 'to the archaeologist the frontier as an identifiable regional space is imperceptible'. He takes this to be a fault of the concept itself, rather than a limitation of his evidence. Thus, without the state, its goals, and its narratives, the frontier becomes a place like any other: 'a framework where processes of interaction and exchange took place between communities', given that 'in the medieval periods, there were no linear boundaries'.[12] In the end, Eger has to deny the existence of the very subject of his book. In the Conclusions, he despairs of defining the frontier as anything more specific than 'the simultaneous accumulation of several layers of perception', a definition that can be applied to anything that human beings do, anywhere and at any time. This is precisely one of the problems of the paradigm of fluidity: if frontiers are nothing but processes of exchange, then, as Eger recognises, there is no difference between them

[10] For example, Paul Lemerle, 'Invasions et migrations dans les Balkans depuis la fin de l'époque romaine jusqu'au VIIIe siècle', *Revue historique* 211 (1954), 264–308, here 273.

[11] A. Asa Eger, *The Islamic–Byzantine Frontier: Interaction and Exchange among Muslim and Christian Communities* (London: I. B. Tauris, 2015), 2, 312–13, and the subtitle.

[12] Eger, *The Islamic–Byzantine Frontier*, 20, 310–11.

and any other place.[13] This does not help us understand borders but rather dissolves them away as an analytical category.

By contrast, the Romans themselves clearly understood the border to mark the limits of their polity (or 'empire', as we call it). Their borders were constituted and maintained by statal institutions and demarcated the limits of their territorial power and jurisdiction. It was this understanding, and the interventions of the state that sustained it, which formed the bedrock on which any and all other 'layers of perception' of the border rested. If the archaeology cannot by itself generate such a view, its findings and analytical concepts will have to adjust to it. Put differently, if archaeology cannot 'see' the border, that does not mean that it did not exist.

A final qualification is in order. The argument of this chapter will be rooted in empirical reality, in the testimony of the sources in many languages, and in the concepts that the east Romans themselves used to describe their borders. I will not be discussing an alternative approach that recruits long-standing ideologies about 'Byzantium' to dismiss the idea that it had any borders at all. In this view, which not only flirts with fantasy but is self-consciously embedded in it, borders are a modern phenomenon with no ancient or medieval equivalent. They are allegedly a feature of modern nation states, whereas Byzantium was an ecumenical (Christian) empire with no sense that its jurisdiction was spatially limited. This idea effectively denies that a geographically limited, institutionally defined Roman state existed at all. It largely dispenses with empirical evidence for the definition, operation, and perception of borders, and turns instead to theological, poetic, and rhetorical texts, often those that purvey apocalyptic fantasies of the End Times. The Roman state is obscured behind a theological project of universal salvation.[14] Yet any

[13] Eger, *The Islamic–Byzantine Frontier*, 312, 10.

[14] Strains of this theory can be found in Charles Richard Whittaker, *Frontiers of the Roman Empire: A Social and Economic Study* (Baltimore: Johns Hopkins University Press, 1994), while the full symphony is in Gilbert Dagron, 'Byzance et la frontière: Idéologie et réalité', in Outi Merisalo (ed.), *Frontiers in the Middle Ages* (Louvain-la-Neuve: Fédération Internationale des Instituts d'Études Médiévales, 2006), 303–18, a rare lapse in judgment by a great scholar. See also David Olster, 'From Periphery to Center: The Transformation of Late Roman Self-Definition in the Seventh Century', in Ralph W. Mathisen and Hagith S. Sivan

society with a firmly delimited institutional existence can still produce and consume theological fantasies in which its authority is projected globally, and the Roman empire always projected 'soft power' beyond its borders. This does not mean that the latter did not exist on the ground.[15] In Romanía, *horia* meant more or less what we mean by 'borders', and ecumenical readings are rapidly losing ground as a framework for interpreting the realities of the east Roman state, so I will not spend more time on them here.

Borders as State Artefacts

Greatrex and others have demonstrated that the Romans of the eastern empire in antiquity believed that their state had definite, linear borders, which the armies and emperors were expected to defend. This did not change in the middle Byzantine period. Narrative and other sources refer often to the *horia* of the Romans or the Roman state that were violated when barbarians invaded, or that were extended when the Romans annexed more territory. There are so many such passages that only illustrative ones need be cited here. For example, the Bulgar ruler Omurtag 'boldly crossed inside the *horia* of the Romans' with his army in 822.[16] The campaigns of Ioannes Kourkouas in the early tenth century 'extended the Roman *horia*', and our source specifies the former and current geographical limits of those borders.[17] When Bardas Skleros lost his bid for the throne in 979, 'he went off to the Roman *horia* and

(eds), *Shifting Frontiers in Late Antiquity* (Aldershot: Variorum, 1996), 93–101; for the selective use of sources made by this school of thought, see Dimitris Krallis, 'The Army that Crossed Two Frontiers and Established a Third', in Merisalo (ed.), *Frontiers*, 335–48, here 343–4; for the problems of ecumenical readings of Byzantium, see Anthony Kaldellis, 'Did the Byzantine Empire have "Ecumenical" or "Universal" Aspirations?', in Clifford Ando and Seth Richardson (eds), *Ancient States and Infrastructural Power: Europe, Asia, and America* (Philadelphia: University of Pennsylvania Press, 2017), 272–300.

15 Greatrex, 'Roman Frontiers', 145; Cecily Hilsdale, *Byzantine Art and Diplomacy in an Age of Decline* (Cambridge: Cambridge University Press, 2014).

16 *Theophanes Continuatus*, ed. Immanuel Bekker, Corpus Scriptorum Historiae Byzantinae 48 (Bonn: Weber, 1838), Book II: 17, 65; *Chronographiae quae Theophanis Continuati nomine fertur libri I–IV*, ed. and trans. Michael Featherstone and Juan Signes-Codoñer, Corpus Fontium Historiae Byzantinae 53 (Berlin: De Gruyter, 2015), 96.

17 *Theophanes Continuatus*, ed. Bekker, Book VI: 40–1, 426–7.

defected to the Assyrians with his men'.[18] The emperor Basil II 'took himself off to the most afflicted *horia* in both east and west, to clear them of barbarians'.[19] In his epitaph, Basil II proclaimed that he had 'protected the children of New Rome' by campaigning 'in the west and to the very *horoi* of the east'.[20] Cities were designated as 'inside our *horia*' whereas barbarians lived 'on all sides around us and pressed upon the Roman *horia*'.[21] Ideally, the boundary separating Romans and barbarians was firmly and clearly demarcated by gorges, rivers, and mountains, or by man-made obstacles or markers, such as cities and forts: the *horia* should, in one way or another, be 'walled off'.[22] This was a normative concept that did not always correspond to reality, but it is important to establish its existence nonetheless.

Countless more such references could be given. It is useless to deny that the east Romans lacked a well-developed concept of a border that divided them from the 'barbarians'. Denials are made anyway, but they take curious, evasive forms. Consider for example the observation that the allegedly 'porous' state of the borders after the seventh century led to a 'lack of protracted literary attention to . . . "frontiers" as physical barriers or limits or as dividing lines'.[23] It is not clear how to evaluate this claim. Borders had never received 'protracted literary attention', so why expect it now? Moreover, what is 'protracted literary attention'? Do countless small references in narratives, letters, and epigrams (touched on above) not count? We can also add passages in military manuals from precisely this era – 'forts should be erected near the

[18] Michael Psellos, *Chronographia*, vol. 1: *Einleitung und Text*, ed. Diether Roderich Reinsch, Millenium Studies 51 (Berlin: De Gruyter, 2014), Book I: 9, 6–7.

[19] Psellos, *Chronographia*, Book I: 22, 14.

[20] Marc Lauxtermann, *Byzantine Poetry from Pisides to Geometres* (Vienna: Austrian Academy of Sciences, 2003), 236–7.

[21] Psellos, *Chronographia*, Book IV: 19, 60, and Book VI: 9, 110.

[22] Michael Psellos, *Epistulae*, ed. Stratis Papaioannou (Berlin: de Gruyter, 2019), Letter 88. For the role played by the Tauros mountains in the east, see Ralph-Johannes Lilie, 'The Byzantine–Arab Borderland from the Seventh to the Ninth Century', in Florin Curta (ed.), *Borders, Barriers, and Ethnogenesis: Frontiers in Late Antiquity and the Middle Ages* (Turnhout: Brepols, 2005), 13–21, here 14.

[23] Jonathan Shepard, 'Emperors and Expansionism: From Rome to Middle Byzantium', in Abulafia and Berend (eds), *Medieval Frontiers*, 55–82, here 58–61.

horoi',[24] and 'the job of those who are posted by the frontier provinces is to preserve and protect the territories of the Romans secure and unharmed from enemy invasion'[25] – as well as saint's lives: when the Arabs attacked in 838, 'the *horia* that defined and divided the Romans from the Ishmaelites were torn down'.[26]

The emperor and his foreign counterparts such as the Bulgar khan, Bulgarian tsar, and Muslim caliph, as well as the minor emirs, needed to know exactly who controlled what, where it was agreed that soldiers could be stationed, who owned which forts, what lands went with those forts, through what customs offices trade had to pass, what actions constituted provocations, how religious minorities on either side were to be treated, how the movement of people (refugees, deserters, captives) was to be regulated, and so on. Warfare along the border was not continual but was instead punctuated by long periods of tense watchfulness or even peace. Minor raiding did not change these arrangements; it merely moved slaves and cattle around. Major wars and invasions did change them, whereupon a different status quo emerged. Border agreements were frequently spelled out explicitly in treaties, of which we know many, including their specific clauses and territorial demarcations. Oddly, there is no comprehensive study that focuses on the treaties between Romanía and its neighbours regarding borders and related matters. Again, only a small selection can be mentioned here.

The treaty of 716 between the Romans and the Bulgars specified the boundary and made stipulations regarding trade. The treaty of 816 also delineated the border (using the term *horothesia*, 'a border definition') and was carved on inscriptions as well. Where there was no landmark at the location, the border was demarcated as 'in the middle between' (*meson*) two named sites. The Bulgars also constructed a 121-kilometre-long earthwork from the

[24] *The Anonymous Byzantine Treatise on Strategy*, in *Three Byzantine Military Treatises*, ed. and trans. George T. Dennis, Corpus Fontium Historiae Byzantinae 25 (Washington, DC: Dumbarton Oaks, 1985), c. 9, 28.

[25] Nikephoros II Phokas, *On Skirmishing*, in ibid., c. 1, 150.

[26] Euodios, *The 42 Martyrs of Amorion* (Version Z), ed. P. Nikitin and V. Vasilievskij, *Skazanija o 42 amorijskih mučenikah* (St. Petersburg, 1906), 61–78, here 64.

Black Sea to the Maritsa River, ensuring that this border was 'neither imprecise nor zonal'.[27] Also, 'epigraphical evidence suggests that Simeon [tsar of Bulgaria, 893–927] sought demarcation of the borders near Thessalonike'.[28] Such definition made it possible for the Romans and Bulgarians to engage in fairly precise adjustments to their borders. In the negotiations over Boris' conversion in the 860s, the empress Theodora ceded to the Bulgarians 'the empty land from Sidera, which happened to be the *horion* between them and the Romans at the time, all the way to Develtos, which they now call Zagora'.[29] Similar precise negotiations, based on prior written documents, over the control of specific forts and territories occurred between Constantinople and its Caucasian client-princes.[30]

Arrangements with the Arabs could be just as specific, and sometimes even more complex. A case in point is the island of Cyprus, which was shared by treaty between Romans and Arabs. The Romans did not surrender their sovereignty over it, but it was demilitarised, accepted an Arab presence, and split its taxes between the two states. This arrangement lasted for three centuries before Nikephoros II Phokas ended it in the 960s. In the meantime, the Cypriots could be described as 'on the border (*methorioi*)

[27] Florin Curta, *Southeastern Europe in the Middle Ages, 500–1250* (Cambridge: Cambridge University Press, 2006) 83, 154–7; earthworks: Florin Curta, 'Linear Frontiers in the 9th Century: Bulgaria and Wessex', *Quaestiones Medii Aevi Novae* 16 (2011), 15–31, quotation from 16. For the texts of treaties in general, see Jonathan Shepard, 'Past and Future in Middle Byzantine Diplomacy: Some Preliminary Observations', in Michel Balard, Élizabeth Malamut and Jean-Michel Spieser (eds), *Byzance et le monde extérieur: Contacts, relations, échanges* (Paris: Sorbonne, 2005), 171–91.

[28] Jonathan Shepard, 'Bulgaria: The Other Balkan "Empire"', in Timothy Reuter (ed.), *The New Cambridge Medieval History* (Cambridge: Cambridge University Press, 2000), 3: 567–85, here 571.

[29] *Theophanes Continuatus*, ed. Bekker, Book IV: 15, 165.

[30] For example, Konstantinos VII Porphyrogennetos, *De administrando imperio*, ed. Gyula Moravcsik and trans. Romilly J. H. Jenkins, Corpus Fontium Historiae Byzantinae 1 (Washington, DC: Dumbarton Oaks, 1967), c. 44, ll. 99ff, 210; cf. Evangelos Chrysos, 'Η βυζαντινή ἐπικράτεια καί τά σύνορα τῆς αὐτοκρατορίας (Σχόλιο στό DAI, κεφ. 45, *Περὶ Ἰβήρων*)', in Athanasios Markopoulos (ed.), *Κωνσταντίνος Ζ΄ ὁ Πορφυρογέννητος καί ἡ ἐποχή του* (Athens: European Cultural Center of Delphi, 1989), 15–24.

between the Roman and Saracen powers'.[31] We have detailed information about the treaty imposed by the Romans on the emirate of Aleppo in 970, and on the treaties between the Romans and the Fatimids that established peace in Syria and Palestine in the late tenth and early eleventh centuries. These treaties featured specific clauses about border demarcation, trade taxation and regulation, and the treatment of groups of interest such as religious minorities.[32] The Romans aimed for similar clarity and definition in southern Italy too, when they could. The capable governor and administrator Basileios Boioannes (early eleventh century) established and demarcated what historians call an 'artificial' frontier in Capitanata, and he used both military and legal means (for example, forts and decrees regulating the movement of people).[33] Of course it was artificial: all borders are. State planning here imposed realities on the ground. The Roman border was an artefact of state operations.

We should not have expected anything different from an empire that was Roman, and I say this for a number of reasons. First, in the Roman context landownership and control was subject to a sophisticated apparatus of administration and law, including techniques of land measurement that continued into Byzantine times, as well as complex legal doctrines of ownership, possession, and use. It is unlikely that the Romans were precise and legalistic when it came to private land but fuzzy about the territorial extent and rights of their *res publica*. The mentality of demarcation was ingrained in their culture, as shown by the boundary markers that

[31] Nikolaos Mystikos, *Nicholas I Patriarch of Constantinople, Letters*, ed. and trans. Romilly J. H. Jenkins and Leendert G. Westerink, Corpus Fontium Historiae Byzantinae 6 (Washington, DC: Dumbarton Oaks, 1973), Letter 1, ll. 146–7, 10; see David Michael Metcalf, *Byzantine Cyprus, 491–1191* (Nicosia: Cyprus Research Center, 2009).

[32] Anthony Kaldellis, *Streams of Gold, Rivers of Blood: The Rise and Fall of Byzantium, 955 A.D. to the First Crusade* (Oxford: Oxford University Press, 2017), 74–5, 127–30; greater detail in Werner Felix, *Byzanz und die islamische Welt im frühen 11. Jahrhundert: Geschichte der politischen Beziehungen von 1001 bis 1055* (Vienna: Austrian Akademy of Sciences, 1981).

[33] Catherine Holmes, *Basil II and the Governance of Empire (976–1025)* (Oxford: Oxford University Press, 2005), 441–3; Jean-Marie Martin, *La Pouille du VIe au XIIe siècle* (Rome: École française de Rome, 1993), 258–64.

individuals, churches, and monasteries placed around their properties.[34] It stands to reason that legal notions of possession and ownership would also be applied to international relations.[35] For example, a transfer of territory to the empire by an Armenian prince in the tenth century was carried out in a way that 'implies the adoption of Roman legal practice'.[36] Second, since the time of the Republic the Romans generally assumed that a specific territory corresponded to each city-state, people, or kingdom with which they dealt, and that these territories were defined by definite borders. A notional border around the Roman *res publica* was not only presupposed but required by a number of Roman–Byzantine legal concepts, such as that of *postliminium*, pertaining to the loss and recovery of civic rights through enslavement by foreigners and forcible transportation across the border.[37]

Third, borders defined the limits of the operation of key state institutions, such as taxation and law. The state did not survey, census, or tax lands beyond the border, nor did people who live outside them typically enjoy the rights, or bear the responsibilities, of Roman citizenship. These were the *termini iurisdictionis Romanae* – the limits of Roman jurisdiction – as authors and emperors

[34] For example, Salvatore Cosentino, 'Boundary Marks and Space Organization in Early Byzantine Epigraphy', in Christos Stavrakos (ed.), *Inscriptions in the Byzantine and Post-Byzantine History and History of Art* (Wiesbaden: Harrassowitz, 2016), 95–109. Byzantine *agrimensores*: Jacques Lefort *et al.* (eds), *Géométries du fisc byzantin* (Paris: Lethielleux, 1991); ownership: George C. Maniatis, 'On the Validity of the Theory of Supreme State Ownership of All Land in Byzantium', *Byzantion* 77 (2007), 566–634.

[35] Chrysos, ‘Ἡ βυζαντινὴ ἐπικράτεια’.

[36] Tim Greenwood, 'Social Change in Eleventh-Century Armenia: The Evidence from Taron', in James Howard-Johnston (ed.), *Social Change in Town and Country in Eleventh-Century Byzantium* (Oxford: Oxford University Press, 2020), 196–219, here 199.

[37] Clifford Ando, 'Aliens, Ambassadors, and the Integrity of the Empire', *Law and History Review* 26 (2008), 491–519, here 505; for the importance of borders, see also Greatrex, 'Roman Frontiers', and Niki Koutrakou, '"Sagene" – "Network": A Byzantine Perception of the International Legal Order', in Spyridon Flogaitis and Antoine Pantélis (eds), *The Eastern Roman Empire and the Birth of the Idea of the State in Europe* (London: Esperia Publications, 2003), 175–96, here 187. On Byzantine *postliminium*, see Yuval Rotman, *Byzantine Slavery and the Mediterranean World* (Cambridge, MA: Harvard University Press, 2009), 27–39, 52–3; and see *Basilika*, Book 34, in *Basilicorum Libri LX*, eds Herman Jan Scheltema and Nicolaas van der Wal, Series A (Groningen: J. B. Wolters, 1962), 4: 1552–6.

admitted.[38] This distinction was replicated fractally within the empire as well: the borders of individual provinces limited the jurisdiction of the authorities stationed within each, for example their governors; the same was true for civic and ecclesiastical territories. Provincial borders had to be clearly defined to avoid administrative chaos, and the imperial border was made up, in effect, by a series of outward-facing provincial borders.[39] For example, in the eleventh century, the bridge called Zompos over the Sangarios river was the recognised boundary between the themes (provinces) of Anatolikon and Kappadokia.[40]

We turn now to the experience of the international border by those who wanted to cross it. The first category of experience was the state's regulation and taxation of trade. Some maps of medieval trade feature graceful arcs linking the places of production to those of consumption, but in reality all trade crossing the empire's borders had to pass through specific customs offices, a different one designated for each trade route. At these places merchants had to pay a tax – around 10 per cent on the value of their goods – and obtain proof of payment, otherwise they were liable to be fined or their goods impounded at the next checkpoint or at their destination. These points-of-entry were staffed by imperial officials and generated revenue for the Roman state.[41] We

38 Ammianus Marcellinus, *Rerum gestarum libri qui* supersunt, ed. Wolfgang Seyfarth (Leipzig: Teubner, 1978), Book 18: 4.5, 140. Justinian, *Novel* 7 (epil.), in *Corpus Iuris Civilis*, vol 3: *Novellae*, eds Rudolf Schoell and Wilhelm Kroll (Berlin: Weidmann, 1895), 62–3.

39 The borders of individual provinces are discussed, for example, in Justinian's reform legislation from the 530s, for example, *Novel* 28 on Helenopontus. Provincial boundaries, sometimes specific ones, are mentioned in Konstantinos VII Porphyrogennetos, *De thematibus*, ed. Agostino Pertusi (Vatican City: Biblioteca Apostolica Vaticana, 1952); for the military aspect, see John Haldon, *Warfare, State and Society in the Byzantine World, 565–1204* (London: University College London Press, 1999), 113. For the origins of the territorially bounded Roman provinces, see John Richardson, '*Fines Provinciae*', in Oliver Hekster and Ted Kaizer (eds), *Frontiers in the Roman World* (Leiden: Brill, 2010), 1–11; and Kate Da Costa, 'Drawing the Line: An Archaeological Methodology for Detecting Roman Provincial Borders', ibid., 49–60. Similar work has not yet been carried out on the Byzantine provinces.

40 Michael Attaleiates, *History*, ed. and trans. Anthony Kaldellis and Dimitris Krallis (Washington, DC: Dumbarton Oaks, 2012), c. 23, 336–7.

41 Helen Antoniadis-Bibicou, *Recherches sur les douanes à Byzance: L'"octava", le 'kommerkion' et les commerciaires* (Paris: Librairie Armand Colin, 1963); Federico Montinaro, 'Les premiers commerciaires byzantins', *Travaux et mémoires* 17 (2013), 351–537.

have revenue figures for those of Trebizond, Adranoutzin (in the Caucasus), Attaleia, and others. For merchants going directly to Constantinople, the customs offices were at Abydos in the Hellespont and Hiereia in the Bosporos.[42] The workings of the officials at Abydos are revealed in the trading privileges granted by Basileios II to the Venetians in 992.[43] Thus, the mere existence of trade and exchange is no argument for 'open borders'.[44] These borders were quite firm and policed. Historians of institutions know that 'the movement of shipping was in many respects determined by political boundaries'.[45]

Border control over trade could be manipulated by the Roman state to promote policy objectives, such as to monopolise certain sectors. Youval Rotman has argued that the emperors established a monopoly over the slave trade passing through their territories between the West and the Muslims, and that some western Europeans, in particular a group called the Radhaniyya, looked for detours to circumvent the empire's custom offices; conversely, some Muslim rulers imposed higher tariffs (10%) on Roman traders than on others 'since', as one Muslim author explained, 'they take the same from foreign merchants who pass through their lands'.[46]

The Roman state monitored and regulated the movements and activities of foreign merchants, not just their bottom line. We know from a set of

[42] Nikolas Oikonomides, 'Πόλεις-Commercia στην Μικρά Ασία του 10ου αιώνα', in Stylianos Lambakis (ed.), *Η βυζαντινή Μικρά Ασία (6ος–12ος αι.)* (Athens: National Hellenic Research Foundation, 1998), 67–72; Nikolas Oikonomides, 'Le *kommerkion* d'Abydos: Thessalonique et le commerce bulgare au IXe siècle', in Catherine Abadie-Raynal *et al.* (eds), *Hommes et richesses dans l'empire byzantin* (Paris: P. Lethielleux, 1989–91), 2: 241–8; Angeliki E. Laiou, 'Exchange and Trade, Seventh–Twelfth Centuries', in A. E. Laiou (ed.), *The Economic History of Byzantium* (Washington, DC: Dumbarton Oaks, 2002), 697–770, here 727–8. Justinian: Prokopios, *Procopii Caesariensis Opera Omnia*, vol. 3: *Historia quae dicitur arcana*, ed. Jakob Haury, add. et corr. Gerhard Wirth (Leipzig: Teubner, 1963), c. 25. 3, 153.

[43] David Jacoby, 'Review of Pozza and Ravegnani', in *Mediterranean Historical Review* 9 (1994), 139–43, here 140–2.

[44] As assumed by Alison Vacca, *Non-Muslim Provinces under Early Islam: Islamic Rule and Iranian Legitimacy in Armenia and Caucasian Albania* (Cambridge: Cambridge University Press, 2017), 92, reading an Arabic text that identifies Trebizond as the required point of entry.

[45] Leslie Brubaker and John Haldon, *Byzantium in the Iconoclast Era c. 680–850: A History* (Cambridge: Cambridge University Press, 2011), 515.

[46] Rotman, 'Byzantium and the International Slave Trade', 137.

tenth-century trade treaties with the Rus that the Romans could and likely did regulate how many foreign merchants could be in Constantinople at any given time (unarmed and escorted, of course); how long they could stay; the volume of their trade; and how they could move around in the city. The urban authorities kept lists of such visitors and we know of at least one occasion when these lists were used: when the Rus ruler Jaroslav the Wise attacked Constantinople in 1043, all the Rus who happened to be in the city were rounded up and detained, which means that their identities and locations were known.[47] It is likely that similar rules applied to Bulgarians and to Arabs/Muslims, though we lack precise documentary evidence. According to the treaties of 716 and 816, Bulgar and Roman merchants both needed official 'diplomas and seals' in order to trade in each other's realms.[48] In the late ninth century, the imperial authorities required Bulgarian trade to pass through Thessalonike, not Constantinople, and they raised the taxes on it, which sparked a war with tsar Simeon. This implies that the state retained the same level of control over Bulgarian merchants as it did the Rus. Similarly, Muslim traders were likely confined to the *metata* in Constantinople that were designated for their exclusive use.[49] When Aleppo became a Roman protectorate in 970, trade passing through it to Romanía was heavily regulated by treaty.[50] Thus, insofar as the state was successful in enforcing these regulations, it was consciously acting in the opposite

[47] Rus treaties: Laiou, 'Exchange and Trade', 724 (from the *Russian Primary Chronicle*); Jonathan Shepard, 'Constantinople – Gateway to the North: The Russians', in Cyril Mango and Gilbert Dagron (eds), *Constantinople and its Hinterland* (Aldershot: Variorum, 1995), 243–60, here 253. Attack in 1043: Kaldellis, *Streams of Gold*, 186. For foreigners in Constantinople in general, see Kaldellis, *Romanland*, 225–7, 258–60.

[48] Theophanes the Confessor, *Chronographia*, ed. Carolus de Boor (Leipzig: Teubner, 1883–5), 497 (AM 6305).

[49] Bulgarian incident: Shepard, 'Bulgaria', 570; Muslims: David Jacoby, 'Constantinople as Commercial Transit Center, Tenth to Mid-Fifteenth Century', in Magdalino and Necipoğlu (eds), *Trade in Byzantium*, 193–210, here 196; Stephen William Reinert, 'The Muslim Presence in Constantinople, 9th–15th Centuries: Some Preliminary Observations', in Helène Ahrweiler and Angeliki E. Laiou (eds), *Studies on the Internal Diaspora of the Byzantine Empire* (Washington, DC: Dumbarton Oaks, 1998), 125–50.

[50] Laiou, 'Exchange and Trade', 724–5.

direction of 'fluidity', and it brought to bear considerable institutional means to achieve that end.

The *Book of the Eparch* is a set of regulations from circa 910 issuing out of the office of the prefect of Constantinople (*eparchos*); many of them focus on the regulation of trade and the guilds of the city. This text provides official confirmation that foreign trade was tightly regulated and that 'Syrian' merchants were limited to three-month stays in the capital.[51] Merchants from 'outside' were also monitored and regulated, though it is unclear whether this means from outside the empire or the city. But the state took a particular interest in the distribution of silk garments and banned the sale of its higher-quality products to foreigners.[52] An unhappy experience in this regard is recounted by the Western envoy Liudprand of Cremona, who illegally purchased some fine silks in the city, only to have them confiscated right before his departure.[53] Apart from his outrage, the operation of these institutions did not merit literary attention by our sources, which is why we do not hear about them much. Surviving literary texts do not deal with the hum-drum operation of the state bureaux, especially in the provinces.

There were certain items whose export the Roman state banned altogether, whether at specific moments or as a general rule; these were called *kekolymena*, or 'interdicted' items. The reasoning was laid out by Leon VI (886–912) in his

[51] For example, Leo VI, *Das Eparchenbuch Leons des Weisen*, ed. and trans. Johannes Koder, Corpus Fontium Historiae Byzantinae 33 (Vienna: Austrian Academy of Sciences, 1991), c. 10.2, 110–11; c. 5.5, 96–7 (Syrians).

[52] 'Outsiders:' Leo VI, *Eparchenbuch*, c. 6.5, 98–9, c. 8.3, 104–5, c. 8.5, 104–5, c. 8.7, 104–5, c. 10.2, 110–11, c. 20.1–2, 132–5; silk: ibid., c. 4.1, 90–1, c. 6.5, 96–7, c. 6.16, 100–1; debate: David Jacoby, 'The Byzantine Outsider in Trade (*c.*900–*c.*1350)', in Dion C. Smythe (ed.), *Strangers to Themselves: The Byzantine Outsider* (Aldershot: Ashgate, 2000), 129–47, here 133. For the silk industry and trade, see Anna Muthesius, 'The Byzantine Silk Industry: Lopez and Beyond', *Journal of Medieval History* 19 (1993), 1–67; prohibition: Angeliki E. Laiou, 'Monopoly and Privileged Free Trade in the Eastern Mediterranean (8th–14th Century)', in Damien Coulon *et al.* (eds), *Chemins d'outre-mer: Études d'histoire sur la Méditerranée médiévale offerts à Michel Balard* (Paris: Sorbonne, 2004), vol. 2, 511–26, here 514–16.

[53] Liudprand of Cremona, *Embassy to Constantinople*, in *The Complete Works of Liudprand of Cremona*, trans. Paolo Squatriti (Washington, DC: Catholic University of America Press, 2007), c. 54–5, 271–3.

law on the penalties for violators: some goods were not to be sold because they 'make the enemy stronger and more aggressive'.[54] Roman imperial law, which was still valid in the Byzantine period, outlawed, on pain of death, teaching barbarians how to make ships and selling weapons to them.[55] Additional specific prohibitions were sometimes put into effect in the early Byzantine period, for example against selling iron to the Persians and other nations.[56] In the middle period, the emperor Ioannes Tzimiskes (963–9) sent envoys to Venice demanding that they stop selling wood and weapons to Muslims. Venice duly complied, issuing a decree in 971 that gives a detailed list of the contraband items. The Romans burned three Venetian ships that seemed about to violate this restriction.[57] Some of these restrictions possibly lapsed during the eleventh century, whereas that on selling timber to Muslims, if not others, may have lasted until at least the late thirteenth century.[58]

[54] Leon VI, *Οι Νεαρές Λέοντος Ϛ του Σοφού*, ed. and trans. Spyros N. Troianos (Athens: Herodotos, 2007), Novel 63, 208–9.

[55] Theodosius II in *Codex Theodosianus*, Book 9, Title 40. 24 (419 AD) and Marcian in *Codex Iustinianus*, Book 4, Title 41. 2 (c. 455–7 AD). For more information and sources, see Hugh Elton, *Warfare in Roman Europe, AD 350–425* (Oxford: Clarendon Press, 1996), 58, n. 31, 205. Byzantine period: *Basilica* 19.1.85–86, 56.1.11, 56.1.18; *Synopsis Basilicorum* K: 10 in *Jus Graecoromanum*, ed. Ioannes and Panagiotes Zepos (Athens: Fexis, 1931), 5: 346; in general, see Laiou, 'Monopoly', 512–16.

[56] Libanios, *Libanii Opera*, vol. 4: *Orationes LI–LXIV*, ed. Richard Förster (Leipzig: Teubner, 1908), *Oration* 59: 66–70, 240–3; *Expositio totius mundi et gentium*, ed. J. Rougé, Sources chrétiennes 124 (Paris: Éditions du Cerf, 1966), c. 22; Prokopios, *Procopius Caesariensis, Opera Omnia*, vol. 1: *De bellis libri I–IV*, ed. Jakob Haury, add. et corr. Gerhard Wirth (Munich: Saur, 2001), Book 1, 19: 25, 104.

[57] Sources in Laiou, 'Exchange and Trade', 723; Marco Miotto, *Ο ανταγωνισμός Βυζαντίου και Χαλιφάτου των Φατιμίδων στην εγγύς ανατολή και η δράση των Ιταλικών πόλεων στην περιοχή κατά τον 10ο και τον 11ο αιώνα* (Thessalonike: Center for Byzantine Research, 2008), 183–4; David Jacoby, 'Byzantine Trade with Egypt from the Mid-Tenth Century to the Fourth Crusade', Thesaurismata 30 (2000), 25–77, here 36. For the Byzantine regulation of Italian trade, see Rotman, 'Byzantium and the International Slave Trade', 140.

[58] Lapsed: Kostis Smyrlis, 'Trade Regulation and Taxation in Byzantium, Eleventh–Twelfth Centuries', in Magdalino and Necipoğlu (eds), *Trade in Byzantium*, 65–87, here 67; continued: Cécile Morrisson, 'Trading in Wood in Byzantium: Exchange and Regulations', in ibid., 105–27, here 119–20.

The Roman state was also capable of shutting down the border to *all* trade with Muslim lands. A basic fact has to be emphasised here: for all that scholars today want to talk about 'contacts', the border between Romanía and Muslim-ruled Syria was immensely more restrictive to all movement and exchange than that same region had been as a merely provincial divide before the Arab conquests. Contacts were fewer, more difficult, and more policed. According to John Haldon, 'such an estrangement was undoubtedly reinforced by the deliberate actions of the Byzantine government', which wanted to 'control access to and egress from the empire'. Roads were watched and guarded, some borderlands were deliberately vacated, and so on, on both sides.[59] The Romans imagined the Muslim side of the border to be much like their own. At the Council of Nicaea II in 787, a bishop told a story about thirty-two Cypriots who had recently sailed to Syria in two ships, presumably for trade, where they were assigned Arab soldiers to escort them.[60] In the *vita* of the ninth-century saint Ioannikios, an apparition of the saint appeared to some Romans in Muslim captivity and 'led them safely away from all the sentry posts and watchtowers that the wicked Hagarenes [Muslims] are accustomed to place on all the essential roads', until they made it across the border.[61]

This border, guarded and monitored, could even be closed. For example, in advance of the expedition of 911 against the Arabs of Syria officials were instructed 'to maintain security and vigilance (*asphaleia kai akribeia*), and not to allow anyone unknown to them to go away to Syria, and [thereby] for information to be carried from Romanía through them to Syria'.[62] The general and military theorist Nikephoros Ouranos (c. 1000), who had served in Syria, noted in his manual on tactics that generals along the border should

[59] John Haldon, *The Empire that Would Not Die: The Paradox of Eastern Roman Survival, 640–740* (Cambridge, MA: Harvard University Press, 2016), 134–5. Eger, *The Islamic–Byzantine Frontier*, argues for less devastation and abandonment of frontier regions.

[60] *Concilium Universale Nicaenum Secundum, Concilii Actiones VI–VII*, ed. Erich Lamberz, Acta Conciliorum Oecumenicorum, series 2, vol. 3, pars 2 (Berlin: De Gruyter 2016), 410.

[61] Petros the Monk, *Life of Ioannikios*, trans. Denis F. Sullivan, in Alice-Mary Talbot (ed.), *Byzantine Defenders of Images: Eight Saints' Lives in English Translation* (Washington, DC: Dumbarton Oaks, 1998), c. 62, 330.

[62] Konstantinos VII Porphyrogennetos, *The Book of Ceremonies*, trans. Ann Moffatt and Maxeme Tall (Canberra: Australian Association for Byzantine Studies, 2012), Book 2, 44, 2: 660.

block all trade when the empire has besieged a city. 'The forces of the frontier *themata* [the militarised provinces] must be arranged in relays to maintain a constant guard over the roads leading to this fortress, for as a result the entry of anything at any time into Syria will be completely prevented' – the word is *kolythei*, the same as in *kekolymena* (interdicted goods).[63]

The state could close the border to all trade even in the absence of ongoing military operations. Leon V (813–20) is said in Western sources to have prohibited all trade with Syria and Egypt and to have imposed this restriction on the empire's Italian clients. Our information is late and hazy, and its historicity is doubted.[64] What cannot be doubted, however, is the global embargo on travel and trade with Syria and Egypt imposed by Basil II in 1016. It brought his enemies in Syria to heel and so he lifted it for them in circa 1020, but he refused to lift it for Egypt even when envoys from the Fatimids appealed to him in the early 1020s.[65] Basil II was acting from a position of unprecedented strength, but we find again that the border was a zone of potentially significant state intervention, subject to the priorities of central policy.

This meant that individuals crossing the border for personal reasons, including religious reasons, could be stopped or questioned by officials. Such experiences are frequently attested. Emissaries of Pope Gregory III (731–41), carrying letters to Constantinople against the policy of Iconoclasm, were repeatedly detained and confined by the governor of Sicily.[66] Some followers of Thomas the Slav, a rebel defeated in 823, tried to flee to Syria 'but the governors of the frontier regions arrested and impaled them'.[67] In 867,

[63] Nikephoros Ouranos, *Taktika*, in *Sowing the Dragon's Teeth: Byzantine Warfare in the Tenth Century*, ed. and trans. Eric McGeer (Washington, DC: Dumbarton Oaks, 1995), c. 65.4, 65.9, 154–7.

[64] Miotto, *Ο ανταγωνισμός*, 181–2; Juan Signes Codoñer, *The Emperor Theophilos and the East, 829–842: Court and Frontier in Byzantium during the Last Phase of Iconoclasm* (Farnham: Ashgate, 2014), 41–2.

[65] Kaldellis, *Streams*, 129–30, for context and sources.

[66] Liber Pontificalis, *Gregorius III* in *The Lives of the Eighth-Century Popes*, trans. Raymond Davis (Liverpool: Liverpool University Press, 1992), c. 2–4, 19–21.

[67] Skylitzes, *Synopsis*, ed. Thurn, 42, *John Skylitzes: A Synopsis of Byzantine History, 811–1057*, trans. John Wortley (Cambridge: Cambridge University Press, 2010), 44; also, *Theophanes Continuatus*, ed. Bekker, Book II, 72.

papal envoys were again turned back: 'between the borders of Bulgaria and the Constantinopolitans they came upon Theodoros, who guarded that frontier, and he would let them go no further'. They waited there for forty days, before returning to Rome.[68] We must remember that the borders were usually guarded on both sides, not just the Roman one. In the ninth century, Pope Nicholas wrote to the Bulgarian king Boris that 'You claim that it is part of the custom of your country that guards always stand on the alert between your country and the boundaries of others; and if a slave or freeman [manages to] flee somehow through this watch, the guards are killed without hesitation because of this.'[69] The difficulty of crossing the border was thus doubly enforced.

In his youth, the tenth-century saint Loukas of Steiris was arrested by a harbour master in the Peloponnese 'who was not allowing ships to cross the borders (*horia*) of Greece on account of the enemy raids'. The saint was caught in violation of this policy, trying to find a ship with which to cross, and was beaten severely.[70] In around 1010 some political refugees from the rule of the Fatimid caliph al-Ḥākim wanted to enter the empire and so they wrote to the *doux* at Antioch asking for permission; he said that he had to refer this to the emperor, but they did not have time, so they emigrated to Iraq instead.[71] A few years later, some Christians fleeing from the reign of al-Ḥākim had to bribe the border guards to let them pass into Roman territory.[72]

There was yet another way by which the state controlled and monitored movement into and out of the empire. It is a technology that many historians would deny even existed, given the low view that prevails of the infrastructural and bureaucratic capabilities of premodern states, but it is amply attested in

[68] Liber Pontificalis, *Nicholas I* in *The Lives of the Ninth-Century Popes*, trans. Raymond Davis (Liverpool: Liverpool University Press, 1995) c. 71–72, 242–3 (modified).

[69] Pope Nicholas I, *Letter* 99, in *Monumenta Germaniae Historica, Epistolae*, vol. 6, *Epistolae Karolini Aevi IV*, ed. Ernst Perels (Berlin: Weidmann, 1925), 568–600, here 579; trans. online by William L. North (accessible at https://sourcebooks.fordham.edu/basis/866nicholas–bulgar.asp).

[70] *The Life and Miracles of Saint Luke of Steiris*, ed. and trans. Carolyn L. and W. Robert Connor (Brookline, MA: Hellenic College Press, 1994) c. 38, 58–9.

[71] Yahya of Antioch, *Histoire de Yahya-ibn-Sa'ïd d'Antioche, continuateur de Sa'ïd-ibn-Bitriq, fascicule II*, ed. and trans. Ignace Kratchovsky and Alexander Vasiliev, Patrologia Orientalis 23.3 (Turnhout: Brepols, 1976), 347–520, here 501.

[72] Yahya of Antioch, *Histoire*, 519.

the sources, though it has been little studied. According to John Haldon, 'each traveler generally required formal letters authorizing their departure . . . for laypersons, these papers were known as *sigillia* [or *sphragides*] . . . and without them the traveler could encounter serious problems'.[73] Bulgarian merchants, for example, were required to bear proper *sigillia* according to the aforementioned treaties of 716 and 816. A passage in the *vita* of saint Gregorios Dekapolites (early ninth century) implies that travel to the Slavic borderlands in the Balkans required imperial permission and a *sphragis*.[74] In the eleventh and twelfth centuries, groups of Westerners who wanted to pass through the empire on the way east had to apply for permission and, if it was granted, received formal documents to that effect. There was 'a network of control posts where passports and transit visas had to be presented or had to be applied for'.[75] Soon after 1099, some travellers from Rome to Jerusalem put in at Athens, where they were arrested by the local official who suspected them of being hostile to the emperor (Alexios I Komnenos). The local saint, Meletios the Younger, intervened on their behalf and they then obtained 'an imperial letter' authorising them to continue their travels.[76]

[73] Haldon, *The Empire that Would Not Die*, 116 (the notes, however, do not give extensive documentation); a general reference in Ihor Ševčenko, 'Constantinople Viewed from the Eastern Provinces in the Middle Byzantine Period', *Harvard Ukrainian Studies* 3–4 (1978–80), 712–47, here 720; for more references, see Ioannis Dimitroukas, *Reisen und Verkehr im Byzantinischen Reich vom Anfang des 6. bis zur Mitte des 11. Jhs.* (Athens: Basilopoulos, 1997), 108–12; for the later period, see Chrysa Maltezou, "Άδειες ἐλεύθερης κυκλοφορίας (12ος–15ος αἰ.): Συμβολή στήν ἔρευνα τοῦ θεσμοῦ τῶν διαβατηρίων ἐγγράφων', in *Θυμίαμα στη Μνήμη της Λασκαρίνας Μπούρα* (Athens: Benaki Museum, 1994), 1: 173–9; for the formulaic patterns and terminology of *sigillia* in the imperial chancery, see Otto Kresten, 'Der Geleitbrief. Ein wenig beachteter Typus der byzantinischen Kaiserurkunde. Mit einem Exkurs: Zur Verwendung des Terminus Sigillion in the byzantinischen Kaiserkanzlei', *Römische Historische Mitteilungen* 38 (1996), 41–83. I thank Alexander Beihammer for bringing the chancery practice, and the reference, to my attention.

[74] Ignatios the Deacon, *Ignatios Diakonos und die Vita des Hl. Gregorios Dekapolites*, ed. Georgios Makris (Stuttgart: Teubner, 1997), 49.

[75] Krijnie N. Ciggaar, *Western Travellers to Constantinople: The West and Byzantium, 962–1204* (Leiden: Brill, 1996), 37–8, citing a number of cases.

[76] Nikolaos of Methone, *Life of Meletios the Younger*, ed. V. G. Vasil'evskij, 'Nikolaja episkopa Mefonskogo i Feodora Prodroma pisatelej XII stoletija zitija Meletija Novogo', *Pravoslavnij Palestinskij Sbornik* 6 (1886), 1–39, here 33.

These kinds of arrests on suspicion alone were more frequent that we might imagine. It happened, for example, to many saints who, for reasons known only to saints, looked foreign or dressed strangely, and it tended to happen near the border or at ports from which one might enter or leave the empire, where the authorities were looking for spies. One historian who studied these encounters found that 'it appears that they arrested everyone unable to produce a written permit to account for his presence near the border',[77] especially the eastern border, though this policy was probably not so uniform, extensive, or comprehensive.

Conclusions: Borders as Institutions, not Lines on a Map

The Romans (Byzantines included) often used physical features of the terrain such as rivers and mountains to demarcate borders, whether for practical purposes or in the imagination. But borders as such are not natural: they are state mechanisms, created and maintained by institutions within the limits of operational contingency to serve specific policy goals. Even when terrain features were pressed into service, they became, for the purpose of defining the borders, annexes of state institutions. Thus, we should not define borders in terms of geography or primarily ask *where* they were, though that is a valid question for any particular moment. Instead, we should define them in terms of the institutions that created and maintained them and ask *how* and *why* they operated as they did.

Thus, borders were a function of institutions and not geography. This was especially the case in the Byzantine empire, whose geography was defined so much by the sea. Its maritime borders included all lands washed by the Mediterranean, the Aegean, and the Black Sea, as well as the straits between them, the Hellespont and Bosporos. Constantinople itself was a kind of border city, and we saw above that many border-institutions operated there too. Thus, if we define borders as the sum of those institutions that regulated

[77] Francis Dvornik, *Origins of Intelligence Services* (New Brunswick, NJ: Rutgers University Press, 1974), 152–3. For fuller references, see Niki Koutrakou, 'Diplomacy and Espionage: Their Role in Byzantine Foreign Relations, 8th–10th Centuries', *Graeco-Arabica* 6 (1995), 125–44, here 128–9; and Niki Koutrakou, '"Spies of Towns": Some Remarks on Espionage in the Context of Arab–Byzantine Relations', *Graeco-Arabica* 7–8 (2000), 243–66, here 263–4.

the passage of people and goods between the polity of the Romans and its neighbours, then such borders operated in many places of the empire, not just where the land armies were stationed and fortresses built. They operated at the customs stations of Attaleia and Abydos, in the capital, or wherever state officials were on the lookout for suspicious strangers, which was pretty much everywhere. They sometimes operated beyond the physical border defined by the row of armies and forts (as some modern states will operate their customs offices in foreign airports). Even so, this extended institutional matrix was not uniform in density or presence: armies and forts received far more investment by the Roman state than customs houses or patrols of the countryside, and so they demarked borders for most practical and ideological purposes.

We should also question the paradigm of 'fluidity', which, in most of its appearances in this field, lacks methodological rigour and so has become little more than a trendy pose. Roman borders cannot be *defined* as fluid zone of interactions, as many publications imply; in fact, they should not even be primarily *characterised* that way. To be sure, the border with Syria was not always closed or impermeable, nor was everyone interrogated who approached it (and no one has proposed that it was quite like that). However, the border was also not always open, fluid, and free. The emperor and his officials decided how open it would be at any moment, relative to which goods or people. Now, it might be argued that such policies could not be enforced given the practical limitations of premodern governments. But this common misunderstanding is little more than an a priori assumption about premodern states. It cannot be invoked to just override all the evidence presented above. The Roman state, which operated at the higher end of premodern state efficiency, was evidently capable of doing exactly what the sources say that it was. State intervention was generally effective.

It might also be objected that those policies were more effective against large groups seeking to cross the border, especially on merchant ships, diplomatic delegations, and large groups of pilgrims, who could not easily sneak across, than it was against individuals. To this we may answer that in premodern times people tended to travel in groups for safety and support, which facilitated state monitoring; moreover, there is ample evidence for the surveillance and arrest of small groups and individuals too.

Borders were not zones of fluid contact: they were zones of state-regulated contact that could be more open or more closed depending on policy. There was, of course, a lot of movement of peoples, goods, and ideas across them: this by itself does not refute the existence of borders or make them fluid. Borders exist if (and only if) a state authority has the ability to intervene and regulate or restrict that movement. That is what a border is, and there is every indication that for most of its long history the Roman state had the infrastructural capability to operate them to its advantage.

6

A CHRISTIAN INSURGENCY IN ISLAMIC SYRIA: THE JARĀJIMA (MARDAITES) BETWEEN BYZANTIUM AND THE CALIPHATE

Christian C. Sahner

Introduction

In the century following the Arab conquest, the Byzantine Empire launched several campaigns aimed at retaking lost territory across the Middle East. Perhaps the most threatening of these relied on the muscle of a group known as Jarājima in Arabic and as Mardaites in Greek.[1] These were mountain Christians who helped the Byzantines re-establish control over the coastal highlands between Antioch and Jerusalem at the end of the seventh century. Although their success was short-lived, the Jarājima managed to create a Christian guerilla zone on the doorstep of the Umayyads' most important

I wish to thank Phil Booth and Andrew Marsham for their helpful comments on an earlier draft of this article.

[1] Throughout this chapter, I will refer to them as 'Jarājima' in the interest of simplicity and because most of our surviving accounts of the group are in Arabic, which do not use the term 'Mardaites' (with the exception of the later Maronite sources). For general introductions, see H. Lammens, 'Mardaites', in M. T. Houtsma *et al.* (eds), *The Encyclopaedia of Islam*, 5 vols (Leiden: Brill, 1913–38) , 3: 272–3; M. Canard, 'Djarādjima', in Peri Bearman *et al.* (eds), *Encyclopaedia of Islam, second edition,* 13 vols (Leiden: Brill, 1954–2009) (hereafter: *EI²*), 2: 456–8; Paul A. Hollingsworth, 'Mardaites', in Alexander Kazhdan (ed.), *The Oxford Dictionary of Byzantium*, 3 vols (Oxford: Oxford University Press, 1991) (hereafter: *ODB*), 2: 1297.

province. In the process, they terrified caliphs, gave hope to emperors, and left a deep impression on the historical record of the period.

The Jarājima are familiar to many students of Byzantine and early Islamic history. Indeed, there exists more than a century of serious academic research about them.[2] Yet in significant respects, they have yet to be properly contextualised. In this article, I hope to give a fresh re-reading of the premodern sources about the Jarājima – Islamic and Christian alike, scattered across Arabic, Greek, and Syriac texts. I hope this rereading will be novel for several reasons. First, building on the work of Georges Chalhoub (whose book is the most comprehensive study to date), my aim is to establish a clear chronology for the Jarājima from the time they first appear in the historical record during the Arab conquest of the 630s, to their last gasp as a militarised movement during the little-studied revolt of Theodore in 759–60.[3] Second, my goal is to explore

[2] For the major studies, see Henri Lammens, *Études sur le règne du calife omaiyade Moʿâwiya Ier* (Paris: Paul Geuthner, 1908), 14–22; Muḥammad Kurd ʿAlī, *Kitāb khiṭaṭ al-Shām* (Damascus: al-Maṭbaʿa al-Ḥadītha bi-Dimashq, 1925–8), 1: 149–53; Eduard Sachau, 'Zur historischen Geographie von Nordsyrien', *Sitzungsberichte der königlich preussischen Akademie der Wissenschaften zu Berlin* (1892), 313–38, here 320–5; Chrats M. Mpartikian, 'Hē lysē tou ainigmatos tōn Mardaïtōn', in Nia A. Stratos (ed.), *Byzantion: Aphierōma ston Andrea N. Strato* (Athens: no pub., 1986), 2: 17–39; ʿUmar ʿAbd al-Salām al-Tadmurī, *Lubnān min al-fatḥ al-Islāmī ḥattā suqūṭ al-dawla al-Umawiyya* (Tripoli: Jarrūs Briss, 1990), 100–4, 116–31, 137–8; Keiko Ohta, 'The Expansion of the Muslims and Mountain Folk of Northern Syria: The Jarājima in the Umayyad Period', *Orient* 27 (1991), 74–94; Andreas Kaplony, *Konstantinopel und Damaskus: Gesandtschaften und Verträge zwischen Kaisern und Kalifen, 639–750* (Berlin: Klaus Schwarz Verlag, 1996), 77–136; James Howard-Johnston, 'The Mardaites', in Tony Goodwin (ed.), *Arab–Byzantine Coins and History: Papers Presented at the 13th Seventh Century Syrian Numismatic Round Table Held at Corpus Christi College Oxford on 11th and 12th September 2011* (London: Archetype Publications, 2012), 27–38; *Theophilus of Edessa's Chronicle and the Circulation of Historical Knowledge in Late Antiquity and Early Islam*, trans. with an introduction and notes by Robert G. Hoyland (Liverpool: Liverpool University Press, 2011), 169–70, 180–2, 186; A. Asa Eger, *The Islamic–Byzantine Frontier: Interaction and Exchange among Muslim and Christian Communities* (London: I. B. Tauris, 2015), 295–300; Miloš Cvetković, 'The Settlement of the Mardaites and their Military-Administrative Position in the Themata of the West: A Chronology', *Zbornik radova Vizantološkog instituta* 54 (2017), 65–85.

[3] Georges Chalhoub, *Recherches sur les Mardaïtes-Ǧarāǧima* (Kaslik: Université Saint-Esprit de Kaslik, 1999), whose greatest strength is its analysis and translation of the relevant sources,

the afterlife of the Jarājima until the tenth century, when for all intents and purposes, they disappear from our historical radar. Virtually nothing is known about this period, but a careful reading of Maronite and Byzantine sources reveals, if not a treasure trove of new information, then certainly a small haul which extends the story later than has been told before.

Third, I hope to use this article to weigh in on a few outstanding questions about the Jarājima which have piqued the interest of scholars before me: what was their confessional background? (Unclear, but possibly Chalcedonian.) What was their ethnic and cultural makeup? (Heterogeneous, but probably with a core of Aramaic-speaking locals who were deeply rooted in Syria's coastal mountains.) Did they have a strong ideological programme? (Not really; they seem to have been more opportunistic than principled, including in their dealings with the Byzantines.)

Fourth, along with these questions, I hope to examine the Jarājima against a wider backdrop that will take us beyond Syria and the Byzantine frontier: why was Byzantine revivalism so uncommon in the post-conquest period, in contrast to Sasanian revivalism in the Iranian world? (For myriad reasons, especially certain strategic and ideological factors.) Did the Jarājima rise up in a moment of widespread nativist unrest elsewhere in the empire? (Yes.) Why were Christian insurgencies like that of the Jarājima so uncommon? (Also, for myriad reasons, the most important being that Christians, while numerically dominant in many parts of the new empire, were largely demilitarised, and thus incapable of vying for serious political power like other outsider groups.) And finally, can the Jarājima help us say something about the difficulties of conquest and state-building in mountainous regions outside of Syria? (Again, yes.)

1. History

1.1. Origins

The name 'Jarājima' (s. *jurjumānī*) comes from the city where the group allegedly originated, al-Jurjūma, located in the region of Jabal al-Lukkām (the Amanus Mountains, average height, c. 1100 metres) of northern Syria, close to Antioch

though some historical reports are missing (see two sections below, *1.6. The rebellion of Theodore*, and *1.7. Afterlife*).

and between Bayās and Būqā.[4] This is significant because it suggests that the group was known mainly by its geographic origins, not by its ethnicity or some other cultural characteristic. Interestingly, the Greek sources do not use the term 'Jarājima' at all, but instead refer to 'Mardaites' (*mardaitai*). This is probably a loanword from Syriac or Arabic meaning 'rebel' (Syr. *marīdā*, *mardyānā*; Ar. *mārid*).[5] Writing in Syriac, Michael the Great (d. 1199) refers to the group as 'Līpūrē'. This term is more puzzling, and scholars have suggested that it may derive from the Greek *laphyra*, meaning 'spoils', or *leipontes*, meaning 'deserters', though neither is certain.[6] Some have suggested there may be a distinction between Jarājima and Mardaites, but there is nothing in the sources to support

4 For al-Jurjūma, see Aḥmad ibn Yaḥyā al-Balādhurī, *Liber expugnationis regionum auctore Imámo Ahmed ibn Jahya ibn Djábir al-Beládsorí*, ed. Michael Jan de Goeje (Leiden: Brill, 1866), 159 (Arabic); *The Origins of the Islamic State*, trans. Philip Khûri Ḥitti (New York: Columbia University Press, 1916), 246 (English); Shihāb al-Dīn Abū ʿAbdallāh Yaʿqūb ibn ʿAbdallāh al-Ḥamawī Yāqūt, *Muʿjam al-buldān* (Beirut: Dār Ṣādir, 1977), 2: 123. For the broader region, see M. Streck, 'al-Lukkām', *EI²*, 5: 810–11; Clifford Edmund Bosworth, 'Payās', *EI²*, 8: 288; Janine Sourdel-Thomine, 'Būḳa', *EI²*, 1: 1292; Guy Le Strange, *Palestine under the Moslems: A Description of Syria and the Holy Land from A.D. 650 to 1500* (London: Alexander P. Watt, 1890), 81–2. The geographer al-Muqaddasī (fl. 4th/10th century) remarks that Jabal al-Lukkām was 'the most populous mountain area of Syria' (Shams al-Dīn Abū ʿAbdallāh Muḥammad ibn Aḥmad al-Muqaddasī, *The Best Divisions for Knowledge of the Regions: A Translation of* Ahsan al-Taqasim fi Maʿrifat al-Aqalim, trans. Basil Anthony Collins with Muhammad Hamid al-Tai (Reading: Centre for Muslim Contribution to Civilization & Garnet Publishing Limited, 1994), 172).

5 Robert Payne Smith, *Thesaurus Syriacus* (Hildesheim: G. Olms, 1981), 2216–19; Edward William Lane, *An Arabic–English Lexicon* (Beirut: Librairie du Liban, 1968), 7: 2706; on the origin of the name, see Chalhoub, *Mardaïtes-Ǧarāǧima*, 101–16.

6 Michael the Great, *Chronique de Michel le Syrien: Patriarche jacobite d'Antioche (1166–1199)*, ed. and trans. Jean-Baptiste Chabot (Paris: Ernest Leroux, 1899–1910), 2: 455 (French), 4: 437 (Syriac); Bar Hebraeus, Ibn al-ʿIbrī Abū ʾl-Faraj Ghrīghūriyūs, *Gregorii Barhebræi Chronicon Syriacum e codd. Mss. emendatum ac punctis vocalibus adnotationibusque locupletatum*, ed. Paul Bedjan (Paris: Maisonneuve, 1890), 109; with comment on the etymology in David Woods, 'Corruption and Mistranslation: The Common Syriac Source on the Origins of the Mardaites', in Elizabeth Jeffreys (ed.), *Proceedings of the 21st International Congress of Byzantine Studies, 2006*, accessible online: http://www.syriacstudies.com/AFSS/Syriac_Articles_in_English/Entries/2011/1/9_Corruption_and_Mistranslation__The_Common_Syriac_Source_on_the_Origin_of_the_Mardaites_David_Woods.html.

this assertion.[7] In fact, some writers such as Michael the Great make clear that the two groups were one and the same.[8]

At the outset, it is interesting to note that the Jarājima were rarely described as Christians (though as we shall see below, there is little doubt that this was the case). In the eyes of later Muslim writers, the group's geographic identity was more remarkable than its religious one. Indeed, the Jarājima were rarely lumped together with other Christian groups who were active during the seventh and eighth centuries, and they were almost never assigned conventional labels such as *naṣārā, ahl al-kitāb*, or *ahl al-dhimma*. Another basic point is that the sources rarely identify specific leaders of the Jarājima (that is, until the revolt of Theodore in 759–60). This is significant because early Muslim writers often identified rebel movements through the figures who instigated or inspired them (e.g. the Kaysāniyya, so named for the general Abū ʿAmra Kaysān who supported the revolt of al-Mukhtār al-Thaqafī in Kufa in 66–7/685–7; or the Muslimiyya, the partisans of the murdered leader of the Abbasid revolution, Abū Muslim al-Khurāsānī, d. 137/755). The Jarājima, by contrast, are consistently portrayed as a relatively faceless movement, more distinguished by the geographic milieu from which they came than by any one figure who led them.

There is almost no information about the pre-Islamic history of the Jarājima, contrary to the claims of some Byzantinists who would see them as Armenian Christians or as deserters from the imperial army.[9] Mohsen

[7] For instance, James Howard-Johnston, *Witnesses to a World Crisis: Historians and Histories of the Middle East in the Seventh Century* (Oxford: Oxford University Press, 2010), 494; Robert G. Hoyland, *In God's Path: The Arab Conquests and the Creation of an Islamic Empire* (Oxford: Oxford University Press, 2015), 128.

[8] Along with Michael the Great (see above, note 6), it is revealing that the Arab Christian chronicler Agapius (d. c. 941–2) refers to the group as 'Jarājima', despite his source's dependence on earlier Greek and Syriac chronicles, which presumably referred to them as 'Mardaites'. The point is that he clearly regarded them as one and the same group. See Agapius, Maḥbūb ibn Qusṭanṭīn al-Manbijī, *Kitab al-ʿUnvan, Histoire universelle, écrite par Agapius (Mahboub) de Menbidj, seconde partie*, ed. and trans. Alexandre Vasiliev, Patrologia Orientalis 8/3 (Paris: Firmin-Didot, 1912), 399–547, here 492–3, 497; Theophilus of Edessa, *Chronicle*, trans. Hoyland, 319–23.

[9] For the Armenian thesis, see Mpartikian, 'Lysē tou ainigmatos tōn Mardaïtōn'; for the military thesis, see Woods, 'Corruption and Mistranslation'.

Zakeri has also suggested that the Jarājima began life as Persian soldiers who settled in Syria during the Sasanian period, though this theory strikes me as far-fetched.[10] As far as I can tell, Abū'l-Faraj al-Iṣfahānī (d. 356/967) is the earliest author to connect the Jarājima with Iran. He links them with other well-known Sasanian or quasi-Sasanian groups such as the Banū Aḥrār of Sanaa, the Abnā' of Yemen, the Aḥāmira of Kufa, the Asāwira of Basra, and the Khaḍāmira of the Jazīra, all of whom were active before the rise of Islam.[11] Another legendary report comes from the great historian of Aleppo Ibn al-ʿAdīm (d. 660/1262), who identifies the Jarājima as the ancient inhabitants of Syria and Palestine during the time of Darius and Alexander. He presents them as counterparts of the Copts and Berbers in the Maghrib and the Romans and the Slavs (*ṣaqāliba*) in the North.[12] Though the anecdote is mythical, it may bring us closer to the heart of the matter, namely, the Jarājima were one of a variety of indigenous communities in Syria who antedated the rise of the Arabs and Islam. Passages in the writings of al-Jāḥiẓ (d. 255/869), al-Balādhurī (d. c. 279/892), and Ibn al-Faqīh (fl. 289–90/902–3) leave the same impression.[13] That being said, the fact that we have no references

[10] Mohsen Zakeri, *Sāsānid Soldiers in Early Muslim Society: The Origins of the ʿAyyārān and Futuwwa* (Wiesbaden: Harrassowitz, 1995), 128–64. Zakeri's argument rests on the apparent similarity between the terms 'Mardaites' and 'Mardoi', the latter being an ancient nomadic tribe from Central Asia who are mentioned in classical sources and whom Zakeri claims settled in the Syrian borderlands during Late Antiquity. In my view, this is highly speculative; indeed, the most concrete evidence in favour of the thesis is a single passage in Abū 'l-Faraj al-Iṣfahānī (see below, note 11), which identifies the Jarājima as one of several armed Sasanian groups who remained in Syria after the Arab conquest. Since this information is otherwise unattested, it strikes me as a ninth-century legend used to explain the origins of the Jarājima.

[11] Abū 'l-Faraj ʿAlī ibn al-Ḥusayn al-Iṣfahānī, *Kitāb al-aghānī* (Būlāq, Cairo: Dār al-Kutub, 1868), 16: 73; Abū 'l-Fayḍ Muḥammad ibn Muḥammad Murtaḍā al-Zabīdī, *Tāj al-ʿarūs min jawāhir al-qāmūs*, eds ʿAbd al-Saṭṭār Aḥmad Farrāj *et al.* (Kuwait: Maṭbaʿat Ḥukūmat al-Kuwayt, 1965–2001), 31: 397 (*qawmun min al-ʿajam bi-'l-jazīra*).

[12] Kamāl al-Dīn Abū 'l-Qāsim ʿUmar ibn Aḥmad Ibn al-ʿAdīm, *Bughyat al-ṭalab fī tārīkh Ḥalab*, ed. Suhayl Zakkār (Damascus: no pub., 1988–9), 4: 1597.

[13] al-Jāḥiẓ, Abū ʿUthmān ʿAmr ibn Baḥr al-Baṣrī, *al-Bayān wa-'l-tabyīn*, ed. ʿAbd al-Salām Muḥammad Hārūn (Cairo: Maṭbaʿat Lajnat al-Taʾlīf wa-'l-Tarjama wa-'l-Nashr, 1948–50), 1: 292–3; Aḥmad ibn Yaḥyā al-Balādhurī, *Ansāb al-ashrāf*, eds Suhayl Zakkār and Riyāḍ

to Jarājima (or Mardaites) until the Islamic period may suggest that we are dealing with a group that acquired historical visibility – if not came into being in some sense – only in the seventh century.

1.2. The Arab conquest

We are on firmer ground when it comes to history of the Jarājima after the emergence of Islam. Our most important sources about the Jarājima in this respect are the writings of the Abbasid historian and courtier al-Balādhurī, including his *Futūḥ al-buldān* and *Ansāb al-ashrāf*.[14] In the case of the former, al-Balādhurī states that he obtained his information from 'old men among the inhabitants of Antioch' (*mashāyikh min ahl Anṭākiya*), suggesting that his account may stem from local knowledge of their history.[15]

Al-Balādhurī writes that al-Jurjūma, the hometown of the Jarājima, was under the jurisdiction of Antioch during the Byzantine period. He also writes that a mine with iron sulphate (*maʿdin al-zāj*) existed nearby, perhaps indicating a source of economic activity that connected the mountain-dwellers to lowland markets.[16] The area around Jabal al-Lukkām was close to the Arab–Byzantine frontier, and thus emerged as a hotbed of military activity during the seventh century.[17] Prior to the rise of Islam, it also had a reputation for lawlessness and independence. As Brent Shaw has shown, the Amanus region – along with neighbouring Isauria – was one of the eastern Mediterranean's great ungovernable areas. Plains-based states had great difficulty in controlling these regions, often granting local strongmen autonomy and tribute in exchange for keeping bandits, pirates (and

Ziriklī (Beirut: Dār al-Fikr lil-Ṭibāʿa wa-ʾl-Nashr wa-ʾl-Tawzīʿ, 1996), 8: 318; Aḥmad ibn Muḥammad al-Hamadhānī ibn al-Faqīh, *Compendium libri Kitâb al-Boldân*, ed. M. J. de Goeje (Leiden: Brill, 1885), 35.

[14] al-Balādhurī, *Liber expugnationis*, 159–63 (Arabic), *Origins*, 246–52 (English); al-Balādhurī, *Ansāb al-ashrāf*, vol. 4, pt 2, eds ʿAbd al-ʿAzīz al-Dūrī and ʿIṣām ʿUqla, Bibliotheca Islamica 28e (Beirut: Dār al-Nashr al-Kitāb al-ʿArabī, in Kommission bei 'das Arabische Buch' Berlin, 2001), 273–86; *Ansāb al-ashrāf*, eds Zakkār and Ziriklī, 8: 318.

[15] al-Balādhurī, *Liber expugnationis*, 159 (Arabic), *Origins*, 246 (English).

[16] al-Balādhurī, *Liber expugnationis*, 159 (Arabic), *Origins*, 246 (English); reproduced in Yāqūt, *Muʿjam al-buldān*, 2: 123.

[17] Generally, Eger, *Islamic–Byzantine Frontier*, and for this region, 294–9.

the strongmen themselves) at bay.[18] None other than Cicero, who was briefly proconsul in Cilicia between 51 and 50 BC, marched Roman troops into the Amanus in the hopes of checking the violence. He remarked that the Amanus was a region 'where news comes in very slowly, because of its remoteness and because of the banditry in the countryside'. As such, it was incumbent upon Rome to 'pacify' the area.[19] In Late Antiquity, nearby Isauria emerged as an important reservoir of military power, providing large contingents of mercenaries for the imperial army. The highlanders became so influential that one of their own eventually ascended to the imperial throne: Zeno the Isaurian, who ruled briefly between 474 and 475. We might view the Isaurians as large-scale, highly successful precursors of the Jarājima, 'private agents of violence, who operated on either side of the law', as Shaw has put it. What characterised these mountain peoples then, as under Islam, was that they were sometime cooperators of the state, and sometime antagonists against it.[20]

The conquest of Antioch occurred in 16/637–8 under the great Arab general Abū ʿUbayda. Initially, the Muslims failed to take notice of the Jarājima, given their isolation in the hills. But when the inhabitants of Antioch reneged on their peace treaty and rebelled, Abū ʿUbayda was forced to subdue the city for a second time, provoking a violent crackdown on the broader area. At this time the new governor, Ḥabīb ibn Maslama al-Fihrī, is said to have raided al-Jurjūma. Much to his surprise, however, the people did not resist, but asked for their own guarantee of safe conduct as well as a peace treaty (*al-amān wa-ʾl-ṣulḥ*). In exchange, they agreed to serve as helpers and scouts (*aʿwān wa-ʿuyūn*) for the Muslims, as well as to man garrisons in the militarily sensitive border region.[21]

[18] Brent D. Shaw, 'Bandit Highlands and Lowland Peace: The Mountains of Isauria-Cilicia', *Journal of the Economic and Social History of the Orient* 33 (1990), 199–233, 237–70; for useful comparisons to later periods and different regions, see James C. Scott, *The Art of Not Being Governed: An Anarchist History of Upland Southeast Asia* (New Haven, CT: Yale University Press, 2009).

[19] Cicero, *Ad familiares*, 2.9.1–2, cited in Shaw, 'Bandit Highlands and Lowland Peace', 224.

[20] On the late antique period, see Shaw, 'Bandit Highlands and Lowland Peace', 237–61, with quote at 258.

[21] al-Balādhurī, *Liber expugnationis*, 159 (Arabic; and for the treaty terms which follow), *Origins*, 246–7 (English).

The Jarājima received extremely favourable terms of surrender: al-Balādhurī states that they did not have to pay the poll tax (*jizya*) and were allowed to keep the booty they had acquired while fighting alongside the Muslims. The idea that a non-Muslim group would avoid paying the *jizya*, retain its weapons, and enjoy the fruits of the battlefield was unthinkable, at least by the standards of the early Abbasid period when al-Balādhurī lived and the classical *dhimmī* regime was first being developed.[22] But such agreements were typical of the improvisational days of the conquests, when no such laws existed and the Muslim authorities were eager to neutralise the threat posed by armed groups such as the Jarājima. Thus, al-Balādhurī also states that the Muslim conquerors allowed the Samaritans of Palestine and Transjordan to pay a special tax rate in exchange for serving as spies and guides for the Muslim army. The powerful Christian tribe of Taghlib, meanwhile, was permitted to pay a tax theoretically reserved for Muslims – the *ṣadaqa* instead of the *jizya* – though at double the normal rate because they wished to remain Christians.[23] We should see the treatment of the Jarājima against the backdrop of these early, ad hoc arrangements (acknowledging, of course, that our picture of these arrangements is filtered through the lens of later periods, when these arrangements would have been considered abnormal).

At this point in the story, we also gain a slightly clearer picture of the social composition of the Jarājima and their followers. Although the Jarājima seem to have been identified mainly by their geographic origins, al-Balādhurī states that they were accompanied by a diverse group of mountain-dwellers, including traders, slaves, and Nabataeans (*anbāṭ*) – a slippery term which usually refers to the Aramaic-speaking peasants of the countryside in Iraq and Syria. These were not Jarājima in the strict sense of the term, but 'hangers-on' (*rawādif*),

[22] On these legal norms, which crystallised during the early Abbasid period, see Antoine Fattal, *Le statut légal des non-musulmans en pays d'Islam* (Beirut: Imprimerie catholique, 1958); Milka Levy-Rubin, *Non-Muslims in the Early Islamic Empire: From Surrender to Coexistence* (Cambridge: Cambridge University Press, 2011).

[23] al-Balādhurī, *Liber expugnationis*, 158 (Samaritans), 181–3 (Taghlib) (Arabic), *Origins*, 244–5, 284–6 (English); discussion in Hoyland, *In God's Path*, 97; Christian C. Sahner, *Christian Martyrs under Islam: Religious Violence and the Making of the Muslim World* (Princeton, NJ: Princeton University Press, 2018), 203–4.

so called because they followed the Jarājima into the Muslims' encampment.[24] There are hints that the term *rawādif* may have been more than simply a pejorative. In future centuries, the mountainous area between Nahr al-Kabīr and Bāniyās in northwestern Syria came to be known as Jabal al-Rawādīf (*sic*). It was dominated by tribes such as the Banū Aḥmar and the Banū Ghannāj, and in the eleventh century, it fell under the control of a local chieftain named Naṣr ibn Musharraf al-Rādūfī. Like the Jarājima centuries earlier, he alternated between fighting for and against the Byzantines, who were then in control of the region.[25] This suggests that the *rawādif* may have formed a discrete group of highlanders long after the Jarājima faded from view.

Other sources highlight the same non-Arab, peasant element within the Jarājima. In a speech by the anti-Umayyad rebel Yazīd ibn al-Muhallab (d. 102/720), for instance, the Syrian troops of Maslama ibn ʿAbd al-Malik

[24] On these various groups, see al-Balādhurī, *Liber expugnationis*, 159 (Arabic), *Origins*, 247 (English); cf. Yāqūt, *Muʿjam al-buldān*, 2: 123. In a later context, the followers of the rebel Theodore are described as being Jarājima and '*anbāṭ* of Mt. Lebanon': Thiqat al-Dīn Abū ʾl-Qāsim ʿAlī ibn Abī Muḥammad Ibn ʿAsākir, *Tārīkh madīnat Dimashq*, ed. ʿAlī Shīrī (Beirut: Dār al-Fikr lil-Ṭibāʿa wa-ʾl-Nashr wa-ʾl-Tawzīʿ, 1995–2000), 18: 267. For background, see David F. Graf and Toufic Fahd, 'Nabaṭ', *EI²*, 7: 834–8; Michael G. Morony, *Iraq after the Muslim Conquest* (Princeton, NJ: Princeton University Press, 1984), 169–80; Zakeri, *Sāsānid Soldiers*, 142–5. On the meaning of *rawādif* (s. *radīf*), see Lane, *Arabic–English Lexicon*, 3: 1068. The term *rawādif* also appears in seventh-century Kufa, where it was used to describe the 'late-comers' who settled in the famous garrison town after the Arabs' initial victories at al-Qādisiyya and Yarmūk: Martin Hinds, 'Kûfan Political Alignments and their Background in the Mid-Seventh Century A.D.', *International Journal of Middle East Studies* 2 (1971), 346–67, here 349.

[25] On Jabal al-Rawādīf and Naṣr ibn Musharraf al-Rādūfī, see Saʿīd ibn al-Baṭrīq Eutychius, *Eutychii patriarchae Alexandrini annales*, eds Louis Cheikho, Bernard Carra de Vaux and Habib Zayyat, Corpus Scriptorum Christianorum Orientalium, Scriptores arabici 6–7 (Beirut: Typographeo Catholico, 1906–9), 2: 257; on Naṣr's dealings with the Byzantines, see John Skylitzes, *A Synopsis of Byzantine History, 811–1057*, trans. John Wortley (Cambridge: Cambridge University Press, 2010), 361–2, 440; also Andrew J. Cappel, 'The Byzantine Response to the 'Arab (10th–11th Centuries)', *Byzantinische Forschungen* 20 (1994), 113–32, here 116–17; Stefan Winter, *A History of the ʿAlawis: From Medieval Aleppo to the Turkish Republic* (Princeton, NJ: Princeton University Press, 2016), 28, 30; Eger, *Islamic–Byzantine Frontier*, 299.

were dismissed as little more than Berbers and Slavs, Jarāmiqa and Jarājima, Copts and Nabataeans, ploughmen and riff-raff (*al-fallāḥūn wa-ʾl-awbāsh*). This was in contrast to Yazīd's largely Arab tribal force, though this itself was probably an exaggeration.[26] Ibn al-Faqīh confirms this impression, describing the Jarājima as the 'ʿ*ulūj* of Syria', a disparaging term meaning 'landless peasants' (or more colloquially, 'non-Arab scum'). In this respect, they were counterparts of the Copts in Egypt, the Jarāmiqa in the Jazīra, the Nabataeans in southern Iraq, the Sabābija of Sind, the Mazūn of Oman, and the Sāmurān of Yemen.[27] The Jarājima were also lukewarm, unreliable allies of the Muslims. In the words of al-Balādhurī, 'At one moment they would be upright with the [Arab] governors, and at the next, crooked', maintaining contact with the Byzantines despite their professed loyalty to the Umayyads.[28]

1.3. The reigns of Muʿāwiya and Constantine

The Jarājima became a problem for the Arabs during the reign of the Umayyad caliph Muʿāwiya ibn Abī Sufyān and his Byzantine counterpart Constantine IV. Interestingly, the episode is described extensively in Christian sources, but referred to only obliquely in Islamic sources.[29] The events transpired in the ninth year of the reign of Constantine, meaning sometime between 676 and 677.[30]

[26] al-Jāḥiẓ, *Bayān wa-ʾl-tabyīn*, 1: 292–3; Abū ʾl-Ḥasan ʿAlī ibn Muḥammad Ibn al-Athīr, *al-Kāmil fī ʾl-tārīkh*, ed. ʿUmar ʿAbd al-Salām Tadmurī (Beirut: Dār al-Kitāb al-ʿArabī, 1997), 4: 127; cf. al-Balādhurī, *Ansāb al-ashrāf*, eds Zakkār and Ziriklī, 8: 318; Abū ʾl-Ḥasan ʿAlī ibn al-Ḥusayn al-Masʿūdī, *Murūj al-dhahab wa-maʿādin al-jawhar (Les prairies d'or)*, ed. Charles Pellat (Beirut: Manshūrāt al-Jāmiʿa al-Lubnāniyya, 1966–79), 3: 299 (*awbāsh*) (Arabic); *Les prairies d'or*, ed. and trans. Charles Barbier de Meynard (Paris: L'Imprimerie Nationale, 1861–1917), 5: 224 (French).

[27] Ibn al-Faqīh, *Kitâb al-Boldân*, 35–6; on the term ʿ*ulūj*, see Zakeri, *Sāsānid Soldiers*, 144–5.

[28] al-Balādhurī, *Liber expugnationis*, 159–60 (Arabic), *Origins*, 247 (English); cf. Yāqūt, *Muʿjam al-buldān*, 2: 123.

[29] For these oblique allusions, in which ʿAbd al-Malik is said to have copied an earlier peace treaty that Muʿāwiya had signed with the Byzantines, see al-Balādhurī, *Liber expugnationis*, 160 (Arabic), *Origins*, 247 (English); al-Balādhurī, *Ansāb al-ashrāf*, vol. 4, pt 2, eds Dūrī and ʿUqla, 275.

[30] For a summary of these events, see Kaplony, *Konstantinopel und Damaskus*, 77–97.

During this time, the Jarājima rebelled and spread south, establishing control over a vast highland territory located between Antioch and Jerusalem.[31] Mount Lebanon seems to have been the centre of their rebellion. This was probably due to its proximity to the Umayyad capital of Damascus, as well as its strategic position between the ports of the Mediterranean coast and the inland cities of Syria, which relied on each other for trade and communication. Once again, the Jarājima's forces were heterogeneous – in the words of Theophanes (d. c. 817), they were made up of 'slaves, prisoners, and native peasants (*autochthones*)', who fled to the Jarājima for protection and soon numbered in the thousands.[32] Along with these native elements, the Jarājima were reinforced by Byzantine soldiers from abroad. Agapius (d. c. 941–2) and the *Chronicle of 1234* specify that the Byzantines came by ship, landing on the coast near Tyre and Sidon, from which they presumably climbed the slopes of Mount Lebanon.[33] They then wreaked havoc on the region, distracting the Arabs from their raids on Byzantine territory.[34] James Howard-Johnston connects these events with the Byzantine naval victory over the Arabs in 674 – what he calls 'the Romans' Trafalgar'.[35] This led to the destruction of the Arab expeditionary fleet and seems to have created an opening for the Byzantines to sneak into Syria and sow chaos.

The creation of a full-blown Christian insurgency in the Umayyad heartlands forced Muʿāwiya to sue for peace.[36] The caliph took the initiative by

[31] On the geographic range, see Chalhoub, *Mardaïtes-Ǧarāǧima*, 21–9.

[32] Theophanes Confessor, *Theophanis Chronographia*, ed. Carolus de Boor (Leipzig: Teubner, 1883–5), 1: 355 (Greek), *The Chronicle of Theophanes Confessor: Byzantine and Near Eastern History AD 284–813*, trans. Cyril Mango and Roger Scott with Geoffrey Greatrex (Oxford: Clarendon Press, 1997), 496 (English).

[33] Agapius, *Kitab al-ʿUnvan*, 492; *Anonymi auctoris Chronicon ad annum Christi 1234 pertinens*, eds and trans. Jean-Baptiste Chabot, Aphram Barsaum, J. M. Fiey and Albert Abouna, Corpus Christianorum Scriptorum Orientalium 81–2, 109, 354, Scriptores Syri 36–7, 56, 154 (Louvain: L. Durbecq, 1952–74), 1: 288 (interestingly, this detail is not attested in the other Syriac chronicles).

[34] Agapius, *Kitab al-ʿUnvan*, 492.

[35] Howard-Johnston, *Witnesses to a World Crisis*, 227.

[36] Theophanes, *Chronographia*, 355 (Greek), *Chronicle*, 496 (English); cf. Constantine Porphyrogenitus, *De administrando imperio*, ed. Gyula Y. Moravcsik and trans. Romilly J. H. Jenkins (Washington, DC: Dumbarton Oaks Center for Byzantine Studies, 1967), 84–7.

dispatching envoys to the emperor, who reciprocated by sending the high-ranking patrician John Pitzigaudes to Syria to negotiate.[37] There he met a delegation of 'emirs and Qurashīs' (*amēraiōn kai korasēnōn*), with the caliph offering the Byzantines an annual payment of 3,000 pieces of gold, fifty prisoners, and fifty thoroughbred horses in exchange for a suspension of hostilities. (Interestingly, the patriarch Nikephoros, d. 828, mentions the same treaty, but without any reference to the Jarājima; he gives the Arabs' abortive siege of Constantinople as the main reason for the negotiations.)[38] It seems that other enemies of the Byzantines, including the Avars, took note of the treaty and also sued for peace, intimidated by what had happened with the Jarājima.

1.4. The reigns of ʿAbd al-Malik and Justinian II

Despite the peace settlement, the Jarājima never disappeared from their mountain lairs. As Islamic and Christian sources both make clear, the conflict between the two sides was renewed during the reigns of ʿAbd al-Malik and Justinian II.[39] The precipitating event was the advent of the second Arab Civil War (60–72/680–92), specifically the conflict between ʿAbd al-Malik in Syria and Muṣʿab ibn al-Zubayr – brother of the famous ʿAbdallāh ibn al-Zubayr – in Iraq.[40]

With ʿAbd al-Malik distracted in the east, Justinian saw an opportunity to break his father's peace treaty and reactivate the Jarājima. Indeed, as Nikephoros puts it, the emperor 'dislodged the armed men who had since olden times been lurking in the mountains of Lebanon', who promptly resumed their waves of guerilla attacks.[41] Theophanes hints that this unleashed bedlam so fearsome that Syria quickly descended into plague and famine.[42] Although it does not name the Jarājima explicitly, the *Kitāb al-fitan* of Nuʿaym ibn Ḥammād (d. 228/843) – a

[37] Ralph-Johannes Lilie *et al.*, after preliminary work by Friedhelm Winkelmann, *Prosopographie der mittelbyzantinischen Zeit. Erste Abteilung (641–867)* (Berlin: De Gruyter, 1998–2002), *Zweite Abteilung (867–1025)* (Berlin: De Gruyter, 2009–13), no. 2707.

[38] Nikephoros, Patriarch of Constantinople, *Short History*, ed. and trans. Cyril Mango (Washington, DC: Dumbarton Oaks Research Library and Collection, 1990), 84–7.

[39] For a summary of these events, see Kaplony, *Konstantinopel und Damaskus*, 99–137.

[40] For the background, see esp. al-Balādhurī, *Ansāb*, eds al-Dūrī and ʿUqla, 323–63.

[41] Nikephoros, *Short History*, 92–5.

[42] Theophanes, *Chronographia*, 361 (Greek), *Chronicle*, 503 (English).

collection of Umayyad- and Abbasid-era hadith about the apocalypse – gives a flavour for the kind of terror this must have sown:

> The Byzantines will descend on the plain of Acre and overcome Palestine, the heart of Jordan, along with Jerusalem. But they will not cross the Pass of Afīq for forty days. Then the imām of the Muslims will go to them and drive them to the Field of Acre. There they shall fight until the blood reaches the fetlocks of the horses, then God will defeat them and kill them, other than a small number who will go to Mount Lebanon, then to a mountain in the land of the Byzantines.[43]

> The courier (*al-barīd*), who came from Iraq, shall pass by Homs, and there they shall discover that some of the non-Muslims (*al-aʿājim*) had locked [the gates of the city] upon the offspring of the Muslims who were inside. And there came to them news that the Arabs had perished . . . Then the ruler (*al-wālī*) shall say: 'Should we expect anything other than that every city in Syria would lock [its gates] upon those who are inside them?' . . . [The enemy] shall come to the coast, but not find any relief there to save them. Therefore, it is as if I am looking at the Muslims striking their necks on the coast of Acre until they reach at Mount Lebanon [in flight]. But only around two hundred of them shall escape, reaching Mount Lebanon until they reach the mountains of Byzantine territory. The Muslims, meanwhile, shall return to Homs and besiege it . . . From that very day, it shall be left in ruins, uninhabited. They shall say: 'How can we dwell in a place where our women were dishonored?'[44]

Here, it is important to note that the Jarājima were not the only example of Byzantines trying to exploit the chaos of the Arab Civil War for their own

[43] Nuʿaym ibn Ḥammād al-Khuzāʿī al-Marwazī, *Kitāb al-fitan*, ed. Suhayl Zakkār (Beirut: Dār al-Fikr lil-Ṭibāʿa wa-ʾl-Nashr wa-ʾl-Tawzīʿ, 2003), 267 (Arabic); *'The Book of Tribulations': The Syrian Muslim Apocalyptic Tradition*, ed. and trans. David Cook (Edinburgh: Edinburgh University Press, 2017), 253 (English, adapted). Even if this does not refer to the Jarājima, it does seem to reflect actual knowledge of the escape routes that would have enabled certain groups to flee to Byzantium via the mountains.

[44] Nuʿaym ibn Ḥammād, *Fitan*, 268–9 (Arabic); *Book of Tribulations*, 273 (English, adapted). The idea that non-Muslims would lock the gates of the cities and wreak havoc on Muslims, and in the process, violate their women and children, is a recurring trope in the sources (e.g. *Book of Tribulations*, 253, 263, 269, 275, 309, 313).

gain: around the same time, the Byzantines also attacked Caesarea on the Mediterranean coast, as well as Melitene and Germanikeia (Marʿash) along the frontier in Anatolia.[45]

As under Constantine, Justinian sparked his insurgency by dispatching a group of Byzantine soldiers to lead the Jarājima. According to Ibn ʿAsākir (d. 571/1176), these troops were led by a patrician named *f-l-q-ṭ*, possibly 'Polyeuktos', who anchored at Wajh al-Ḥajar near Byblos.[46] He then scattered his commanders across the coastal highlands while he marched for the Black Mountain near Antioch, presumably to be close to al-Jurjūma, the Jarājima's base. A state of lawlessness and banditry descended on the region, with the Jarājima in control of many of the major peaks, including Mount Lebanon, Sanīr (between Homs and Baalbek), Jabal al-Thalj (Mount Hermon), and the Golan Heights.[47] This more or less corresponded to the territory in which the Jarājima were active during the first wave of attacks during the 670s. Al-Masʿūdī (d. 345/956) remarks on the makeup of the rebels at this time, consisting of 'the slaves, riff-raff, and criminals (*ʿabīdahā wa-awbāshahā wa-duʿʿārahā*) of Damascus who rebelled against [the city's] inhabitants, [along with those who] descended from the mountain'.[48]

ʿAbd al-Malik was in no position to fight on two fronts, and so, 'terrified that [the emperor] might come to Syria and prevail over him', he sued for peace.[49] The loss of the Syrian coast must have been especially devastating for the caliph because it prevented him from resupplying his army via sea-born

45 al-Balādhurī, *Liber expugnationis*, 143 (Caesarea), 185 (Melitene), 188 (Germanikeia) (Arabic), *Origins*, 219, 289, 294 (English); discussion in Stephanie Forrest, '"Destroying the Brazen Wall": Byzantium and the Umayyad Caliphate in the First Reign of Justinian II, 685–695', MPhil thesis, University of Oxford, 2018, 56–7.

46 Ibn ʿAsākir, *Tārīkh madīnat Dimashq*, 20: 144–5; see also al-Balādhurī, *Liber expugnationis*, 160 (which does not name the commander) (Arabic), *Origins*, 248 (English); al-Balādhurī, *Ansāb*, eds al-Dūrī and ʿUqla, 275 (which does not name the commander, but describes him as *qāʾid min quwwād al-ḍawāḥī*, suggesting he may have been responsible for border areas). On the reconstruction of the name 'Polyeuktos', see Theophilus of Edessa, *Chronicle*, trans. Hoyland, 169 n. 437. On the location of Wajh al-Ḥajar, see Yāqūt, *Muʿjam al-buldān*, 5: 363.

47 On Sanīr, see Yāqūt, *Muʿjam al-buldān*, 3: 269–70; on Jabal al-Thalj (Mount Hermon), see Le Strange, *Palestine*, 79.

48 al-Masʿūdī, *Murūj al-dhahab*, 3: 299 (Arabic); *Prairies d'or*, 5: 225 (French).

49 al-Balādhurī, *Liber expugnationis*, 160 (Arabic), *Origins*, 247 (English).

shipments from Egypt.[50] At this point, Muslim historians mention how ʿAbd al-Malik modelled his agreement with Justinian on the one that had been contracted between Muʿāwiya and Constantine several years before: in it, he offered the emperor a weekly tribute of a thousand *dīnārs*, payable each Friday. He also promised to dispatch Byzantine captives to Baalbek, presumably so they could rendezvous with Byzantine troops there or the Jarājima. Islamic sources name ʿAbd al-Malik's envoys as Ḥumayd ibn Ḥurayth al-Kalbī and Kurayb ibn Abraha the Ḥimyarite.[51]

The Christian historians give far more details about the treaty, which was designed to last for ten years.[52] They confirm the weekly payment of a thousand *dīnārs*, as stipulated in the Arabic texts, along with an annual payment of 365 slaves and thoroughbred horses. Crucially, they also claim the agreement stipulated that the emperor would remove the Jarājima from Mount Lebanon and halt their attacks on the Arabs. Outside the Levant, the treaty arranged for the two sides to split the tax revenues of Cyprus, Armenia, and Georgia, which were contested areas claimed by both sides, though the details of these arrangements vary by the source. The texts name the magistrianus Paul as Justinian's main envoy. The date for the treaty is given as around 685–6.

In the end, we read that the emperor honoured his agreement with the caliph, removing some 12,000 Jarājima to Byzantine territory, not counting women and children. The *De administrando imperio* specifies that the emperor resettled them in Armenia, thus 'destroying the brazen wall' (*chalekon teichos dialysas*) of defences which had protected the empire from Arab incursions until that point.[53] Theophanes expresses disapproval of this resettlement, writing

[50] Forrest, 'Destroying the Brazen Wall', 57.

[51] al-Balādhurī, *Liber expugnationis*, 160 (Arabic), *Origins*, 247 (English); al-Balādhurī, *Ansāb*, eds al-Dūrī and ʿUqla, 275; Ibn al-Athīr, *Kāmil*, 3: 361.

[52] For the Greek sources, see Theophanes, *Chronographia*, 363 (Greek), *Chronicle*, 506–7 (English); Constantine Porphyrogenitus, *De administrando imperio*, 92–5. For the Christian Arabic, see Agapius, *Kitab al-ʿUnvan*, 497; Theophilus of Edessa, *Chronicle*, trans. Hoyland, 321. For the Syriac, see Michael the Great, *Chronique*, 2: 469 (French), 4: 445–6 (Syriac); *Chronicon ad annum 1234*, 1: 294; Bar Hebraeus, *Chronicon*, 111.

[53] Constantine Porphyrogenitus, *De administrando imperio*, 94–5; this is an allusion to a famous motif in classical literature, i.e. Donald E. W. Wormell, 'Walls of Brass in Literature', *Hermathena* 58 (1941), 116–20.

that Justinian's actions weakened Roman power in the region. Indeed, he notes that while the Jarājima were active, they managed to depopulate the frontier zone between Mopsuestia and Fourth Armenia, creating a strategic buffer between the empire and the caliphate. Ever since the removal, however, 'Roman land endured terrible evils at the hands of the Arabs'.[54]

Islamic sources confirm that not all was rosy for the Byzantines in the wake of the treaty. Determined to flush the Jarājima out of the mountains, ʿAbd al-Malik dispatched a trusted deputy named Suḥaym ibn al-Muhājir, who was based in Tripoli, to confront the Byzantine commander Polyeuktos.[55] According to Ibn ʿAsākir, who provides the most detailed account of the incident, Suḥaym tracked Polyeuktos to a mountain village where he was holed up with his men.[56] Allegedly disguising himself as a Byzantine *patrikios*, Suḥaym found Polyeuktos eating and drinking in a church. He ingratiated himself to the commander, falsely slandering ʿAbd al-Malik in order to win his trust. Suḥaym then offered to stand guard over the Byzantines' encampment at night. As darkness descended and the troops fell asleep, Suḥaym killed them all by his own sword (despite the presence of a large group of Umayyad soldiers and *mawālī* waiting in the wings). He then turned his sword on Polyeuktos. Only a few Byzantines survived, fleeing to their ships, which were still moored at Wajh al-Ḥajar. Following the attack, some Jarājima were scattered among the villages of Homs and Damascus, while a majority simply returned to their homes in Jabal al-Lukkām. Thus, some portion of the Jarājima remained inside Islamic territory after the treaty, while others were resettled in Byzantium. Their Nabataean allies also returned to their villages, while the fugitive slaves who had joined the revolt were returned to

54 Theophanes, *Chronographia*, 363 (Greek), *Chronicle*, 506 (English); with comment in Howard-Johnston, *Witnesses to a World Crisis*, 497 (with background on the now-lost chronicle of Trajan at 306–7).

55 The Islamic sources do not always clarify the sequence of events, though Ibn al-Athīr (*Kāmil*, 3: 361) states that Suḥaym's attack occurred directly after the treaty was signed; thus, it may have been a consequence of it.

56 Ibn ʿAsākir, *Tārīkh madīnat Dimashq*, 20: 144–46; cf. al-Balādhurī, *Liber expugnationis*, 160 (Arabic), *Origins*, 248 (English); al-Balādhurī, *Ansāb*, eds al-Dūrī and ʿUqla, 275–6. The detail of Suḥaym's false slander against ʿAbd al-Malik is found only in al-Balādhurī and not in Ibn ʿAsākir. The detail of the freed slaves comes from al-Balādhurī, *Futūḥ*.

their masters. Ibn al-Athīr (d. 630/1233) adds that some of these slaves were offered manumission in exchange for enrolling as soldiers in the Umayyad *dīwān*.[57] Needless to say, the whole story is fanciful and may be an anecdotal explanation for a series of observable events: the death of Polyeuktos, the retreat of the Byzantines, and the survival of the Jarājima, however this actually unfolded.

The affair was not completely over, however, for in around 690–1, Justinian broke the peace treaty again. Theophanes states that he did so because he was upset with Arab plans to transfer the population of Cyprus off of the island. He was also incensed by ʿAbd al-Malik's new aniconic coins, which diverged dramatically from the pseudo-Byzantine issues the Muslims had been minting since the conquest. The caliph sued for peace, not necessarily to placate the emperor, but to stop him from mobilising the Jarājima for a third time. Clearly, ʿAbd al-Malik knew that the Jarājima had kept their weapons and could be called upon to fight at a moment's notice.[58]

1.5. The battle of Ṭuwāna

In the years after the three peace treaties, it seems the remaining Jarājima were pacified and transformed into Arab allies. Indeed, as the geographer Yāqūt puts it, 'The Muslims sought help from the Jarājima in numerous areas during the reigns of the Umayyads and ʿAbbasids, granting them wages and taking intelligence from them.'[59] We see this new dynamic clearly during the siege of the fortress of Ṭuwāna (Greek Tyana) in Anatolia, located on the road between Cappadocia and the Cilician Gates. This took place around the year 707.[60] In and of itself, the battle was unremarkable,

[57] Ibn al-Athīr, *Kāmil*, 3: 361.

[58] Theophanes, *Chronographia*, 365 (Greek), *Chronicle*, 509–10 (English). On the role of coinage in the rivalry between the Byzantines and the Umayyads, see Luke Treadwell, 'Byzantium and Islam in the Late 7th Century AD: A "Numismatic War of Images"', in Tony Goodwin (ed.), *Arab–Byzantine Coins and History: Papers Presented at the 13th Seventh Century Syrian Numismatic Round Table Held at Corpus Christi College Oxford on 11th and 12th September 2011* (London: Archetype Publications, 2012), 145–56; Michael Humphreys, 'The "War of Images" Revisited. Justinian II's Coinage Reform and the Caliphate', *The Numismatic Chronicle* 173 (2013), 229–44.

[59] Yāqūt, *Muʿjam al-buldān*, 2: 123.

[60] Clive Foss, 'Tyana', *ODB*, 3: 2130; Yāqūt, *Muʿjam al-buldān*, 4: 45–6.

one of a great series of skirmishes that occurred along the border throughout the Umayyad period.[61] The Arab commanders included the new caliph's half-brother, Maslama ibn ʿAbd al-Malik, along with his son al-ʿAbbās ibn al-Walīd.[62] One of their deputies was a man named Maymūn al-Jurjumānī, who appears in both Islamic and Christian sources (where he is referred to as 'Maiouma').[63]

This Maymūn is an interesting figure: he began life as a Byzantine slave, we are told, serving in the household of one Umm al-Ḥakam al-Thaqafī, a sister of none other than the caliph Muʿāwiya. Her family's fortunes were on the rise at precisely the moment ʿAbd al-Malik was fending off the Zubayrids in the east and the Jarājima in the west, for we read how Umm al-Ḥakam's son, ʿAbd al-Raḥmān ibn ʿAbdallāh, was entrusted with command of Damascus.[64] As for Maymūn, it is said that he 'was named for the Jarājima [viz. al-Maymūn al-Jurjumānī] because he associated with them and rebelled with them in

[61] Ṭuwāna was the site of later battles between the Byzantines and the Muslims, including during the reign of Hārūn al-Rashīd (AM 6298/AD 805–6), who led a mixed force including Maurophoroi (wearers of black, meaning Abbasids, or in this context Rāwandiyya, per note 118 below) and built a 'house of blasphemy', that is to say, a mosque: Theophanes, *Chronographia*, 482 (Greek), *Chronicle*, 661 (English).

[62] K. V. Zettersteen and F. Gabrieli, 'al-ʿAbbās b. al-Walīd', *EI*², 1: 12–13.

[63] For references to the battle and Maymūn's role in Arabic sources, see Khalīfa ibn Khayyāṭ al-ʿUṣfurī, *Tārīkh Khalīfa ibn Khayyāṭ*, eds Muṣṭafā Najīb Fawwāz and Ḥikmat Kishlī Fawwāz (Beirut: Dār al-Kutub al-ʿIlmiyya, 1995), 184 (Arabic), *Khalifa ibn Khayyat's History on the Umayyad Dynasty (660–750)*, trans. Carl Wurtzel and Robert G. Hoyland (Liverpool: Liverpool University Press, 2015), 159 (English); al-Balādhurī, *Liber expugnationis*, 160–1 (Arabic), *Origins*, 248–9 (English); al-Balādhurī, *Ansāb*, eds al-Dūrī and ʿUqla, 274; Abū Jaʿfar Muḥammad ibn Jarīr al-Ṭabarī, *Annales quos scripsit Abu Djafar Mohammed ibn Djarir at-Tabari cum aliis*, ed. M. J. de Goeje (Leiden: Brill, 1879–1901), 8: 1185 (Arabic), *The History of al-Ṭabarī (*Taʾrīkh al-rusul waʾl-mulūk*)*, vol. 23: *The Zenith of the Marwānid House*, trans. Martin Hinds (Albany, NY: State University of New York Press, 1990), 134 (English). In Greek: Theophanes, *Chronographia*, 376–7 (Greek; called 'Maiouma'), *Chronicle*, 525–6 (English); Nikephoros, *Short History*, 104–7. In Syriac: Michael the Great, *Chronique*, 2: 478 (French), 4: 451 (Syriac).

[64] al-Balādhurī, *Ansāb*, eds al-Dūrī and ʿUqla, 274. ʿAbd al-Raḥmān was especially prominent during the reign of his maternal uncle Muʿāwiya, when he served as governor of Mosul, Kufa, and Egypt, and led a winter raid against Byzantium: al-Ṭabarī, *Annales*, 7: 128, 157, 192, 196.

Mount Lebanon'.[65] Therefore, he may have been one of the runaway slaves who joined the Jarājima according to a number of sources.

News of Maymūn's bravery eventually reached ʿAbd al-Malik, who instructed his *mawālī* to manumit him when the conflict was over. Maymūn was thus clearly among the slaves who had been freed and enrolled in the *dīwān* after the Jarājima's revolt, per the account in Ibn al-Athīr.[66] Indeed, one wonders whether his elite connections to members of the Umayyad family saved him from a more unpleasant fate in the wake of the uprising. From there, Maymūn seems to have gone north, where he was given command of a group of a thousand soldiers from Antioch, possibly Jarājima, who fought on behalf of the Muslims. He fell on the battlefield at Ṭuwāna – the Islamic sources state 'he was martyred' (*ustushhida*), hinting that he may have died a Muslim. Regardless of his religion, Maymūn was clearly a valued ally, for ʿAbd al-Malik dispatched a large force against Byzantium to avenge his death.[67]

The story of Maymūn nicely reflects the flexibility of the Jarājima as a group of mercenaries on the marches between two empires. Although they were most famous for fighting on behalf of the Byzantines, we should not forget that they initially served as scouts and soldiers on behalf of the Arabs. In Maymūn and his men, therefore, the Jarājima were merely restoring the status quo ante. But part of the Jarājima's character was their tendency to flip-flop, and indeed, within only a few years of Maymūn's death, they were at it once again, aiding and abetting the Byzantines.

In 89/708–9, we read how the Syrian Jarājima joined with a group of Byzantine troops who had come across the border near Alexandretta and Rūsis.[68] The

[65] For the quote and background on Maymūn's masters, see al-Balādhurī, *Liber expugnationis*, 160–1 (Arabic), *Origins*, 248 (English); cf. al-Balādhurī, *Ansāb*, eds al-Dūrī and ʿUqla, 274.

[66] Ibn al-Athīr, *Kāmil*, 3: 361.

[67] al-Balādhurī, *Liber expugnationis*, 161 (Arabic), *Origins*, 249 (English).

[68] al-Balādhurī, *Liber expugnationis*, 161 (Arabic), *Origins*, 249 (English); with a possible allusion in Abū ʾl-ʿAbbās Aḥmad ibn Abī Yaʿqūb al-Yaʿqūbī, *Ibn Wādih qui dicitur al-Jaʿqubī Historiae*, ed. M. T. Houtsma (Leiden: Brill, 1883), 2: 338–9 (no year given, merely the reign of al-Walīd ibn ʿAbd al-Malik, 86–96/705–15), *The Works of Ibn Wāḍiḥ al-Yaʿqūbī*, trans. Matthew S. Gordon, Chase F. Robinson, Everett K. Rowson and Michael Fishbein (Leiden: Brill, 2018), 3: 989–90 (English). For Rūsis, a rural district in the *ʿAwāṣim* between Antioch and Tarsus, see Yāqūt, *Muʿjam al-buldān*, 3: 83.

caliph al-Walīd ibn ʿAbd al-Malik dispatched a large army to quash the threat. Desperate to contain the Jarājima at all costs, he granted them extremely favourable terms of surrender (mirroring some of the terms they received in the aftermath of the initial conquest in the 630s): they could settle wherever they liked in Syria; they would receive a payment of eight *dīnārs* per head; each household would receive rations of wheat and oil; and not a single one of them would be compelled to renounce his or her Christianity. What is more, the wives and children of the Jarājima would be exempted from the *jizya*, and they would keep whatever portion of the booty they had acquired while raiding with Muslims. Despite this, not all was rosy: in the wake of the insubordination, Maslama destroyed the city of al-Jurjūma, and the Jarājima were once again scattered, this time to different areas in and around the floodplain of al-ʿAmq (near Antioch). These included the regions of Jabal al-Ḥawwār, Sunḥ al-Lūlūn (?), and ʿAmq al-Tīzīn.[69] The destruction of al-Jurjūma and the displacement of its inhabitants seems to have done the trick, for the sources mention no further rebellions with Byzantine cooperation.

1.6. The rebellion of Theodore

The last gasp of the Jarājima is a little-known revolt which occurred in Baalbek and Mount Lebanon after the Abbasid Revolution in 142–3/759–60.[70] Interestingly, no study of the Jarājima seems to be aware of the connection. The

[69] On the broader area (including discussion of ʿAmq Tīzīn), see Dominique Sourdel, 'al-ʿAmḳ', *EI*², 1: 446–7. On Ḥawwār (or Ḥuwwār), see Yāqūt, *Muʿjam al-Buldān*, 2: 315 (a district of Aleppo between ʿAzāz and al-Jūma); Le Strange, *Palestine*, 451–2. I have been unable to find Sunḥ al-Lūlūn, and indeed, judging from de Goeje's edition of al-Balādhurī, the name may be a copyist's error. I note that Yāqūt (*Muʿjam al-buldān*, 5: 26) mentions a 'Luʾlūʾa,' apparently a fortress near Tarsus in Cilicia. Given its proximity to the homeland of the Jarājima, this may be the site in question.

[70] The most extensive discussion is found in Paul M. Cobb, *White Banners: Contention in ʿAbbāsid Syria, 750–880* (Albany: State University of New York Press, 2001), 112–15; see also Kurd ʿAlī, *Khiṭaṭ al-Shām*, 1: 179–81; Philip K. Hitti, *History of Syria, including Lebanon and Palestine* (London: MacMillan & Co., 1951), 542–3 (Hitti discusses the episode with similar detail across several works, this one being the earliest); Farouk Omar, *The ʿAbbāsid Caliphate, 132/750–170/786* (Baghdad: The National Printing and Publishing Co., 1969), 316–17; Kamal Salibi, *Syria under Islam: Empire in Trial, 634–1097* (Delmar:

most extensive account of the revolt comes from Ibn ʿAsākir (and to a lesser extent, al-Balādhurī), but Theophanes also includes an interesting report that fleshes out certain details of the incident. According to Robert Hoyland, this is one of a series of notices which Theophanes derived from a now-lost continuation of Theophilus of Edessa's chronicle that focused on the affairs of the Chalcedonian Christians of Syria.[71]

Ibn ʿAsākir states that the Jarājima had lain quiet in Mount Lebanon until the appearance of a man named 'Bundār'. Theophanes identifies him as 'Theodore', and indeed, one can imagine how a later Arabic scribe might have miscopied the letters *th-y-d-ā-r* (ثيدار) to read *b-n-d-ā-r* (بندار) instead.[72] Whatever his actual name, Theodore, as I shall call him, hailed from al-Munayṭira, located high above Byblos near the villages of al-Laqlūq,

Caravan Books, 1977), 35–7; Patricia Crone, *Slaves on Horses: The Evolution of the Islamic Polity* (Cambridge: Cambridge University Press, 1980), 71; Iḥsān ʿAbbās, *Tārīkh bilād al-Shām fī ʾl-aṣr al-ʿAbbāsī* (Amman: Manshūrāt Lajnat Tārīkh Bilād al-Shām – al-Jāmiʿa al-Urdunniyya – Jāmiʿat Yarmūk, 1992), 136–8. One of the most important Christian martyrs of the early Islamic period, Elias of Helioupolis (d. 779), seems to have been born in Baalbek in precisely the year of Theodore's revolt. For more, see Sahner, *Christian Martyrs under Islam*, 53–9. There were apparently plans to produce a television drama about the incident in Lebanon, which would have starred the actor Fadi Ibrahim. The series would have highlighted the role of the jurist al-Awzāʿī in promoting good relations between Muslims and Christians in the wake of the revolt (see below). Prime Minister Rafiq al-Hariri seems to have promised funding, but the project never came to fruition after Hariri was assassinated in 2005. I thank Hussein Abdulsater for bringing this to my attention.

71 For the Arabic account, see Ibn ʿAsākir, *Tārīkh madīnat Dimashq*, 18: 267–8; cf. al-Balādhurī, *Liber expugnationis*, 162 (a shortened version which does not mention Theodore by name; the account is difficult to understand, since al-Balādhurī's chronology jumps around) (Arabic), *Origins*, 250–1 (English). For the Greek, see Theophanes, *Chronographia*, 431 (Greek), *Chronicle*, 597 (English). On the possible Chalcedonian source underlying Theophanes' report, see Theophilus of Edessa, *Chronicle*, trans. Hoyland, 310–12.

72 Scribal errors almost certainly explain why the manuscript of Ibn ʿAsākir gives the name of the rebels as *al-ḥarāḥiyya* (الحراحية) instead of *al-jarājima* (الجراجمة) (Ibn ʿAsākir, *Tārīkh madīnat Dimashq*, 18: 267 n. 2). While 'Bundār' may be a copyist's error, it is also a Persian word meaning 'firm, solid, or certain' (an appropriate name for a rebel leader, particularly if Zakeri is right about the Iranian origins of the Jarājima, per *Sāsānid Soldiers*, 128–64); see F. Steingass, *A Comprehensive Persian–English Dictionary* (New Delhi: Manohar Publishers & Distributers, 2008), 202; Kurd ʿAlī, *Khiṭaṭ al-Shām*, 1: 180 n. 1.

al-ʿĀqūra, and Afqā.[73] He is said to have possessed a strong frame and been very charismatic. Theophanes describes him as 'Syrian [and] Lebanese' (*syros libanitēs*), suggesting he may have been a native speaker of Aramaic, as opposed to Arabic or Greek.[74] His followers hailed him as a 'king' (*malik*), and he wore a crown and displayed a cross as symbols of his sovereignty. His supporters included the same Aramaic-speaking peasants who had taken part in the revolts of the Jarājima (here called *anbāṭ jabal Lubnān*). This time, however, their grievances were mainly political and financial.

Ibn ʿAsākir states that Theodore's Christians initially went to Baalbek to complain about taxes before two local officials, one Ismāʿīl ibn al-Azraq and one al-Jazarī, the latter of whom was in charge of the *kharāj*, or land tax. These men mistreated the peasants, who reacted by seizing several villages in the Beqaa Valley. They also killed Muslims and plundered widely. The people of Baalbek managed to muster 5000 cavalrymen to fight them, killing many rebels and putting the remainder to flight. Theodore went into hiding in a nearby citadel. The threat was serious enough that the Abbasid governor of Damascus, Riyāḥ ibn ʿUthmān al-Murrī, along with his brothers Yazīd and al-Walīd, raised an army to confront Theodore.[75] They besieged his fortress and vanquished most of his followers. Despite their efforts, Theodore managed to escape to Byzantium, following the well-trod path of countless Jarājima before him.

What followed reverberated even more loudly in the annals of early Islamic history. Ṣāliḥ ibn ʿAlī – the great-uncle of the caliphs al-Saffāḥ and al-Manṣūr – who was then the senior Abbasid in Syria – ordered the Christians of Mount Lebanon to be removed from their villages and scattered into the districts of Syria.[76] This was in apparent retaliation for Theodore's revolt. Ṣāliḥ's actions, however, provoked an angry letter from al-Awzāʿī (d. 157/774), the leading

[73] The site is marked on many modern maps, half-way between Byblos and Baalbek at the top of the mountain (cf. Salibi, *Syria under Islam*, 35 n. 12). Yāqūt, *Muʿjam al-buldān*, 5: 21, says it is a fortress (*ḥiṣn*) near Tripoli, which is almost certainly wrong.

[74] With parallels in contemporary Greek texts discussed in Sahner, *Christian Martyrs under Islam*, 18, 55.

[75] On Riyāḥ ibn ʿUthmān, who later became famous for serving as governor of Medina, see Khalīfa ibn Khayyāṭ, *Tārīkh*, 276, 283, 286; Cobb, *White Banners*, 114.

[76] Adolf Grohmann and Hugh Kennedy, 'Ṣāliḥ b. ʿAlī', *EI*^{2}, 8: 985.

jurist in Syria at the time, who resided in Beirut.[77] Al-Awzāʿī objected to the indiscriminate punishment of all local Christians on account of the crimes of the few, citing Qurʾan 6: 164 as his justification. Christians were *dhimmīs*, he explained, entitled to certain basic rights under the covenant of protection with the Muslims. Ṣāliḥ had violated this covenant by imposing corporate punishment on the innocent as well as the guilty.[78] The letter of al-Awzāʿī seems to have circulated widely, for it was excerpted in al-Balādhurī's *Futūḥ*, as well as two ninth-century fiscal texts, one by Abū ʿUbayd (d. 224/838) and the other by Ibn Zanjawayh (d. 251/865).[79] These authors were mainly interested in the dispute as a legal precedent for the proper treatment of *dhimmīs*.

There is a possible epilogue to the story in a text known as *Madīḥa ʿalā jabal Lubnān*, a verse poem by the famous Maronite priest and writer Jibrāʾīl ibn al-Qilāʿī (d. c. 1516). Despite its late date and quasi-legendary contents, the poem is the oldest surviving 'history' of the Maronite Church, containing garbled accounts of events that may have actually happened in the early Islamic period. One such event was a revolt by an unnamed Christian king (*malik*) who lived in a village called Baskintā, located between modern Jounieh and Baalbek at the top of Jabal Ṣannīn.[80] Ibn al-Qilāʿī states that the king dispatched troops to plunder the Beqaa Valley, killing men and women along

[77] Steven C. Judd, 'al-Awzāʿī', in Kate Fleet *et al.*, *Encyclopaedia of Islam, 3rd edn* (Leiden: Brill, 2007–present) (hereafter *EI3*).

[78] Al-Awzāʿī had a positive reputation among *dhimmīs*, perhaps owing to this incident: his funeral procession was attended by large numbers of 'Jews, Christians, and Copts' (Ibn ʿAsākir, *Tārīkh madīnat dimashq*, 35: 227). Qurʾan 6: 164: 'no soul shall bear the burden of another'.

[79] al-Balādhurī, *Liber expugnationis*, 162 (Arabic), *Origins*, 251 (English); slightly longer text in Abū ʿUbayd Qāsim ibn Sallām, *The Book of Revenue (*Kitāb al-Amwāl*)*, trans. Imran Ahsan Khan Nyazee (Reading: Garnet, 2002), 170–1; Abū Aḥmad Ḥumayd ibn Makhlad Ibn Zanjawayh, *Kitāb al-amwāl*, ed. Shākir Dhīb Fayyāḍ (Riyad: Markaz al-Malik Fayṣal lil-Buḥūth wa-ʾl-Dirāsāt al-Islāmiyya, 1986), 419–21; reprinted in ʿAbbās, *Bilād al-Shām fī ʾl-ʿaṣr al-ʿabbāsī*, 219.

[80] Ibn al-Qilāʿī, *Zajaliyyāt Jibrāʾīl ibn al-Qilāʿī*, ed. Buṭrus al-Jumayyil (Beirut: Manshūrāt Dār Laḥd Khāṭir, 1982), 91–2; with discussion in Kamal Salibi, *Maronite Historians of Mediæval Lebanon* (Beirut: American University of Beirut, 1959), 35–7, 42–4 (including English translation of the relevant verses); Salibi, *Syria under Islam*, 36–7; general background of the text in Moukarzel, *Gabriel Ibn al-Qilāʿī*, 417–30 (esp. 421), plus Salibi, *Maronite Historians*, 23–87.

the way. He then took up residence in a village called Qab Ilyās, just beside the modern city of Chtoura at the base of the mountain. Eventually news of the bedlam reached an unnamed ruler (*al-sulṭān*, presumably a Muslim), who dispatched envoys with a robe of honour for this king. This was a ruse, however, for soldiers came with the envoys ready to pounce, promptly killing the king and his men. From this point onward, the Muslims took possession of the Beqaa. Ibn al-Qilāʿī blames this tragedy on the king's drunkenness and his fixation on a certain singing girl. Indeed, he explains that the king's drunkenness accounted for why his name was not recorded in works of history.[81] The story is typical of the poem as a whole, in the sense that it contains few dates and specific names. Ibn al-Qilāʿī's goal was to explain how the Maronites lost control of the Beqaa, as well as to show how immorality and faithlessness sowed misfortune within the Church.[82]

There are many similarities between the tale of this Christian king and Theodore; it is tempting to see them as one and the same. Yet the Lebanese historical tradition is divided over the king's identity, with none of the leading theories suggesting that it was Theodore. This may owe to the accessibility of our texts; the reports in Theophanes, al-Balādhurī, and Ibn ʿAsākir seem to be unknown to many later Lebanese chroniclers. The closest we get is the Maronite historian Ḥaydar al-Shihābī (d. 1835) – who despite his late date, seems to have preserved a significant amount of rare early information – who identified the king as a Christian chieftain (*muqaddam*) and rabble-rouser named Ilyās (whence the name 'Qab Ilyās'), who was killed in 135/752 on the orders of Caliph al-Ṣaffāḥ. This Ilyās was buried beside the Friday Mosque of a village originally called 'al-Murūj', whose name was later changed to 'Qab Ilyās' to honour the slain chieftain.[83] The dates for Theodore (759–60)

[81] Ibn al-Qilāʿī, *Zajaliyyāt*, 92–3 goes on to explain that the king's nephew, a *muqaddam* known as Simʿān, continued to fight Muslims after his uncle's death. He was named 'king of Khārija (i.e. Kisrawān)' by the 'king of Jubayl (Byblos)' and the Maronite patriarch. That being said, the chronology is extremely confused: despite being named as a nephew of the eighth-century king, this Simʿān seems to be a figure from the Crusader period (Salibi, *Maronite Historians*, 48–53).

[82] Salibi, *Maronite Historians*, 43–4.

[83] Ḥaydar Aḥmad al-Shihābī, *Kitāb tārīkh al-amīr Ḥaydar Aḥmad al-Shihābī, Kitāb al-ghurar al-ḥisān fī tawārīkh ḥawādith al-azmān*, ed. Naʿūm Mughabghab (Cairo: Maṭbaʿat al-Salām, 1900), 100.

and Ilyās (752) do not line up exactly, nor do their long-term fates: Theodore is said to have escaped to Byzantium, whereas Ilyās was killed in the Beqaa. Yet given the late date of these traditions and their legendary contents, we may be dealing with a garbled account of an actual revolt known from earlier Byzantine and Islamic sources. If this is so, it suggests that memory of Theodore endured in Lebanon well beyond the eighth century.

1.7. Afterlife

Thereafter, we hear very little about the Jarājima. Al-Balādhurī states that their *jizya* exemption came to an end during the reigns of al-Wāthiq (r. 227–32/842–7) or al-Mutawakkil (r. 232–47/847–61), when they presumably started to be taxed as normal Christians.[84] We have already heard about the destruction of their hometown, al-Jurjūma, at the hands of Maslama at the start of the eighth century. This, coupled with their resettlement across Syria and Byzantine Armenia, must have contributed signnificantly towards destroying their power. It must have also weakened their identity as a geographically concentrated group.

That being said, Eduard Sachau and Henri Lammens both knew of a village in the vicinity of Antioch named 'Gurgum'.[85] This may be what Friedrich Hild and Hansgerd Hellenkemper identified as 'Çomçom', a village situated twelve kilometres north of modern Iskenderun.[86] Such names hint at the town's survival long after the Umayyad period, though unfortunately, no comprehensive archaeological survey of the Amanus range has taken place. Therefore, to my knowledge, there is no archaeological evidence pointing one way or another. The continued survival of the community is also suggested by the presence of a monastery named for the Jarājima and the Mother of God in Jabal al-Lukkām during the tenth century. This detail comes from the *Life* of the martyred

[84] al-Balādhurī, *Liber expugnationis*, 161 (Arabic), *Origins*, 249–50 (English).

[85] Sachau, 'Geographie von Nordsyrien', 320–5; Lammens' discovery is mentioned in Canard, 'Djarādjima', *EI2*, though I have been unable to track down the original reference. See also René Dussaud, *Topographie historique de la Syrie antique et médiévale* (Paris: P. Geuthner, 1927), 235 (on a 'king of Gourgoum' in the valley of Marʿash in Assyrian texts), 469, 513.

[86] Friedrich Hild and Hansgerd Hellenkemper, *Kilikien und Isaurien*, Tabula Imperii Byzantini 5 (Vienna: Verlag der Österreichischen Akademie der Wissenschaften, 1990), 1: 263.

patriarch Christopher of Antioch (d. 967), whose disciple Jeremiah apparently founded the community.[87] Finally, as is well known, the Maronites of Lebanon and Syria developed a rich tradition linking themselves to the Mardaites/Jarājima (whom they referred to as 'Marada'). By and large, however, the connection between the two groups is tenuous and mostly a product of later Maronite mythmaking, as scholars before me have pointed out.[88]

Despite this, the Maronite tradition is not completely devoid of authentic historical information, for as we have already seen in the case of Theodore, it seems to contain plausible details about the Jarājima (again, called 'Marada') which are not attested elsewhere.[89] A good example are reports about conflicts between the Marada and Arab tribes in Lebanon during the early Abbasid period. These come from the chronicle of Ṭannūs ibn Yūsuf al-Shidyāq (d. 1861), a member of the famous Maronite family

[87] Joshua Mugler, 'The Life of Christopher', *Al-ʿUṣūr al-Wusṭā* 29 (2021), 112–80, here 149 (Arabic), 177 (English). Joseph Nasrallah, 'Deux auteurs melchites inconnus du Xe siècle', *Oriens Christianus* 63 (1979), 75–86, here 81–2 n. 29, is inclined to see the term 'Jarājima' as referring to the region where the group was once active as opposed to the makeup of the monastery's inhabitants.

[88] The principal study is Matti Moosa, 'Relation of the Maronites of Lebanon to the Mardaites and al-Jarājima', *Speculum* 44 (1969), 597–608; also Kamal Salibi, *A House of Many Mansions: The History of Lebanon Reconsidered* (London: I. B. Tauris & Co, 1988), 82–6; Chalhoub, *Mardaïtes-Ǧarāǧima*, 9–19; Mariam De Ghantuz Cubbe, 'Quelques réflexions à propos de l'histoire ancienne de l'église maronite', *Parole de l'Orient* 26 (2001), 3–69, here 18–23; William W. Harris, *Lebanon: A History, 600–2011* (New York: Oxford University Press, 2012), 52–3. The originator of this idea was the Maronite patriarch Isṭifān al-Duwayhī (d. 1704). While the theory has been discredited, it continues to be repeated, e.g. Elias El-Hāyek, 'Struggle for Survival: The Maronites of the Middle Ages', in Michael Gervers and Ramzi Jibran Bikhazi (eds), *Conversion and Continuity: Indigenous Christian Communities in Islamic Lands, Eighth to Fifteenth Centuries* (Toronto: Pontifical Institute of Mediaeval Studies, 1990), 407–21, here 415–17. For an in-between view, which imagines the Jarājima and the Maronites as having mixed sometime later, see Philip K. Hitti, *Lebanon in History: From the Earliest Times to the Present* (London: MacMillan & Co., 1957), 247; also Kurd ʿAlī, *Khiṭaṭ al-Shām*, 1: 68–9; Kamal Salibi, 'The Maronites of Lebanon under Frankish and Mamluk Rule (1099–1516)', *Arabica* 4 (1957), 288–303, here 288–90.

[89] For a detailed overview of the Maronite sources, though without discussion of the following episode, see Chalhoub, *Mardaïtes-Ǧarāǧima*, 67–70.

which was heavily involved in church politics and the literary *Nahḍa* of the nineteenth century. Despite its late date, Shidyāq's history contains interesting details about Lebanon during the early Islamic period, much of it culled from otherwise-lost earlier histories of notable families, as Kamal Salibi showed.[90]

The passage in question is Shidyāq's report on the arrival of the Banū Arslān in Lebanon. An Arab tribe originally from Maʿarrat al-Nuʿmān in northwestern Syria, the Arslān would become in later centuries one of the most powerful Druze clans in Lebanon. Shidyāq states that they initially came to Lebanon on the invitation of the Abbasid caliph al-Manṣūr in 142/759, settling in the regions of al-Gharb, Beirut, and Sinn al-Fīl. Their task was to stop the raiding of the Marada, whose banditry had reportedly reached all the way to Hama and Homs. It seems that the strategy was for the Arslān to implant themselves in precisely the same areas where the Marada were active, thereby depriving them of the ability to sow chaos. The Arslān confronted the Marada in several battles, the last of which took place in 875. After this point we hear nothing more about them as a serious threat.[91] If this information is correct, and if the Marada are indeed to be identified with the Jarājima, as seems likely, it suggests that they remained a disruptive force with plenty of military power through at least the ninth

[90] Salibi, *Maronite Historians*, 161–233.

[91] Ṭannūs ibn Yūsuf al-Shidyāq, *Kitāb akhbār al-aʿyān fī jabal Lubnān*, ed. Fuʾād Afrām al-Bustānī (Beirut: Manshūrāt al-Jāmiʿa al-Lubnāniyya, 1970), 2: 495–9; with discussion in Salibi, *Maronite Historians*, 179; see also Kurd ʿAlī, *Khiṭaṭ al-Shām*, 1: 68–9; Nejla M. Abu-Izzeddin, *The Druzes: A New Study of their History, Faith and Society*, 2nd edn (Leiden: Brill, 1993), 142–5 (which summarises these events without citing a source, though clearly Shidyāq). The major encounters took place at Antelias (c. 775–85, which rid the coast of the Marada), Sinn al-Fīl (791, which led to the destruction of many Marada villages), and Nahr Bayrūt (875, per the discussion below, note 92). The Banū Arslān were also responsible for repelling a Byzantine naval attack on the village of al-Awzāʿī (the site of the tomb of the famous jurist) near Beirut in 801. Interestingly, Shidyāq states that in 831, Hānī, the son of the emir Masʿūd, led troops to Egypt to take part in the suppression of the Copts, a clear reference to the famous Bashmūric revolts (see below, note 122). The Banū Arslān clearly specialised in controlling unruly Christians. Shidyāq's section on the Arslān emirs contains two further references to conflicts with the Marada: in 1081, where they are mentioned in connection with the Franks, and in 1293, in connection with the Mamluks. Given the time period and the well-known conflation of the terms 'Marada' and 'Maronites', these probably refer to the latter, not the former (in the sense of 'Jarājima'); see al-Shidyāq, *Akhbār al-aʿyān*, 1: 506, 509.

century. It also suggests that the Abbasid state attempted to check their influence by settling Arab tribesmen from outside in their historic domains – a classic strategy for neutralising a rural military threat.

Shidyāq's account is convincing because, despite its late date, it complements the story of the Jarājima found in earlier sources in two particular ways. First, Shidyāq states that the Arslān showed up in Lebanon in 759, precisely the year of Theodore's revolt. If true, this suggests that the two events were linked; indeed, it is possible that al-Manṣūr moved the Banū Arslān into Lebanon to contain Theodore and/or to forestall future revolts after his. Second, Shidyāq states that in 875, the Arslān fought the last of their major battles against the Marada at Nahr Bayrūt. Many rebels were killed or taken captive. He then reports that the leaders of the Marada, along with numerous prisoners, were dispatched to Baghdad, where they were presented to Caliph al-Mutawakkil as trophies of war. Al-Mutawakkil reacted by sending a letter to the emir of the Arslān, al-Nuʿmān, praising him for his bravery and skill. Along with this he dispatched a sword, a girdle and a black screen as gifts, presumably as symbols of the emir's sovereignty over the area. If this is true, then the battle of Nahr Bayrūt and the arrival of the Marada prisoners in Baghdad may help explain why the Jarājima lost their *jizya* exemption during the reign of al-Mutawakkil, as al-Balādhurī states.[92]

We do not have much information about the afterlife of the Jarājima on the Byzantine side of the frontier. What we do know has recently been analysed by Miloš Cvetković in a very thorough article.[93] We have already seen how Justinian II resettled 12,000 Jarājima in Byzantine Armenia in the wake of his peace treaty with ʿAbd al-Malik.[94] Thereafter, Theophanes describes the Byzantine guerillas who helped fend off the Arab siege of Constantinople in 717–18 as being 'like Mardaites', suggesting that they had inspired the fighting tactics of the imperial army, if not also joined it.[95] Stronger evidence comes from the *De administrando imperio* ascribed to Constantine Porphyrogenitus,

[92] For this passage, see al-Shidyāq, *Akhbār al-aʿyān*, 1: 399; cf. al-Balādhurī, *Liber expugnationis*, 161 (Arabic), *Origins*, 249–50 (English), though one wonders whether the *jizya* exemption was just a way of describing the impossibility of taxing a remote mountain population.

[93] Cvetković, 'Settlement of the Mardaites'.

[94] Constantine Porphyrogenitus, *De administrando imperio*, 94–5.

[95] Theophanes, *Chronographia*, 397 (Greek), *Chronicle*, 546 (English).

which mentions the existence of a 'captain general (*kapitanō*) of the Mardaites of Attaleia', a city on the southern coast of Asia Minor not far from the Arab frontier. In the tenth century, the emperor Alexander (r. 912–13) was persuaded to appoint a man named Aberkios to this post. Aberkios apparently belonged to a distinguished family which 'sprang from the race of the Saracens and continued as true Saracens in thought, manners, and religion'. This suggests that Aberkios and his high-ranking relatives may have been of Arab or Middle Eastern stock. If the title 'captain general of the Mardaites' was anything more than an honorific, therefore, it is possible they were descendants of the very Jarājima who had been resettled during the Umayyad period.[96]

Another work patronised by Constantine Porphyrogenitus, the *De ceremoniis*, specifies that the Mardaites of Attaleia took part in Byzantine naval offences against Syria. The group seems to have manned warships under the aforementioned captain general, and these were deployed as part of the empire's anti-Arab defences. The source also mentions the presence of Mardaite soldiers in the Peloponnesus, Nikopolis, and Cephalonia. It is unlikely that these groups came directly from Syria, but were probably resettled there via Attaleia. They numbered over 5,000 men.[97] It is important to note that these were not the only soldiers of eastern origin to be resettled in the western part of the empire: a century earlier, the Byzantines had stationed Khurramī troops in roughly the same area, that is, recruits from the failed quasi-Zoroastrian revolts that had rocked the Jibāl region during the 830s.[98] Again, it is hard to say whether these soldiers were Mardaites in the original sense of the term. By the tenth century, when the source was composed, it is

[96] Constantine Porphyrogentius, *De administrando imperio*, 240–3. If this Aberkios was indeed of Arab ancestry, it is tempting to imagine his name as a corruption of an Arabic *kunya*, i.e. 'Abū so and so'.

[97] Constantine Porphyrogenitus, *The Book of Ceremonies*, trans. Ann Moffatt and Maxeme Tall (Canberra: Australian Association for Byzantine Studies, 2012), 2: 654–7, 659–60, 662, 665, 668.

[98] Cvetković, 'Settlement of the Mardaites', 78; more broadly, Evangelos Venetis, 'Korramis in Byzantium', *Encyclopaedia Iranica*, https://iranicaonline.org/articles/korramis-in-byzantium (last accessed 28 February 2022); Patricia Crone, *The Nativist Prophets of Early Islamic Iran: Rural Revolt and Local Zoroastranism* (Cambridge; Cambridge University Press, 2012), 41–2, 46–76.

possible that the term 'Mardaite' referred mainly to units with loose origins among a particular people, but were now made up of diverse groups of fighters (not unlike the Scottish Highland regiments in the modern British army). By the same token, the Mardaites may have survived as a discrete community in Byzantium long after their relocation from Syria, and this may explain the continued use of the name.

2. Analysis and Conclusion

2.1. Confessional and social background

How does the foregoing help us answer some of the big questions surrounding the Jarājima in the history of Byzantium and the Islamic caliphate, particularly concerning life along the frontier of these two great empires?

Many scholars have puzzled over the religious identity of the Jarājima. Henri Lammens and Marius Canard both called them 'lukewarm Christians' (whatever that means), and there is also a long tradition of linking them with the Maronites, as we have seen.[99] The problem is that the medieval sources leave no hints as to what kind of Christians the Jarājima actually were. Given their geographic origins, it is safe to say that their native language was probably Aramaic rather than Greek or Arabic.[100] But as to whether they were Miaphysites or Chalcedonians is anyone's guess (and frankly, in the grand scheme of things, not very important). There was nothing stopping the Byzantines from forging alliances with non-Chalcedonians, as we see with Aksūmites, the Ghassānids, and the Armenians. But then again, the Miaphysites' real centre of gravity during the seventh and eighth century was not the mountainous area around Antioch – home to a proud and powerful Chalcedonian patriarchate – but the rural areas further to the east and north, especially the great monasteries where the bishops were often based.[101] The Chalcedonian

[99] Lammens, 'Mardaites', *EI*[1]; Canard, 'Djarādjima', *EI*[2].

[100] Later confirmation may come from the historian of Aleppo Ibn al-ʿAdīm (d. 660/1262), who remarks that Jabal al-Lukkām was locally known as 'Bayt Lāhā', which he says means 'House of God' in Syriac (*Bughyat al-ṭalab fī tārīkh Ḥalab*, 1: 420); this may be legendary, but by the same token it may say something about the region's Aramaic culture.

[101] Wolfgang Hage, *Die syrisch-jakobitsche Kirche in frühislamischer Zeit nach orientalischen Quellen* (Wiesbaden: Otto Harrassowitz, 1966), esp. 95–109 (for lists of bishoprics and monasteries).

connection is only slightly more plausible based on the close relationship between the Jarājima and the Byzantine Empire, the pro-Chalcedonian slant of the Greek reports about Theodore in Theophanes' *Chronicle*, and the reference to a monastery of the Jarājima in the *Life* of Christopher of Antioch, a Chalcedonian Melkite patriarch. If there is any reality to the claim that the Jarājima were connected to the Maronites, it lies in Jack Tannous's observation that the Monothelite position may have simply been the leading expression of Chalcedonian Orthodoxy in Syria during the early Islamic period.[102] This waned over time, however, due to the influx of Byzantine slaves during the Umayyad period and to the Byzantine reconquest of northern Syria in the tenth century.[103] Both of these events tilted the demographic scales towards Dyothelitism (that is, the Byzantine Orthodox or Melkite position on Chalcedon) and away from Monothelitism (that is, the Maronite position).

We are on firmer ground when it comes to the social background of the Jarājima. As the sources make clear, the broader 'Jarājima movement' was made up of several distinct camps. At the centre were the Jarājima themselves, presumably long-time residents of Jabal al-Lukkām, Christians in faith, probably Aramaic in culture, and most likely with a long tradition of banditry or mercenary activity before the rise of Islam. Indeed, we should see the Jarājima as part of the same lawless mountain world as Isauria, which was resistant to centralised political and military control for much of antiquity, as Brent Shaw has shown.[104]

The Jarājima came from the city of al-Jurjūma, meaning they had very local origins, even as they spread throughout the rest of the coastal mountains during the second half of the seventh century. Around them were local hangers-on. The most important of these were the 'Nabataeans' (*anbāṭ*), fellow Aramaic-speakers, but probably landless peasants without a strong

[102] Jack Tannous, 'In Search of Monothelitism', *Dumbarton Oaks Papers* 68 (2014), 29–68.

[103] On Byzantine captives changing the religious demography of Syria during the eighth century, see Tannous, 'In Search of Monothelitism', 34; Muriel Debié, 'Christians in the Service of the Caliph: Through the Looking Glass of Communal Identities', in Antoine Borrut and Fred M. Donner (eds), *Christians and Others in the Umayyad State* (Chicago: Oriental Institute of the University of Chicago, 2016), 53–71, here 63–4. On the Byzantine conquest of northern Syria in the tenth century and its alleged displacement of the Maronites, see Kamal Salibi, 'Mārūniyya', *EI2*, 12: 602–3; Salibi, *House of Many Mansions*, 90–1.

[104] Shaw, 'Bandit Highlands and Lowland Peace'.

tradition of fighting and warfare of their own. There were also escaped slaves, who like Maymūn may have originally been Byzantines, and were thus drawn to the Jarājima as an anti-Arab movement. The sources give the impression that the Jarājima accumulated these followers as time went on, providing refuge to groups who, like themselves, felt threatened by the rise of the Islamic state and saw something to be gained by giving it a bloody nose. It is less clear whether any of these hangers-on actually fought the Arabs. I am disinclined to think so, partly because al-Balādhurī states how the Jarājima, the Nabataeans, and the escaped slaves were separated by the Muslims once the revolt was over, suggesting that they may have never unified as a coherent fighting force (though of course, we must allow for polemical distortion in the description of the Jarājima as a magnet for the rural down-and-outs).[105] Instead, I am inclined to see the Jarājima as a magnet for a loose agglomeration of disenfranchised, rural Christians in the mountains. As we shall see below, we might compare theirs to other nativist uprisings in the early Islamic period, which drew on a similar cross-section of aggrieved rural communities. We might also compare the Jarājima and their allies to various colonial-era revolts in the New World centuries later, when African slaves and native Indians found common cause in resisting Spanish rule.[106]

2.2. A Byzantine revival?

What role did the Byzantines play in all this, and in what manner are the Jarājima representative of life along the imperial frontier? Specifically, would the Jarājima have rebelled had it not been for Byzantine instigation? The sources give the clear impression that the Jarājima were activated, coordinated, and led from outside. One suspects this also involved payments from the Byzantines, or at least promises of security, as we see fulfilled in the campaign to resettle the Jarājima in Byzantine Armenia after the peace treaty with ʿAbd al-Malik, or their evident resettlement in the region of Attaleia.[107]

[105] al-Balādhurī, *Liber expugnationis*, 160 (Arabic), *Origins*, 248 (English).

[106] For instance, see Erin Woodruff Stone, 'America's First Slave Revolt: Indians and African Slaves in Española, 1500–1534', *Ethnohistory* 60 (2013), 195–217, which chronicles a mixed African-Indian uprising in the colony of Santo Domingo in 1521.

[107] Constantine Porphyrogenitus, *De administrando imperio*, 94–5, 240–3.

Several sources describe Byzantine commanders reaching the Jarājima by sea, mooring on the coast of Lebanon, and ascending the mountains to meet them; in only one case do we read about Byzantine soldiers reaching the Jarājima by land.[108] There must have been much coordination across the border which goes unmentioned in the sources. By the same token, the absence of concrete information may also suggest that travel across the frontier was very perilous.

As we have already seen, the Byzantines attempted to reclaim territory from the Arabs several times during the course of the seventh century. We should see the Jarājima as an extension of this strategy, indeed, its most successful outcome.[109] Alexandria, for instance, was conquered by the Arabs in 21/642, but the city rebelled in 25/645 and was briefly retaken by the Byzantines. The Arabs managed to recover the city, repulsing a second Byzantine invasion in 31–2/652.[110] The Byzantines targeted other coastal cities, too, including Caesarea and Ascalon, but with little success.[111] Towns along the land frontier in Anatolia also switched sides, including Melitene and Germanikeia.[112] There were also fierce battles for control of strategic buffer zones such as Cyprus, Georgia, Armenia, and Caucasian Albania. In fact, the Byzantines may have had a hand in fomenting rebellions in these places during the seventh century.[113] On balance, however, with the exception of the Caucasus, the Byzantines do not seem to have succeeded in mobilising

[108] For sea landings, see Agapius, *Kitab al-ʿUnvan*, 492; *Chronicon ad annum 1234*, 1: 288; Ibn ʿAsākir, *Tārīkh madīnat dimashq*, 20: 145. For land crossing, see al-Balādhurī, *Liber expugnationis*, 161 (Arabic), *Origins*, 249 (English).

[109] For discussion of a possible Byzantine recovery, see Hoyland, *In God's Path*, 126–8.

[110] Gary Leiser, 'Alexandria (early period)', *EI3*. Booth has recently cast doubt on whether this reconquest actually happened: 'The Last Years of Cyrus, Patriarch of Alexandria († 642)', in Jean-Luc Fournet and Arietta Papaconstantinou (eds), *Mélanges Jean Gascou. Textes et études papyrologiques*, Travaux et Mémoires 20/1 (Paris: Association des Amis du Centre d'Histoire et Civilisation de Byzance, 2016), 509–58, here 515–17.

[111] M. Sharon, 'Ḳayṣariyya, Ḳayṣāriyya', *EI2*, 4: 841–2; al-Balādhurī, *Liber expugnationis*, 143 (Arabic); *Origins*, 219 (English).

[112] al-Balādhurī, *Liber expugnationis*, 185 (Melitene), 188 (Germanikeia) (Arabic), *Origins*, 289, 294 (English).

[113] Discussion in Forrest, 'Destroying the Brazen Wall', 56–7.

indigenous Christian resistance to Arab rule. This makes the Jarājima very unique.

But were the Jarājima and their foreign handlers actually interested in re-establishing Byzantine control over Syria? The sources, both Islamic and Christian, leave the abiding impression that the Jarājima were little more than hired guns, committed to sowing chaos in the Umayyads' backyard far more than in laying the foundations for renewed Byzantine rule. Theirs was a relationship of opportunity more than ideology. The highland spine stretching from Antioch in the north to Jerusalem in the south where the Jarājima were active was hardly a suitable base for a Christian statelet (as the French knew very well when they extended the borders of Mount Lebanon to include the coast and the Beqaa Valley, thereby forming *Le Grand Liban* for their Maronite Christian clients). We read of no efforts to conquer other regions of Syria, whether Tyre, Beirut, or Sidon on the coast, or Aleppo, Homs, or Damascus on the edge of the desert. There is also no evidence that the Jarājima or the Byzantines ever attempted to tax or otherwise administer the guerilla zone they temporarily controlled. This suggests that both groups were content to operate as gadflies – albeit very painful gadflies – rather than to launch the kind of operation that would lead to a full-scale Byzantine recovery from the frontier (comparable to what the Byzantines would achieve in precisely this area several centuries later).

The early Islamic period was marked by sporadic Christian protest against Arab rule. Interestingly, almost none of this opposition invoked the memory of the Byzantine Empire. This is in stark contrast to the situation in Iran, where local dynasties often invoked the memory of the Sasanian kings and the ancient Persian past. This was true from the third/ninth century onward – interestingly, at precisely the same moment that Iran was becoming more Islamic and less Zoroastrian. We see this clearly in the case of figures such as Mardāwīj ibn Ziyār (d. 323/935), founder of the Ziyārid dynasty in the Caspian, as well as the Būyids, *condottieri* from the highlands of Daylam who subjugated the Abbasid caliphs and styled themselves 'kings of kings'.[114] The

[114] Christian C. Sahner, 'Ending Islamic Rule in Medieval Iran? The Life and Times of Mardāwīj b. Ziyār (d. 323 H/935 CE)', in Stefan Heidemann and Katharina Mewes (eds), *The Reach of Empire: The Early Islamic Empire at Work* (Berlin: De Gruyter, 2023) (forthcoming);

obvious difference between Syria and Iran, of course, was that the Sasanian Empire was completely wiped out by the conquests, whereas the Byzantine Empire kept on keeping on, albeit in much diminished form.[115] Paradoxically, one wonders whether the disappearance of the Sasanian Empire rendered it a more malleable and palatable symbol for would-be rebels. It was appealing precisely because it had ceased to exist as a reality, and could thus be appropriated for a range of possible agendas, utopian, nativist, or otherwise.

By contrast, would-be Christian rebels in Syria had a far harder time channelling the symbolic power of Byzantium. Byzantium was still a living empire on the other side of the frontier, and its symbolic power was therefore less flexible. To nail one's colours to the mast of Byzantium was to form a potentially dependent relationship with a strong-willed foreign power. This brought possible benefits in the form of weapons and treasure, but it also meant that Byzantium might take control. What is more, Byzantium's agenda may not have aligned with that of a Christian insurgency on the Islamic side of the frontier; the fact that both parties were Christian did not necessarily mean they shared the same goals. Needless to say, Byzantium was completely off-limits for would-be Muslim rebels in Syria, even the most ferociously nativist ones. While some may have cooperated with the Byzantines from time to time as a matter of convenience, they did not invoke the pre-Islamic, Roman culture of Syria for symbolic ends (say, in the way that modern Syrian nationalists have done with figures such as Zenobia, Philip the Arab, or Julia Domna).

Wilferd Madelung, 'The Assumption of the Title *Shāhānshāh* by the Būyids and the "Reign of Daylam (*Dawlat al-Daylam*)"', *Journal of Near Eastern Studies* (1969) 28: 2, 84–108; 28: 3, 168–83; Clifford Edmund Bosworth, 'The Heritage of Rulership in Early Islamic Iran and the Search for Dynastic Connections with the Past', *Iran* 11 (1973), 51–62; Deborah G. Tor, 'The Long Shadow of Pre-Islamic Iranian Rulership: Antagonism or Assimilation?', in Teresa Bernheimer and Adam Silverstein (eds), *Late Antiquity: Eastern Perspectives* (Oxford: Oxbow Books, 2012), 145–63.

115 A point made famously by Walī ʾl-Dīn ʿAbd al-Raḥmān ibn Muḥammad Ibn Khaldūn, *The Muqaddimah: An Introduction to History*, trans. Franz Rosenthal (Princeton, NJ: Princeton University Press, 1969), 1: 329; on the reasons for the resilience of the Byzantine Empire, see now John Haldon, *The Empire That Would Not Die: The Paradox of Eastern Roman Survival, 640–740* (Cambridge, MA: Harvard University Press, 2016).

2.3. *The Jarājima and other nativist movements in the caliphate*

The only clue that the Jarājima had an ideological element in their revolt is the uprising of Theodore in the Beqaa Valley during the early Abbasid period. As we have already seen, Theodore was referred to as a 'king', wore a crown, and displayed a cross in public. Ibn ʿAsākir gives no further details about his programme, but it seems obvious that these were symbols of his imagined sovereignty and were designed to express his antipathy for Arabs and Islam. Paul Cobb has argued that Theodore may have been portraying himself as a messianic leader, not unlike the Emperor of the Last Days who is frequently mentioned in Christian apocalyptic literature of the period.[116] If this is so, the figure of the messianic king obviously incorporates symbols from the Byzantine imperial repertoire. Given the Jarājima's ancient connections with the Byzantines, this may be the precedent Theodore wished to invoke.

We should not forget that Theodore appeared at a time of messianic protest across the Abbasid caliphate, including the quasi-Zoroastrian revolts in Iran and Central Asia chronicled by Patricia Crone.[117] These movements mixed and matched elements of Islamic and pre-Islamic beliefs, often with the hopes of establishing utopian societies free from Arab rule. In his brief notice about Theodore, the Byzantine historian Theophanes interestingly notes that AM 6253/AD 759–60 also witnessed a revolt at Dābiq in northern Syria by a group known as the Maurophoroi ('wearers of black') – identifiable as the famous Rāwandiyya of early Islamic history. The Rāwandiyya were extreme partisans of the Abbasid family (hence the reference to 'black,' the colour of the Abbasid Revolution), going so far as to 'proclaim the caliph's son [i.e. al-Mahdī] to be a god, inasmuch as he was their provider'.[118] Clearly,

[116] Cobb, *White Banners*, 115; on the apocalyptic milieu of the period, see now Stephen J. Shoemaker, *The Apocalypse of Empire: Imperial Eschatology in Late Antiquity and Early Islam* (Philadelphia: University of Pennsylvania Press, 2018).

[117] Crone, *Nativist Prophets*, esp. 31–188.

[118] Theophanes, *Chronographia*, 431 (Greek), *Chronicle*, 597 (English). Elsewhere in Theophanes' *Chronographia*, 430 (Greek), *Chronicle*, 595 (English), the Rāwandiyya are described as Magians who threw themselves from walls in the expectation that they could fly to heaven, presumably as angels. This matches descriptions of the group found in Islamic sources, per Crone, *Nativist Prophets*, 86–91.

Theodore and the Jarājima revolted in an atmosphere of eschatological expectation connected with the changing of the political guard.

There are very few examples of violent unrest among Christians in the early Islamic period.[119] Rather, what we tend to find is unrest among marginalised Muslim groups, that is, aggrieved members of the broader ruling class who found themselves barred from accessing the highest echelons of political, economic, and military power. A classic example were the partisans of the Abbasid Revolution itself. These included Khurāsānī tribesmen – Arabs who resented the dominance of the Umayyads and their Syrian troops – and the recent Persian converts among whom they lived – who resented being treated as second-class citizens by their Arab overlords. Such groups were dangerous in the sense that, although outsiders to the immediate affairs of empire, they were still members of the broader Muslim elite. This meant they could mobilise armies and contest for political power. Christians and other non-Muslims, at least in the core territories of the empire, enjoyed few of these advantages, and therefore rarely rebelled.

When it comes to Christian resistance during the Umayyad and Abbasid periods, we do have examples of 'martyrs' who protested the dominance of Islam through dramatic acts of apostasy and blasphemy, as I have shown in my recent book. Despite their potential as symbols of resistance, however, they never inspired revolts or other acts of organised disobedience (with the possible exception of the so-called 'Córdoba martyrs', c. 850–9).[120] The early Islamic period also witnessed a series of uprisings which the sources characterise as tax revolts, and these were only slightly more successful. During these episodes, Christians protested the financial burdens imposed on them by the state in their capacity as *dhimmīs*.[121] A number of uprisings were quite disruptive. The revolt of Theodore and the Jarājima in 759–60 was a revolt against financial abuse – this abuse being the most obvious and aggressive way in which the state interfered in people's lives. So were the more famous Coptic uprisings in Egypt between the 720s and the 830s. The last of these, known as the Bashmūric Revolt, was especially devastating not only

[119] Sahner, *Christian Martyrs under Islam*, 191–8.

[120] Sahner, *Christian Martyrs under Islam*, 140–59, 216–21.

[121] For instance, a Christian revolt in Homs in 241/855, which was brutally suppressed by al-Mutawakkil, see al-Ṭabarī, *Annales*, 12: 1422–4; with discussion and further references in Moshe Gil, *A History of Palestine, 634–1099* (Cambridge: Cambridge University Press, 1992), 296–7.

because of its location in semi-inaccessible reaches of the Nile delta, but also because it drew in a wide cross-section of disenfranchised groups, not just Christians. This included Arab tribesmen who were also aggrieved by the fiscal policies of the state.[122]

Ultimately, however, none of these movements posed an existential threat to Muslim rule. Christians – and in particular Christian peasants – had limited ability to raise armies of their own and thus challenge the Arabs' hold on power. One of the very few examples other than the Jarājima is the uprising of a man named John of Dadai, who operated in the region of Mayyāfāriqīn in the 750s. He is mentioned in the *Chronicle of Zuqnīn* in Syriac, a source rich in detail about daily life in northern Mesopotamia at the start of the Abbasid period. John is said to have exploited a dispute between local Arabs and the new Abbasid power brokers, wreaking havoc and going so far as to kill the local governor. Throughout his revolt, he profited from a highly strategic base of operations: a mountainous village about a day's march from Mayyāfāriqīn, which was difficult for the Arabs to reach. Based on what we know, John was remarkably successful for a time, winning a number of battles and even foiling a plot to kill him. John's ambitions, however, were mainly local and never extended beyond his mountain base. The most one can say about John's ideology was that he was proudly self-sufficient, at one point telling his followers: 'Today, you know that there is no king to avenge our blood on these people [i.e. the Arabs]. If we ignore them, they will gather against us to remove us from the land along with all we have!'[123]

[122] Keiko Ohta, 'The Coptic Church and Coptic Communities in the Reign of al-Maʾmūn: A Study of the Social Context of the Bashmūric Revolt', *Annals of the Japan Association for Middle East Studies* 19 (2004), 87–116; Yaacov Lev, 'Coptic Rebellions and the Islamization of Medieval Egypt (8th–10th Century): Medieval and Modern Perceptions', *Jerusalem Studies in Arabic and Islam* 39 (2012), 303–44; Maged S. A. Mikhail, *From Byzantine to Islamic Egypt: Religion, Identity and Politics after the Arab Conquest* (London: I. B. Tauris, 2014), 75–6, 118–27, 189–91.

[123] *Incerti auctoris Chronicon Pseudo-Dionysianum vulgo dictum*, eds and trans. Jean-Baptiste Chabot, Ernest Walter Brooks and Robert Hespel, Corpus Scriptorum Christianorum Orientalium 91, 104, 121, 507, Scriptores Syri 43, 53, 60, 213 (Louvain: L. Durbecq, 1952–89), 3: 196–9 (Syriac); *The Chronicle of Zuqnīn, Parts III and IV, A.D. 488–775*, trans. Amir Harrak (Toronto: Pontifical Institute of Mediaeval Studies, 1999), 181–3 (English) (quote below at 181); discussion in Hoyland, *In God's Path*, 211; Sahner, *Christian Martyrs under Islam*, 194–5.

Mayyāfāriqīn was not far from the frontier, and one wonders whether John could have rallied troops from Byzantium if he had wanted to do so. Regardless, he did not call on the emperor or any governor, and this is the crucial difference between him and the Jarājima. The Jarājima were successful precisely because they had managed to link up with a great power on the other side of the frontier. We might think of the Byzantines as 'supercharging' what would have otherwise been a fairly minor mountain insurgency. This transformed the Jarājima from bandits and gadflies into a very serious threat to Umayyad rule.

Like a modern sectarian militia in Lebanon or Iraq, which rises above the obscurity of local politics thanks to funding from abroad (e.g. from Iran or the Gulf states), the Jarājima were transformed into the single most successful indigenous Christian insurgency of the period thanks to their Byzantine patrons. Here, geographic proximity was the key. The fundamental reason we do not see copycat movements like the Jarājima in Palestine or Egypt was that they were too far away from the Byzantine frontier to realistically supply them with men and arms (though a number of anti-Arab uprisings in seventh-century North Africa allegedly combined Berber and Byzantine troops, including those led by Kusayla and al-Kāhina, though there is no evidence of coordination with Constantinople).[124] The Jarājima were useful because they lived on the border. They were thus capable of communicating with the Byzantines, but also of extending their reach deep into Islamic territory. There were few groups who could accomplish something similar.

To sum up, the Jarājima were quintessential inhabitants of the frontier between the two empires. Although usually loyal to the Byzantines, they were opportunistic and fought on behalf of both sides throughout their history. They are emblematic of other groups along the border who found their political and strategic fortunes shaped by their liminal position between two great powers. Although the Jarājima were Christians, religion does not seem to have been a significant factor in their uprisings. Nor does ethnic identity.

[124] Yves Modéran, 'Kusayla, l'Afrique et les Arabes', in Claude Briand-Ponsart (ed.), *Identités et culture dans l'Algérie antique* (Mont-Saint-Aignan: Publications des universités de Rouen et du Havre, 2005), 423–57; Yves Modéran, 'De Masties à la Kâhina', *Aouras* 3 (2006), 159–83.

Rather, they were defined mainly by their geographic origins and sphere of activity, namely the coastal mountains of Syria and Lebanon.

Ultimately, it is not clear where the Jarājima came from. They are unknown to us from before the Arab conquests, when they suddenly step into the light of history, as if fully formed. The Jarājima did not appear overnight, of course. One suspects that, if we had the sources, there would be an interesting pre-history of the group to tell. But the circumstances of the seventh century prompted them to coalesce as a group in a way that had not happened before or at least had not been apparent to outsiders. The creation of a new border near their territory – a frontier between empires, religions, languages, and much else – seems to have been the electric spark that catalysed their sudden emergence.

7

THE CHARACTER OF UMAYYAD ART: THE MEDITERRANEAN TRADITION

Robert Hillenbrand

Introduction

The art of the Umayyads (661–750) has long been a magnet for scholarly attention, especially from around 1900 onwards, and with a particular focus on architecture and its decoration, since that accounts for most of what survives. Some of the greatest scholars of Islamic art, such as Creswell, Herzfeld,[1] Sauvaget,[2] Ettinghausen[3] and Grabar,[4] have sought to chronicle

[1] Ernst Herzfeld, 'Die Genesis der islamischen Kunst und das Mschatta-Problem', *Der Islam* I (1910), 27–63, 105–44; for an English translation by Fritz Hillenbrand and Jonathan M. Bloom, see 'The Genesis of Islamic Art and the Mshattā Problem', in Jonathan M. Bloom (ed.), *Early Islamic Art and Architecture* (Aldershot: Variorum, 2002), 7–86.

[2] See his review of Creswell's *Early Muslim Architecture* in *Revue des Études Islamiques* 12 (1938), 74–6; see Julian Raby, 'Reviewing the Reviewers', *Muqarnas* VIII (1991), 8–9. See also Jean Sauvaget, 'Châteaux umayyades de Syrie: Contribution à l'étude de la colonisation arabe aux Ier et IIe siècles de l'hégire', *Revue des Études Islamiques* (1967), 1–49, a posthumous assessment of Umayyad secular architecture; but his overview does not include either Umayyad religious architecture or the non-architectural material.

[3] Richard Ettinghausen, *Arab Painting* (Geneva: Skira, 1962) and Richard Ettinghausen, 'The Throne and Banquet Hall of Khirbat al-Mafjar', in Ettinghausen, *From Byzantium to Sasanian Iran and the Islamic World: Three Modes of Artistic Transference* (Leiden: Brill, 1972), 17–65.

[4] From his unpublished doctoral dissertation ('Ceremonial and Art at the Umayyad Court', Princeton University, 1954) to his final book, his engagement with Umayyad art could

that material and to unravel its complexities. In particular, Creswell's magisterial survey of that subject, first published in 1932 and then re-issued in expanded form in two gargantuan volumes in 1969,[5] has provided a solid foundation for all subsequent research, though of course not the last word.[6] And Grabar devoted perhaps his finest work to a comprehensive assessment of early Islamic art in its full historical, social, economic, religious and cultural context, and the Umayyad period was central to his argument.[7] More recently, the Umayyad contribution to textiles,[8] manuscript production[9] and

justifiably be regarded as the leitmotif of his scholarly career. In that book he had his final say on the monument to which he had returned at intervals throughout his adult life: Oleg Grabar, *The Dome of the Rock* (Cambridge, MA: Harvard University Press, 2006).

5 For a conspectus of how these books were received, see Raby, 'Reviewers', 5–11.

6 It is worth noting that the update of Creswell's work undertaken by James W. Allan, *K. A. C. Creswell, A Short Account of Early Muslim Architecture. Revised and supplemented by James W. Allan* (Aldershot: Scolar Press, 1989) faithfully reproduced the layout of Creswell's 1969 version of his *Early Muslim Architecture*, thereby signalling the widely accepted authority of that work.

7 Oleg Grabar, *The Formation of Islamic Art* (New Haven: Yale University Press, 1973), 2nd edn (New Haven: Yale University Press, 1987); for detailed comments on the changes made in the second edition, see the review by Robert Hillenbrand, *Oriental Art* N.S. XXXV/1 (1989), 46–7.

8 Avinoam Shalem, '"The Nation Has Put on Garments of Blood": An Early Islamic Red Silken Tapestry in Split', in Gudrun Bühl and Elizabeth D. Williams (eds), *Catalogue of the Textiles in the Dumbarton Oaks Byzantine Collection* (Washington, DC: Dumbarton Oaks, 2019), https://www.doaks.org/resources/textiles/essays/shalem.

9 François Déroche, *Qur'ans of the Umayyads: A First Overview* (Leiden: Brill, 2014); Ursula Dreibholz, 'Early Quran Fragments from the Great Mosque in Sanaa', *Hefte zur Kulturgeschichte des Jemen* 2 (Sanaa: Deutsches Archäologisches Institut Orient-Abteilung Aussenstelle Sanaa/Deutsche Botschaft Sanaa, 2003); Hans-Caspar Graf von Bothmer, 'Architekturbilder im Koran: Eine Prachthandschrift der Umayyadenzeit aus dem Yemen', *Pantheon* 45 (1987), 4–20; Hans-Caspar Graf von Bothmer, 'Spätantike Voraussetzungen der frühislamischen Koran-Handschriften in Sanaa', *Eothen: Jahreshefte der Gesellschaft der Freunde islamischer Kunst und Kultur* 2/3 (1991/2) [published 1994], 7–12; Hans-Caspar Graf von Bothmer, 'Die Anfänge der Koranschreibung: Kodikologische und kunsthistorische Beobachtungen an den Koranfragmenten in Sanaa', in Hans-Caspar Graf von Bothmer, Karl-Heinz Ohlig und Gerd-Rüdiger Puin (eds), 'Neue Wege der Koranforschung', *Magazin Forschung der Universität des Saarlandes* 1 (1999), 33–47.

metalwork[10] has attracted greater interest and has made a more nuanced appreciation of Umayyad art possible.[11]

Nevertheless, the great bulk of the published work on Umayyad art has taken the form of close-focus studies of individual monuments and their decoration, to the detriment of sustained attempts to identify the immanent characteristics of Umayyad art as a whole. The relatively few ventures in this latter direction have either been too brief,[12] as in some of the handbooks of Islamic art,[13] or have been too focused on a single building to permit extended reflections of more general import.[14] That latter approach

[10] See the inlaid ewer from Baʿlabakk dated 122/739–40 recently acquired by the Dar al-Athar, Kuwait, and the iron and bronze brazier found in seven pieces in a palatial context in al-Fudayn, now in the Jordan Archaeological Museum (for a web page on this object, see Aida Naghawy, 'Brazier', in *Discover Islamic Art, Museum With No Frontiers*, 2022, https://islamicart.museumwnf.org/database_item.php?id=object;ISL;jo;Mus01;6 (accessed 7 January 2022).

[11] For reasons of space there will be no attempt to provide exhaustive documentation for the arguments presented in this chapter. In most cases (principally studies of architecture) the publications cited in the footnotes have a signposting function only and are merely intended to be triggers for further reading.

[12] K. Archibald C. Creswell, *A Short Account of Early Muslim Architecture* (Harmondsworth: Penguin Books, 1958), 156–8, and K. Archibald C. Creswell, *Early Muslim Architecture. Umayyads A.D. 622–750*, 2 vols (Oxford: Oxford University Press, 1969) II, 650–1. These summaries are little more than perfunctory so far as the Umayyad aesthetic is concerned, for their steady focus is on architectural elements and techniques. The minds that conceived the changes are left out of account.

[13] Katharina Otto-Dorn, *L'Art de l'Islam*, trans. Jean-Pierre Simon (Paris: Éditions Albin Michel, 1968), 64–5; Richard Ettinghausen and Oleg Grabar, *The Art and Architecture of Islam 650–1250* (Harmondsworth and New York: Penguin and Viking Penguin, 1987), 74; Jonathan M. Bloom and Sheila S. Blair, *Islamic Arts* (London: Phaidon Press, 1997), 36–8; Richard Ettinghausen, Oleg Grabar and Marilyn Jenkins-Madina, *Islamic Art and Architecture 650–1250* (New Haven: Yale University Press, 2001), 50–1; Rina Talgam, *The Stylistic Origins of Umayyad Sculpture and Architectural Decoration* (Wiesbaden: Harrassowitz Verlag, 2004), ix, 121–5; Jonathan M. Bloom and Sheila S. Blair (eds), *The Grove Encyclopedia of Islamic Art and Architecture* (Oxford: Oxford University Press, 2009), III, 370; Robert Hillenbrand, *Islamic Art and Architecture*, revised and expanded edn (London: Thames and Hudson, 2021), 14–19, 35–9.

[14] Daniel Schlumberger, 'Les fouilles de Qasr el-Heir Gharbi', *Syria* XX (1939), 357–60, which (as he fully acknowledges) is significantly indebted to Herzfeld, 'Genesis', especially 32. See also Robert Hillenbrand, 'Umayyad Woodwork in the Aqsa Mosque', in Jeremy Johns (ed.), *Bayt al-Maqdis: Jerusalem and Early Islam*, Oxford Studies in Islamic Art, IX, Part Two (Oxford: Oxford University Press, 1999), 303–8 ('The Umayyad Aesthetic').

has indeed consistently yielded significant results,[15] but it is nevertheless too easy to lose sight of their wider application. So, there is still ample room for an assessment of Umayyad art as a whole, concentrating on the wood rather than the trees, let alone the twigs. The evidence cited in the present chapter is for the most part familiar enough. But it is used here in an attempt to define an Umayyad aesthetic by probing the rationale that governed what was borrowed from earlier Mediterranean traditions.[16]

The Historical Context

It is worth recalling very briefly the political backcloth to this artistic process, familiar as it is. The whirlwind Arab conquests in the exact century following the death of the Prophet Muḥammad in 632 saw Muslim territory expand continuously, until it stretched from central France to the borders of China, the greatest empire the world had yet seen. Such conquests engendered a superb self-confidence. This was fostered by the apparently irresistible spread of Islam and by the limitless wealth which these conquests generated. Greater Syria, which encompassed modern Syria, Palestine, Israel, Lebanon and Jordan, a land thoroughly Hellenised over the previous millennium, became the centre of the new empire, with Damascus as its capital. So, these lands were favoured above all others by successive Umayyad caliphs, and indeed the history of Umayyad art can be written in its virtual entirety by material produced within them. That is why the classical heritage, whose works – Greek, Roman, Early Christian, Byzantine – were still to be seen so plentifully everywhere in this region, exerted such a powerful influence. In the course of the Umayyad century Greater Syria was transformed by glamorous religious buildings like the Dome of the Rock in Jerusalem and the Great Mosque of Damascus, and by massive investment in the countryside in the form of hydraulic installations, villas, hunting lodges and luxurious 'desert palaces'.[17]

[15] For example, Alain George, *The Umayyad Mosque of Damascus: Art, Faith and Empire in Early Islam* (London: Gingko, 2021), 185–213.

[16] For a stirring, inspirational *tour d'horizon* that contextualises the present chapter, see Peter Brown, *The Making of Late Antiquity* (London: Thames and Hudson, 1971); the last chapter focuses on the Umayyads.

[17] For the most comprehensive account of these monuments, see Denis Genequand, *Les Établissements des Élites Omeyyades en Palmyrène et au Proche-Orient* (Beirut: Institut Français du Proche-Orient, 2012).

The Umayyad Response to the Art of the Mediterranean World

This enquiry into the nature of Umayyad art, then, will be conducted in the particular context of what happened to the heritage of classical Graeco-Roman art (a term here used to include early Christian and Byzantine art as well) under Umayyad rule. The art of this century takes the Graeco-Roman, early Christian and Byzantine heritage down many unexpected paths, with its time-honoured conventions variously copied, adapted and thoroughly reworked in accordance with a constantly evolving aesthetic. That aesthetic used not only Graeco-Roman art but also the various subsets of Byzantine art[18] – Italian, Balkan, Syrian and Egyptian among them – in unprecedented ways. It also looked to the east, to the art of the recently defunct Sasanian empire and its provinces, and while that is a strand of Umayyad art that will not be explored in this chapter, its importance – which extends throughout the Umayyad period – should not be overlooked, and deserves separate and extended treatment.[19] The constant surprises that result from this rich pictorial patrimony reflect an art that was in a state of permanent flux for almost a century, and in which the rhythms of change varied from one medium to the next. In coinage and in epigraphy they were much faster than in architecture. A key factor in all these changes is that the princely patrons of this art had well-nigh bottomless financial resources at their disposal. So they had deep pockets – but also open minds, and it seems that somehow they were able to transmit that freedom of expression to the craftsmen who worked for them. Umayyad art reveals a joyous lack of unthinking dependence on the models of the past, an absence of the constraints imposed by long-established artistic conventions. It rejoices in bold juxtapositions of forms previously kept separate from each other, in familiar motifs changed beyond recognition by being greatly enlarged or greatly reduced, or transposed from familiar to unfamiliar

[18] These are outlined with exemplary clarity and depth in Ernst Kitzinger, *Early Medieval Art* (repr. London: British Museum, 1983), a classic account which has worn very well and lost none of its significance.

[19] Alastair Northedge, *Studies on Roman and Islamic ʿAmmān: The Excavations of Mrs C.-M. Bennett and Other Investigations. Volume I: History, Site and Architecture* (Oxford: Oxford University Press for The British Institute at Amman for Archaeology and History, 1992), 100–4, and Ettinghausen and Grabar, *Art and Architecture*, 74.

contexts in which changes of setting (from cramped to open, from urban to rural) or scale (from large to small and vice versa), of location and of material all played their part. This art ignores the borders that separated distinct pictorial traditions and had long served to police them. Artists from many different traditions now worked together on these Umayyad buildings,[20] many of them conscripted by the corvée or *leiturgia* system, with consistently unpredictable results. They would have been intrigued and inspired by these unlooked-for encounters, spurred to emulate and outdo each other. Yet this eclectic and experimental art, with its delicious lack of inhibition and its occasional vein of parody, could also take on a political and proclamatory role of the utmost seriousness.

Three Guiding Principles

So much for the wider context of this chapter. It is now time to investigate in more detail the guiding principles behind the Umayyad art that developed out of the Mediterranean tradition. The arguments developed in this chapter suggest that they can be summarised in three words: imitation, adaptation and transformation. This is not to suggest that some master plan based on these three headings was in operation – as Hamilton somewhat ironically observed, 'Arabia bred no art historians'[21] – and no doubt other themes could be proposed. But for the purposes of the present enquiry, it seems worthwhile to test the validity of these three guiding principles against the surviving evidence and to explore their implications. To cite merely one or two examples would not suffice to prove the point, so the net will be cast as widely as the limitations of space in this chapter will allow. The more that the evidence reveals the outworking of these principles across multiple media and contexts, the more their validity is corroborated. Naturally there will be overlap between these three categories, nor should one expect them to unfold in smooth chronological sequence. Examples of imitation are apt to contain elements of adaptation,

[20] Mshattā provides the clearest case; see Herzfeld, 'Genesis', 142; his training in classical architecture sharpened his eye for mouldings (a skill which is rare among Islamic art historians; see his fig. 18) and allowed him to demonstrate that masons from the northern Jazīra had worked on the site (Herzfeld, 'Genesis', 113–6, 139–40).

[21] Robert W. Hamilton, 'Khirbat al Mafjar: the Bath Hall reconsidered', *Levant* 10 (1978), 128.

while some aspects of adaptation can easily shade over into transformation. After all, what Umayyad art presents is not a set of three carefully packaged and policed categories, each clearly demarcated in both time and nature from the next. Rather should one view it as a spectrum, and the pace of change along that spectrum is uneven: sometimes fast, sometimes slow.

Imitation

Imitation is obviously the first category and also the least controversial. It stands to reason that the dizzying speed of the Arab conquests would very quickly have brought the new lords of Greater Syria face to face with hundreds of monuments and artefacts of a kind not readily to be found in Arabia. This is not to deny that Arabia had a material culture of its own, nor even that this culture included elements of Mediterranean origin.[22] Byzantine coinage circulated there; the churches of southern Arabia bore, if only at several removes, the imprint of Byzantine culture; and some temples employed basic components (columns, capitals, mouldings) derived from the Graeco-Roman and Byzantine heritage. But, in general, the sheer quantity and sophistication of the material culture of Greater Syria would have created an immediate problem for the Umayyad elite, steeped as its members were in the very different cultures of pagan and early Islamic Arabia. How were they to respond to a challenge that was primarily cultural rather than political, though of course it was big with political implications? Imitation was obviously the speediest and also the most practical solution, for the conquerors did not bring with them an army of Arabian craftsmen. The existing local workforce, moreover, had its own well-established traditions and practices, and these could not be changed overnight. Nor did the Arab conquerors immediately find their feet in their new environment. It is no accident that the first major example of Islamic architecture in Greater Syria – the Dome of the Rock in Jerusalem, 691–2 – was built almost sixty years after the conquest of that city.[23] So it took two generations to

[22] Barbara Finster, 'The Material Culture of Pre- and Early Islamic Arabia', in Finbarr B. Flood and Gülru Necipoğlu (eds), *A Companion to Islamic Art and Architecture. Volume I. From the Prophet to the Mongols* (Hoboken, NJ: Wiley Blackwell, 2017), 61–88.

[23] For the exact date, see Sheila Blair, 'What is the Date of the Dome of the Rock?', in Julian Raby and Jeremy Johns (eds), *Bayt al-Maqdis: ʿAbd al-Malik's Jerusalem. Part One*, Oxford Studies in Islamic Art IX (Oxford: Oxford University Press, 1992), 59–87.

formulate the first monumental response to the implied challenge to the Muslims posed by the innumerable temples, churches and other monuments of Greater Syria.[24] And it is generally agreed that in its plan and structure the Dome of the Rock is a thoroughly Byzantine monument (Figure 7.1).[25] Its elevation places it squarely within the same family of buildings as the premier Christian structure in late antique Jerusalem, namely the Church of the Holy Sepulchre erected by the Emperor Constantine (Figure 7.2).[26] And there is more. For just as the Holy Sepulchre, a commemorative centralised structure, has a basilical church for communal prayer beside it, so does the Dome of the Rock, also a commemorative centralised structure, have the Aqṣā Mosque,

Figure 7.1 Jerusalem, Dome of the Rock, exterior.

[24] Since so much has disappeared in the last century, it is appropriate to cite the work, remarkably comprehensive in its own time, of Howard C. Butler, based on fieldwork carried out in the first two decades of the twentieth century: Howard C. Butler and Earl B. Smith, *Early Churches in Syria, Fourth to Seventh Centuries – Part One, History; Part II. Analysis* (Princeton, NJ: Princeton University Press, 1929).

[25] The issue is dealt with in encyclopaedic fashion by Creswell, *Early Muslim Architecture* I, 101–31.

[26] Charles Couasnon, *The Church of the Holy Sepulchre Jerusalem* (London: Oxford University Press for the British Academy, 1973); the resemblance is clearest in a reconstruction of its appearance c. 348; see William L. MacDonald, *Early Christian & Byzantine Architecture* (London: Studio Vista, 1968), fig. 10.

Figure 7.2 Jerusalem, Holy Sepulchre, reconstruction of its fourth-century form.

intended for communal prayer, nearby. The difference lies in the setting. The Christian site is cramped (Figure 7.3); the Muslim site is expansive and makes full use of the ample space of the Ḥaram al-Sharīf (Figure 7.4). Imitation was at work; but so was emulation, and the Muslims thought big.

The same formula of large-scale imitation modulated by minor alterations occurs at ʿAnjar (Figure 7.5), essentially a Muslim version of a Roman *colonia* (Figure 7.6)[27] complete with two colonnaded main streets which divide the urban space into quarters and whose intersection is marked by a public monument.[28]

[27] Such as Timgad: Mortimer Wheeler, *Roman Art and Architecture* (London: Thames and Hudson, 1964), 48–52 and figs 27–8.

[28] For a convenient summary, see Creswell, *Early Muslim Architecture* II, 478–81; Barbara Finster, 'Anjar: spätantik oder frühislamisch?', in Karin Bartl and ʿAbd al-Razzāq Moaz (eds), *Residences, Castles, Settlements: Transformation Processes from Late Antiquity to Early Islam in Bilad al-Sham* (Rahden: Verlag Marie Leidorf, 2008), 229–42; and Beatrice Leal, 'ʿAnjar: An Umayyad image of urbanism and its afterlife', in John Mitchell, John Moreland and Beatrice Leal (eds), *Encounters, Excavations and Argosies: Essays for Richard Hodges* (Oxford: Archaeopress, 2017), 172–89.

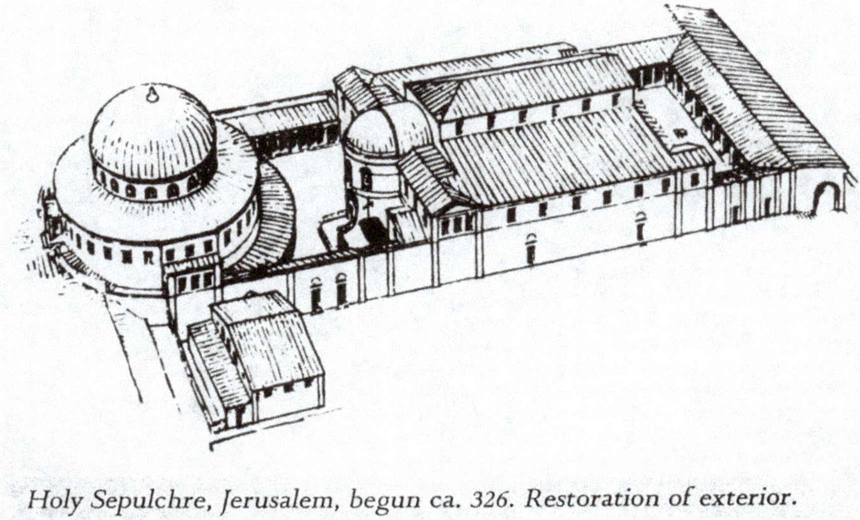
Holy Sepulchre, Jerusalem, begun ca. 326. Restoration of exterior.

Figure 7.3 Jerusalem, Holy Sepulchre and adjacent basilica, reconstruction.

Figure 7.4 Jerusalem, Ḥaram al-Sharīf, aerial view.

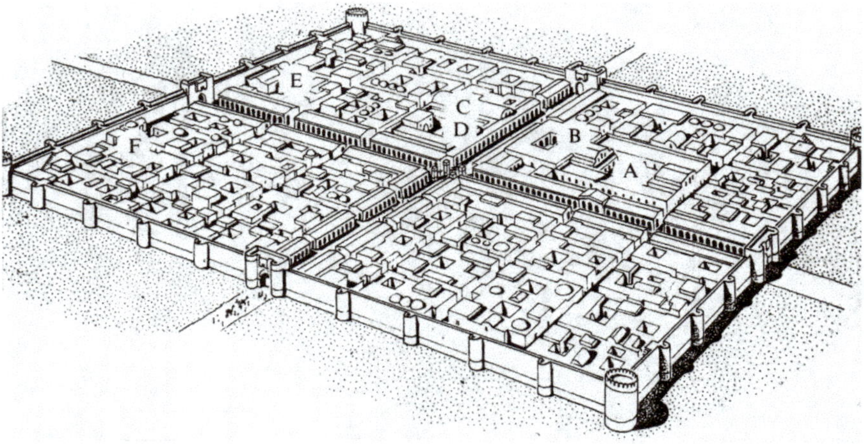

Figure 7.5 ʿAnjar, reconstruction.

Figure 7.6 Timgad, Algeria, aerial view.

Figure 7.7 ʿAnjar, main street.

But shoe-horned into that familiar Roman model, and respecting the overall grid that is the defining characteristic of this site, is a monumental palace. Like the shops behind the colonnaded streets (Figure 7.7), this is an unexpected variation on an established model. Recent excavations have uncovered earlier structures on this site,[29] but there is no doubt that ʿAnjar is essentially an Umayyad foundation.

A third example of what might be termed imitation plus is Quṣair ʿAmra. This is a bath house whose major accent externally is a triple row of barrel vaults (Figure 7.8), a formula illustrated some five centuries earlier in the hunting baths at Leptis Magna on the Libyan coast (Figure 7.9); both structures, though diminutive, are a study in powerful solid geometry.[30] In both sites the paintings of the interior feature hunting scenes.[31] But the addition of a miniaturised audience hall

[29] Aila Santi, 'ʿAnjar in the shadow of the church? New insights on an Umayyad urban experiment in the Biqāʿ Valley', *Levant* 50 (2019), 1–14.

[30] Claude Vibert-Guigue and Ghazi Bisheh, *Les Peintures de Qusayr ʿAmra: Un bain omeyyade dans la* bâdiya *jordanienne* (Beirut: Institut Français du Proche-Orient, 2007), pl. 90 (Quṣair ʿAmra); Wheeler, *Roman Art and Architecture*, 16, 57 and pl. 38 (Leptis Magna).

[31] Martin Almagro, Luis Caballero, Juan Zozaya and Antonio Almagro, *Qusayr ʿAmra: Residencia y Baños Omeyas en el Desierto de Jordania* (Madrid: Ministerio de Asuntos Exteriores, Dirección General de Relaciones Culturales; Junta para la Protección de Monumentos y

Figure 7.8 Quṣair ʿAmra, exterior.

Figure 7.9 Leptis Magna, hunting baths.

at Quṣair ʿAmra takes the Roman model into new territory, so that once again something more than straight imitation of art work.

Bienes Culturales en el Exterior; Instituto Hispano-Árabe de Cultura, 1975), 178 (Quṣair ʿAmra); Wheeler, *Roman Art and Architecture*, 39 (Leptis Magna).

The principle of imitation extends into other media, as two examples illustrate. The first is coinage.[32] In the decades following the Arab conquest of Greater Syria, the decision was taken to make no change in the gold coinage. The first Umayyad caliph, Muʿāwiya, issued an experimental Islamic coinage early in his reign which triggered such a furious backlash that he speedily withdrew it from circulation, and indeed no specimens of these coins have survived.[33] Moreover, the Umayyads were constrained to rely on Byzantium for their denominations in gold. The standard design had an obverse featuring the Byzantine emperor flanked by two junior co-emperors of slightly smaller stature. They wore crowns with crosses and held orbs which also bore a cross. At some stage (these coins bear no dates) these crosses, which were clearly offensive to Muslim tastes, were removed – a minor but assuredly strategic change.[34] In the same way the cross on steps on the reverse had its cross-bar removed so that it became a staff or pole.[35] These changes were small, so that the overall appearance of these coins at first glance (which was probably what mattered most) was not seriously affected; but they were not trivial.

32 Luke Treadwell, 'The Formation of Religious and Caliphal Identity in the Umayyad Period: The Evidence of the Coinage', in Flood and Necipoğlu, *Companion*, 89–108.

33 Andrew Marsham, *Rituals of Islamic Monarchy: Accession and Succession in the First Muslim Empire* (Edinburgh: Edinburgh University Press, 2009), 87, citing the anonymous Maronite Chronicle.

34 The basic source is John Walker, *A catalogue of the Arab–Byzantine and post-reform Umaiyad coins* (London: Trustees of the British Museum, 1956). For a fine overview, see Michael L. Bates, 'History, Geography and Numismatics in the First Century of Islamic Coinage', *Revue Suisse de Numismatique* 65 (1986), 231–62; Michael L. Bates, 'The Coinage of Syria Under the Umayyads, 692–750 A.D.', in Muḥammad A. Bakhīt and Robert Schick (eds), *The History of Bilad al-Sham During the Umayyad Period, Fourth International Conference, 1987, Proceedings of the Third Symposium* (ʿAmmān: Bilad al-Sham History Committee, 1989), 195–228; Luke Treadwell, 'The Formation of Religious and Caliphal Identity in the Umayyad Period: The Evidence of the Coinage', in Flood and Necipoğlu, *Companion*, 89–108. See also the papers in Tony Goodwin (ed.), *Arab–Byzantine Coins and History. Papers presented at the Seventh Century Syrian Numismatic Round Table held at Corpus Christi College, Oxford on 10th and 11th September 2011* (London: Archetype Publications, 2012).

35 Nadia Jamil, 'Caliph and *qutb*: Poetry as a source for interpreting the transformation of the Byzantine Cross on Steps on Umayyad coinage', in Johns, *Bayt al-Maqdis*, 11–58.

A final example is the famous embroidered *ṭirāz* silk in the name of the Umayyad caliph Marwān, probably of late Umayyad date.[36] It employs a familiar late antique formula, namely a repetitive series of double concentric medallions, each circular band filled with decorative motifs, in this case dots. In Byzantine and Coptic textiles such medallions typically contain a figural centrepiece – affronted or addorsed horsemen, winged horses, putti, pagan divinities, busts or Christian religious scenes.[37] In this Umayyad textile, however, the figural theme is replaced by an abstract one, a saltire cross superimposed on a rosette,[38] and this emphasis recurs in the red silk from Split for which an Umayyad date has been proposed.[39] In the case of the Marwān silk the alteration does not change the rhythm of repeated double medallions, but the removal of figural motifs does entail a lack of iconographic charge.[40] In

[36] Albert F. Kendrick, *Catalogue of Muhammadan Textiles of the Medieval Period* (London: HMSO, 1924), 34, and Gillian Vogelsang-Eastwood, 'Embroidered tiraz', in Gillian Vogelsang-Eastwood (ed.), *Encyclopedia of Embroidery from the Arab World* (London: Bloomsbury Academic, 2016), 140–50, especially 140–1. For comparable material in the Metropolitan Museum of Art, see Daniel Walker, 'Textiles in the Metropolitan Museum of Art', *The Metropolitan Museum of Art Bulletin*, n.s., 53/3 (1995–6), 15. Recent research has demonstrated a far wider variety of themes, including figural ones, in textiles that are either certainly or probably Umayyad than earlier scholarship had suggested; see Elizabeth D. Williams, 'A Taste for Textiles: Designing Umayyad and ʿAbbāsid Interiors', in Bühl and Williams, *Catalogue*, especially figs. 3–13 (https://www.doaks.org/resources/textiles/essays/Williams). Indeed, the groundbreaking articles by Shalem and Williams propel the study of Umayyad textiles to a new level of sophistication and reinstate the important role of that medium in the art of that time. For the role of textiles in architecture, see Kathrin Colburn, 'Loops, Tabs, and Reinforced Edges: Evidence for Textiles as Architectural Elements', in Bühl and Williams, *Catalogue*, https://www.doaks.org/resources/textiles/essays/colburn.

[37] W. Fritz Volbach, *Early Decorative Textiles*, trans. Yuri Gabriel (Feltham: Paul Hamlyn, 1969), pls. 27 and 33–7, 47 and 50–2; Pierre du Bourguet, *Coptic Art*, trans. Caryll Hay-Shaw (London: Methuen, 1971), 78; Klaus Wessel, *Coptic Art*, trans. Jean Carroll and Sheila Hatton (London: Thames and Hudson, 1965), pls. 104 and 115.

[38] Coptic parallels for this feature do exist as in Wessel, *Coptic Art*, pls. XX and XXI, but in conjunction with a figural centrepiece. It is the move from background motif to main motif that is typically Umayyad.

[39] Shalem, 'Garments of Blood', last paragraph.

[40] It is important to recognise that the Marwān silk, as its inscription indicates, is the product of princely patronage; at the more everyday level, early Islamic textiles in Egypt maintain much

each of these cases, then, simple imitation is enriched by an extra factor not present in the pre-Islamic model.

Adaptation

The next stage, which can be encountered at almost any time in the Umayyad century, can be covered by the umbrella term 'adaptation'. This tends to express itself in one of two ways. The first way is the adoption of an earlier form which is then given an extra element or a new function. The second way, which is a pervasive Umayyad characteristic, typically involves no change of the form itself, but uses it in an unexpected way, and this will be analysed below.

An outstanding example of the first type of adaptation is the so-called 'desert castle'. As the Arab armies poured out of Arabia into Byzantine territory, they would have encountered the fortresses which the Romans had erected to protect the southern frontier of Greater Syria: the *Limes Arabicus*.[41] These were not glamorous buildings; they were strategically sited to control the major long-distance routes with a minimum of resources. A set formula quickly evolved: a walled square of seventy metres per side with corner bastions and a portal flanked by towers. The stone masonry and high walls discouraged opportunistic attacks. Inside, the facilities were spartan: basic accommodation for a small garrison disposed around an open courtyard. One might consider this an unpromising model for the super-rich luxury-loving Umayyad elite to adopt. But by a stroke of imaginative genius that unpromising interior took on the lineaments of the standard Roman or late-antique villa furnished with the appurtenances of gracious living (Figure 7.10). The interior was remodelled, sometimes on two floors with the princely apartments upstairs and with the courtyard articulated by pillars or arcades with accommodation for the princely retinue in a series of adjoining chambers set

of the Coptic preference for figural designs (Georgette Cornu and Marielle Martiniani-Reber, *Tissus d'Egypte. Témoins du monde arabe VIIIe–XV siècles. Collection Bouvier* (Paris: Société Présence du Livre, 1993), 29, 40–1, 43, 46–7, 50–1, 54–5, 62–5, 67, 71, 78–83, 94–5, 97–107, 109–11, 113).

41 S. Thomas Parker, *Romans and Saracens: A History of the Arabian Frontier* (Philadelphia: American Schools of Oriental Research, 1986).

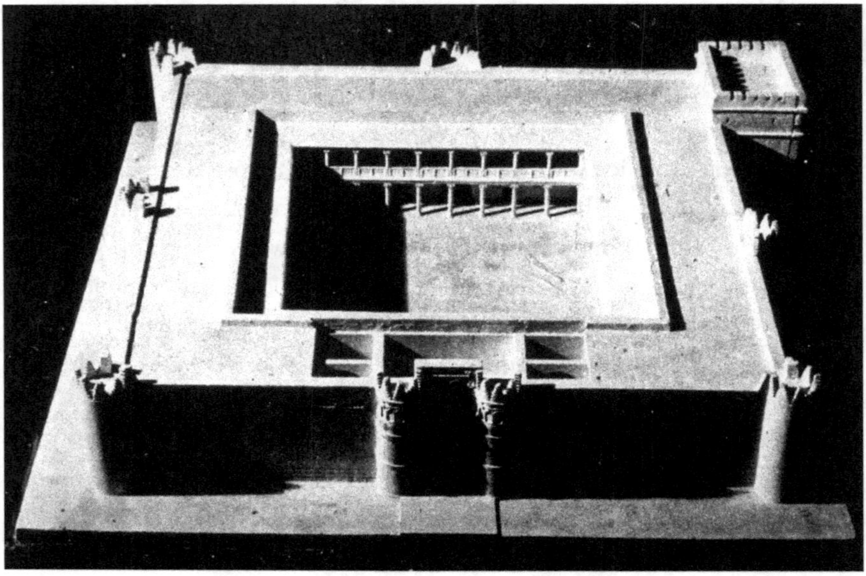

Figure 7.10 Qaṣr al-Ḥair al-Gharbī, model.

further back. A new system was introduced for these, involving units (*baits*) comprising rooms disposed symmetrically around a miniature courtyard, an echo of a Roman villa (Figure 7.11).[42] Luxurious painted or carved decoration proclaimed the owner's wealth and status. The austere military gateway, with its Syrian machicoulis, was sometimes incorporated with little change into Umayyad palatial architecture,[43] but it could also lose all pretension to a defensive purpose and be festooned with overall ornament (Figure 7.12).[44] This was essentially a shotgun marriage between two building types that were kept far apart in their parent culture. The scale of these forts was well suited for a compact secular palace, and its fortified character was especially suitable for a princely Arab elite that ruled an overwhelmingly Christian population and for whom security was a critical factor. That elite did not adapt the

[42] Creswell, *Early Muslim Architecture* II, 386, 588. For a colour view of a typical Roman townhouse, see Wheeler, *Roman Art and Architecture*, fig. 106.

[43] As at Qaṣr al-Ḥair al-Sharqī (Creswell, *Early Muslim Architecture* II, 526–7, 540–2).

[44] The outstanding example is Qaṣr al-Ḥair al-Gharbī; it is noteworthy that its gaudy façade retains its upper ramparts. But these are for show only, for there was no walkway behind them.

Figure 7.11 Pompeii, villa of the Vettii.

forts themselves to new purposes, as distinct from converting churches into mosques,[45] but instead erected new buildings closely based on these forts, for example in their dimensions and their external military aspect. Moreover, in several cases these new palaces became the centres of agricultural estates with an expensive infrastructure of dams, irrigation canals and even game parks.

What of the second type of adaptation, in which the basic form remains recognisable? Here the change is one of context, location, material or scale. That might sound innocuous, but in practice such apparently minor changes spring major surprises because a familiar form is being used in an unfamiliar

[45] The classic case of this process is at Ḥamā; see Poul J. Riis, 'Temple, Church and Mosque', *Historisk-filosofiske Meddelelser udgivet af Det Kongelige Danske Videnskabernes Selskab* 40: 5 (1965), 3–49. See also Mattia Giudetti, 'Sacred Topography in Medieval Syria and its Roots between the Umayyads and Late Antiquity', in Antoine Borrut and Paul M. Cobb (eds), *Umayyad Legacies: Medieval Memories from Syria to Spain* (Leiden: Brill, 2010), 343–52; Mattia Giudetti, 'Sacred Spaces in Early Islam', in Flood and Necipoğlu, *Companion,* I, 130–50.

Figure 7.12 Qaṣr al-Ḥair al-Gharbī, gateway.

way, and this changes its nature. Any one of the four subsets of change just enumerated would have forced viewers long accustomed to pre-Islamic conventions to perform a double take.

But when such a viewer encountered more than one of these subsets used together, the surprise would have been intensified. For such changes demanded some serious lateral thinking. Take, for example, the surface of the inner drum of the Dome of the Rock – an immense band, almost a quarter of a kilometre in length and some six metres in height. Its mosaic decoration comprises regularly spaced bejewelled vases from which sprout concentric circles formed of half-open buds, each producing a replica of itself.[46] The effect is of an immense jungle of dense vegetation. A close parallel for a single scroll of this kind, executed in mosaic tesserae of similar colours, can be found tucked away inconspicuously in the spandrel of a minor vault in an upper room of Haghia Sophia in Constantinople (Figure 7.13).[47] Thus the essence of this spectacular drum decoration in Jerusalem is borrowed from Byzantine art. But it has been magnified a thousandfold and now has not just a place of honour in the interior, but has become its single dominant accent. That gives an abstract vegetal motif a previously unheard-of prominence. In terms of scale, it is a promotion from the tiny to the gigantic; in terms of setting, a promotion from an easily overlooked afterthought to pride of place

Figure 7.13 Haghia Sophia, scroll in vault of upper room.

[46] The core design of this immense, apparently endless unfolding scroll is best appreciated in a detail; see Richard Ettinghausen, *Arab Painting* (Geneva: Skira, 1962), 21.

[47] For a colour plate, which emphasises the close link with the Jerusalem mosaic, see Ekrem Akurgal, Cyril Mano and Richard Ettinghausen, *Treasures of Turkey: The Earliest Civilizations of Anatolia. Byzantium. The Islamic Period* (Geneva: Éditions d'Art Albert Skira, 1966), Akurgal, 96.

(Figure 7.14). These two changes work in tandem to powerful dramatic effect. A broadly similar double change, involving both context and scale, can be seen at the palace of Mshattā.[48] Here a zigzag motif with an infill of rosettes, embedded in a small-scale geometric panel found in a vault of the Great Temple at Baʿlabakk,[49] is applied to the decoration of the entire external façade of the central, royal section of the palace. But now it is on a hugely magnified scale, some thirty-three metres long and about five metres high (Figure 7.15). A third example is the Great Mosque of Damascus, which uses the multiple naves of a standard basilical church but changes the orientation of prayer from west–east to north–south, so that the spatial experience of the worshipper is decisively different. It also moves the main triple-arched entrance block, which was a standard feature of monumental Syrian churches,[50] from the west

Figure 7.14 Jerusalem, Dome of the Rock, drum.

[48] Creswell, *Early Muslim Architecture* II, pls. 1112b, 113a.

[49] Creswell, *Early Muslim Architecture* I, fig. 114.

[50] Andrée Claire and Marc Balty, *Pierres Chrétiennes de Syrie* (Paris: Éditions Eric Koehler, 1998), 34 (Kharab Shams), 79 (Dair Semaan), 88–9 (St Simeon) and 151 (Baqirba).

Figure 7.15 Mshattā, façade.

front to the centre of the southern courtyard façade, thereby asserting the new importance of the transverse axis facing Mecca.

The Sub-sets of Adaptation: Context, Location, Medium and Scale

So much for the impact of these apparently minor changes when used in concert. Shortage of space forbids a fully detailed assessment of the four subsets of the theme of 'adaptation' listed above, so a single example of each must suffice. What of context? The frontier fort was not the only building type that was given an unexpected makeover and a new function in Umayyad times. The bath hall at Khirbat al-Mafjar illustrates how the Roman triumphal arch, found in scores of sites across the entire Mediterranean world (Figure 7.16), was pressed into service as a portal, losing its distinctive free-standing character in the process.[51] Thus a long-familiar form found a new lease of life in an unexpected context. Nonetheless, it retained its characteristic division into

[51] Robert W. Hamilton, *Khirbat al Mafjar: An Arabian Mansion in the Jordan Valley* (Oxford: Clarendon Press, 1959), 92–103 and pl. CVII.

Figure 7.16 Leptis Magna, triumphal arch of Septimius Severus, reconstruction.

a sequence of horizontal superposed tiers, and also its emphasis on figural decoration (Figure 7.17). So the Roman origin of the design is plain enough. Minor changes can easily be identified – the round arch acquires a pointed profile; the fluting of the columns is replaced by a series of horizontal bands, each with a different kind of ornament; the design is complicated by squeezing in three niches; and it is rounded off by crenellations which lend the whole a mildly military aspect. The most important change is that the entire layout is dominated by a centrally placed princely image, in all probability depicting al-Walīd ibn Yazīd, the heir apparent and the patron of the entire site.[52]

[52] Robert W. Hamilton, 'Who built Khirbat al Mafjar?', *Levant* I (1969), 61–7.

Figure 7.17 Khirbat al-Mafjar, bath hall, portal, reconstruction.

The next subset to be considered is location, which may seem a trivial matter but well illustrates the ability of the craftsmen working under Umayyad direction to invigorate forms which had become stale by dint of frequent use in the same place. Thus Creswell demonstrated that the marble grilles of the Great Mosque of Damascus were laid out in a scheme based on equilateral triangles in the same way as many a Roman and late antique floor mosaic.[53] Geometric window grilles are commonly found in Byzantine architecture[54] but none of them approach the complexity of the Damascus examples, whereas complex geometric patterns are a standard feature of Roman and Byzantine floor mosaics in Greater Syria.[55] The critical change was to borrow inspiration from floor mosaics for a new use as window grilles, and to intensify the impact of that change in location by the choice of a new material and technique, namely carved openwork marble.

The switch of a given motif from one medium to another is the third subset of the adaptation theme, and it is pervasive in Umayyad art. One of its boldest expressions is the floor painting at the palace of Qaṣr al-Ḥair al-Gharbī featuring a personification of the goddess of the earth, Ge or Gaia (Figure 7.18).[56] The theme itself, executed in roundel form, was a sufficiently familiar one in Coptic textiles,[57] in Roman art[58] and in the floor mosaics of Syrian churches.[59] But because of its idolatrous flavour one would not

[53] Creswell, *Early Muslim Architecture,* I, 202–4, fig. 92 and pl. 59a-d; cf. the floor mosaic of the probably late fourth-century church at Shiloh; see Rina Talgam, *Mosaics of Faith: Floors of Pagans, Jews, Samaritans, Christians, and Muslims in the Holy Land* (Jerusalem and University Park, PA: Yad Ben-Zvi Press and The Pennsylvania State University Press, 2014), 158–9 and fig. 250.

[54] Richard Krautheimer, *Early Christian and Byzantine Architecture* (Harmondsworth: Penguin Books, 1965), pls. 69, 74, 80–2, 86–7, 109, 111A, 115; Heinrich G. Franz, 'Die Stuckfenster im Qasr al-Hair al-Gharbi', *Wissenschaftliche Annalen* 5 (1956), 468–72 and figs. I and II.

[55] Doro Levi, *Antioch Mosaic Pavements* I (Princeton, London and The Hague: Princeton University Press, Oxford University Press and Martinus Nijhoff, 1947), 373–489; Michele Piccirillo, *The Mosaics of Jordan* (ʿAmmān: American Center of Oriental Research, 1993), *passim*; and Talgam, *Mosaics of Faith, passim.* For the wider context of decorated floors in antiquity, see Fabio Barry, 'Walking on Water: Cosmic Floors in Antiquity and the Middle Ages', *The Art Bulletin* 89: 4 (2007), 627–56.

[56] Daniel Schlumberger, 'Deux Fresques Omeyyades', *Syria* XXV (1946–8/1–2), 86–102, remains the classic account, supplemented by Ettinghausen, *Arab Painting,* 33–7.

[57] Du Bourguet, *Coptic Art,* 78.

[58] Talgam, *Mosaics,* 65, 73, 209 and fig. 64.

[59] Talgam, *Mosaics,* 137, 181, 189, 207, 210, 277, 384 and fig. 277. Her fig. 268 (in colour) depicts a now partially defaced image of Ge in the Chapel of the Priest John at Khirbat al-Mukhayyāt, dated 565. Piccirillo, *Mosaics,* discusses this on 38 (with a drawing, fig. xxiii) and on 78; his fig. 226 shows its original state. His fig. 368 depicts another damaged Ge. The relatively frequent presence of personifications of Ge and other classical deities on church

Figure 7.18 Qaṣr al-Ḥair al-Gharbī, floor painting.

so readily expect to find it decorating the palace of a Muslim prince, let alone the caliph himself. It is likely to have offended pietistic Islamic visitors unschooled in the local artistic traditions.[60] But the most curious aspect of

floors in Greater Syria, especially in the sixth and seventh centuries, might suggest that these images were not regarded as idolatrous by Christian worshippers (but see the next note). Perhaps, then, the presence of this divinity in Hishām's palace would not have startled some contemporary viewers.

60 And possibly also pious Christians when images of classical deities were used in their floor mosaics; the early church specifically forbade such personifications as Ge, Thalassa Oceanus and Selena in the decoration of churches (Talgam, *Mosaics*, 192).

this work is its medium: paint. In contemporary Greater Syria, if floors were to be decorated with figural or vegetal ornament, the commonest medium was mosaic. Painted floors with such ornament, vulnerable as they were to regular footfall, were apparently unknown. So this is a dramatic break from convention. Here the location at the base of a stairwell, visible from above by those climbing the staircase that led to the royal apartments, would have protected it to some extent from daily wear and tear, but it would not have lasted long. Its preservation is the result of the great earthquake of 747 that brought down the whole palace. The reason for this novel and cheapskate solution to how to decorate a floor falls into place in the wider context of this entire palace and its decoration.[61] That palace was constructed of mud brick instead of stone; its principal decoration was in carved plaster rather than carved stone; and its walls bore broad and simplified approximations, executed in paint on plaster, of the complex natural graining of marble slabs used as a costly form of wall decoration in the elite buildings of late antiquity[62] – yet another switch of medium (Figure 7.19). This was a palace built in a hurry that employed numerous short cuts to keep costs down. That fits well with the famed stinginess of its lord, the caliph Hisham.[63]

The last subset of adaptation to be considered is scale. The drum mosaic of the Dome of the Rock and the façade of Mshattā have already been cited as examples of the metamorphosis of small-scale motifs to gigantic size. But the opposite process – a dramatic reduction in scale of a motif borrowed from an earlier tradition – is also frequently encountered in Umayyad art.

[61] See Robert Hillenbrand, 'Hishām's Balancing Act: The Case of Qaṣr al-Ḥair al-Gharbī', in Alain George and Andrew Marsham (eds), *Power, Patronage, and Memory in Early Islam: Perspectives on Umayyad Elites* (Oxford: Oxford University Press, 2018), 103.

[62] For example, the interior of San Vitale, Ravenna; see Jean Lassus, *The Early Christian & Byzantine World* (London: Paul Hamlyn, 1967), pl. 40. For the meanings that late antique viewers felt able to read into such decoration, see John Onians, 'Abstraction and Imagination in Late Antiquity', *Art History* 3: 1 (1980), 1–24.

[63] Francesco Gabrieli, *Il Califfato di Hisham: Studia di Storia omeyyade* (Alexandria: Société de publications égyptiennes, 1935), 133, 137; Julius Wellhausen, *The Arab Kingdom and its Fall*, trans. Margaret G. Weir (Beirut: Khayyats, 1963), 348–9; Khalid Y. Blankinship, *The End of the Jihād State: The Reign of Hishām ibn ʿAbd al-Malik and the Collapse of the Umayyads* (Albany: State University of New York Press, 1994), 79, 227, 302.

Figure 7.19 Qaṣr al-Ḥair al-Gharbī, painted walls.

The gateway of Qaṣr al-Ḥair al-Gharbī, prinked out with a farrago of stucco motifs, is a good example. Its heterogeneous assemblage of motifs, a true rag-bag – a feature it shares with the portal of the bath hall of Khirbat al-Mafjar – includes two unrelated borrowings from Palmyrene stone sculpture, totally decontextualised as if they were mere filler motifs. Here they are rendered in stucco, not stone, and above all much reduced in scale. They are marooned somewhat uncomfortably in an upper tier of the gateway, so high up that it would have been hard to distinguish them from ground level. One sculpture depicts a boy carrying a sheep; the other depicts that favoured Palmyrene theme, the funerary repast.[64] To make the necessary visual impact that its

[64] For the first, see Daniel Schlumberger, *Qasr el-Heir el Gharbi* (Paris: Librairie Orientale Paul Geuthner, 1986), 67f, identified as a shepherd carrying a lamb, and formerly part of the parapet decoration (there is no further discussion); for the second, ibid., 21 and pl. 64b; for a brief commentary on this theme, see Daniel Schlumberger, *L'Orient Hellenisé* (Paris: Éditions Albin Michel, 1970), 84. For a comparable Palmyrene example, see Annie Caubet, *Aux Sources du Monde Arabe* (Paris: Réunion des Musées Nationaux/Institut du Monde Arabe, 1990), 84; for more detail on the Palmyrene connection, see Talgam, *Umayyad Sculpture*, 118–9.

serious religious subject matter demands, such sculpture needs to be much larger and much more easily accessible to the viewer, as indeed it was in its original religious and funerary contexts. But the subject matter of these sculptures would of course have evoked no corresponding reverence from a Muslim audience. To diminish their scale so radically, and for good measure to place them virtually out of sight, is also to diminish their importance and indeed to trivialise them.[65] Once again, then, two subsets of adaptation, in these two cases changes in both location and scale, operate in tandem.

Transformation

The third and last major theme to be explored in this chapter could be termed 'transformation'. As with 'imitation' and 'adaptation', this is not a hard and fast category; it is not easy to define and it can be a matter of judgment to determine exactly where one category shades into another. A case in point is the bath hall at Khirbat al-Mafjar (Figure 7.20), whose core is clearly derived from a specific kind of Byzantine quincunx church whose popularity began in the sixth century with the celebrated Nea[66] and continued for a millennium and more in numerous variations. That aspect of the borrowing could be regarded as simple imitation. But the change of function from a building for religious worship to a building for musical and poetic performances, and for other entertainments, including erotic ones, is indeed a radical move, and is certainly a major adaptation. But the addition of bathing facilities, a kind of Star Chamber, a portal with imperial associations, a plunge bath designed to be filled with wine, and an entrance chamber whose upper reaches are enlivened by a half-naked gymnast[67] and a bevy of topless girls – all this surely adds up to a transformation.[68]

[65] The balustrades of Khirbat al-Mafjar, and the elaborately framed oculus which served as a window, illustrate respectively the diminution and the magnification of familiar motifs (Hamilton, *Khirbat al-Mafjar*, 241–81, fig. 213 and pls. XII/1, LXV/1 and LXVI/1 (balustrades) and pl. XII/5) and Robert Hamilton, *Walid and his Friends: An Umayyad Tragedy*, Oxford Studies in Islamic Art VI (Oxford: Oxford University Press, 1988), 59 (window). This latter feature deserves much more detailed study than it has received in print.

[66] Krautheimer, *Architecture*, 259, 261.

[67] Suspended uncomfortably as he is from a pendentive, he could be interpreted as a broad parody of the classical caryatid as on the Erechtheum on the Athenian Acropolis in Athens.

[68] Hamilton, *Khirbat al Mafjar*, 45–105, 227–41, 292–3, 327–42.

Figure 7.20 Khirbat al-Mafjar, bath hall, axonometric view.

Equally, one might argue that while Mshattā is to some degree a version of the Roman frontier fort, and could thus be seen as an adaptation of it, the other changes imposed on that putative model go much further. One is a doubling of the usual dimensions, from 70 metres per side to nearly 144 metres per side internally. Another is a system of symmetrical and successive subdivision into three which totally reworks the interior arrangement found in other Umayyad *quṣūr*. This has powerful political implications, since its function is to exalt the majesty of the prince in unmistakable spatial terms. A third is the combination of stone for the lower walls and brick, especially for the vaults. Most dramatic of all is the unprecedentedly lavish embellishment of the exterior of the central or royal tract by a tapestry of filigree stone carving incorporating geometric, vegetal and figural elements. Surely this ensemble of changes qualifies as transformation. The frontier fort has become a machine both for luxurious living and for the exercise of despotic power,[69] a

[69] For the debt Mshattā owes to earlier cultures, see Sergio Bettini, 'Il Castello di Mschatta in Transgiordania nell' ambito dell' "Arte di Potenza" tardoantica', in Sergio Bettini *et al.* (eds), *Anthemon. Scritti di archeologia e di antichità classiche in onore di Carlo Anti* (Florence: G. C.

move for which the early fourth-century palace of Diocletian at Split provides a useful parallel.[70]

A Test Case: Writing

But rather than expatiate on the two undeniably original and thought-provoking reworkings of earlier models at Khirbat al-Mafjar[71] and Mshattā, it is perhaps preferable to tackle the theme of transformation in a much simpler context. This is the use of writing on a capital. In sixth-century Byzantine architecture it was common practice to include in the design of a densely carved capital an inconspicuous monogram that referred in suitably modest, elliptical and coded terms to the patron of the building (Figure 7.21).[72] It was not easily readable; to make sense of it, prior knowledge of the conventions employed was necessary. Nor did it call attention to itself by size or by colour.

To compare this with the inscription carved onto the capital and the column shaft at the cistern of al-Muwaqqar (720) is to move from one civilisation to another, from one thought-world to the next.[73] Here the writing is abundant, not sparse (Figure 7.22). It is easily legible; there is no attempt at sophistication.

Sansoni, 1955), 321–66; Volkmar Enderlein and Michael Meinecke, 'Graben – Forschen – Präsentieren: Probleme der Darstellung vergangener Kulturen am Beispiel der Mschatta-Fassade', *Jahrbuch der Berliner Museen* 34 (1992), 137–72; see also Stefan Weber and Eva-Maria Troelenberg, 'Mschatta im Museum: Zur Geschichte eines bedeutenden Monuments frühislamischer Kunst', *Jahrbuch Preussischer Kulturbesitz* 46 (2010), 104–32.

[70] For a reconstruction in colour, see Wheeler, *Roman Art and Architecture*, fig. 127.

[71] Here the unpredictable, almost random juxtaposition of architectural elements brings to mind such Roman sites as the Hadrianic palatial complex at Tivoli or Piazza Armerina in Sicily (Alex Boethius and John B. Ward-Perkins, *Etruscan and Roman Architecture* (Harmondsworth: Penguin Books, 1970), 254–6 and 529–33 respectively).

[72] For example, the monogram of Justinian on a capital in Haghia Sophia, Constantinople; see Jean Lassus, *The Early Christian & Byzantine World* (London: Paul Hamlyn, 1967), colour pl. 48. See also Antony Eastmond, 'Monograms and the Art of Unhelpful Writing in Late Antiquity', in Brigitte M. Bedos-Rezak and Jeffrey Hamburger (eds), *Sign and Design: Script as Image in Cross-cultural Perspective (300–1600 CE)* (Washington, DC: Dumbarton Oaks Research Library and Collection, 2016), 219–35 and especially 229, b and f.

[73] Robert W. Hamilton, 'An eighth-century water-gauge at al-Muwaqqar', *Quarterly of the Department of Antiquities in Palestine* XII (1948), 70–2 and pl. XXIII/1; for the inscription, see Leo A. Mayer, 'Note on the inscription from al-Muwaqqar', *Quarterly of the Department of Antiquities in Palestine* XII (1948), 73–4 and pl. XXIII/1–2.

Figure 7.21 Haghia Sophia, capital with monogram.

It is not there as a covert allusion to the patron but rather to inform the viewer about water levels in the cistern. So the architectural elements – the column and the capital that crowns it – are merely a convenient surface for the message. There is no attempt to accommodate message and surface to each other. The person

Figure 7.22 Al-Muwaqqar, inscribed column and capital.

who carved the inscription probably had no sense of flouting an iron convention which dictated that column shafts should be kept free of applied ornament.[74] And so the writing spreads like a rampant infection right across and far down the column, virtually obliterating its structural role. The core elements of the

[74] Thus the 867 plates in Rudolf Kautzsch, *Kapitellstudien. Beiträge zu einer Geschichte des spätantiken Kapitells im Osten vom vierten bis ins siebente Jahrhundert* (Berlin: Verlag von Walter de Gruyter & Co., 1936) include not one example of a decorated shaft. Despite the odd exception to this rule in the Justinianic period (Martin Harrison, *A Temple for Byzantium: The Discovery and Excavation of Anicia Juliana's Palace Church in Istanbul* (Austin: University of Texas Press, 1989)), it was in Umayyad times that the principle of a plain shaft was jettisoned. Al-Muwaqqar was not an isolated case. Decorated shafts occur at the Aqsa mosque (Robert W. Hamilton, *The Structural History of the Aqsa Mosque: A Record of the Architectural Gleanings from the Repairs of 1938–1942* (Jerusalem, Oxford and London: Oxford University Press for the Government of Palestine, 1949), pl. III/3 and 4), and similar themes occur in the woodwork of the Aqṣā mosque (Hillenbrand, 'Umayyad Woodwork', 306 and figs. 58–62) and the portal of the bath hall at Khirbat al-Mafjar (Hamilton, *Khirbat al Mafjar*, pl. CVIII). A surviving column from the Umayyad mosque at Wāsiṭ of 703 takes the process much further: it is completely drowned in applied decoration (George, *Damascus*, 188).

capital – its volutes and its leaves – have been overrun and rendered void and irrelevant by writing. In place of the exquisitely mannered execution of the capital at Haghia Sophia is a rough and ready column and capital that pay the merest lip service to the classical tradition while downplaying its components. There could be no better illustration of the extent to which Islam exalted the Word. For the inscription contains not a public proclamation of rank or faith, but workaday information about water levels in the cistern. Exactly the same process of the ascendancy of the word can be recognised in the evolution of Umayyad coinage. In the medium of gold, the sequence is crystal clear – first, using Byzantine coins without changing them in any way; second, tinkering almost invisibly with their design; third, experimenting briefly with figural designs of Islamic import; and fourth and last, instigating a root and branch reform of the gold coinage by introducing a brand new type with no figural elements at all, and comprising writing and writing alone on both obverse and reverse – writing, moreover, that was overwhelmingly of religious content (Figure 7.23). This turned the entire numismatic tradition of the Mediterranean world, a venerable tradition over a millennium old, upside down in the most radical fashion. And that entire process was telescoped into a mere sixty years. Indeed, coinage was the medium in which Umayyad art most rapidly and triumphantly found its distinctive voice.

Figure 7.23 *Dīnār* of ʿAbd al-Malik.

And here the crucial steps are the same as those proposed earlier in this chapter: imitation, adaptation and transformation.

Conclusion

It is time to step back from the scrutiny of detail and to attempt to define the key characteristics of Umayyad art. The evidence marshalled above indicates clearly enough that the engagement of Umayyad art with the Graeco-Roman, early Christian and perhaps especially Byzantine artistic tradition was close, intimate and anything but deferential. Indeed, at times it comes close to parody and burlesque. As the dominant local artistic tradition at the time of the Arab conquest, it was the obvious point of departure for future developments. But change was not immediate, and it took time for the new Islamic regime to digest its conquests and to take on board the ensuing challenges. The situation in Syria was, after all, very different from that in Arabia in confessional, demographic and administrative terms. The choice of Damascus as the capital of the newly established Umayyad dynasty was a turning point, heralding as it did the ultimate eclipse of the political role of the holy cities of Arabia. As time passed and the Umayyad dynasty gradually saw off the menace of its external and internal foes, and established its power base in Greater Syria ever more securely, the ruling elite grew in confidence and embraced the notion of asserting themselves culturally as well as politically. The key decade here was the 690s, which saw a hardening of attitudes to Byzantium coupled with the defeat of the anti-caliph Ibn al-Zubair. With the erosion of his power-base in Arabia, Greater Syria became dominant. The political, military and financial power of the Umayyad elite did not merely enable these princes to become patrons of architecture but turbocharged an astonishing building boom. It is no accident that this boom began no earlier than the 690s. In their different ways, the Dome of the Rock and the coinage reform both express this new-found confidence.

The successive stages of imitation, adaptation and transformation analysed in this chapter do not tell the whole story of Umayyad art and its complex relationship with the classical and Byzantine tradition. For alongside these varied Umayyad responses to that tradition another equally marked reaction makes itself felt. It can be very simply defined as the desire to outdo the masterpieces of the past in scale and in splendour. That desire had both a political and a financial edge – for the demonstration of wealth had clear political implications. A few examples will make this clear. In Jerusalem, the Umayyad take-over of the huge empty space within which had stood the temple originally built by Solomon and later modified in various ways, and which was now renamed al-Haram al-Sharif, was a masterstroke. So too was the decision to give the exterior of the Dome of the Rock a carapace of golden mosaic,[75] and to clothe the courtyard facades and the sanctuary of the Great Mosque of Damascus with mosaics, an enterprise of unprecedented scale. Similarly, the centrepiece of the immense mosaic floor of the bath hall at Khirbat al-Mafjar displays the largest Catherine wheel design known from ancient times (Figure 7.24). This was a favoured motif in both secular contexts and in churches, so to surpass these multiple models was a significant

Figure 7.24 Khirbat al-Mafjar, bath hall, central mosaic.

[75] H. R. Allen, 'Some Observations on the Original Appearance of the Dome of the Rock', in Johns, *Bayt al-Maqdis Part Two*, colour pl. on 202–3; even Old St Peter's in distant Rome, perhaps the greatest of all Western churches, had its decoration concentrated in the interior (Krautheimer, *Architecture*, 43).

technical and artistic achievement. Finally, the *dīwān* mosaic at the same site depicts a tree with affronted animals – a theme that had become a cliché in the mosaic floors of the churches of Greater Syria. But it greatly increases its size, magnificence and complexity, infusing it not only with new drama but also with a new set of meanings, while not losing those that had become firmly associated with this design for centuries.[76]

It would be mistaken to present Umayyad art as dominating the lands of Greater Syria under that dynasty. For the largely Christian population, little changed, as the rich array of post-conquest floor mosaics in churches proves. Moreover, abundant archaeological evidence indicates that the transition from Byzantine to Islamic rule in material culture at the non-elite level was often so gentle as to be virtually invisible.[77] And while the great sacred foundations in Jerusalem and Damascus designedly proclaimed the arrival of a new power and a new religion, the secular aspect of elite Umayyad art was much less visible given the clear preference of Umayyad patrons for rural and even remote sites rather than urban ones, even for spectacular palaces.

It is very likely that much more Umayyad art was on display in the cities than is suggested by what has survived. But an assessment of Umayyad art as a whole must depend principally on what has actually survived, however skewed the accidents of survival might be. It takes a fresh and inquisitive mind, one untrammelled by the shackles of convention, to make fresh connections between bodies of material long kept apart, and it is this very freshness that is the distinctive hallmark of Umayyad art. Many a classical or Byzantine theme or motif developed under Umayyad tutelage in directions that those raised in its conventions could scarcely have predicted. The clue to those changes of direction lies in the lack of inhibition, the indifference to the dictates of

[76] Ettinghausen, *Arab Painting*, 36, 38–40; Ettinghausen, 'Throne and Banquet Hall', 44–7; Doris Behrens-Abouseif, 'The Lion-Gazelle Mosaic at Khirbat al-Mafjar', *Muqarnas* 14 (1997), 11–18.

[77] This is the thrust of a ground-breaking book by Alan Walmsley, *Early Islamic Syria: An Archaeological Assessment* (London: Gerald Duckworth & Co., 2007), which deliberately eschews a discussion of elite art in favour of focusing on the evidence of a much wider range of material culture. For a more detailed account of this process within the single province of Filastin, see Gideon Avni, *The Byzantine–Islamic Transition in Palestine: An Archaeological Approach* (Oxford: Oxford University Press, 2014).

convention, and the capacity for lateral thinking displayed by the craftsmen who worked for Umayyad patrons. The interplay in the world of ideas between patron and artist remains obscure. But the explosion of new ideas that transformed the classical and Byzantine tradition in art speaks for itself. This chapter has tried to show how Umayyad art, while rooted in the Mediterranean world and thus using visual idioms instinctively familiar to a Western observer – the arch and the vault, the column and the capital, complex mouldings and *ajouré* decoration – nevertheless found its own distinctive voice by 750. In so doing it created the foundation on which all later Islamic art rests.

8

BYZANTINE HEROES AND SAINTS OF THE ARAB–BYZANTINE BORDER (NINTH–TENTH CENTURIES)

Sophie Métivier

The poorly documented Byzantine–Arab border acquires a real visibility moulded through various literary works that relate it to places, people, events, and social practices, especially warfare. The way the border has been defined over the last century, as a region with its own representations and characteristics, is largely a historiographical construction, to which two articles of the scholar Henri Grégoire, 'L'âge héroïque de Byzance' and 'Études sur l'épopée byzantine', both published in 1933,[1] have largely contributed by considering the frontier as closely related to epic literature. More recently, when Gilbert Dagron comments on the military treatise *De Velitatione*, a treatise on the Arab–Byzantine wars and border written at the end of the tenth century, he also contributes to the creation of common representations of the border. Not only does he evoke the landscapes of the Taurus mountains' canyons and mention military contacts and skirmishes between Arabs and Byzantines, well-known thanks to the book of Vasiliev

[1] Henri Grégoire, 'L'âge héroïque de Byzance', in *Mélanges offerts à M. Nicolas Iorga par ses amis de France et des pays de langue française* (Paris: J. Gamber, 1933), 382–97; Henri Grégoire, 'Études sur l'épopée byzantine', *Revue des études grecques* 46 (1933), 29–69, in which he describes the most famous hero Digenis Akritas as 'le fabuleux gardien de la frontière'.

and Canard,[2] but he also describes the bilingual, even bicultural, society that lives on the frontier.[3] For him, the Arab–Byzantine border is not a gap that separates two civilisations, but a space between them, that creates continuity and unity from one empire to the other.

Most of these stereotypes, shaped by modern historians, share a common source, the late work *Digenis Akritas*. Yet this poem is as problematic as the border itself. Not only do several forms of it exist, but we do not know when, where, and by whom the two medieval versions were composed.[4] The story collates many confused allusions to historical events and people which belong to the 'Byzantine heroic age of the wars against the Arabs'.[5] However, the world it creates is impressive enough to be accessible to modern readers. It is a peculiar world, both Arab and Byzantine,[6] made of war, violence, and wealth.

2 Alexander A. Vasiliev, *Byzance et les Arabes*, vol. 1: *La dynastie d'Amorium (820–867)*, trans. Henri Grégoire and Marius Canard (Brussels: Éditions de l'Institut de philologie et d'histoire orientales, 1935); Alexander A. Vasiliev and Marius Canard, *Byzance et les Arabes*, vol. 2/1: *La dynastie macédonienne (867–969)* (Brussels: Éditions de l'Institut de philologie et d'histoire orientales et slaves, 1968).

3 *Le traité sur la guérilla (De velitatione) de l'empereur Nicéphore Phocas (963–969)*, eds and trans. Gilbert Dagron and Haralambie Mihăescu (Paris: Éditions du Centre national de la recherche scientifique, 1986). Gilbert Dagron perpetuates a long tradition that also included Marius Canard, Irène Mélikoff, and Agostino Pertusi. For instance, see Agostino Pertusi, 'Tra storia e leggenda; akritai e ghâzi sulla frontiera orientale di Bizanzio', in Mihai Berza and Eugen Stanescu (eds), *Actes du XIVe congrès international des études byzantines. Bucarest, 6–12 septembre 1971* (Bucarest: Editura Academiei Republicii Socialiste România, 1974), 1: 238–83.

4 See Roderick Beaton, 'An epic in the making? The early versions of *Digenes Akrites*', in Roderick Beaton and David Ricks (eds), *Digenes Akrites: New Approaches to Byzantine Heroic Poetry* (Aldershot: Ashgate, 1993), 55–72, here 64–5 ('a *terminus post quem* for the core, which cannot predate by very much the revival of the romance in the mid-twelfth century'). In the same volume, see also Paul Magdalino, '*Digenes Akrites* and Byzantine Literature: The Twelfth Century Background to the Grottaferrata Version', 1–14.

5 Corinne Jouanno, 'Shared Spaces: 1 Digenis Akritis, the Two-Blood Border Lord', in Carolina Cupane and Bettina Krönung (eds), *Fictional Storytelling in the Medieval Eastern Mediterranean and Beyond* (Leiden: Brill, 2016), 260–84.

6 The hero is called Digenis, because his father is Arab, and his mother is Byzantine. I do not think that the word *digenis*, hardly used in Byzantine literature (only twice in the Thesaurus

It gives no place to central institutions, emperor, or church; on the contrary, it is dominated by local powers, outlaws, and fabulous or legendary creatures, like dragons or Amazons. Digenis Akritas' romance has been viewed as a distorting mirror of a reality that, in fact, we know very little about.[7]

In short, I would say that the Arab–Byzantine border has developed as an object and a theme of Byzantine literature and modern historiography. It has been elaborated and studied as a world of heroes.[8] The hero, as collective and cultural product, can be defined as the one who is both the main character, on whom the narration is focused, and the model *par excellence*, distinguished by his capacity for acting (until death) and by his chosen relationship to the divine.[9] Heroic figures indeed began to appear in ninth-century literary works, long before the eldest versions of *Digenis Akritas*. Why make the ninth- and tenth-century border the matrix of heroes? Who was interested in such a process? Can we define the cultural productions of this time, associated with the frontier, as the expression of a border society? As the consequence of contacts between the Byzantine empire and the Islamic world? This last

Linguae Graecae, for Leo V, 'Assyrian' and 'Armenian', and for Theophobos, whose mother was Byzantine and whose father was Persian), refers to men who had also a double origin. The stake may be elsewhere: the hero is compared to Christ, another *digenis*. See Corinne Jouanno, *Digénis Akritas, le héros des frontières: Une épopée byzantine* (Paris: Brepols, 1998), 160.

7 Paul Magdalino, '*Digenes Akrites* and Byzantine Literature', 1: 'the poem preserves and exalts the memory of a frontier society which was vital to the empire's existence for 400 years, maintaining defence against the main ideological enemy and providing the military leadership for the *reconquista* on all fronts in the ninth and tenth centuries.' He speaks about a 'matière de Cappadoce' or 'akritic material' (ibid., 2, 5). When he discusses the place of composition, Constantinople or the East, he asserts that 'Digenes' parentage (reflects) the realities of an older and quintessentially provincial aristocratic world' (ibid., 9). On the contrary, Anthony Bryer, 'The Historian's *Digenes Akrites*', in Beaton and Roderick (eds), *Digenes Akrites*, 99, remarks that 'this work lacks the contextual credibility of its other Anatolian counterparts [Sayyid al-Battal, the Melik Danishmend]'.

8 The perspective changed recently. See Koray Durak, 'The Cilician Frontier: A Case Study of Byzantine–Islamic trade in the Ninth and Tenth Centuries', in Niels Gaul *et al.* (eds), *Center, Province and Periphery in the Age of Constantine VII Porphyrogennetos: From* De Ceremoniis *to* De Administrando Imperio (Wiesbaden: Harrassowitz Verlag, 2018), 168–83.

9 See Daniel Fabre, 'L'atelier des héros', in Pierre Centlivres *et al.* (eds), *La fabrique du héros* (Paris: Éditions de la Maison des sciences de l'homme, 1999).

supposition is appealing, since a phenomenon of heroisation also characterises the Islamic world as early as the Umayyad age and at different periods.[10]

Indeed, this phenomenon appeared later in Byzantium for obvious military and political reasons. The empire was unsuccessful until the eighth century; the champion of the Arab failure before Constantinople in 717 was the iconoclast and soon-condemned emperor Leo III.[11] The vanquisher of the battle of Akroinon in 741 was the accursed Constantine V. The first Byzantine figures who come close to heroes are the few martyrs noticed by the early ninth-century chronicler Theophanes.[12] He briefly mentions the capture and death of two imperial officers: Eustathius (*PmbZ*, no. 1751), son of a *patrikios*,[13] made prisoner at Sideron in Byzantium on the occasion of an Arab raid and killed in Harran in 739/740 on the order of Caliph Hisham;[14] Theophilus (*PmbZ*, no. 8194), *strategos* of the Kibyrrheotai theme, caught by Arabs and martyrised by Hārūn al-Rashīd in 789/790.[15] The famous Forty-Two Martyrs of Amorion are much better known. Several Passions narrate their collective confrontation

[10] Antoine Borrut, *Entre mémoire et pouvoir: L'espace syrien sous les derniers Omeyyades et les premiers Abbassides (v. 72–193/692–809)* (Leiden: Brill, 2011), 229–82, deals with the Umayyad hero Maslama b. ʿAbd al-Malik as model of a ghāzī warrior. The memory of Maslama is related to specific Byzantine locations, a fact which is understood as symbolically taking possession of Constantinople.

[11] Borrut's analysis shows how the Byzantine sources, such as Theophanes, Nicephorus, and Germanus of Constantinople, ignore Leo's role, whereas the Syriac and Armenian chronicles, such as the Chronicle of Zuqnin and Łewond, highlight his role: ibid., 247–59. He supposes a 'memory competition' (for heroisation) between the caliphate and the empire.

[12] Note that the chronicler does not highlight the chiefs of the Byzantine armies, contrary to the Arab ones.

[13] For an explanation of this and similar terms, refer to the *Oxford Dictionary of Byzantium* (Oxford: Oxford University Press).

[14] Theophanes Confessor, *Theophanis Chronographia*, ed. Carolus de Boor (Leipzig: Teubner, 1883), 411, 414. For *PmbZ* references, see Ralph-Johannes Lilie *et al.*, nach Vorarbeiten von Friedhelm Winkelmann, *Prosopographie der mittelbyzantinischen Zeit. Erste Abteilung (641–867)* (Berlin: De Gruyter, 1998–2002), *Zweite Abteilung (867–1025)* (Berlin: De Gruyter, 2009–13).

[15] Theophanes, Chronographia, 465. On Theophilus, see also *Synaxarium Ecclesiae Constantinopolitanae e codice Sirmondiano nunc Berolinensi*, ed. Hippolyte Delehaye, Propylaeum ad Acta Sanctorum Novembris (Brussels, 1902), 30 January, 3, col. 434, Synaxaria selecta, col. 431–3.

with the Arab armies, which besieged the Anatolian town in 838, and subsequently with the Islamic authorities, when they were put to death in Samarra seven years later. However, only one of these Passions focused on the life of a given martyr, Kallistos, which I have already treated elsewhere.[16] These martyrs, who point to the existence of a new and mature Byzantine perception of the Islamic world,[17] combine both categories of ninth- and tenth-century Byzantine heroes related to the Byzantine–Arab border and Byzantine–Arab wars, that emerge at this same period or slightly later in Byzantine literature: heroised generals and saints.

Significantly, the political and cultural context has changed: since the battle of Akroinon (741), Byzantine armies could again be victorious; and it is not coincidental that precisely at this period some old martyrs – Roman soldiers who were venerated for having refused to sacrifice to pagan gods – began to be honoured as military saints. They are now depicted as fighters (with armour and military costume) and not as martyrs; they can also appear as being at the head of troops – in short, they have acquired a military role, which is a completely novel depiction of them.[18] This cultural change is well attested by Arabic writers as well. According to al-Masʿūdī, who quotes a converted Byzantine, Arab heroes would have been portrayed in Byzantine churches.[19]

16 On Kallistos (Melissenos), see Sophie Métivier, *Aristocratie et sainteté à Byzance (viiie–xie siècle)* (Brussels: Société des Bollandistes, 2019), 95–101.

17 See also the well-known story of Leo the philosopher, a ninth-century Byzantine scholar, who became renowned in the Byzantine Empire for his fame at the caliph's court.

18 See Christopher Walter, *The Warrior Saints in Byzantine Art and Tradition* (Aldershot: Ashgate, 2003); Monica White, *Military Saints in Byzantium and Rus, 900–1200* (Cambridge: Cambridge University Press, 2013); Vincent Déroche, 'Origines et développement du culte des saints militaires: les lignes de force', in Jean-Pierre Caillet *et al.* (eds), *Des dieux civiques aux saints patrons (ive–viie siècle)* (Paris: Editions A&J Picard, 2015), 257–73.

19 Al-Masʿūdī, *Les prairies d'or*, trans. Charles Barbier de Meynard and Abel Pavet de Courteille, rev. Charles Pellat (Paris: Geuthner, 1997), 5: 1294, §3201: 'D'après ce que m'a raconté un Byzantin converti et devenu excellent Musulman, ses compatriotes ont placé dans une de leurs églises l'image de dix Musulmans célèbres pour leur énergie, leur courage, leurs stratagèmes et leurs ruses contre les Chrétiens; on remarque parmi eux cet homme que Muʿāwiya avait chargé d'enlever de Constantinople un certain patrice à l'aide d'une ruse, et qui l'y ramena après qu'il eut été frappé en vertu de la loi du talion. Les autres personnages

As this could hardly be a question of heroes shared by Arabs and Byzantines, it likely refers to icons or wall paintings of military saints, confused by al-Masʿūdī or his source with Arab fighters' portraits. Besides a misinterpretation, it may also reflect how the Byzantines understood these armed saints' introduction in the church decoration within the context of the ongoing Byzantine–Arab wars.

This chapter examines two types of heroes related to the Arab–Byzantine border, which made their appearance at that time, namely the Byzantine general and the saint. I will show that, in contrast to what is commonly held, the border heroes of the ninth- and tenth-century Byzantine literature were not produced in the border provinces, for families concerned to integrate into the capital's aristocracy, but in Constantinople where the border constituted a new stake. Several scholars, including Alexander Kazhdan, Athanasios Markopoulos, and more recently Luisa Andriollo,[20] have highlighted the process which, in this context, tends towards the heroisation of Byzantine generals in tenth-century literature.[21] We find its traces first and

représentés sont: ʿAbd Allāh al-Battāl, Umar b. ʿUbayd Allāh, ʿAlī b. Yahyā al-Armanī, al-Ghuzayyil b. Bakkār, Ahmad b. Abī Qatīfa; Korbeas (Qurbyās) le Paulicien (al-Baylaqānī) – chef de la ville d'Ibrīq qui appartient aujourd'hui aux Byzantins; ce Korbeas, qui était le patrice des Pauliciens (Bayāliqa), mourut en 249/863–864. On remarque aussi dans la même église Chrysocheir (Kh. r. s. khār) sœur du précédent; Yāzmān al-Khādim, dans son équipage et entouré de ses guerriers, et enfin Abū l-Qāsim ibn ʿAbd al-Bāqī.' See Olof Heilo, 'Seeing Eye to Eye: Islamic Universalism in the Roman and Byzantine Worlds, 7th to 10th Centuries', Dissertation, University of Vienna, 2010, 119; Olof Heilo, 'The Holiness of the Warrior: Physical and Spiritual Power in the Borderland between Byzantium and Islam', in Johannes Koder and Ioannis Stouraitis (eds), *Byzantine War Ideology Between Roman Imperial Concept and Christian Religion* (Vienna: Austrian Academy of Sciences Press, 2012), 44.

20 Luisa Andriollo, *Constantinople et les provinces d'Asie Mineure, ixe–xie siècle: Administration impériale, sociétés locales et rôles de l'aristocratie* (Leuven: Peeters, 2017), 372–9.

21 I prefer speaking of a trend because these glorious men do not constitute a specific category. The 'paganising' Greek word ἥρως is hardly used by Byzantine writers. Other terms are not systematically employed (like 'illustrious men' or 'grands hommes'). It would be useful to examine the posterity of these heroised men: have they been famous in the next centuries, like the sixth-century general Belisarius during the Macedonian period (ninth–eleventh centuries)? *Digenis Akritas* gives up some clues.

foremost in Byzantine historiography, which had previously been characterised by the place given to other figures than these imperial ones.[22] It is true particularly in the last part of the tenth-century chronicle published under the title of *Theophanes Continuatus*,[23] which features a few high commanders of the late ninth and the tenth century: Nikephoros Phokas the Elder (*PmbZ*, no. 25545), his grand-son, the eponymous emperor (*PmbZ*, no. 25535),[24] Eustathius Argyros (*PmbZ*, no. 21828), John Kourkouas (*PmbZ*, no. 22917), and Constantine Doukas (*PmbZ*, no. 23817). All of them are described in the same way, according to classical standards, bequeathed by antique or late antique literature: feats, victories against the Arabs, a fame so great that it terrifies enemies, and outstanding virtues.[25] For instance, two of them are said to be *agrypnoi*, namely 'wakeful', a word which is also used

[22] Alexander Kazhdan, 'Chivalresque historiography: Leo the Deacon and his contemporaries', in Alexander Kazhdan, *A History of Byzantine Literature (850–1500)*, ed. Christine Angelidi (Athens: National Hellenic Research Foundation, Institute for Byzantine Research, 2006), 273–94. He mentions the 'noble warriors in the late tenth-century chronography' (ibid., 273). Athanasios Markopoulos, 'From narrative historiography to historical biography: new trends in Byzantine historical writing in the 10th–11th centuries', *Byzantinische Zeitschrift* 102 (2009), 697–715; Athanasios Markopoulos, 'Sur les deux versions de la chronographie de Syméon Logothète', in Athanasios Markopoulos, *History and Literature of Byzantium in the 9th–10th centuries* (Aldershot: Ashgate, 2004), no. VI. Luisa Andriollo, 'Aristocracy and literary production in the 10th century', in Aglae Pizzone (ed.), *The Author in Middle Byzantine Literature: Modes, Functions and Identities* (Berlin: De Gruyter, 2014), 119–38.

[23] The concerned parts of the chronicle would have been written around 963. See Herbert Hunger, *Die hochsprachliche profane Literatur der Byzantiner* (Munich: C. H. Beck, 1978), 1: 339–43, and, more recently, Warren Treadgold, *The Middle Byzantine Historians* (New York: Palgrave Macmillan, 2013), 211.

[24] See lastly, Denis Sullivan, *The Rise and Fall of Nikephoros II Phokas: Five Contemporary Texts in Annotated Translations* (Leiden: Brill, 2018).

[25] *Theophanes Continuatus*, ed. Immanuel Bekker, Corpus Scriptorum Historiae Byzantinae 48 (Bonn: Weber, 1838), Book VI, Leo imp. 10, 359 (Nikephoros Phokas the Elder), Book VI, Leo imp. 22, 368–369, and 374 (Eustathius Argyros), Book VI, Rom. imp. 40, 426–8, and Rom. imp. 42, 428 (Theophilos Kourkouas, compared to Justinian's general Salomon). These standards are applied to the emperors. On classical rhetoric, see Laurent Pernot, *La rhétorique dans l'Antiquité* (Paris: Le livre de poche, 2000), 230–7.

for Christian ascetics;[26] according to the same chronicle, the mere name of Eustathius Argyros used to scare the Arabs.[27] The most outstanding example of this trend is John Kourkouas, a general of Emperor Romanos Lekapenos for over twenty years, who reconquered Melitene in 934. He is described as follows:[28]

Ἐπειδὴ δὲ ὁ ῥηθεὶς Ἰωάννης μάγιστρος καὶ δομέστικος τῶν σχολῶν ἄριστος ἐγένετο εἰς τὰ πολέμια, καὶ πολλὰ καὶ μεγάλα ἀνέστησε τρόπαια, καὶ τὰ Ῥωμαϊκὰ ἐπέκτεινεν ὅρια, πλείστας τε πόλεις ἐπόρθησεν τῶν Ἀγαρηνῶν, καὶ διὰ τὸ περιφανὲς τῆς τοῦ ἀνδρὸς ἀρετῆς, ἠβουλήθη ὁ βασιλεὺς Ῥωμανὸς εἰς τὸν ἑαυτοῦ ἔκγονον Ῥωμανὸν τὸν ἐκ Κωνσταντίνου τοῦ υἱοῦ αὐτοῦ θυγατέρα ἀναλαβεῖν. ἡ οὖν θυγάτηρ τοῦ Κουρκούα ἦν ἡ Εὐφροσύνη, ὁ δὲ υἱὸς τοῦ Κωνσταντίνου ἦν Ῥωμανὸς ὁ εὐνουχισθεὶς παρὰ Κωνσταντίνου τοῦ Πορφυρογεννήτου, καὶ ἐτιμήθη πατρίκιος καὶ πραιπόσιτος. φθόνου δὲ αὐτῷ τῆς τοιαύτης ἕνεκεν ὑποθέσεως τῶν λοιπῶν βασιλέων κινηθέντος, παύει τῆς ἀρχῆς, εἴκοσι καὶ δύο χρόνους καὶ μῆνας ἑπτὰ δομέστικος ἀδιάδοχος τελέσας. πλὴν οὖν ἄξιον εἰπεῖν τό τε γένος καὶ τὴν ἀγωγὴν αὐτοῦ καὶ τὸ ἐπιτήδευμα καὶ τὸ φύσει τῆς ψυχῆς καὶ τοῦ σώματος αὐτοῦ καὶ τὴν πρᾶξιν, καὶ ὁποῖος πιστὸς καὶ ὀρθὸς ἀνεφάνη τῇ γενεᾷ ἡμῶν. οὗτος ἐκ γένους τῶν Ἀρμενιακῶν ἦν ἀπὸ Δόκιαν χωρίου Δαρβιδοῦν, πατρὸς μὲν τῶν οὐκ ἀσήμων παλατίνου πάνυ πλουσίου υἱοῦ Ἰωάννου δομεστίκου τῶν ἱκανάτων. λέγεται δὲ καὶ τὰ ἱερὰ γράμματα ἐκπεπαιδεῦσθαι παρά Χριστοφόρου μητροπολίτου Γαγγρῶν τοῦ συγγενοῦ αὐτοῦ. ὡς ᾄδεται δὲ ὁ λόγος, ὅτι ἔφη ὁ ἀρχιερεὺς ‘οὗτος ὁ Ἰωάννης εἰς λύτρωσιν καὶ ἄνεσιν τῶν Ῥωμαίων γενήσεται.’ πολλὰς γὰρ καὶ πλείστας πόλεις καὶ κάστρα καὶ χώρας καὶ καστέλλια καὶ τόπια τῶν Ἀγαρηνῶν ἐχειρώσατο, καὶ τὴν Ῥωμανίαν διπλῆν κατεστήσατο, πρότερον οὖσαν

[26] The word is used for John Kourkouas and Nikephoros Phokas the Elder: *Chronographiae quae Theophanis Continuati nomine fertur liber quo Vita Basilii imperatoris amplectitur*, ed. and trans. Ihor Ševčenko, Corpus Fontium Historiae Byzantinae 42 (Berlin: De Gruyter, 2011), c. 71, 244, l. 14.

[27] *Theophanes Continuatus*, Book VI, Leo imp. 22, 369, ll. 3–5: Εὐστάθιον Ἀργυρὸν οἱ Ἀγαρηνοὶ ἐδεδίεσαν, ὡς τὸ τούτου ὄνομα ἔκπληξιν καὶ φόβον αὐτοῖς λέγεσθαι, 374, ll. 18–19: καὶ τὸ ὄνομα αὐτοῦ φημιζόμενον καταπτήσσειν καὶ τρέμειν.

[28] *Theophanes Continuatus*, Book VI, Rom. imp. 40, 426–8.

καὶ κατεχομένην ὑπὸ τῶν ἀρνητῶν τοῦ Χριστοῦ μέχρι τοῦ Χαρσιανοῦ κάστρου καὶ τῆς Ὑψηλῆς καὶ τοῦ Ἅλυ ποταμοῦ. ὁ δὲ πιστὸς καὶ σπουδαῖος πρὸς Ῥωμανὸν αὐτοκράτορα Ἰωάννης δομέστικος τῶν σχολῶν μέχρι τοῦ Εὐφράτου καὶ τοῦ Τίγρη τὰ ὅρια τῶν Ῥωμαίων ἐστήσατο καὶ προῖκα καὶ δῶρα τῇ Ῥωμανίᾳ προσήνεγκεν, καὶ λαὸν καὶ στρατὸν ὁ βασιλεὺς ἐκεῖθεν προσεκτήσατο, καὶ φόρους πολλοὺς ἐτησίως λαμβάνειν ἐτύπωσεν, καὶ πολλῶν λαφύρων καὶ ἁρμάτων καὶ αἰχμαλώτων Ἀγαρηνῶν ἐκεῖθεν ἀπήνεγκεν. Μεγίστοις γὰρ ἀγῶσιν ἑαυτὸν παραθεὶς τὰς πόλεις τῶν ἀρνητῶν Χριστοῦ ἐπόρθησεν· καὶ τίς ἂν ἐξείπῃ κατ᾽ ὄνομα ταύτας ἃς χειρωσάμενος ὑποφόρους τοῖς Ῥωμαίοις Ἰωάννης ὁ Κουρκούας καὶ δομέστικος τῶν σχολῶν [ἐποιήσατο;] τοῖς εἴκοσι καὶ δύο χρόνοις πόλεις χιλίας σχεδὸν καὶ πλέον κατεστήσατο καὶ τῇ Ῥωμανίᾳ προσήγαγεν· καὶ ἦν ἰδεῖν τὸν ἄγρυπνον Ἰωάννην τὸν Κουρκούαν ἐπὶ παρατάξεως πολεμικῆς διαλαλιαῖς καὶ παραινέσεσι πιθαναῖς τοῖς Ῥωμαίοις χρώμενον, καὶ ἄλλον Τραϊανὸν ἢ Βελισάριον εἰκάσαι καὶ ὀνομάσαι τοῦτον. καὶ εἴ τις πρὸς τούτους παραθήσει τὸν ἄνδρα, εὑρήσει πλείονας τὰς τοῦ Κουρκούα ἀνδραγαθίας καὶ ἀριστείας. οἱ δὲ λαμπρῶς ποθοῦντες καὶ θέλοντες μαθεῖν τὰς τοῦ Ἰωάννου Κουρκούα ἀριστείας καὶ συγγραφὰς εὑρήσουσιν ἐν ὀκτὼ βιβλίοις ἐκτεθείσας παρὰ Μανουὴλ πρωτοσπαθαρίου καὶ κριτοῦ.

Since the said John, magister and *domestikos* of the Scholes, excelled at war, won many brilliant victories, extended the Roman frontiers, and plundered many of the Arabs' towns, because of the famous excellence of this man, the emperor Romanus wanted to marry his grandson Romanus born of his son Constantine with the daughter of that one. Kourkouas' daughter was Euphrosyne, Constantine's son was the Romanus made eunuch by Constantine Porphyrogenitus and honoured as *patrikios* and *praepositus*. Due to the jealousy aroused by the other emperors against him, he ceases commanding after having been *domestikos* for twenty-two years and seven months continuously. But he is worthy of speaking of his kin, his conduct, his way of life, the nature of his soul and his body, and his doings, and how he was trusty and true to our race. He was from the Armeniac theme by his kin, from the village of Dokeia Darbidoun,[29] and his father was not an obscure individual, but a very

[29] The chronicler does not assert that John is from Armenian origins, but that his family comes from the Armeniac theme, precisely from the village of Dokeia, which is indeed in the Armeniac theme, exactly in Paphlagonia, like Gangrai, mentioned a little later. Opposite view in *PmbZ*, no. 22917, and Luisa Andriollo, 'Les Kourkouas (ixe–xie siècle)', *Studies in Byzantine Sigillography* 11 (2012), 58, n. 53.

> rich palatine, son of John, the *domestikos* of the Hikanatoi. They say that he was educated in the Scriptures by his relative Christopher, the metropolitan of Gangrai. According to the tradition, the bishop said that 'this John was born for the redemption and the remission of the Romans.' He seized many Hagarene cities and fortresses, villages and castles and lands, and he doubled Romania's territory, which was previously shut in by the faith's enemies (lit. 'Christ's deniers') between Charsianon kastron and the Hypseles and Halys rivers. But the *domestikos* of the Scholes John, loyal and zealous to the autocrat Romanus, enlarged the Roman frontiers to the Euphrates and to the Tigris, and he brought gifts and presents to Romania. Thence the emperor gained soldiers and an army, he ordered to raise annually many taxes, and brought back many spoils, arms, and prisoners from the Hagarenes. Applying himself to great struggles, he plundered the cities of the Christ-deniers. Who could name all the towns that the *domestikos* of the Scholes John Kourkouas conquered and subjected to Romans? Within twenty-two years he brought down nearly thousands of towns and more and brought them into Romania. And you should have seen the vigilant John Kourkouas facing the enemy ranks, giving orders, exhorting, and persuading the Romans; you could have compared him to another Trajan or Belisarius, and have called him this way. And if you compare this man to them, you will find that Kourkouas' prowess and feats are greater. Those who want to learn of the magnificence of John Kourkouas' deeds will find them collected in eight books, written by the protospatharios and judge Manuel.[30]

His case has been well studied by Luisa Andriollo, both in a contribution specially dedicated to John Geometres as well as in her book published in 2017, in which she aimed to 'trace a specifically aristocratic-inspired literature in tenth-century Byzantium', and insisted on the hero's noble birth, his military achievements, and the Christian character of the Byzantine–Muslim war.[31] In the chronicle, John Kourkouas is indeed presented through an expanded biographical notice, rightly taken for an *encomium* by Luisa Andriollo, which

[30] This is Andriollo's translation (in Andriollo, 'Aristocracy and literary production', 128), completed (l. 1–12, 16–17, 23–9) and modified slightly by me.

[31] Andriollo, 'Aristocracy and literary production', 119, 127. The tenth-century poet John Geometres indeed 'gives voice the ideology of the military aristocracy, just as contemporary chronicles do in a number of passages' (ibid., 130). Andriollo, *Provinces d'Asie Mineure*, 373–4, 378. See also Andriollo, 'Les Kourkouas', 61–2.

deals with his origin (l. 14–16), his *paideia* (l. 16–18), his deeds in warfare (l. 19–38), and, finally, his kin on the following page.[32] Feats, conquests, and virtues are mentioned; the Byzantine general moreover is compared to antique or late-antique forerunners, such as Trajan and Belisarius (l. 35–8).[33] Moreover, Kourkouas' glory is rooted in the border area, since clear allusion is made to the frontier: the word itself, ὅρια, is employed (l. 3, l. 25). Lastly, Kourkouas' legend is the only example around which an entirely literary work was built, now lost but historically well attested. Warren Treadgold, whose argumentation is partly convincing, rejects the idea of a John Kourkouas secular Vita written by Manuel.[34] However, the reference in the passage cited above is obviously biographical, and Treadgold himself does not hesitate to suppose the existence of 'saints' lives of Theophilos' generals Manuel the Armenian and Theophobos the Persian'.[35] In the eleventh century, Michael Psellos, extolling Constantine X Doukas (1059–67), whose advisor he was, reminds the reader of the ancient glory of the Doukai Andronikos and his father Constantine in the following words: 'Through the συγγραφαί (writings) that celebrate them, they are known to all until now.'[36]

[32] See also *Symeonis Magistri et Logothetae Chronicon*, ed. Stephan Wahlgren, Corpus Fontium Historiae Byzantinae 44: 1 (Berlin: De Gruyter, 2006), c. 136. 76, 337, ll. 585–93: only the first lines are introduced, the laudatory and the biographical parts (l. 1–10), borrowed from Manuel's work, are missing.

[33] This remarkable parallel may be borrowed from the late-antique comparisons between both Roman emperors Trajan and Theodosius I. On this point, see Maria Pilar García Ruiz, 'Rethinking the political role of Pliny's *Panegyricus* in the *Panegyrici Latini*', *Arethusa* 46 (2013), 195–216, especially 212–16 (see ibid., 216: 'panegyrists and historians were to laud Theodosius as an *alter Traianus* because of his Spanish background and his uncompromising defence of the borders of the empire').

[34] Treadgold, *Byzantine Historians*, 197–203, here 198: 'Although Curcuas was doubtless an important and capable general, as far as we know no other Byzantine who was not an emperor ever became the subject of a biography in multiple books. Our only Byzantine biographies are of saints and emperors, and Curcuas belonged to neither group . . . Much more likely than that Manuel wrote an unprecedented eight-book biography of a single general is that he composed a history of the type of Genesius and the author of *Theophanes continuatus* . . .' It is indeed difficult to conceive such a wide work dedicated to only one man.

[35] Ibid., 147–8.

[36] Michael Psellos, *Chronographie ou Histoire d'un siècle de Byzance (976–1077)*, ed. E. Renault (Paris: Les Belles Lettres, 1928), 2: 140.

Thus, even if nothing is said about his death, Kourkouas is seen and described as a hero:[37] he has distinguished himself by his ceaseless fight, at the service not only of the emperor, but also of Romania. He is clearly related to a civic and political community, the Roman community (Romania is mentioned three times on lines 21, 26 and 33), to the history of which he contributes. He is associated with the divine, as his mission is decided by God (l. 18–19).

Likewise, after him, his brother Theophilos is celebrated in very similar terms: he is extolled for having plundered many Arabs' places and he is compared to another general of Justinian, Solomon. Furthermore, two other relatives are mentioned in the chronicle: John Tzimiskes, John's grandson, and Romanos Kourkouas, John's son. For this reason, its source, Manuel's work, is supposed to be partly a family's praise, meant to strengthen the authority of the Kourkouases and serve the family's interests.[38]

This heroisation of secular figures is not limited to secular literature. In the *Life of Saint Basil the Younger*, the general-in-chief Constantine Doukas is described as a heroic figure: after the emperor's death, with the Bulgarians very close to Constantinople, the people protest against the government and want to appeal to the general because of his fame: '[T]his man was truly most successful and fearsome in wars, so that often even the barbarians, when questioned by captives, told how one man, the one indeed discussed here, put them to flight: "Whenever he comes against us to engage in war, we see a burning fire coming from his horse's breath, as well as from his weapons, that burns us [and] dashes us to the ground."' Then the hagiographer explains that the horse and the weapons were given as a gift to Doukas by the Theotokos.[39] Wonder, which is a habitual feature in hagiographic texts, transfigures the Byzantine military chief too, whose evocation acquires here an epic dimension.

37 See Caillet *et al.* (eds), *Des dieux civiques aux saints patrons*, especially Peter Brown, 'Concluding Remarks', 375–84.

38 On the role of literature and writing in aristocratic power, see, for instance, Patricia Karlin-Hayter, 'Études sur les deux histoires du règne de Michel III', *Byzantion* 41 (1971), 452–96, who supposes (493), that '[l]es Vies d'hommes illustres constituaient une [des] sources de prédilection [des historiens byzantins]'; Catherine Holmes, *Basil II and the Governance of the Empire (976–1025)* (Oxford: Oxford University Press, 2005).

39 *The Life of Saint Basil the Younger*, eds Denis F. Sullivan, Alice-Mary Talbot and Stamatina McGrath, Dumbarton Oaks Studies 45 (Washington, DC: Harvard University Press, 2014), I: 14, 92–3.

The understanding until now of such heroic figures has typically been in the context of a supposed competition and conflict among several aristocratic clans, and the glorification of these generals has been understood as a way to justify the power of the new Anatolian aristocracy, which in the tenth century controlled the most important military posts.[40] According to this interpretation, such depictions were a form of weapon in a conflict between centre and periphery. Even the elaboration of epic literature has been understood as a sign of the expansion of a new aristocracy in Byzantium, that would have emerged from the Arab–Byzantine frontier. Yet the reading may be more complex.

As Luisa Andriollo, in the case of poetry, and I, regarding hagiographic texts,[41] have shown, some aristocratic people, either civil officers or military commanders, chose to devise literary works to protect or promote their social position. The trend is not restricted to a specific aristocratic group, and it is, at least, a century old by the time of the late-tenth-century aristocratic conflicts. The case of Manuel, the uncle of the empress Theodora, who saved the emperor Theophilus from the Arabs at the battle of Dazimon in 838, and who is closely associated, rightly or not, with the restoration of the images in 843, is a well-known example of such glorification.[42]

The heroisation of these men is foremost a Constantinopolitan trend. The literary works which exalt them were composed in the capital city. This is true in the case of *Theophanes Continuatus*, including its last part; and, of course, other sources record the fame of these men, and all are Constantinopolitan.

[40] Andriollo, *Les provinces d'Asie Mineure*, 376: 'Si la valorisation de la bravoure au combat et la christianisation des vertus militaires peuvent être l'expression d'une culture plus proprement provinciale, elles furent vite mises à profit comme moyen de légitimation du pouvoir politique et social acquis par l'aristocratie orientale au cours du xe siècle.'

[41] Andriollo, 'Aristocracy and literary production'; Sophie Métivier, 'Peut-on parler d'une hagiographie aristocratique à Byzance (viiie–xie siècle)?', in Antonio Rigo *et al.* (eds), *Byzantine Hagiography: Texts, Themes and Projects: Moscow, 12–14 November 2012* (Turnhout: Brepols, 2018), 179–99; Métivier, *Aristocratie and Sainteté*.

[42] *PmbZ*, no. 4707. Henri Grégoire, 'Manuel et Théophobe ou la concurrence de deux monastères', *Byzantion* 9 (1934), 183–204 (Grégoire, ibid., 183, speaks of a 'personnage de légende'). Warren Treadgold, 'The Chronological Accuracy of the *Chronicle* of Symeon the Logothete for the Years 813–845', *Dumbarton Oaks Papers* 33 (1979), 180–2; Métivier, *Aristocratie and Sainteté*, 107–10.

For instance, in a letter addressed to the emir of Damascus, Arethas of Caesarea, a Constantinopolitan scholar, refers to Constantine Doukas as having killed 18,000 Arabs.[43] Manuel, the author quoted in *Theophanes Continuatus* as the source of his information about John Kourkouas, may well be the *protospatharios* and judge Manuel, said *Byzantios*, namely Constantinopolitan, by John Skylitzes.[44] Constantinopolitan provenance holds true also for *The Sack of Crete*, a long poem written by Theodosius the Deacon to the glory of the general Nikephoros Phokas around 963 (just before his advent).[45]

Only one text is invoked and very often quoted by modern historians to defend the idea that the works that were written to the glory of these men were local compositions from the border region:[46] namely, a *scholion* written by the famous scholar Arethas at the beginning of the tenth century and copied in the margins of two manuscripts of the third-century Philostratus' *Vita Apollonii* (V 20, 2). According to Ryan Bailey, Philostratus 'accused a shipowner of trafficking images of the gods and parading statues from city to city in hope of turning a profit'. Commenting on this passage, Arethas calls such statue dealers *agyrtai* ('beggars'), whom he compares to 'the accursed Paphlagonians who make up songs about the adventures of famous men and sing them for pennies from door to door' (Τοὺς ἀγείροντας λέγει, ἤτοι ἀγύρτας, ὧν καὶ νῦν δεῖγμα οἱ κατάρατοι Παφλαγόνες ᾠδάς τινας συμπλάσαντες πάτη περιεχούσας ἐνδόξων ἀνδρῶν καὶ πρὸς ὀβολὸν ᾄδοντες καθ᾽ἑκάστην οἰκίαν).[47] Clearly, the *scholion* attests to the existence of some epic compositions. Bailey reminds us that this note has been considered by modern scholars as 'the earliest attestation of the beginnings of the Akritan oral cycle'. However, can we conclude that the songs were

[43] Arethas' Letter to the emir of Damascus, in Karl Förstel, *Schriften zum Islam von Arethas und Euthymios Zigabenos und Fragmente der griechischen Koranübersetzung* (Wiesbaden: Brill, 2009), 36.

[44] John Skylitzes, *Synopsis historiarum*, ed. Johannes Thurn, Corpus Fontium Historiae Byzantinae 5 (Berlin: De Gruyter, 1973), 3, l. 27. See Treadgold, *Byzantine Historians*, 202.

[45] Theodosius the Deacon, *La prise de la Crète (960–961)*, trans. René-Claude Bondoux and Jean-Pierre Grélois (Paris: ACHCByz, 2017).

[46] It is also true for the later *Digenis Akritas*.

[47] Ryan Bailey, 'Arethas of Caesarea and the scholia on Philostratus' *Vita Apollonii* in *codex Laurentianus Pluteus* 69.33', *Byzantion* 86 (2016), 53–89, here 54–5.

dedicated to heroes of Arethas' time? Is the *scholion* a proof of the existence of a provincial literature in favour of people from the ninth- or tenth-century aristocracy? I would say no.[48]

The identity of these generals who were honoured as heroes must also be discussed. They have been considered by modern historians as representatives of the provincial aristocracy. Of course, they were established in Anatolia, particularly in Cappadocia and in Paphlagonia: there they had offices, fought Arab armies, owned properties, and built churches and monasteries; but they usually lived in Constantinople.[49] Even if their families originally had a provincial or even a foreign origin, like the Argyroi or the Phokas, they had already arrived in the capital city when the sources mention them for the first time.[50] When the tenth-century writers praise and glorify their feats against the Arabs, these men are no longer *akritai*, namely border fighters, if they ever had been.

[48] See Andriollo, *Les provinces d'Asie Mineure*, 372–9. Luisa Andriollo, who highlights the rhetorical standards of the cultural model (she alludes to the influence of the *basilikos logos* and the rules of Menander Rhetor), prefers to speak of a mixed form which combined 'haute culture' and 'matière provinciale', which expressed values of Anatolian aristocracy (war culture and Christianisation of the war). This paradigm is attractive, but she herself realises the tenuous evidence on which it stands, in Andriollo, 'Aristocracy and literary production', 131: 'Unfortunately, for lack of better evidence, we can just assume the provincial character of aristocratic and family literature, while we are left assessing the influence of aristocratic warrior culture only through its Constantinopolitan expressions.' The author herself gives examples which are not distinctive of a specific aristocratic group: emperors like Heraclius or Leo VI insisted on the war's religious dimension. In the same perspective, see Homère-Alexandre Théologitis, 'Digénis Akritas et la littérature byzantine: problèmes d'approche', in Bernard Pouderon (ed.), *Les personnages du roman grec: Actes du colloque de Tours, 18–20 novembre 1999* (Lyon: Maison de l'Orient et de la Méditerranée Jean Pouilloux, 2001), 393–405, here 401 (about the 'matière de Cappadoce').

[49] Andriollo, *Les provinces d'Asie Mineure.*

[50] It is true for the oldest Cappadocian family, Saint Eudokimos' family. At the beginning of his Vita, Eudokimos, who lived under Theophilos' reign (829–42), is said to be from Cappadocia and to live with his parents in Constantinople. See Sophie Métivier, 'Aristocrate et saint, le cas d'Eudokimos', in Béatrice Caseau (ed.), *Les réseaux familiaux: Antiquité tardive et Moyen Âge. In memoriam A. Laiou et E. Patlagean* (Paris: ACHCByz, 2012), 101; Andriollo, *Les provinces d'Asie Mineure*, 321–5.

So, in my view, it seems very difficult to assert that the works I referred to aimed to justify or legitimate the social ascension of provincials or people from the border. Furthermore, in the same period, we know of some foreign people who actually were imperial officers at the court or in the border provinces, and none are put forward in the way that John Kourkouas or the Argyroi are. The best example is the Armenian Melias (*PmbZ*, no. 25041). In two of his works, *De thematibus* and *De administrando imperio*, Emperor Constantine VII presents in detail his military deeds to explain the expansion of the Byzantine empire in the Taurus mountains. Thanks to Melias and his companions, the Lykandos country between Cappadocia and Upper Mesopotamia had just been included in the empire, first as a *kleisoura*, then a *thema*. Melias is said to be well-born and famous; he is rewarded by the important dignity of *magistros* for his loyalty to the emperor and for his victories against the Arabs, but nothing else.[51] In *Theophanes Continuatus*, he is only mentioned next to Byzantine generals such as John Kourkouas.[52]

Therefore, I am led to conclude that the Arab–Byzantine border was only a pretext for making heroes out of some Byzantine aristocrats, and not the place where heroic or epic literature is produced. There existed no Byzantine equivalents to Arab poets like al-Mutanabbī or Abū Firās, who wrote for the Ḥamdānid prince Sayf al-Dawla. Yet it is also true that we cannot compare the Byzantine toparchs, who are hardly known, or the archons, with the Syrian and Mesopotamian emirs, who governed their lands with full autonomy.

Byzantine literature produced another type of border hero, figured this time as a holy man. The link between the man of the Arab–Byzantine border *par excellence*, Digenis Akritas, and hagiography was brought to light and studied by Erich Trapp. In 1976, he highlighted the literary borrowings made by

[51] Constantine Porphyrogenitus, *De Thematibus*, ed. Agostino Pertusi (Vatican City: Biblioteca Apostolica Vaticana, 1952), c. 12, 75–6. Constantine Porphyrogenitus, *De administrando imperio*, ed. Gyula Moravcsik and trans. Romilly J. H. Jenkins (Washington, DC: Dumbarton Oaks Center for Byzantine Studies, 1967), c. 50, 238–41.

[52] *Theophanes Continuatus*, Book VI, Const. imp. 10, 389, ll. 5–10, and Const. imp. 24, 416, ll. 14–17. About Melias, see Gérard Dédeyan, 'Mleh le Grand, stratège de Lykandos', *Revue des Études Arméniennes*, NS 15 (1981), 73–102.

Digenis Akritas from various hagiographic texts, such as the *Life of Theoktiste* and the *Passions of Theodore*.[53] Like *Digenis Akritas*, hagiography may celebrate the double origin of a saint and his belonging to two worlds, because as a go-between, an intercessor, the saint is, by definition, an outsider standing apart. He is, at least symbolically, a border hero too.[54]

Thus, it does not come as a surprise that men of the border – at least some of whom were strangers to Byzantium – are included among the Byzantine saints, and that Byzantine hagiographers often honour foreign saints, especially from Palestine.[55] The best-known cases are the hymnograph Andrew of Crete in the early eighth century, the three confessors of the Second Iconoclasm, Michael the *synkellos*, and the two *graptoi* brothers.[56] This also seems to be true of Basil the Younger, mentioned before: even if his Life takes place in the imperial city, he is a foreigner. He was arrested by two imperial officers of the emperors Leo VI and Alexander in Anatolia because of 'his foreign character and appearance' (τὸ ξένον τοῦ ἔθους καὶ τοῦ σχήματος αὐτοῦ), then he was brought to the capital, because he was suspected of being a spy. There, he was interrogated by the *parakoimomenos* Samonas, whom the author of the Life twice calls an Arab. The foreign prisoner, Basil, is probably suspected of being an Arab too. Because he refuses to reveal his identity, he is thrown into the sea, and miraculously rescued.[57]

[53] Erich Trapp, 'Hagiographische Elemente im Digenes-Epos', *Analecta Bollandiana* 94 (1976), 275–87.

[54] Peter Brown, 'The Rise and Function of the Holy Man in Late Antiquity', *The Journal of Roman Studies* 61 (1971), 80–101. See also Lennart Rydén, 'New Forms of Hagiography: Heroes and Saints', in *The 17th International Byzantine Congress: Major Papers* (New York: Aristide D. Caratzas Pub., 1986), 537–51. All the heroes Rydén's article concerns are also saints.

[55] More generally, concerning the place of Arabs in hagiographic texts, see Nike Koutrakou, 'Language and Dynamics of Communication in Byzantium: the "Image" of the Arabs in Hagiographical Sources', in Barbara Crostini and Sergio La Porta (eds), *Negotiating Co-Existence: Communities, Cultures and* Convivencia *in Byzantine Society* (Trier: Wissenschaftlicher Verlag Trier, 2013), 45–62.

[56] *Life of Andrew*, in *Ανάλεκτα ἱεροσολυμιτικῆς σταχυλογίας*, ed. Athanasios Papadopoulos-Kerameus, vol. 5 (St Petersburg, 1898), 169–79. *The Life of Michael the Synkellos*, ed. and trans. Mary B. Cunningham (Belfast: Belfast Byzantine Enterprises, 1991).

[57] *The Life of Saint Basil the Younger*, I. 4–9, 70–83. The author of the Life used rather the word ξένος than the unequivocal ἐθνικός (see ibid, I. 26, 116, l. 2, concerning Barbaros), probably because Basil, as a saint, can be also said ξένος in the secular world.

If nothing is said explicitly about the foreign origin of Basil in his Life, this is, on the contrary, clearly stated in the case of two other saints of Arab origin who lived during the reign of Michael II (820–9) and his successors, Antony the Younger and Barbaros (*PmbZ*, no. 745). The latter, an African fighter who, after a defeat, becomes not only Christian but a monk in Byzantine Greece, is known only through a late praise written by Constantine Akropolites in the late thirteenth century.[58] For this reason, I prefer to examine here the case of the former, Antony the Younger (*PmbZ*, no. 534).[59] Who is he? First a Palestinian boy, then a Byzantine officer based in Attaleia, finally a monk in Anatolia, then in Constantinople. Born in Palestine to a Christian family, he takes refuge in the Byzantine empire after his mother's death and his father's remarriage. Recruited in the army, as delegate (ἐκ προσώπου) of the *strategos* of Kibyrrhaiotai, he supports the emperor Michael II during the rebellion of Thomas the Slav and he protects the town of Attaleia (in Pamphylia) against a naval attack of the Arabs. When he is about to marry at the age of forty, he decides instead to become a monk. He becomes a recluse on Mount Olympus, and through his advice, leads the general Petronas to victory against the Arabs in 863.

For the author of Antony's Life, the question of his hero's identity is an important matter. First, we learn that Antony was born in Palestine from

[58] Constantine Akropolites, *Life of St. Barbaros* (*BHG* 220), in Ανάλεκτα ἱεροσολυμιτικῆς σταχυλογίας, ed. Athanasios Papadopoulos-Kerameus (St. Petersburg, 1891), 1: 405–20. After having been a soldier of the Islamic armies of Ifriqiyya, which were defeated by Byzantines, Barbaros became a robber in the country of the Ambracian Gulf, then a hermit. The story takes place in the reign of Michael II (820–9). About the author, see Donald Nicol, 'Constantine Akropolites: A Prosopographical Note', *Dumbarton Oaks Papers* 19 (1965), 249–56.

[59] *Life of Antony the Younger*, in *Συλλογὴ παλαιστινιακῆς καὶ συριακῆς ἁγιολογίας*, ed. Athanasios Papadopoulos-Kerameus, vol. 1, *Pravoslavnyi palestinskij sbornik* 19 (1907), 186–216. François Halkin, 'Saint Antoine le Jeune et Pétronas le vainqueur des Arabes en 863 (d'après un texte inédit)', *Analecta Bollandiana* 62 (1944), 187–225. Due to its originality, the text has been analysed by several scholars in different ways. For instance, see Alexander Kazhdan, *A History of Byzantine Literature (650–850)*, with Lee E. Sherry and Christine Angelidi (Athens: National Hellenic Research Foundation, Institute for Byzantine Research, 1999), 291–4; Martha Vinson, 'Gender and Politics in the Post-Iconoclastic Period: The Lives of Antony the Younger, the Empress Theodora and the Patriarch Ignatios', *Byzantion* 68 (1998), 469–515.

Christian parents, second that he spoke to the Arab commander who attacked Attaleia in the Syrian language (τῇ Σύρᾳ φωνῇ), probably Arabic rather than Syriac;[60] lastly that the first name of Antony, now a monk, was Echimos. It is an Arabic sounding name, maybe Hakim or Hashim. Being bilingual in Greek and Arabic, with a name in either language, Echimos, then Antony, in the service of both the emperor and God, his identity is ambivalent. So, like Basil the Younger, he is questioned at least three times about who he is.

We can assume that in the eyes of his hagiographer he is a man of the Arab–Byzantine border. Like the romance of *Digenis Akritas*, his Life includes three main groups: outlaws, Arabs, and soldiers. Because the author knows nothing about Antony's childhood, he prefers recalling the adventures of his spiritual father, John, who predicts both his military career and his subsequent conversion. John is an outlaw (ἀρχιληστής/ληστής) who becomes a monk as an act of repentance, after he has killed the champion of the Syrian governor (called the '*protosymboulos* of Syria', the 'Saracens' *boularchos*', or the '*syriarchos*') in single combat. Once a monk at the Great Lavra of Mar Saba, he brings six robbers (λῃσταί) down. The subject of the outlaws who belong to no political community,[61] which appears at least twice in this Life – John himself, then the robbers – refers not only to edifying stories but also directly to *Digenis Akritas*. Indeed, Lennart Rydén compared John's story with the first part of the romance, the Lay of the Emir.[62] As for Arabs, they are mentioned again further in the Life, both when they attack Attaleia and when

60 Some parallels have been found: Theodoret of Cyrrhus, *L'histoire des moines de Syrie*, eds Pierre Canivet and Alice Leroy-Molinghen (Paris: Le Cerf, 1979), vol. 2, XXI. 15, 94, ll. 14–15 (Syriac); Leontius of Neapolis, *Vie de Syméon le Fou et Vie de Jean de Chypre*, ed. and trans. André-Jean Festugière (Paris: Geuthner, 1974), 73, l. 22 (Syriac). Photius, *Bibliothèque*, ed. and trans. R. Henry (Paris: Les Belles Lettres, 1962), 3: 91, l. 42 (Syriac). Leo the Deacon, *Leonis Diaconi Caloënsis Historiae libri decem*, ed. Carolus Benedictus Hase, Corpus Scriptorum Historiae Byzantinae 33 (Bonn, 1828), 165, l. 21 (probably Arabic: the expression is used for the name of the town of Mempetze).

61 Here the author employs the term Arabs, elsewhere he chooses the words Saracens, Hagarens, or Ismailites to refer to the Byzantines' military enemies. See below.

62 Rydén, 'New Forms of Hagiography', 543.

they fight the Byzantine army led by Petronas.[63] Finally, the army has an important space in the Life through three officers who play important roles in it: the saint himself, the *strategos* of the Kibyrrhaiotai, and Petronas, *strategos* of the Thrakesioi and the emperor's uncle (*PmbZ*, no. 5929).[64] The author also uses military words such as *ekspedeton* or *prokoursa*.[65] He even describes the military costume that Antony wears,[66] even if the latter prefers taking off his military costume and wearing an ascetic's clothing to protect Attaleia's town.[67] In short, robbers, Arabs, and soldiers belong to the social formation of Antony in the same way as to that of Digenis Akritas.

We also, as with Digenis Akritas, meet women and monsters. Antony is about to get married when he is recalled by his spiritual father to his vocation: he leaves his wedding feast in secret to become a monk. During his crossing of Anatolia, he even sees a dragon, but, unlike Digenis, he does not need to kill it. It is obvious that the Life of Antony the Younger roots the hero, a saint, in a universe similar to that of Digenis Akritas. Both texts reveal a distinctive imaginary world associated with the Arab–Byzantine border in a characteristic, although not unique, way. Yet the Life, which contributes to the creation of representations of men of the border or men beyond the border,[68] was not

[63] *Life of Antony the Younger*, ed. Papadopoulos-Kerameus, c. 17, 198, l. 30 (ὁ τῶν Σαρακηνῶν στόλος). *Life of Antony the Younger*, ed. Halkin, c. 14, 218, ll. 9–10 (δύο φοσσᾶτα τῶν ἀθέων Ἰσμαηλιτῶν) and c. 15, 219, ll. 14–15 (τὸ ἐκσπέδετον τῶν Σαρακηνῶν), l. 21 (κατεδίωξεν ὀπίσω τῶν Ἀγαρηνῶν).

[64] *Life of Antony the Younger*, ed. Papadopoulos-Kerameus, c. 10–11, 193–4 (the *strategos* of Kibyrrheotai). *Life of Antony the Younger*, ed. Halkin, c. 14, 218, ll. 8–9 (Petronas).

[65] *Life of Antony the Younger*, ed. Halkin, c. 14, 218, l. 14 (τὰ ἐθνῶν πρόκουρσα). Ibid., c. 15, 219, l. 14–15 (τὸ ἐκσπέδετον τῶν Σαρακηνῶν).

[66] *Life of Antony the Younger*, ed. Papadopoulos-Kerameus, c. 18, 199, ll. 17–20 (τὴν ἀρχικὴν . . . περιβολὴν).

[67] Ibid., c. 16–17, 198, ll. 24–7, 199, l. 11.

[68] It is a theme, as said before, which occurred many times. In the same period, Emperor Theophilus would have forced Byzantine widows to marry *ethnikoi* men. An imperial decree is mentioned in the *Life of Athanasia of Aegina* (see Franz Dölger, *Regesten der Kaiserurkunden des oströmischen Reiches von 565–1453*, vol. 1/1: *Regesten 565–867*, 2nd edn Andreas E. Müller (Munich: C. H. Beck, 2009), no. 430b (422)). This decision is alluded to in the *Passio* of the Forty-Two martyrs of Amorion written by Michael the Synkellos (*BHG* 1213), in V. Vasilievskij and P. Nikitin, *Skazanija o 42 amorijskih mučenikah* (St Petersburg, 1905),

written on the empire's margins, on the Arab–Byzantine frontier, by and for men who are from this border. On the contrary: François Halkin suggested that it was composed by an anonymous follower of Patriarch Ignatios, on the order of his *higoumen*, at the end of the ninth century. As with the Lives of other Palestinian saints,[69] it was produced in Constantinople, probably to support some aristocratic circle: Antony is Petronas' spiritual father.[70]

This is an important point, because it prevents us from concluding that the making of 'border heroes' was meant to glorify and legitimate the upward mobility of some provincials. This trend seems to be a Constantinopolitan matter, one which does not exclude an old and foreign influence, coming from Palestine in the case of hagiographic texts. It also reveals the strategic value of the Arab–Byzantine border and the importance of military commands in the *cursus honorum* and for the fame of the tenth-century Byzantine aristocrats, as the recurrence of the theme of 'East-Anatolian origin' to describe this aristocracy also shows.

But what is at stake here seems to be a different issue. The development of these heroes takes place within the context of the territorial expansion of the Byzantine empire. They are heroes of the conquests, not resistance fighters.[71] John Kourkouas, compared with Trajan and Belisarius, 'seized many Hagarene cities and fortresses, villages and castles and lands, and he doubled Romania's territory'.[72] On the contrary, Petronas, who defeated an Arab army at the heart of the empire, is not extolled in a specific work.[73]

27, ll. 5–7; see also *Chronographiae quae Theophanis Continuati nomine fertur libri I–IV*, ed. and trans. Michael Featherstone and Juan Signes-Codoñer, Corpus Fontium Historiae Byzantinae 53 (Berlin: De Gruyter, 2015), Book III. 21, 162, ll. 7–8, and Joseph Genesios, *Regum libri quattuor*, ed. Annie Lesmüller-Werner and Johannes Thurn, Corpus Fontium Historiae Byzantinae 14 (Berlin: De Gruyter, 1978), Book III. 3, 38, ll. 55–6.

69 See André Binggeli *et al.* (eds), *Les nouveaux martyrs à Byzance* (Paris: Éditions de la Sorbonne, 2021).

70 See Métivier, 'Hagiographie aristocratique', 191–4. Métivier, *Aristocratie et sainteté*, 113.

71 In the older Byzantine chronography on the seventh and eighth centuries, the Byzantine generals are often named, but it is not always the case; their role during military campaigns, either negative or positive, is just noticed. They are shadowy figures (Kazhdan, *Byzantine Literature (850–1000)*).

72 See p. 213.

73 See *PmbZ*, no. 5929. In the case of Manuel, his feats against the Arabs are added to his political role in 843.

The aim of these wars of conquest is finally the control of new spaces. Who was to control them? The emperor? Or his commanders and their heirs, who belonged to his aristocracy?[74] With the Byzantine expansion in Upper Mesopotamia, Cilicia, and Syria, the emperors took control of these territories: they went there;[75] they turned them into state domains;[76] they favoured the establishment of foreign soldiers.[77] They asserted and displayed their control against foreign enemies and Byzantine aristocracy,[78] even if these regions were administered 'through indirect means'.[79] The creation of new heroes in these texts, heroes who claim and remind the reader of the role of the late ninth- and tenth-century officers in the ongoing border warfare, may be meant as a symbolic seizure of these spaces by the Byzantine aristocracy.

[74] The idea of competition, even opposition, has been proposed by Alexander Kazhdan regarding the chronicler's position, hostile or well-inclined towards some important aristocratic families. See Kazhdan, *Byzantine Literature (850–1500)*, 167.

[75] This was the case with Nikephoros II Phokas, John I Tzimiskes, and Basil II.

[76] *Theophanes Continuatus*, Book VI, Rom. imp. 24, 416–17. On the *kouratoria* of Melitene, see Jonathan Shepard, 'Constantine VII, Caucasian openings and the road to Aleppo', in Anthony Eastmond (ed.), *Eastern Approaches to Byzantium: Papers from the Thirty-Third Spring Symposium of Byzantine Studies, University of Warwick, Coventry, March 1999* (Aldershot: Ashgate, 2001), 30; James Howard-Johnston, 'Crown Lands and the Defense of Imperial Authority in the Tenth and Eleventh Centuries', *Byzantinische Forschungen* 21 (1995), 75–100; Jean-Claude Cheynet, '*Épiskeptitai* et autres gestionnaires des biens publics (d'après les sceaux de l'IFEB)', *Studies in Byzantine Sigillography* 7 (2002), 87–117, here 116–17; Jean-Claude Cheynet, 'Les gestionnaires des biens impériaux: étude sociale (xe–xiie siècle)', *Travaux et mémoires* 16 (= *Mélanges Cécile Morrisson*) (Paris: ACHCByz, 2010), 163–204, especially 175–6.

[77] Alexander Beihammer, 'Strategies of Diplomacy and Ambassadors in Byzantine–Muslim Relations on the Tenth and Eleventh Centuries', in Audrey Becker and Nicolas Drocourt (eds), *Ambassadeurs et ambassades au cœur des relations diplomatiques. Rome – Occident médiéval – Byzance (viiie siècle av. J.-C.–xiie siècle après J.-C.)* (Metz: Centre régional universitaire lorrain d'histoire, 2012), 382–3.

[78] Andriollo, *Les provinces d'Asie Mineure*, 264–5.

[79] Catherine Holmes, '"How the East was Won" in the Reign of Basil II', in Eastmond (ed.), *Eastern Approaches*, 41–56, here 54. The author intended to show that Basil II, shortly after the conquests, depended on local intermediaries and figures. Yet, her reasoning concerning a new meaning of the word *kouratores* is less convincing (ibid., 47: as 'plenipotentiary figures placed at the head of an infrastructure of indigenous administrators', and not as 'estate officials').

9

A COSMOPOLITAN FRONTIER STATE: THE MARWĀNIDS OF DIYĀR BAKR, 990–1085, AND THE PERFORMANCE OF POWER

Carole Hillenbrand

Introduction

The dissolution and fragmentation of ʿAbbāsid power in the tenth and eleventh centuries led to the appearance of a number of small dynasties across many areas of the Muslim world. Various Kurdish groups formed principalities which were in practice autonomous from the Baghdad caliphate. Such Kurdish dynasties included the Shaddādids (c. 951–1174) in Armenia and Caucasian Albania, with their centre in Arrān,[1] who waged jihad against Christian Georgians, Armenians and Byzantines, but also intermarried with them and ruled over them, and the Ḥasanwayhids (c. 960–1014) who flourished in the central Zagros area and supplied troops for the Būyid *amīr*s of Persia and Iraq.[2] In northern Syria, Diyār Bakr and Armenia, territories which lay near or on the eastern borders of the Byzantine empire or the fringes of the Fāṭimid empire, small states, ethnically diverse, whose peoples spoke Arabic,

1 Thomas Ripper, *Die Marwāniden von Diyār Bakr* (Würzburg: Egon Verlag, 2000), 41–2, 323–6.

2 Ripper, *Marwāniden*, 63–6, 68–70; Vladimir Minorsky, *Studies in Caucasian History* (London: Taylor's Foreign Press, 1953), 1–59.

Armenian, Kurdish, Persian or Turkish, clustered together in close proximity, sometimes forming temporary and volatile alliances, and at other moments engaged in fierce hostilities with each other.[3] Some of these small dynasties, such as the Ḥamdānids of Aleppo, the Mazyadids of Ḥilla, the ʿUqaylids of Mosul and the Mirdāsids of Aleppo, depended on Bedouin Arab tribal support, whilst others such as the Ḥasanwayhids and the Marwānids relied on Kurdish nomadic groups[4] (see Figure 9.1).

Ibn al-Azraq on the Marwānids

The historical sources dealing with the Marwānids include some information from well-known medieval Arabic geographical works, such as that of al-Muqaddasī,[5] as well as more especially the *Kāmil fī ʾl-tāʾrīkh* of Ibn al-Athīr.[6] However, the major source for the study of the Marwānids of Diyār Bakr is without doubt the long section about them in the still little-used Arabic chronicle entitled *Tāʾrīkh Mayyāfāriqīn wa Āmid* of Ibn al-Azraq al-Fāriqī (d. after 1176–7).[7] He worked as a scribe for the Artuqids of Mayyāfāriqīn and wrote this detailed history of his home town from early Islamic times. In this work Ibn al-Azraq provides detailed coverage of the Marwānid dynasty, 990–1085. This part of the chronicle, well edited by ʿAwād in 1959,[8] still remains untranslated, but its contents were outlined in some detail in a long

[3] Alexander D. Beihammer, *Byzantium and the Emergence of Muslim–Turkish Anatolia, c.1040–1130* (Abingdon: Ashgate, 2017), 57–61; Catherine Holmes, '"How the east was won" in the reign of Basil II', in Antony Eastmond (ed.), *Eastern Approaches to Byzantium* (Aldershot: Ashgate, 2001), 41–56.

[4] Hugh Kennedy, *The Prophet and the Age of the Caliphates: The Islamic Near East from the Sixth to the Eleventh Century* (Harlow: Longmans, 2016), 264.

[5] Shams al-Dīn Abū ʿAbdallāh Muḥammad b. Aḥmad al-Muqaddasī, *Aḥsan al-taqāsīm fī maʿrifat al-aqālīm*, trans. Basil A. Collins as *The Best Divisions for Knowledge of the Regions* (Reading: Garnet Publishing, 2001), 119.

[6] ʿIzz al-Dīn Ibn al-Athīr, *Al-Kāmil fī ʾl-Tāʾrīkh*, ed. Carl J. Tornberg (repr. Beirut: Dār Bairūt, 1979), IX, 35–8, 71–3, 349, 362, 397 and X, 10, 17–18.

[7] British Library manuscript Or. 5803.

[8] Aḥmad ibn Yūsuf ibn ʿAlī Ibn al-Azraq, *Tāʾrīkh Mayyāfāriqīn wa-Āmid*, ed. Badawī ʿAbd al-Laṭīf ʿAwad (Cairo: General Organisation for G.P.O.s, 1959), 15.

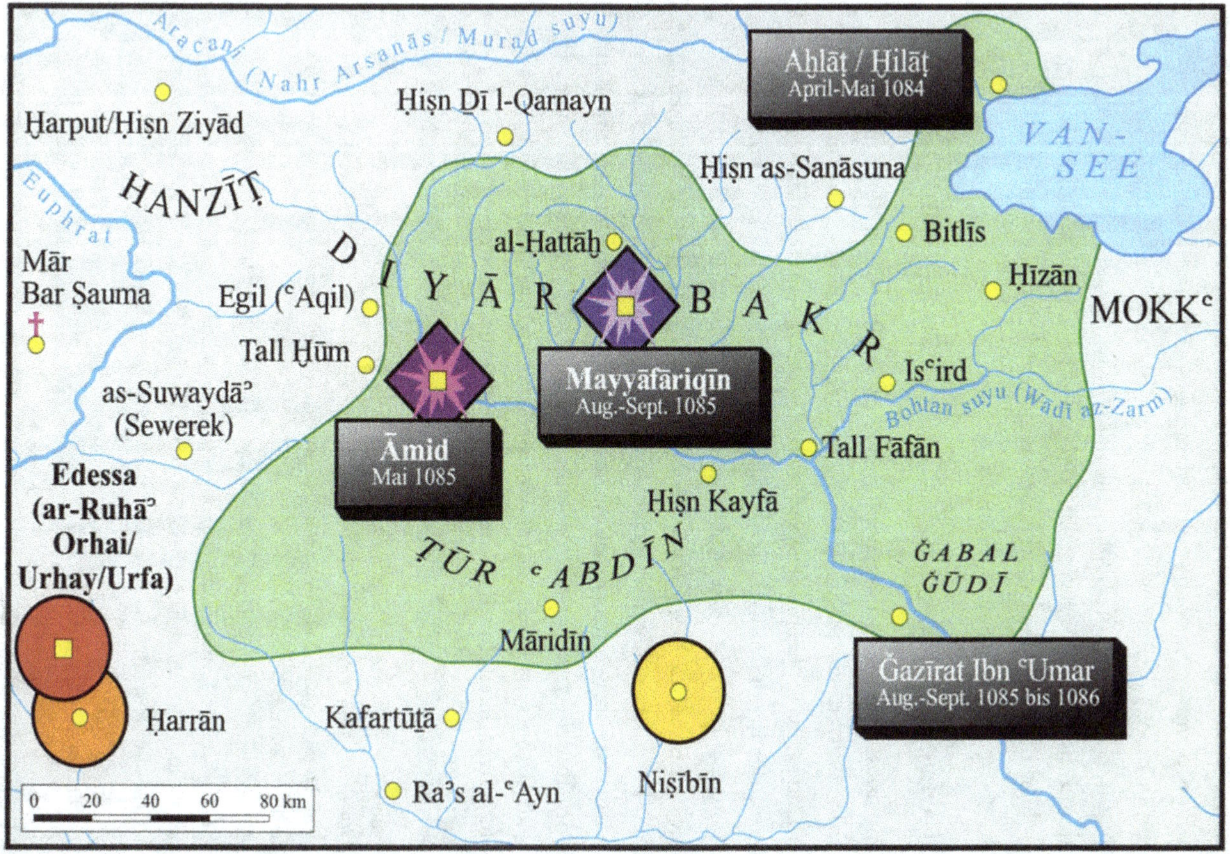

Figure 9.1 Map of the Marwānid territories, 990–1 to 1085–6.

(After Ripper, *Die Marwāniden von Diyār Bakr*, fig. 3.)

article by Amedroz in 1903.[9] When recording the history of the Marwānids, Ibn al-Azraq's account is essentially focused on Mayyāfāriqīn, which was their capital. It chronicles the violent events which preceded the establishment of a Kurdish state centred on the city. It then moves on to record the short periods in power of the first two Marwānid *amīrs*, Bādh the Kurd and Mumahhid al-Dawla, before dealing in great detail with the apogee of Marwānid rule, the fifty-one-year-long reign of Naṣr al-Dawla. The subsequent downfall of Marwānid power is also covered by Ibn al-Azraq.[10]

It must be admitted that Ibn al-Azraq's chronicle is disordered and at times repetitive. Small snippets of information about local events in Diyār Bakr are more frequent than occasional longer narratives; this is especially the case when he is dealing with Naṣr al-Dawla. Moreover, Ibn al-Azraq does not produce many insights into the characteristics of the society he is describing. The impact of the nomads, who lived in the hinterlands of Diyār Bakr, on the settled urban populations is scarcely mentioned, and he shows little interest in the lives of the predominantly Christian population in the cities of Mayyāfāriqīn and neighbouring Āmid. It seems that he took for granted the ethnic, linguistic and religious diversity of the society in which he lived.

The Marwānid Dynasty

The Marwānids ruled from 380/990 until 478/1085. This dynasty established itself in the province of Diyār Bakr, seizing territory situated on the southern and western fringes of Armenia and Kurdistān. Their dynasty began with a Kurdish chief known as Bādh the Kurd, who came from the hills near Hizan, in the province of Bidlīs. After the death of the principal Būyid *amīr*, ʿAḍud al-Dawla, in 373/983, Bādh took possession of Mayyāfāriqīn and thereafter

[9] Henry F. Amedroz, 'The Marwānid dynasty at Mayyāfāriqīn in the tenth and eleventh centuries A.D.', *Journal of the Royal Asiatic Society of Great Britain and Ireland* (1903), 123–54. See also Paul A. Blaum, 'A History of the Kurdish Marwānid Dynasty (983–1085), Part I', *Kurdish Studies: An International Journal* 5: 1–2 (1992), 54–68, and Paul A. Blaum, 'A History of the Kurdish Marwānid Dynasty (983–1085), Part II', *Kurdish Studies: An International Journal* 6: 1–2 (1993), 40–65.

[10] Carole Hillenbrand, 'Marwānids', *Encyclopaedia of Islam, 2nd edn* (*EI*²), vi (Leiden: Brill, 1991), 626–7; for the wider context, see Carole Hillenbrand, 'Mayyāfāriqīn', *EI*², vi, 930–2.

seized the cities of Āmid, Naṣībīn and Akhlāṭ, despite the efforts of Būyid and Ḥamdānid troops to unseat him.[11] In 380/990, however, after he had tried unsuccessfully to take Mosul, Bādh was killed in a battle against a coalition of Ḥamdānid and ʿUqaylid troops. After Bādh's death, members of his family succeeded in establishing the Kurdish Marwānid dynasty (five rulers in all) which lasted almost a hundred years.

Bādh's sister had married a mill owner called Marwān, from whom the name of the dynasty derived. Three of their sons – al-Ḥasan, Saʿīd and Aḥmad – are mentioned in the Arabic sources. The eldest son, al-Ḥasan, known as Abū ʿAlī, had been with Bādh when he died. He made his way to Mayyāfāriqīn with his uncle's widow, a woman from Daylam, whom he subsequently married. He took possession of Mayyāfāriqīn and Āmid and became the first ruler of the Marwānid dynasty in the province of Diyār Bakr. After his murder at Āmid in 387/997, his brother Saʿīd, known as Mumaḥḥid al-Dawla, ruled until 401/1011. These two precarious reigns paved the way for the accession of the third brother, Aḥmad, known by the honorific title of Naṣr al-Dawla. His reign of fifty years marked the crowning period of Marwānid power and prestige. After his death, his son and grandson ruled. The dynasty came to an end in 478/1085.

Mumaḥḥid al-Dawla was able to rule for twice as long as his elder brother, and it was in his reign that the beginnings of a foreign policy involving his neighbours took shape. But much more was to come in the heyday of Marwānid power under Naṣr al-Dawla, who ruled long and very successfully from 401/1010 until 453/1061. The Marwānid state at this time stretched as far south as Akhlāṭ, the borders of Lake Vān and Jazīrat ibn ʿUmar.[12] The Marwānids controlled the key routes from the eastern Anatolian plateau to the plains of the Jazīra, with Mayyāfāriqīn in the centre, Arzan and Siʿird to the east and Āmid to the west. The Byzantines seem to have accepted the Marwānids, like the Ḥamdānids and the Mirdāsids further to the south-west, as a buffer state between them and the wider Muslim world.[13]

[11] Ibn al-Athīr, *Tāʾrīkh*, IX, 35–6; Ibn al-Azraq, *Tāʾrīkh*, 49–52.

[12] Carl F. Lehmann-Haupt, *Armenien einst und jetzt: Reisen und Forschungen* (Berlin: Behr's Verlag, 1910), I, 423.

[13] Kennedy, *Age of the Caliphates*, 264.

How the Marwānids Proclaimed their Power

In the thirteen-year reign of the second Marwānid ruler, Mumahhid al-Dawla (387/997–401/1010), the state gradually began to stabilise and to assert its power vis-à-vis its subjects and neighbouring polities in various ways. The Marwānids expressed their military power by building castles and fortifying city walls; to trumpet their political power and their legitimacy, they obsessively festooned both the exterior and the interior of those walls with their names and official titles; and they also exploited diplomacy and knew how to orchestrate court ceremonial so as to present themselves as a good deal more important than they really were. These various devices can be seen as a calculated performance of power whose various expressions worked in concert. Each of them deserves some discussion.

The military and legitimising aspects

The military and legitimising aspects of the proclamation of Marwānid power worked quite naturally in tandem. During his reign Mumaḥḥid al-Dawla built up the walls of Mayyāfāriqīn, including the cylindrical tower (dated 1000–1 in a surviving inscription)[14] at the north-east corner of the walls, where a Ḥamdānid attack might be expected. Ibn al-Azraq records seeing his name on the outside of the wall in twenty-two places and on a number of further places on the inside wall.[15] This remarkable epigraphic overload offers further evidence of his marked tendency towards self-promotion. Even the much bigger city of ʿAmid cannot rival this proliferation of inscriptions, although it is likely that ʿAmid formerly had many more inscriptions on its walls than now survive.[16]

[14] Lehmann-Haupt, *Armenien*, I, 424, with plate.

[15] Aḥmad b. Muḥammad Ibn Khallikān, *Kitāb Wafayāt al-Aʿyān*, trans. Baron William MacGuckin de Slane as *Ibn Khallikān's Biographical Dictionary*, 4 vols (repr. Beirut: Librairie du Liban, 1970) I, 157–8.

[16] For the inscriptions on the walls of Āmid, see Max van Berchem, 'Matériaux pour l'épigraphie et l'histoire musulmanes du Diyar-Bekr', in Max van Berchem and Josef Strzygowski, *Amida* (Heidelberg and Paris: Carl Winter's Universitätsbuchhandlung and Ernest Leroux, 1910), 6–74; Samuel Flury, *Islamische Schriftbänder: Amida – Diarbekr XI. Jahrhundert. Beilage zu den Jahresberichten des Gymnasiums, der Realschule und der Tochterschule in Basel. Schuljahr 1919/20* (Basel: Frobenius A.G., 1920); Sheila S. Blair, 'Decoration of city walls in the medieval Islamic world: The epigraphic message', in James D. Tracy (ed.), *City Walls: The Urban Enceinte in Global Perspective* (Cambridge: Cambridge University Press, 2000), 510–25.

It is worth investigating how Naṣr al-Dawla built up Mayyāfāriqīn into a well-defended capital city. The medieval Arab geographer al-Muqaddasī describes Mayyāfāriqīn as a fine city, with a sturdy stone wall, battlements, a deep ditch and extensive suburbs.[17] Early on in the reign of Naṣr al-Dawla, since his palace had been destroyed, he decided to renovate the existing castle, which had belonged to the Ḥamdānids, and to build next to it a *burj al-mulk* or centre of government adjoining it. He thus ensured the safety of his official residence.[18] The castle was situated high up on a hill, thereby offering the ruler ample protection and allowing guards to warn of any approaching troops or caravans. The Marwānid principality was after all a buffer state, and buffer states were justifiably nervous of their neighbours and therefore needed to take precautions against potential hostilities. So, it is not surprising that the celebrated vizier of Naṣr al-Dawla, Abū'l-Qāsim al-Maghribī, advised him to build this tower in a position dominating the whole city. Clearly this strategy would impress and intimidate the population both of the town and of the neighbouring settlements in the area, as well as any non-local travellers, merchants, ambassadors and other visitors. But even more importantly these buildings would serve as prestige symbols emphasising his power and grandeur. So, an alternative translation for the Arabic name of this structure could well be 'tower of power'.

According to Ibn al-Azraq, Naṣr al-Dawla ordered work on the castle and tower to begin in the year 403/1012 and he spent a lot of money on it. He even embellished the interior of the castle, placing gold on its walls and ceilings. He constructed an elaborate water system for the castle and placed pools and a bath there. What is extraordinary is that the work was begun and completed within a single year.[19] That is a truly remarkable achievement. It testifies not only to the *amīr*'s determination but also to his wealth and the efficiency of his administration. The building of the tower and the reconstruction of the castle alone (Figure 9.2) would have required the quarrying, transport and dressing of a huge quantity of stone, which would have needed larger numbers of unskilled labourers. The internal decoration of these buildings

[17] Al-Muqaddasī, *Best Divisions*, 140.

[18] Ibn al-Azraq, *Tā'rīkh*, 107.

[19] Ibn al-Azraq, *Tā'rīkh*, 108.

Figure 9.2 Two views of a tower on the walls of Mayyāfāriqīn, now called Silvan.

called for yet more specialised craftsmen. Many spectators came to admire these innovations, so it is clear that this was no run-of-the-mill project.

No detailed examination of the fortifications of Mayyāfāriqīn has yet been carried out, and the dating of its component surfaces is uncertain, though it is very likely that what survives is largely of Marwānid and Artuqid construction, since those were the glory days of the city.[20] Happily the observant and well-travelled Persian Ismāʿīlī writer, Nāṣir-i Khusrau, visited Mayyāfāriqīn in 1046, and his reactions are worth quoting:

> The place has an enormous fortification made of white stone . . . The top of the rampart is all crenellated and looks as though the master builder had just finished work on it. The city has one gate on the west side set in a large gateway with a masonry arch and an iron door with no wood in it. It has a Friday mosque that would take too long to describe [Figure 9.3].[21]

[20] For the topography of the city, see Josef Markwart, *Südarmenien und die Tigrisquellen nach griechischen und arabischen Geographen* (Vienna: Mechitharisten-Buchdruckerei, 1930), 193–8.

[21] Nāṣir-i Khusrau, *Nāṣer-e Khosraw's Book of Travels (Safarnāma)*, trans. Wheeler M. Thackston Jr (Albany: Bibliotheca Persiana/State University of New York Press, 1986), 7.

Figure 9.3 Two views of the exterior of the Friday Mosque of Mayyāfāriqīn.

Clearly, Nāṣir-i Khusrau was struck by the sheer scale of the fortifications, and that chimes with the tenor of Ibn al-Azraq's comments. He notes the whiteness of the stone, a stark contrast to the black basalt of the walls of Āmid, which he praises in hyperbolic terms. And he lays special stress on the iron gate with no wood in it. This obviously added much to the strength of the city's defences; the norm in medieval cities of the Mashriq was to have gates of wood reinforced with iron spikes. But this was still the most vulnerable point in the defences. A gate made entirely of iron was a significant technical undertaking. There is now no trace of the ramparts admired by Nāṣir-i Khusrau, but the largest surviving tower of whitish stone, dressed in large blocks carefully fitted together, strengthened by molten lead and furnished with projecting bosses, again represents a significant technical achievement. So much for the military aspect of the Marwānid proclamation of power.

Diplomacy and ceremony

The Byzantine historian Michael Psellus records that the emperor Basil 'spent the greater part of his reign serving as a soldier on guard at our frontiers'.[22] So

[22] Michael Psellus, *Fourteen Byzantine Rulers: The Chronographia of Michael Psellus*, trans. Edgar R. A. Sewter (London: Penguin Books, 1966), 46.

it is not surprising that Ibn al-Azraq records rather elliptically that in 390/999 the Byzantine emperor Basil II (976–125) went to Āmid and Mayyāfāriqīn. His behaviour on this occasion proved to be in keeping with his regular policy towards his empire's eastern neighbours, which often involved the exercise of peaceful diplomacy rather than military means. Clearly, he well understood the value of face-to-face contact. Basil met Mumaḥḥid al-Dawla and they swore oaths to each other and reached an agreement.[23] Ibn al-Azraq does not mention any more details about the reasons for this visit but he records that Mumaḥḥid al-Dawla then wrote to various rulers and to the caliph in

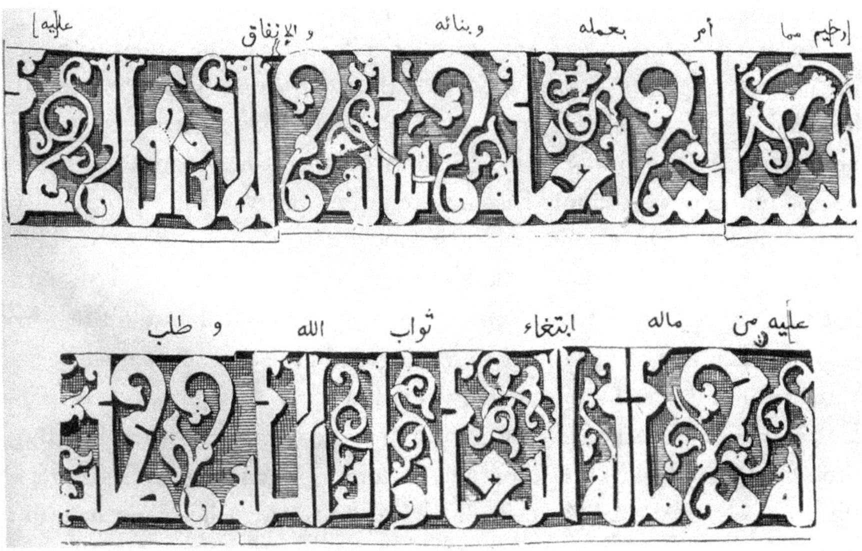

Figure 9.4 Drawing of an inscription in the name of Naṣr al-Dawla at Āmid, 437/1045–6.

(After Flury, *Islamische Schriftbänder*, pl. 4)

[23] Ibn al-Azraq, *Tāʾrīkh*, 84. This visit is also mentioned in the Armenian chronicle of Stepʿanos Tarōnecʿi: Tim Greenwood, *The Universal History of Stepʿanos Tarōnecʿi: Introduction, Translation and Commentary* (Oxford: Oxford University Press, 2017), 308. However, Bar Hebraeus mentions Basil's successful campaign in the east a few years earlier: Bar Hebraeus, *The Chronography of Gregory Abuʾl-Faraj 1225–1286*, trans. Ernest A. W. Budge (London: Oxford University Press, 1932) I, 180. Ostrogorsky also refers to Basil's return to the east, including Syria and the Caucasus region, 'several years' after 995: George Ostrogorsky, *History of the Byzantine State*, trans. Joan Hussey, 2nd edn (Oxford: Basil Blackwell, 1968), 308.

Baghdad. Clearly, he was eager to assert himself as a power in the land, and a good way of attaining that goal was to cement his relationship with his neighbours near and far, all of whom were of a higher status than he was. This was where his geographical position at a confessional and political crossroads helped him. The caliph and the Būyid *amīr*s, Bahā᾿ al-Dawla and his son Fakhr al-Mulk, honoured him. He also received letters and presents from the Fāṭimid caliph, al-Ḥākim, in Egypt.[24] These high-level contacts with Muslim powers contextualise his meeting with the Byzantine emperor, who would of course have had in mind the Christian population living under Marwānid rule. So these diplomatic overtures show the Marwānid monarch working hard to improve his status vis-à-vis his neighbours.

But much more was to come. Years later, the news of the imposing building projects of Naṣr al-Dawla at Mayyāfāriqīn and Āmid (Figure 9.4) would have spread far and wide, and word of it would certainly have reached his neighbours. Small wonder, then, that ambassadors from all four of the larger neighbouring powers should hasten to test the veracity of these reports. And their visits were timed precisely to coincide with the end of the building programme. So, it is anything but coincidence that we read of the sumptuous reception planned by the *amīr* for the end of the last month of the very year in which he had begun work on this grand project, a project which had clearly from the start been intended to mark the arrival of a new power in the land, a ruler to be reckoned with. And so it proved. The brand-new buildings proclaimed his wealth, his power and his ambition, and the ambassadors of the Fāṭimids, of the caliph in Baghdad, of the Būyids who controlled him, and of the Byzantine emperor were there to appraise the newcomer in his seat of power. The *amīr* must have had faith in the ability of the master builder and his men to complete the work on time, for the simultaneous arrival of ambassadors from four polities that were far away from Mayyāfāriqīn – Baghdad, Constantinople and Cairo – implies that they had received the invitation to attend some considerable time in advance. As Ibn al-Azraq writes:

> On the fourth day of the ʿīd, Naṣr al-Dawla sat on the throne to celebrate the ʿīd. The emissaries of the caliph and the sultan sat on the right and the

[24] Ibn al-Azraq, *Tāʾrīkh*, 86.

> emissaries of Egypt and Byzantium sat on the left. Poets and reciters came. It was a great day and a blessed ʿīd . . . Proclamations were read out to the people in the presence of the envoys and the commanders. The amīr wore robes of honour and he gave robes of honour to the envoys, the like of which there was not.[25]

This account of Ibn al-Azraq vividly evokes a new repurposing of an ancient tradition that stretched back to Sasanian times, namely the family of kings gathered around the throne of their overlord. That was by no means the political reality in 403/1012, but for those local people gathered together to participate in that grand reception, the sight of their *amīr* enthroned amidst the representatives of all the great neighbouring powers, with the seating plan making explicit their lower status on this occasion, would have been unforgettable. The stage management of this occasion, timed to coincide with the first day of the *ʿīd*, compels admiration as a piece of political theatre.

It is interesting to speculate on the background to this grand occasion in Mayyāfāriqīn in 403/1012. It was surely masterminded by Naṣr al-Dawla or his vizier, or by both of them in concert. Perhaps they had spread the news of the achievements of Naṣr al-Dawla across the borders into Iraq, Syria and Byzantium. An alternative possibility would be that the four emissaries had been sent by two caliphs, the Byzantine emperor and a Būyid *amīr* to establish good relations with Naṣr al-Dawla, the new ruler of Diyār Bakr, an important state that bordered or was close to their own territories. But the precise timing of the occasion makes that somewhat unlikely. It is also significant that Naṣr al-Dawla was willing to welcome and honour envoys sent by both Sunni and Shiʿite caliphs as well as the Christian emperor of Byzantium. This event was typical of the strategy of accommodation and self-preservation consistently used by Naṣr al-Dawla vis-à vis the three great powers of the time: Byzantium, Egypt and Baghdad. He made it his business to cultivate friendly relations with all of them, even the redoubtable Byzantine emperor. Within his own territory, as Ibn al-Azraq writes, 'his command was strong. There was nobody who defied him.'[26]

[25] Ibn al-Azraq, *Tāʾrīkh*, 110.

[26] Ibn al-Azraq, *Tāʾrīkh*, 104.

Other Aspects of Marwānid Rule

What of the government, the court and the public works of Naṣr al-Dawla during his extremely long reign? As early as the year 403/1012, according to Ibn al-Azraq, Naṣr al-Dawla was busy ordering that parts of the walls of Mayyāfāriqīn which had collapsed should be built up again, and he placed small dwelling places for the citizens on the walls.[27] In the year 414/1023 he built and endowed a hospital and renovated the Friday mosque.[28] Also in that year he constructed the minaret of the mosque in the suburb. He built an excellent bridge. So clearly, he fulfilled one of the basic duties of a virtuous Muslim ruler, namely to build widely for the public good. Indeed, he increased the amenities of Mayyāfāriqīn substantially. He restored the old observatory, put a clock in the Friday mosque, planted the citadel garden, repaired and added to the city walls,[29] constructed and endowed several bridges, and erected public baths. He also made Mayyāfāriqīn a hub of religious scholarship, and his court was a safe haven for many a political refugee.

Happily, Naṣr al-Dawla also had a lighter side. Ibn al-Athīr provides with obvious relish an account of his lifestyle:

> He lived the life of ease and comfort unheard-of by any other of his contemporaries. He possessed singing girls, some of whom he had purchased for five thousand dīnārs or more. He maintained five hundred concubines, and five hundred eunuchs . . . He sent cooks to Egypt and spent a vast sum on their mission until they had learnt the local cuisine. He sent an enormous present to the Seljūq sulṭān Ṭughril Beg, part of which was the 'Ruby Mountain' which had belonged to the Būyids. In addition he sent with it one hundred thousand dīnārs.[30]

Thus this shrewd and experienced ruler of a small border state knew how to ingratiate himself with an intimidating and dangerous newcomer from the distant east.

[27] Ibn al-Azraq, *Tāʾrīkh*, 110.

[28] Ibn al-Azraq, *Tāʾrīkh*, 122.

[29] Max van Berchem, 'Arabische Inschriften', in Carl F. Lehmann-Haupt, *Materialien zur älteren Geschichte Armeniens und Mesopotamiens*. Abhandlungen der königlichen Gesellschaft der Wissenschaften zu Göttingen. Philologisch-Historische Klasse, Neue Folge Band IX/3 (Berlin: Weidmann, 1906), 129–32.

[30] Ibn al-Athīr, *Tāʾrīkh*, X, 17–18.

Naṣr al-Dawla placed a great deal of responsibility for the governing of his state on his viziers, two of whom were famous in their time. The first one was Abū'l-Qāsim al-Ḥusayn al-Maghribī, who came from a family of famous bureaucrats. Ibn al-Azraq describes him as 'the administrator (*mudīr*) of the state and the lord of its politics'.[31] The other vizier of special note was the even more famous Fakhr al-Dawla Ibn Jahīr, who remained in the position of vizier for the rest of the reign of Naṣr al-Dawla. Both men had served other masters of high rank. These men were brilliantly chosen. Al-Maghribī is warmly praised by Ibn Khallikān, who mentions him in his biography of Naṣr al-Dawla, extolling the vizier's erudition in both the arts and the sciences and mentioning his previous employment as secretary of state to the ʿUqaylid *amīr* and several other dynastic leaders in the area.[32] Even more importance is accorded by Ibn Khallikān to Ibn Jahīr (d. 1090), who went on to exercise great power in Baghdad and to whom he devotes an unusually lengthy biography.[33] So under Naṣr al-Dawla the Marwānid state was in the safest of hands.

Naṣr al-Dawla also enjoyed a harmonious relationship with the citizens of Mayyāfāriqīn, distributing charity on a regular basis, and his rule ushered in a period of great prosperity. Only his death put an end to this idyll. Prestigious marriages were a valuable tool in the political strategy of the Marwānids. A typical example was a marriage arranged between a member of the Marwānid family and an Armenian princess from the noble house of Sanasnaykʿ, the descendants of Sanasar.[34] She owned strong fortresses near Akhlāṭ. Furthermore, Naṣr al-Dawla married a lady called al-Fuḍuliyya, the daughter of Faḍlūn b. Manūchihr, the lord of the province of Arrān and upper Armenia. This wife bore him two sons.[35]

The Marwānids took suitable measures to guard against internal rivals and external threats. In gaining control of the city of Mayyāfāriqīn and their other territorial possessions in Diyār Bakr, the Marwānid rulers were violent and ruthless, not hesitating to banish from the city undesirable and hostile

[31] Ibn al-Azraq, *Tāʾrīkh*, 103.

[32] Ibn Khallikān, *Biographical Dictionary* I, 158.

[33] Ibn Khallikān, *Biographical Dictionary* IV, 280–7.

[34] In Arabic sources the name undergoes a change, in that the province of Sasun becomes *jabal al-sanāsana*.

[35] Ibn al-Azraq, *Tāʾrīkh*, 121.

elements; Ibn al-Azraq records that Naṣr al-Dawla banished from Mayyāfāriqīn 'those who were sinful and harmful and evildoers'.[36] It happened quite frequently that opponents were murdered. Speaking of a potentially dangerous rival of Naṣr al-Dawla, a man called Sharwa, Ibn al-Azraq records laconically that Naṣr al-Dawla 'strangled him and crucified his corpse'.[37]

On the matter of the defence of the Marwānid state and its capital, Mayyāfāriqīn, the city proved to be a most impressive stronghold against possible enemy attacks. The Marwānids would have heard about Turkish nomads streaming into south-eastern Anatolia and threatening Byzantine territories and they were also aware of rumours of even more dangerous threats from the east after the Seljūq leaders Ṭughril and Chaghrı had taken possession of Khurāsān, and Ṭughril and his nomadic followers were moving westwards across Iran. A taste of what was to come occurred in the year 434/1042 and it directly involved the Marwānids. Ibn al-Azraq writes a long account of the arrival in Diyār Bakr of Turkish troops from the east. Ṭughril sent two *amīrs*, or commanders, accompanied by 10,000 horsemen, to Diyār Bakr, having given the area to them as *iqṭā*ʿs (administrative grants whose revenues were for the use of the grantee). They arrived, raided the lands, plundered and then encamped outside the gates of Mayyāfāriqīn, which remained closed for several days. Conversation between those outside the walls and those inside continued for some time. The account of Ibn al-Azraq continues as follows:

> They (the Turcomans) were offered about fifty thousand dīnārs to retreat but they did not agree to that. It happened one night that they drank and got drunk . . . and they quarrelled and came to blows. Each one of them struck his neighbour with a knife and they both fell dead . . . The amīr (Naṣr al-Dawla) and his troops went out, plundered what they had, killed many of them and took a great number of prisoners . . . This was the first appearance of the Turcomans in this country.[38]

[36] Ibn al-Azraq, *Tāʾrīkh*, 102.

[37] Ibn al-Azraq, *Tāʾrīkh*, 103. For the history of Sharwa b. Muḥammad, the chamberlain of Mumaḥḥid al-Dawlah, who briefly usurped the throne and even minted coins in his name, see Stefan Heidemann, 'A new ruler of the Marwānid emirate in 401/1010 – and further considerations on the legitimizing power of regicide', *Aram* 9–10 (1997–8), 599–615.

[38] Ibn al-Azraq, *Tāʾrīkh*, 160–1.

This recalls the words of Matthew of Edessa when the Turks invaded Armenia in 467/1018–19: it was the 'first irruption of fierce bloodthirsty beasts, the savage nation of infidels called Turks'.[39]

It is time to attempt an overview of the reign of Naṣr al-Dawla. He emerges as a flamboyant ruler with plenty of political acumen and extravagant tastes. His religious stance appears to have been a pragmatic one, suitable for the ruler of a vulnerable buffer state which was surrounded by powers of the most divergent ethnic and confessional loyalties. It seems likely that he ruled a predominantly Christian population in the towns of the Diyār Bakr province and that he enjoyed a good relationship with Byzantium. The Marwānid capital attracted prominent Muslim religious figures. It is noteworthy that in the reign of Naṣr al-Dawla, the famous religious scholar ʿAbd Allāh al-Kāzarūnī (d. 455/1063) went to Mayyāfāriqīn and spread the Shāfiʿī *madhhab* throughout Diyār Bakr.[40] Shaykh Abū Naṣr al-Manāzī, a high official of Naṣr al-Dawla, collected books and established *waqfs* for libraries in the mosques of Mayyāfāriqīn and Āmid.[41] Poets, among them al-Tihāmī, sought out Naṣr al-Dawla and they were lavish in their praise of him.[42] Naṣr al-Dawla also took good care to remain on friendly terms with the local Christians. Thus, when he undertook building operations on the hill where the convent and Church of the Virgin had formerly stood, he had their relics transferred to the Melkite church.[43]

Naṣr al-Dawla died in 453/1061. Ibn al-Athīr writes warmly about his rule:

> He was 80 and more years of age, and had been emir for 52 years. He had absolute control over affairs in his lands and kept the frontier provinces

[39] Matthew of Edessa, Parmutʿiwn, trans. Édouard Dulaurier as *Chronique de Matthieu d'Edesse (962–1136) avec la Continuation de Grégoire le prêtre jusqu'en 1162 d'après trois manuscrits de la Bibliothèque impériale de Paris* (Paris: A. Durand, 1858), 40–1.

[40] Matthew of Edessa, *Chronique*, 52.

[41] Ibn al-Azraq, *Tāʾrīkh*, 131.

[42] Ibn al-Azraq, *Tāʾrīkh*, 144.

[43] Ibn al-Azraq, *Tāʾrīkh*, 107–8. However Naṣr al-Dawla repeatedly fought the Byzantines in a bid to control Edessa (Ernst Honigmann, *Die Ostgrenze des Byzantinischen Reiches von 363 bis 1071 nach griechischen, arabischen, syrischen und armenischen Quellen* (Brussels: Éditions de l'Institut de Philologie et d'Histoire Orientales: 1935), 134, 136–8).

> flourishing and in order. He lived a life of ease and comfort unheard of for any other of his contemporaries.[44]

The death of Naṣr al-Dawla in 453/1061 heralded the final stage of Marwānid rule; thereafter, the power and prestige of the dynasty declined markedly. His son, Niẓām al-Dīn Naṣr, succeeded him, at first only in Mayyāfāriqīn and then two years later in Āmid too. On his death (472/1079) his son Nasir al-Dawla Manṣūr, the last Marwānid ruler, came to power. The vizier Ibn Jahīr, who had left Diyār Bakr for Baghdad, turned against the son of his former master, Naṣr al-Dawla, and used his influence with the Seljūq sultan Malikshāh and his vizier Niẓām al-Mulk to persuade them to bring the Marwānid dynasty to an end and to seize their treasures. In 478/1085 Diyār Bakr fell to Ibn Jahīr and direct Seljūq Turkish control was imposed.[45] Ibn Jahīr took their treasury for himself and the last Marwānid ruler, Manṣūr, was given Jazīrat Ibn ʿUmar, where he lived on until 489/1096.

Conclusion

Hugh Kennedy has rightly called the period 950–1050 'a Kurdish interlude'[46] during which Naṣr al-Dawla was renowned for excellent government and for enjoying good relations with local civilian elites. The eastern frontier between the Byzantine empire and the Muslim states on the border remained relatively stable in this period, and much of the credit for this must be laid squarely on the shoulders of this astute and far-sighted ruler who enjoyed the good things of life while keeping an eagle eye on both the big and the little picture. He was in many ways a worthy precursor of Saladin.

44 Ibn al-Athīr, *Tāʾrīkh*, trans. Donald S. Richards as *The Annals of the Saljuq Turks: Selections from al-Kāmil fi'l-Tāʾrīkh of ʿIzz al-Dīn Ibn al-Athīr* (London: RoutledgeCurzon, 2002), 135.

45 Ibn al-Athīr, *Annals*, trans. Richards, 140.

46 Kennedy, *Age of the Caliphates*, 266.

10

BYZANTINE POPULATION POLICY IN THE EASTERN BORDERLAND BETWEEN BYZANTIUM AND THE CALIPHATE FROM THE SEVENTH TO THE TWELFTH CENTURIES[1]

Ralph-Johannes Lilie

Before we consider the borderlands between Byzantium and its Muslim neighbours, it will be necessary to start with a well-known commonplace: when speaking of borders today, we think of definite lines that are largely impenetrable. Well-known modern examples are the Berlin Wall, or the 'Trump Wall' planned between USA and Mexico. Maps in historical atlases invoke a similar impression. In fact, however, in earlier times this was extremely rarely the case, as with the Roman Limes in Germany, Hadrian's Wall between England and Scotland, or the Chinese Great Wall.

These, however, were great exceptions. As a rule, no defined borders existed, except perhaps at a river or a coastline, and even there, they were not impassable. Just one example: although Byzantium was able successfully to defend the border at the Danube in the sixth and early seventh century, it could nevertheless not prevent this line being breached repeatedly by Avars,

[1] For the English translation of this text, I am indebted to Dr Cornelia Oefelein, and for its further English editing to Deborah G. Tor. Of course, any faults that remain are my own.

in particular Slavs. Thus, control of the hinterland was lost almost completely, leading to the very loss of the borderline itself some decades later. The more usual case in the pre-modern world, however, was that borders between different powers were usually blurred: regions that they would control more or less, usually less.

But it is certainly important to differentiate between times of peace and those of warfare: in peace, a closely guarded borderline was unnecessary. It sufficed to establish specific checkpoints, be it directly at the border or in the hinterland, where foreigners, merchants, pilgrims, or other travellers entered or exited imperial territory, or where they were otherwise required to report to authorities. Well-known examples include, in the Balkans, Thessaloniki, or later Belgrade in the Middle Byzantine period; Laodicea and Antioch in Northern Syria; and Trebizond on the Black Sea coast. To Constantinople, access, as a rule, was generally restricted.

Equally important is another factor for the fate of the borderland: controlling border regions became important and at once problematic when confronting powers pursuing inherently aggressive politics. This was almost always the case at the eastern border during the Umayyad and the Abbasid dynasties, and later after the arrival of the Seljuqs and the Turcoman nomads. But what could Byzantium do to ward off these threats? Let us try to analyse more closely the problems confronting a centralised government attempting to control disputed borders. Essentially there were four possibilities:

1. The first option is to garrison additional troops, to strengthen existing fortifications and to build new ones. But what can be done if the enemy has broken through this fortified borderline and entered the hinterland?
2. The second option is the devastation of the border region, which might establish a kind of no man's land. By this means, a policy could make it more difficult for the enemy to cross the area. But in consequence, this region would be lost for any military or economic utilisation.
3. Another option could be to strengthen the region's economics, infrastructure, and population by creating or supporting small buffer states or semi-independent local forces on both sides of the borderline. Obviously, it would create a problem of its own to control those minor local powers, especially in times of need.

4. A final and extreme option is to abandon the whole region and to retreat into the interior provinces. But it is evident that this would only delay the problem, since the former hinterland would become the new border region, producing the same problems as before.

These four possibilities naturally did not exist separately but could occur synchronously or in mixed forms. Over the centuries, the Byzantines actually tried each of these options in turn. This chapter aims to analyse the methods and effects of the particular policies during the different times and options, while keeping in mind, of course, that these different policies most certainly were not well-thought-out strategies designed for longer periods of time, but mostly reactions planned ad hoc in response to prevailing conditions. So let us take a closer look at the developments on the eastern border of Byzantium between the seventh and the twelfth centuries.[2]

1. The Border up to the Mid-seventh Century (640 AD)

From the early Byzantine era up to the end of the sixth century, the eastern border of Byzantium was secured by the stationing of troops and by constructing fortresses and fortified cities, and also through treaties with various local powers, mostly Armenians and Arab Ghassānids. This was only partly successful. Essentially the situation remained largely the same during this period.

This system came to an end during the first twenty years of the seventh century as the Byzantine central government exhausted itself in civil wars, while the

[2] A full documentation is not possible in this short chapter. Still important is the article by John Frederick Haldon and Hugh Kennedy, 'The Arab–Byzantine Frontier in the Eighth and Ninth Centuries: Military Organization and Society in the Borderlands', *Recueil des Travaux de l'Institut d'Etudes Byzantins* 19 (1980), 79–116; see also Ralph-Johannes Lilie, 'The Byzantine–Arab Borderland from the 7th to the 9th Century', in Florin Curta (ed.), *Borders, Barriers, and Ethnogenesis. Frontiers in Late Antiquity and the Middle Ages* (Turnhout: Brepols, 2006), 13–21; for the twelfth century, still useful is Speros Vryonis Jr, *The Decline of Medieval Hellenism in Asia Minor and the Process of Islamization from the Eleventh to the Fifteenth Century* (Berkeley: University of California Press, 1971); Speros Vryonis Jr, 'Nomadization and Islamization in Asia Minor', *Dumbarton Oaks Papers* 29 (1975), 41–71; Alexander Beihammer, 'Defection Across the Border of Islam and Christianity: Apostasy and Cross-Cultural Interaction in Byzantine–Seljuk Relations', *Speculum* 86 (2011), 597–651.

Persians were able to conquer Syria and Palestine, along with large portions of Asia Minor. Herakleios' final victory in the 620s had no impact, since circumstances would be upended immediately with the ensuing Arab expansion.[3]

2. Islamic Expansion and Constant Invasions (Seventh/Eighth Century)

The Arabs had conquered the whole of Syria by 638, and Byzantine troops withdrew to Asia Minor behind the Taurus Mountains. There appear to have been initial attempts to defend the border with fortresses, but the Arabs overcame this line at will. Over the next around 150 years, Arabs were able to invade Asia Minor once, or even several times, every year, with only brief interruptions. Byzantium reacted by increased militarisation of the interior regions also: the fortifications of the cities were strengthened, and a system developed in which so-called peasant soldiers supplemented the paid troops. This system limited the consequences of the Arab invasions, even though it could not prevent them altogether.[4]

But what were the conditions in the border region? Here we find a different situation. Some fortified cities still remained, but not directly at the border. Due to the constant invasions, there was no longer the infrastructure

[3] For the relations between Byzantium and the Arabs until the seventh century, see Irfan Shahîd, *Byzantium and the Arabs in the Sixth Century* (Washington, DC: Dumbarton Oaks Research Library and Collection, 1995–2009).

[4] Ralph-Johannes Lilie, *Die byzantinische Reaktion auf die Ausbreitung der Araber: Studien zur Strukturwandlung des byzantinischen Staates im 7. und 8. Jahrhundert*, Miscellanea Byzantina Monacensia 22 (Munich: Institut für Byzantinistik und Neugriechische Philologie, 1976); for the fate of cities and the countryside during this time, see Wolfram Brandes, *Die Städte Kleinasiens im 7. und 8. Jahrhundert*, Berliner Byzantinistische Arbeiten 56 (Berlin: Akademieverlag, 1989); John Frederick Haldon, 'Die byzantinische Stadt – Verfall und Wiederaufleben vom 6. bis zum ausgehenden 11. Jahrhundert', in Falko Daim and Jörg Drauschke (eds), *Hinter den Mauern und auf dem offenen Land: Leben im byzantinischen Reich* (Mainz: Verlag des Römisch-Germanischen Zentralmuseums, 2016), 9–22; Ralph-Johannes Lilie, 'Die ökonomische Bedeutung der byzantinischen Provinzstadt (8.–12. Jahrhundert) im Spiegel der literarischen Quellen', in Daim and Drauschke (eds), *Hinter den Mauern und auf dem offenen Land*, 55–62; Ralph-Johannes Lilie, 'Theophanes and al-Ṭabarī on the Arab Invasions of Byzantium', in Hugh Kennedy (ed.), *Al-Ṭabarī, a Medieval Muslim Historian and his Work*, Studies in Late Antiquity and Early Islam 15 (Princeton, NJ: Darwin Press, 2008), 219–36.

necessary for larger cities to continue to exist. There are only very few extant sources on this, but these are undisputed. Arab sources, for example, report that the residents of Sision deserted their city in 711, as circumstances did not allow them to lead their lives in safety.[5] In fact, it must have been almost entirely impossible to pursue regular agricultural activities in this region, with invasions occurring every year, or at least threatened. Residents of other cities must have followed Sision's example, so this region would have been relatively depopulated in the eighth century.

3. Byzantine Reaction (Depopulation – Eighth Century)

The emperors even encouraged this development by withdrawing residents from these regions and relocating them to the interior provinces, such as Thrace. There are examples of this especially for the beginning of the eighth century, but also for the middle of the eighth century, as Byzantium became stronger again. The reason for this was probably grounded in the realisation that the Arabs remained more powerful militarily. Byzantium was not strong enough to maintain a stable military presence in the border region, particularly since Emperor Constantine V was concentrating on regaining the Balkans at this time and was continually involved in wars against the Bulgars.[6]

4. Consequence: No Man's Land with Local Powers (Ninth Century, c. 950)

The consequence of this situation was the deterioration of the border region into a kind of no man's land, only occasionally traversed by larger armies, in which neither side was able to build or maintain enduring strongholds. Such a no man's land was, of course, at once attractive for people or groups seeking more or less secure places of refuge. The most well-known example

[5] Al-Balâdhuri, *The Origins of the Islamic State*, trans. Philip Khury Hitti (New York: Columbia University, 1916), 262.

[6] Hans Ditten, *Ethnische Verschiebungen zwischen der Balkanhalbinsel und Kleinasien vom Ende des 6. bis zur zweiten Hälfte des 9. Jahrhunderts*, Berliner Byzantinistische Arbeiten 59 (Berlin: Akademieverlag, 1992), 177–91, 234–7; Ilse Rochow, *Kaiser Konstantin V. (741–775): Materialien zu seinem Leben und Nachleben*, Berliner Byzantinistische Studien 1 (Frankfurt am Main: Peter Lang, 1994), 91–3, 102–5.

in the eighth/ninth century are the Paulicians, who established their state around Tephrike, which they managed to maintain up to the 870s until subjugated by Emperor Basil I.[7] Less tangible are the *akritai*, about whom we have knowledge primarily from the epic of Digenes Akritas and the Akritic songs (*Akritika tragoudia*), which are not very reliable at all. It seems that the *akritai* acted as relatively independent groups of varying size, which would go on raids and pillage, but which also aided in protecting the frontiers. There were similar groups on the Arab side.[8]

If we consult the 'Digenes Akritas' poem two things are particularly notable: first, religious differences between Christians and Muslims in the border region appear to have played no crucial role; second, the *akritai* seem to have formally recognised the emperor but did not allow him to dictate their conduct. Rather, they regarded themselves as equals and acted according to their own interest. This, by the way, was not restricted to Byzantium. Two centuries later in Spain, the 'Cantar del mio Cid' describes his hero, Don Rodrigo de Bivar, as similarly independent and alternating repeatedly between Christians and Muslims.[9]

[7] For Basil I, see Ralph-Johannes Lilie *et al.*, with Friedhelm Winkelmann, *Prosopographie der mittelbyzantinischen Zeit: Erste Abteilung (641–867)* (Berlin: De Gruyter, 1998–2002), *Zweite Abteilung (867–1025)* (Berlin: De Gruyter, 2009–2013), [*PmbZ*] no. 20837 (also available online at http://www.pom.bbaw.de/pmbz: Basileios I). For the Paulicians, see Paul Lemerle, 'L'histoire des Pauliciens d'Asie mineure d'après les sources grecques', *Travaux et Mémoires* 5 (1970), 1–144; Claudia Ludwig, 'Wer hat was in welcher Absicht wie beschrieben? Bemerkungen zur Historia des Petros Sikeliotes', in Albrecht Berger *et al.* (eds), *Varia II*, Poikila Byzantina 6 (Bonn: Habelt, 1987), 149–227; Ralph-Johannes Lilie, 'Zur Stellung von ethnischen und religiösen Minderheiten in Byzanz: Armenier, Muslime und Paulikianer', in Walter Pohl, Clemens Gantner, and Richard Payne (eds), *Visions of Community in the Post-Roman World: The West, Byzantium, and the Islamic World* (London: Routledge, 2012), 301–15.

[8] Agostino Pertusi, 'Tra storia e leggenda; akritai e ghâzi sulla frontiera orientale di Bizanzio', in Mihai Berza and Eugen Stanescu (eds), *Actes du XIVe congrès international des études byzantines, Bucarest, 6–12 septembre 1971* (Bucarest: Editura Academiei Republicii Socialiste România, 1974), 1: 238–83.

[9] Corinne Jouanno, 'Shared Spaces: Digenis Akritis, the Two-Blood Border Lord', in Carolina Cupane and Bettina Krönung (eds), *Fictional Storytelling in the Medieval Eastern Mediterranean and Beyond* (Leiden: Brill, 2016), 260–84.

Such conduct was, naturally, only possible as long as the emperor or caliph were too weak to conquer even the relatively small number of local powers or were not interested enough in doing so. Especially after the death of al-Muʿtaṣim in 842, local powers in the border region between the caliphate and Byzantium gained greater independence, such as, on the Arab side, the Emir of Melitene, who developed a very strong local power in the mid-ninth century, but nothing more. After defeat in the battle of Porson (863), Melitene lost all significance.[10]

5. Byzantine Reconquista (950–c. 1000)

As the power of the caliphs diminished, the Byzantines gained in strength. They were, however, preoccupied with other powers, such as the Bulgarians, preventing them from re-launching an offensive in the East for some time. In the tenth century, they gradually gained military superiority, and were thus able to recapture many regions that had earlier been Byzantine but had been lost to the Arab conquests. By the beginning of the eleventh century, Byzantium reached a truce with the most important Muslim power, the Egyptian Fatimids.[11] The border remained relatively stable from then until the middle of the eleventh century.

6. Consequences and Organisation (900–c. 1050)

The organisation of this border region in the ninth and tenth century is of the greatest interest for the present analysis. There is a general consensus that the empire's structure in this period was organised in so-called themes. In very simple terms, the provinces were governed by a joint civil and military administration, led by a military *strategos* appointed by the emperor and, as a rule, would be recalled sometime later. The *strategos* commanded an essential number of professional soldiers, while semi-professional farmer soldiers

[10] For the emir of Melitene, see *PmbZ*, ʿUmar ibn ʿAbdallāh ibn Marwān al-Aqtaʿ, no. 8552.

[11] Franz Dölger, *Regesten der Kaiserurkunden des Oströmischen Reiches von 565–1453*, vol. 1/2: *Regesten von 867–1025*, revised 2nd edn Andreas E. Müller with Alexander Beihammer, Corpus der griechischen Urkunden des Mittelalters und der neueren Zeit A/1, 2 (Munich: C. H. Beck, 2003), no. 789e, 792b.

formed the lower ranks. This theme organisation encompassed more or less the entire empire, including the border regions.[12]

But what exactly did this border region look like? We have only very few concrete reports, but one of those may perhaps offer some insight: there are precise contemporary records extant for the expedition against Crete in 961 regarding all participating forces. One of these pertains to the theme Charpezikion in the Byzantine–Armenian border region, which sent the following number of soldiers: the *strategos* and the commanding officers, 274 non-commissioned officers, and 428 soldiers. This is a curious distribution, as it allocates more than one higher officer for every two common soldiers. Charpezikion was the only eastern theme participating in the expedition, and the soldiers were paid for their voluntary participation. In all, they received the total sum of around 3,380 *nomismata*, around forty-four pounds of gold, of which the *strategos* alone received more than half.[13]

In my opinion we are not dealing with a 'normal' province here, but rather with a local sovereign with his retainers, who either lived in Charpezikion or had been settled there with his people. This ruler was quasi-incorporated

[12] For the so-called theme organisation, see John Frederick Haldon, 'Military Service, Military Lands, and the Status of Soldiers: Current Problems and Interpretations', *Dumbarton Oaks Papers* 47 (1993), 1–67; John Frederick Haldon, 'Seventh-Century Continuities: the Ajnād and the "Thematic Myth"', in Averil Cameron (ed.), *The Byzantine and Islamic Near East, vol. 3: States, Resources, Armies*, Studies in Late Antiquity and Early Islam 1 (Princeton, NJ: Darwin Press, 1995), 379–423; Ralph-Johannes Lilie, 'Araber und Themen: Zum Einfluß der arabischen Expansion auf die byzantinische Militärorganisation', in ibid., 425–60; Ralph-Johannes Lilie, *Einführung in die byzantinische Geschichte*, Urban Taschenbücher 617 (Stuttgart: Kohlhammer, 2007), 169–89.

[13] *Book of Ceremonies*, chap. 44, in John Frederick Haldon, 'Theory and Practice in Tenth-Century Military Administration: Chapters II, 44 and 45 of the *Book of Ceremonies*', *Travaux et Mémoires* 13 (2000), 201–352 (Greek text 203–35, Engl. trans. 202–34), here 221, 59–62; commentary ibid., 258–65; see also *PmbZ*, Anonymus, no. 31245; for the expedition against Crete, see *PmbZ*, Konstantinos Gongylios, no. 23823; for the theme of Charpezikion, see Friedrich Hild and Marcell Restle, *Kappadokien (Kappadokia, Charsianon, Sebasteia und Lykandos)*, Tabula Imperii Byzantini 2 = Österreichische Akademie der Wissenschaften, phil.-hist. Klasse, Denkschriften 149 (Vienna: Verlag der Österreichischen Akademie der Wissenschaften, 1981), 86, 88.

by Byzantium in its theme organisation: they conferred upon him the title of *strategos* and paid him and his people. The emperor, however, most likely refrained from interfering in their internal affairs. One could, to a certain extent, best compare these rulers with west European vassals, without however the formal implications. As a rule, they only served in their own region. The prince/*strategos* of Charpezikion was therefore paid extra for his participation in the expedition to the far West.[14] There are also some other indications that there were more such vassalages in the border regions, some involving Armenians and perhaps others, such as Georgians or Arabs, and some involving Byzantine noble families who owned large estates in these regions, such as the Phokades.

One cannot, therefore, speak of a normal provincial organisation as found in the remaining empire. Instead, we are dealing with personal bonds of fealty, where the emperor would not interfere in internal affairs, with the exception of tributes the amounts of which were probably negotiated individually, if not, indeed, the emperor was the one paying.

This was by no means a well thought out and stable system, but dependent on the actual situation, as the campaign by Emperor Basil II in 1021/22 demonstrates. The emperor was forced to abort this campaign in the eastern border region prematurely because two generals, Nikephoros Xiphias and Nikephoros Phokas, attempted an insurrection at the emperor's rear in Cappadocia and Rodandos. The emperor therefore interrupted the campaign. He was able to play the two out against each other; one was killed, the other surrendered and was forced to become a monk. It is unlikely that these were normal governors of the region. But as semi-independent feudal lords with large personal entourages, the conspirators were apparently so dangerous that the emperor was forced to eliminate this threat.[15] This episode also shows that the rulers in the border region must have perceived a too powerful imperial presence as a threat to their independence. Control of the border region was ultimately always dependent upon how strong the central government was.

[14] *PmbZ*, Anonymus, no. 31245; similar Haldon, 'Theory and Practice', 327.

[15] See *PmbZ*, Nikephoros Xiphias, no. 25661; Nikephoros Phokas, no. 25675; for Basil II's campaign, see *PmbZ*, Basileios II., no. 20837.

This did not merely apply to Armenians or other ethnic groups, but also to the Byzantines themselves. In particular, Byzantine aristocratic families in the tenth century attempted to establish their own centres of power in the provinces and even maintained their own relations with their Arab neighbours. In the last quarter of the tenth century, for example, Bardas Phokas, who was later to revolt against Emperor Basil II, received Arab envoys at his stronghold in Charsianon in eastern Asia Minor.[16] To take an additional example: another Byzantine chief commander, Bardas Skleros, who had rebelled against Basil II just prior to Bardas Phokas, fled after his insurgence failed to the court of the caliph, returning to Byzantium sometime later to seek reconciliation with the emperor.[17] There are many additional examples of similar conduct at this time. One cannot necessarily go so far as to claim that these individuals maintained bases of power in the border region itself. The Phokas family, however, owned enormous estates in Cappadocia and in the theme of Charsianon, that is in the immediate hinterlands of the border region, and it is therefore without doubt that they must have wielded considerable influence at the border itself.

That the influence of the central government as a consequence necessarily suffered as well is equally indisputable. It was not noticeable initially, since the Arab neighbours, at the time, posed no greater threat. The only power at the beginning of the eleventh century somewhat comparable to Byzantium were the Fatimids of Egypt, and with these Byzantium had concluded a truce in 1001.[18]

[16] Henry Frederick Amedroz, 'An Embassy from Baghdad to the Emperor Basil II', *Journal of the Royal Asiatic Society* 25 (1914), 915–42, 933–4, 940–1, [919–20, 930]; see also Alexander Beihammer, 'Der harte Sturz des Bardas Skleros: Eine Fallstudie zu zwischenstaatlicher Kommunikation und Konfliktführung in der byzantinisch-arabischen Diplomatie des 10. Jahrhunderts', *Römisch Historische Mitteilungen* 45 (2003), 21–57, 41–2; Alexander Beihammer, 'Strategy of Diplomacy and Ambassadors in Byzantine–Muslim Relations in the Tenth and Eleventh Centuries', in Audrey Becker and Nicolas Drocourt (eds), *Ambassadeurs et ambassades au cœur des relations diplomatiques Rome – Occident Médiéval – Byzance (VIIIe s. avant J.-C – XIIe s. après J.-C.)*, Centre de recherche universitaire Lorrain d'Histoire Universitaire de Lorraine 47 (Metz: Presses Universitaires de Lorraine, 2012), 371–400, here 376–8, 383–4; *PmbZ*, Ibn Šahrām, no. 22703.

[17] See *PmbZ*, Bardas Phokas, no. 20784; Bardas Skleros, no. 20785.

[18] Dölger and Müller, *Regesten*, no. 789e, 792b (by Beihammer).

7. The Seljuqs and the Collapse of the Byzantine Provincial Organisation (1050–c. 1100)

Under these circumstances, the general situation at the eastern frontier remained widely stable until the middle of the eleventh century. Then major upheaval ensued as, on the one hand, internal rivalries within the central administration erupted, and, on the other hand, a new power to the east surfaced with the Seljuqs, who within only a brief time overran the empire's eastern defences. They defeated the main Byzantine army in 1071 at Manzikert, and over the following twenty years conquered the greater part of Asia Minor. Not until the First Crusade would Byzantium be able to partially re-conquer at least parts of western Asia Minor.

It is the First Crusade, however, which shows that the old border organisation had not disappeared entirely. The Latin sources report that the Crusaders travelled through areas in southeastern Asia Minor that declared themselves to be Christian, which the Crusaders restored to Byzantium, as they themselves had no interest in them.[19] Some of these might have been ruled by Armenians, who had migrated from Armenia towards Cilicia. This is an indication that these local powers – at least in part – are successors of the old semi-feudal and semi-independent local lordships that had been only superficially subjected by the Seljuqs but retained their old socio-political power structures. The largest of these principalities was Edessa, which soon after was conquered by the Crusaders, who established there the County of Edessa.

In other words, the old provincial structure developed in the tenth century still existed to a certain extent even after the Seljuq invasion, even though the authority of the emperors in Constantinople was here merely theoretical at best – and, for that matter, not for much longer.

8. 'Feudal' Border Defence (1100–1180)

Byzantine rule over Asia Minor had become so porous that practically all of Asia Minor had become a border region. A border defence was hardly possible, since nearly every Byzantine province or city could become an object

[19] Ralph-Johannes Lilie, *Byzantium and the Crusader States 1096–1204*, Engl. trans. J. C. Morris and Jean E. Ridings (Oxford: Clarendon Press, 1993), 30.

of attack. John II and Manuel I Komnenos therefore instigated a change in strategy. Both emperors attempted to force the powers beyond the frontier regions to recognise Byzantine suzerainty and thereby – in a certain continuation of tenth century politics – have them function as bulwarks against enemy invasions. This pertained in particular to the Crusader states, the principalities of Lesser Armenia, the Turkish Dānishmendids in north-east Asia Minor, and the Seljuqs of Ikonion.[20] This strategy was successful only temporarily, for the most part because it failed to control the Turkoman nomads that followed the Seljuqs to Asia Minor. One consequence was a widespread economic desolation of the Byzantine provinces in Asia Minor, even though they officially remained more or less intact as imperial territory.[21]

9. Collapse of the Central Power and the Emergence of Local Powers (1180–1204)

Byzantium during this period was more concerned with politics in the West, leaving Asia Minor more or less to its own devices. This would prove to have extremely adverse effects after Emperor Manuel's death in 1180, when internal conflicts broke out once again, paralysing the central government. The threat of attacks from the West meant the emperors were hardly present in Asia Minor. One consequence was that these provinces increasingly strove

[20] Generally, see Lilie, *Byzantium and the Crusader States*; Ralph-Johannes Lilie, *Handel und Politik zwischen dem Byzantinischen Reich und den italienischen Kommunen Venedig, Pisa und Genua in der Epoche der Komnenen und der Angeloi (1081–1204)* (Amsterdam: Hakkert, 1984), 169–177; Paul Magdalino, *The Empire of Manuel I Komnenos, 1143–1180* (Cambridge: Cambridge University Press, 1993); Ralph-Johannes Lilie, 'Byzanz – Staat, Wirtschaft und Gesellschaft im 12. Jahrhundert', in Karl-Heinz Rueß (ed.), *Die Staufer und Byzanz* (Göppingen: Gesellschaft für staufische Geschichte e. V., 2013), 10–42; Martin Marko Vučetić, 'Das Abkommen zwischen Kaiser Manuēl I. Komnēnos und Sultan Kiliç Arslan II. (1161/1162): Mechanismen zur Absicherung von Verträgen und ihr Scheitern', in Georg Jostkleigrewe and Gesa Wilangowsky (eds), *Der Bruch des Vertrages: Die Verbindlichkeit spätmittelalterlicher Diplomatie und ihre Grenzen*, Zeitschrift für Historische Forschung 55 (Berlin: Duncker & Humblot, 2018), 175–202.

[21] Until now, the basic work still is Vryonis, *Decline of Medieval Hellenism in Asia Minor*; Vryonis, 'Nomadization and Islamization in Asia Minor'; see also now Beihammer, 'Defection Across the Border of Islam and Christianity'.

towards independence, creating a number of small local lordships which, however, were only able to survive because the Seljuqs of Ikonion were also experiencing internal problems at the same time. Then many Byzantines retreated to Asia Minor after Constantinople was conquered in the Fourth Crusade, thereby reinforcing the Byzantine presence there and strengthening the Byzantine position in western Asia Minor. With Nicaea and Trebizond, two successor states of a certain regional strength were established, and these were able to offer some respite from Turkish pressure for a while. That, however, lies beyond the time frame of this presentation.

10. Résumé

So much for our brief review of the chronological developments. What may we conclude from this examination?

Firstly, there is no indication that Byzantium pursued any specific strategy in the frontier provinces. From the middle of the seventh century, Arab pressure was so heavy that Byzantium was left with only one general strategy of defence: the militarisation of practically the entire empire. Particular activities in the borderland cannot be observed. Although we must assume that this region was widely abandoned in order for the empire to devote resources instead to defending the most important interior regions and cities, we have no concrete accounts to confirm this.

This Byzantine inclination to redirect resources from the border with the Muslims tends to increase in the eighth century: we have no knowledge of any troops being stationed at the border. Meanwhile, the number of larger and smaller Arab attacks remained constant up to the middle of the century; there were one or two attacks every year, many of them in the border region. There was a short pause around the middle of the eighth century, when power switched from the Umayyads to the Abbasids, only to resume as before soon after. This continued threat prompted the civilian population either to emigrate to interior regions of Byzantium or, in some instances, to convert and join the caliphate. As a result, the frontier turned into a sort of no man's land. The prevailing lawlessness and insecurity there attracted other groups who found refuge there and, in turn, would exert some control, at least as long as the two major powers lacked either the ability or the will to increase their own control over the region.

Not until the tenth century would Byzantium advance again and expand its territory. The sources indicate, however, that Byzantium stationed only a few of its own professional soldiers in the border region, relying instead on local forces that were formally integrated into the Byzantine provincial organisation. These forces remained de facto largely independent, forcing the emperors to make local concessions that were impossible to avoid.

From the mid-eleventh century onwards, Byzantium lost great portions of Asia Minor to the Seljuqs and was itself no longer able to establish and permanently maintain its own border defence system. The emperors attempted instead to stabilise Byzantine holdings in Asia Minor through treaties with the neighbouring powers, especially the Crusaders and the Seljuqs. This was unsuccessful because the Turkoman nomads who had immigrated in the meantime were impossible to discipline. This, in turn, further worsened the economic situation. As the central imperial government nearly collapsed towards the end of the twelfth century, this state of dissolution led to the independence of many former provinces. Only Trebizond and Nicaea could exist for a longer period of time, while the other local powers remained too weak to prevail permanently.

Observing these developments, we can only conclude that there was no real conceptual or strategic attempt to deal with the insecurities of the borderland. With only very few exceptions, the emperors merely reacted ad hoc and tactically to changing situations. If these circumstances changed, the politics of the central government would change as well, without any recognisable line of continuity.

Secondly, for this reason, one cannot speak of a consistent population policy. There are no extant sources confirming any settlement of populations in the eastern border regions. The same is valid for the opposite. The formation of a no man's land in the eighth century was certainly encouraged by the voluntary departure of many residents, but also by numerous imperial relocations. The motive for these relocations was certainly not to create a no man's land; that was merely a side effect. The primary motive was, rather, the endeavour to redress the lack of population in other territories. Ultimately, one has the impression that the government left the frontier region to its own devices and merely sought to force the inhabitants and their neighbours to acknowledge the imperial authority by means of occasional larger offensives by the army;

as soon as that was achieved, the emperors would retreat again. And in most cases, circumstances remained as they had been before such disruptive events.

Most naturally, this was also due to the fact that medieval states were basically unable to pay a sufficient number of professional full-time soldiers over a longer period of time. Such soldiers were therefore only stationed at sites of special strategic significance, such as the environs of the capital city. Here, for example, the *tagmata* would be stationed, who were professionals and constituted the core of the imperial army. The *tagmata* were not, however, stationed in the theme provinces.[22] Those were defended by local troops, which were only in part formed by local professional full-time soldiers and in large part recruited from the so-called farmer soldiers. Later, the function of the *tagmata* would be replaced by foreign mercenaries, such as Latins from the West or the well-known Varangians. An individual province's capability to defend itself was primarily dependent upon how many soldiers it could maintain or mobilise, and this was especially the case for the border regions.

The size of the population in the border region and its composition was not actually determined by the central government, but rather by how attractive it was for immigrants who might profit from specific local conditions. It goes without saying that this was subject to constant change, according to the current situation.

Thirdly, all in all, one might say that the fate of the borderland of Byzantium was not so much dependent upon local powers, but rather upon the situation in the capital, for the local powers were in general too weak to play a decisive role on their own. This is clearly shown in the following example, described in the Vita of St Antony the Younger who lived in the ninth century: before his conversion to the monastic life, Antony was the military commander of the coastal city of Attaleia. There, he had to face an attack by a Muslim fleet on the city. He negotiated with the Arab admiral for their withdrawal in return for an adequate sum of money, accusing the Arabs of unnecessarily attacking a peaceful city. The admiral defended himself by responding: 'You yourself forced us to, as you sent your soldiers out to rob and plunder the entire coast of Syria.' Antony countered: 'The emperor of the Romans commands his

[22] John Frederick Haldon, *Warfare, State and Society in the Byzantine World, 565–1204* (London: Routledge, 1999), 189–96.

generals whatever he wishes, and it occurs, and he prepares and dispatches fleets and armies for battle against those who resist his rule, whether we want to or not.' He then offered tribute and gifts should the Muslims spare the city. Eventually, the Arab was convinced, the Byzantines paid the agreed tributes, and the enemies withdrew without attacking Attaleia.[23]

Since we are dealing here with a hagiographic text, a certain measure of caution is advised. This text nevertheless reveals that religious conflicts between Christian and Muslim inhabitants of the border regions played no significant role, but rather that both groups preferred peaceful (mutual) cooperation. The major players were the emperors and caliphs while the local inhabitants had to endure their decisions. Emperor Nikephoros II Phokas attempted to introduce a religious element to the confrontations with the Muslims when he demanded that all soldiers who had died in battle against the Muslims be declared martyrs. This was rejected even by the church.[24] As for the population, especially the inhabitants of the border region, these campaigns were chiefly fought by the rulers in the distant capital cities. They themselves were in fact left to suffer the consequences.

The emperors in Constantinople, on the other hand, had to keep their eyes not only on events at the eastern border but also on those in the Balkans and Italy. Their interventions at the eastern border were therefore not just determined by developments there but mainly by prevailing general concerns. In addition, they were repeatedly confronted with internal conflicts, especially with the aristocracy, who essentially sought to increase their independence from the emperors in Constantinople and would even, if necessary, be willing to ally with external powers. On the Arab and later Turkish side this was probably not that different. Thus, it comes as no surprise that under such preconditions we

[23] Βίος Ἀντωνίου τοῦ Νέου, e codice mutilo Atheniensi Suppl. 534, ed. François Halkin, 'Saint Antoine le Jeune et Pétronas le Vainqueur des Arabes en 863 (d'après un texte inédit)', *Analecta Bollandiana* 62 (1944), 187–225 (Greek text: 210–25), here 198, 28–200, 12 (= François Halkin, *Saints moines d'Orient* (London: Variorum Reprints, 1973), no. 8); *PmbZ*, Antonios, no. 534; Anonymus, no. 11534; Lilie, 'Byzantine–Arab Borderland', 19; Lilie, 'Byzanz und der Islam: Konfrontation oder Koexistenz?', in Elisabeth Piltz (ed.), *Byzantium and Islam in Scandinavia*, Studies in Mediterranean Archaeology 126 (Jonsered: P. Åströms Förlag, 1998), 13–26.

[24] Dölger and Müller, *Regesten*, no. 703; *PmbZ*, Nikephoros II. Phokas, no. 25535.

can hardly speak of stable constellations in the border region at any time. Quite the opposite: constant change was actually the norm.

Appendix: The Significance of the Border Provinces in Relation to the Central Regions Around Constantinople and the Ability of the Central Government to Control the Borderlands

While we are rather well informed about major political events and developments between Byzantium and the caliphate, we know little about 'normal' conditions in the provinces of Byzantium, especially in the border regions. There is some hagiographic information, but it is not reliable, and legal regulations, such as laws or specific decrees, are rare. Moreover, it is difficult to assess their impact. Nevertheless, there are a few pieces of evidence from which the basic importance of the border areas for the central government and, conversely, the actual authority of the government in these areas, can be reasonably assessed. In the following discussion, we will attempt, on the basis of a few examples, to analyse the central government's real presence in the border regions. We should bear in mind, of course, that this presence was as much influenced by the respective geographic and political conditions as it was by the strength and interests of the central government.

A decree from the 890s is useful in this context: the government moved the market for Bulgarian merchants from Constantinople to Thessaloniki. There the *kommerkion* (i.e. the trade tax) was to be collected.[25] The Bulgarians did not accept this transfer; war broke out, which the Byzantines lost. We can assume that this measure was withdrawn after the war. But why was it issued in the first place? For Thessaloniki it could have been a gain, but for trade as such it was detrimental, because the main destination for Bulgarian goods remained, of course, Constantinople and its environs. Here the transport of goods via Thessaloniki was a big detour. The merchants had either to use the Via Egnatia, or to transport their goods by ship, both of which made prices considerably more expensive. The government's intention, therefore, may

[25] *Theophanes Continuatus*, ed. Immanuel Bekker, Corpus Scriptorum Historiae Byzantinae 48 (Bonn: Weber, 1838), Book VI. 9, 357, ll. 14–23; for further sources, secondary literature, and the persons involved, see *PmbZ*, Kosmas, no. 24102, Musikos, no. 25458, Staurakios, no. 27179.

have been to control Bulgarian exports more tightly, by collecting at a distant point, than they could possibly have done if the Bulgarian traders had direct access to Constantinople. We find this strategy employed in another case as well: Abydos on the Dardanelles was a checkpoint for the ships of the Italians, where they had to pay duties. Also in the intra-Byzantine trade, access to Constantinople was not completely free but rather under strict control. We can therefore conclude that these trade policy measures served to better protect the empire's core territories, which were located in the wider area of Constantinople.[26] Compared to these considerations of the central provinces, the needs of the other provinces and especially the border regions were only secondary.

This is also reflected in the great privilege awarded to Venice, which was issued in 1082. In return for their help against the Normans, the Venetians were granted freedom from customs charges in a number of specified places. Here the empire was forced to comply with the Venetians' demands, but clearly tried to limit their trade to a few designated places. Had the emperors really wanted to promote the provinces, they would have opened the whole country to the Venetians, not just a few selected places. Only in 1198 was this restriction lifted, at a time when Byzantium had become weaker and had to accept practically everything Venice demanded.[27]

The reason for the central government's concentration on Constantinople was due to the fact that it could not sufficiently control the provinces, as the following example shows. In 1174, the Italian merchant city of Genoa sent the ambassador Grimaldi to Constantinople to request, among other things, compensation for Genoese merchants who had suffered injustice in Byzantium. Interestingly, there are two demands included on behalf of the Genoese merchant Robertus, whose ship had been seized at Rhodes on a pretext by the lord of the island, one Churrus Andronicus (i.e. Kyrios

[26] For the importance of Abydos, see Lilie, *Handel und Politik*, 145–6.

[27] Franz Dölger, *Regesten der Kaiserurkunden des oströmischen Reiches*, vol. 2: *Regesten von 1025–1204*, 2nd revised edn by Peter Wirth (Munich: C. H. Beck, 1995), no. 1081; see in detail Lilie, *Handel und Politik*, 11–16, 50–68; on the dating of the privilege to 1082, which has been doubted in some more recent research, see now in detail the preface to the slightly extended electronic version of this book, 2021, 2–7 (accessible online at https://www.academia.edu/43727600/Handel_und_Politik).

Andronikos). Robertus complained to Emperor Manuel I Komnenos, who ordered the ship to be returned. But Andronikos did not obey, so the envoy Grimaldi presented the case again: '*sarracenales DCCC petere mementote quos idem Robertus in eadem navi de suis amisit que omnia duca Rodi habuit et cum cartam inde recepisset a domino imperatore ut omnia restitueret, nichil inde restituit*'.[28] The same Andronikos had also impounded another Genoese ship at Attaleia, for which Grimaldi demanded restitution: '*Pro Rodoano de Mauro . . . ac ceteris sociis quos Churrus Andronicus de Satalia abstulit in navi eorum quam cepit apud Sataliam et petiam vermeioni et paria XI ciminilium propria Rodoani*'.[29] This Churrus Andronicus, who did not care about the emperor's orders, was none other than Andronikos Komnenos, a cousin of Manuel and himself later emperor (1183–5). Andronikos was at that time governor of the province of Cilicia, which in those years also included Attaleia and Rhodes. Because of its geographical location, this province was very important, controlling the sea route from Italy to the Holy Land.[30] Nevertheless, the emperor was obviously not able to control it effectively.

This lack of central control was not due solely to the specific person of Andronikos but was a consequence of the Byzantine ruling structure in the twelfth century. To put it in a nutshell, the provinces of the empire were controlled by noble families who recognised the emperor but granted him only limited authority in the internal affairs of their lands. Another example is the family Gabras, which had its power base in eastern Asia Minor and cooperated with the Seljuks independently of the emperor.[31] The emperor's authority was concentrated in Constantinople and the surrounding core provinces, which also formed the economic heart of the empire. In the other provinces, his influence was contingent upon the extent to which these

[28] *Codice diplomatico della repubblica di Genova dal 953 al 1163*, ed. Cesare Imperiale di Sant' Angelo (Rome, 1936–42), 2: 217, n. 2; cf. Lilie, *Handel und Politik*, 124.

[29] *Codice diplomatico della repubblica di Genova*, 2: 213; cf. Lilie, *Handel und Politik*, 150.

[30] See Lilie, *Handel und Politik*, 117–18, 246–7.

[31] For the Gabras family, see still Antony A. M. Bryer, 'A Byzantine Family: the Gabrades c. 979–c. 1653', *University of Birmingham Historical Journal* 12 (1970), 164–87, and now Stefan Heidemann and Claudia Sode, 'Iḫtiyār ad-Dīn al-Ḥasan ibn Ġafras: Ein Rūm-seldschukischer Usurpator aus byzantinischem Adel im Jahr 588/1192', *Der Islam* 95 (2018), 450–78.

provinces depended on support from the centre and their rulers were willing to cooperate.[32]

This situation, however, was not confined to the twelfth century but applied, at least with respect to the border areas, also to the Middle Byzantine period, as we have seen above in the case of the province of Charpezikion. Here the *strategos* (i.e. governor) was probably an Armenian prince whose dominion was treated only formally like a *thema* (i.e. province), but who was in fact widely independent in internal affairs. This becomes even clearer in the following example, which has already been mentioned briefly above. In the first years of the reign of Basil II there was a civil war between the emperor and the aristocrat Bardas Skleros. To lead the war against the latter, the emperor appointed Bardas Phokas as *domestikos* of the *scholai* (i.e. commander-in-chief). Bardas Phokas had previously been *strategos* of the frontier provinces of Chaldia and Koloneia, and the Phokas family held large landholdings in the eastern provinces. In the fight against the usurper Bardas, Phokas relied to a lesser degree on the imperial troops. Instead, he gathered the forces of the Phokas family and their followers in eastern Asia Minor, and by this means finally defeated Bardas Skleros, who had to flee into the caliphate. After that, Bardas Phokas did not reside in Constantinople, but in his headquarters in the province of Charsianon, where he was virtually independent and even conducted his own foreign policy.[33] Eventually, he too rebelled and tried to gain the throne in Constantinople, but was defeated by Basil II, who could rely on the support of freshly recruited Varangian mercenaries.[34]

These examples could easily be multiplied. There can be no doubt that the emperors, for whatever reasons, gave smaller and larger estates and sometimes

[32] For details, see Ralph-Johannes Lilie, 'Des Kaisers Macht und Ohnmacht. Zum Zerfall der Zentralgewalt in Byzanz vor dem vierten Kreuzzug', in *Varia I*, Ralph-Johannes Lilie und Paul Speck, Poikila Byzantina 4 (Bonn: Habelt Verlag, 1984), 9–120; a slightly revised and new formatted version of this paper is available online at https://www.academia.edu/43727574/Des_Kaisers_Macht_und_Ohnmacht.

[33] On his position in Charsianon, see the report of Ibn Shahrām in Henry Frederick Amedroz, 'An Embassy from Baghdad to the Emperor Basil II', *Journal of the Royal Asiatic Society* 46 (1914), 915–42, Engl. trans. 919–31, Arabic text 933–42, here 933–4, 940ff [919–20, 930]; on the entire report, cf. also Beihammer, 'Der harte Sturz des Bardas Skleros', 41–2.

[34] For Bardas Phokas, see *PmbZ*, Bardas Phokas, no. 20784.

even entire provinces to influential people. These people usually belonged to the high nobility, but in individual cases they could also be foreigners. This was quite similar to the feudal system in medieval Western Europe, but without the formal regulations that were in place there.[35] As we can conclude from a later source from the early thirteenth century, many provinces must have resembled a patchwork quilt, in which the properties of churches, monasteries and private individuals were mixed with state lands.[36] Here we can see the final result of a development that had already begun in the eighth/ninth century. One thinks, for instance, of the aforementioned *akritai* (semi-independent soldiers living in the borderland); or also, to give a concrete example, of the princess Danelis, who controlled parts of the Peloponnese in the second half of the ninth century. Probably the widow of a Slavic prince, she was the chief of one or more Slavic tribes that had settled in the region in the seventh or eighth century and lived there more or less independently, even though they recognised the emperor as sovereign. This was also true for some other Slavic tribes in these areas.[37]

It becomes clear that under such conditions the emperor had difficulties maintaining control of the provinces. One could say that in fact his control was rather nominal. It was certainly perceived as such, as can be seen from the so-called *Strategikon* of Kekaumenos, a source of the eleventh century. In one chapter, the author explicitly warns against going into the provinces in the service of the emperor, since such an official would not be able to assert himself against the local forces and would only suffer personal harm.[38]

An indication that the emperors themselves were well aware of this situation is provided by a regulation of the ninth/tenth century, according to which the governors of the European provinces and the two frontier districts

[35] See Lilie, 'Des Kaisers Macht und Ohnmacht', 62–70.

[36] It is the agreement regarding the division of the Byzantine Empire made by the Crusaders during the Fourth Crusade 1203–4: *Partitio Terrarum Imperii Romaniae*, a cura di A. Carile, *Studi Veneziani* 7 (1965), 125–305.

[37] For Danelis, *PmbZ*, Danelis, no. 21390.

[38] *Cecaumeni Strategicon et incerti scriptoris de officiis regiis libellus*, ed. B. Wassiliewsky and V. Jernstedt (Petrograd, 1896), c. 96ff, 40ff; new edition with Italian translation: *Kekaumenos. Raccomandazioni e consigli di un galantuomo: Stratēgikon*, ed. and trans. Maria Dora Spadaro (Alessandria: Edizioni dell'Orso, 1998).

of Chaldia and Mesopotamia in eastern Asia Minor did not receive their salaries from the central imperial treasury but collected them directly from the revenues of their provinces. This is to say that, with imperial permission, they could dispose of the public dues of their provinces and pay only a portion to Constantinople.[39]

In the inner provinces of the empire, the emperor's position was probably stronger prior to the later part of the twelfth century, when the central administration's authority progressively corroded and eventually collapsed altogether. In the border regions, this development had begun much earlier. Overall, the emperors apparently exerted only a limited amount of control over the provinces, especially in the border areas. In fact, they controlled only a few well-fortified cities and the main passes. In order to maintain a tight monitoring system, a strong deployment of personnel would have been necessary, which the state could not afford. Thus, the central government was generally content with directly controlling Constantinople and the surrounding core regions, whereas in the rest of the empire it relied rather on indirect rule by regional forces and rulers, and was content, so to speak, with collecting taxes, the amount of which, however, probably also depended on local conditions and in all likelihood changed frequently – if it reached the capital at all.

[39] Generally, see Wolfram Brandes, *Finanzverwaltung in Krisenzeiten: Untersuchungen zur byzantinischen Administration im 6.–9. Jahrhundert*, Forschungen zur byzantinischen Rechtsgeschichte 25 (Frankfurt: Löwenklau, 2002), 489–98.

11

THE ISLAMIC–BYZANTINE FRONTIER IN SELJUQ ANATOLIA

A. C. S. Peacock

Writing in the mid- to late thirteenth century, the Arab geographer Ibn Saʿīd al-Maghribī left a vivid description of the Byzantine–Islamic frontier in western Anatolia that evoked both its distinctive culture of raiding, but also its continuities with the borderlands of Umayyad and Abbasid times:

> The [Turkmen] are a numerous people of Turkish descent who conquered the land of Rūm in the period of the Seljuqs. They have become accustomed to raid the *akritai* who live on the coast, to take their possessions and sell them to the Muslims. Only the existence of a peace treaty (*hudna*) and the force of the sultan holds them back. They make Turkmen carpets which are exported. On their coast is a gulf called Macre which is famous among travellers, from which timber is exported to Alexandria and elsewhere. There is located the river of Baṭṭāl, which is deep. Across it is a bridge, which is lowered when there is peace (*hudna*) and raised when war breaks out, which is the border between the Muslims and Christians. The Baṭṭāl after whom it is named often raided Christians in Umayyad times and is mentioned in books of entertainment; his grave is there. To the north of the aforementioned Antalya are the mountains of Denizli, in which region and its surroundings are said to be around 200,000 Turkmen households, who are the ones called the *ūj*. The distance between it and the castle of Khūnās [Chonai/Honaz] where bows [?] are made is two *farsakh*s. The mountains of the Turkmen adjoin the lands

> of al-Lashkarī [the Lascarid], the ruler of Constantinople, from the gate of Denizli, and between Denizli and the bridge to its west is thirty miles. To its east is the Heraclea river which comes down from mount ʿAlāyā to Sinop, where there is Heraclea by the sea,[1] which [Hārūn] al-Rashīd ruined. In its east is the mountain of the Cave in Rūm, where it is said the Cave [of the Seven Sleepers] is, which is mentioned in the history of al-Wāfiq,[2] when someone was sent to gather intelligence on the ruler of Constantinople. Further east are the famous meadows where al-Muʿtaṣim was eager to pasture his horses from Iraq. There are great springs there; the place is called Qaranbuk by the Turks, and in that region is the town of Angūriyya, which is said to be Amorium that was conquered by al-Muʿtaṣim. Today it belongs to the Muslims.[3]

Ibn Saʿīd's description leaves much to be desired in terms of geographical coherence. His representation, however, of the thirteenth-century frontier as essentially a continuation of that of the early Islamic times through the heroic cult of the deceased Umayyad warrior Baṭṭāl Ghāzī, the references to the frontier locations conquered by the Abbasid caliphs Hārūn al-Rashīd and al-Muʿtaṣim, and the mutual raiding of *akritai* and the *ghāzīs* has had a long legacy in scholarship. It was especially influential on Paul Wittek, who was acquainted with Ibn Saʿīd's text through its quotations by the fourteenth-century historian Abū'l-Fidā'. Although today Wittek is best known for his famous 'Ghāzī thesis' presented in his *Rise of the Ottoman Empire* published in 1938, which continues to inspire debate, this study drew substantially on his earlier works that had concentrated on the thirteenth century – his 1934 monograph on the emirate of Menteshe in southwest Anatolia and his important article 'Deux chapitres de l'histoire des Turcs de Roum'.[4] In this

1 A confusion, it seems, between Heraclea Pontica and Heraclea Cybistra.

2 This seems likely to be a confusion with the name of the Abbasid caliph al-Wāthiq (842–7), who sent an expedition to Anatolia to seek the location of the Cave. See Oya Pancaroğlu, 'Caves, Borderlands and Configurations of Sacred Topography in Medieval Anatolia', *Mésogeios* 25–6 (2005), 254.

3 Ibn Saʿīd al-Maghribī, *Kitāb al-Jughrāfiya*, ed. Ismāʿīl al-ʿArabī (Beirut: al-Maktab al-Tijārī lil-Ṭibʿa wa-l-Nashr wa-l-Tawzīʿ, 1970), 185.

4 Paul Wittek, *Das Fürstentum Mentesche: Studie zur Geschichte Westkleinasiens im 13.–15. Jh.* (Istanbul: Abteilung İstanbul des Archäologischen Institutes des Deutschen Reiches, 1934); Paul Wittek, 'Deux chapitres de l'histoire des Turcs de Roum', *Byzantion* 11 (1936),

latter article, he traced the emergence of the Ottoman empire back to the 'age-old struggle' between Byzantium and Islam which resulted 'in a special organization of the frontier'. This Wittek describes in the following terms:

> In these frontier zones, it was those soldiers, who became permanent residents of the region, who devoted themselves to the defense of the land, to almost daily skirmishes with the enemy, and to incursions – the *ghazwa*, the 'razzia' – in the enemies' territory. This population was reinforced by militant elements flowing from the hinterland, impelled by love of adventure, of glory, and of booty, if not by religious zeal. It is easily understood that on these frontiers a population very distinct from that of the interior would have been created . . .[5]

Wittek goes on to describe the common features of the Byzantine and Muslim frontier societies – a warlike milieu, characterised by the flourishing of heresies, renegades and a culture of raiding. Moreover, the Abbasid border, he argued, was staffed by Turkish military men, meaning that when the Seljuqs arrived 'their predecessors had already, to a certain extent Turkicised the marches: the new arrivals thus found a milieu that would be familiar to them and to whose influence they submitted without resistance'.[6] The true conquerors of the Turkish period were thus

> these frontiersmen the Ghāzīs so acclimatized already in all respects to the territory of Rūm. They did not see themselves as strangers, and on the other side, the Anatolian population could not consider them as foreign intruders . . . Thanks to the fact that, in this Turkish conquest, elements already well prepared for conquest were in the lead, a complete rupture in the cultural traditions of Anatolia was avoided.[7]

285–319. My citations of this article are taken from the English translation, 'Two Chapters in the History of Rum', in Paul Wittek, *The Rise of the Ottoman Empire: Studies on the History of Turkey, Thirteenth to Fifteenth Centuries*, ed. Colin Heywood (London: Routledge, 2015), 97–124.

5 Wittek, 'Two Chapters', 102–3.

6 Ibid., 104.

7 Ibid., 105.

As an example of this cultural continuity, Wittek goes on to cite precisely the example of the cult of Baṭṭāl Ghāzī, the continued encounter between the *ghāzīs* and the *akritai*, where, in 'analogous conditions' 'the ghāzī traditions of the Euphrates survived'.[8] This frontier culture ultimately gave birth to the Ottoman *ghāzī* state.

Modern scholarship has generally followed Wittek in seeing the Seljuq frontier with Byzantium as a zone characterised by its own culture, a region whose Byzantine and Muslim inhabitants had more in common with each other than they did with the culture of the states to which they nominally belonged.[9] Indeed, Muslim-ruled Anatolia as a whole has tended to be conceptualised as a frontier region, an 'espace d'imbrication greco-turque' in Michel Balivet's phrase,[10] or a 'Wild West' of the Muslim world.[11] Certainly in some respects it is easy to trace the continuities, in, for example, the cults in frontier locations of the Cave of the Seven Sleepers and Baṭṭāl Ghāzī, both important in Abbasid times, which were patronised by the Seljuqs.[12] Further, as Ibn Saʿīd mentions, heroic tales of Baṭṭāl Ghāzī circulated too, as we will discuss below. Yet such superficial resemblances have meant the stark discontinuities between the Abbasid and the Seljuq frontier have tended to be disregarded. Especially suspect is Wittek's notion of a pre-Seljuq 'Turkicisation' of the frontier region. While no doubt on occasion Turkish *ghulāms* were present on the Abbasid–Byzantine frontier,[13] forming as they did an important

[8] Ibid., 107.

[9] Claude Cahen, *Pre-Ottoman Turkey: A General Survey of the Material and Spiritual Culture and History c. 1071–1330* (New York: Taplinger, 1968), 202–15. See also the discussion in Alexander D. Beihammer, 'Defection Across the Border of Islam and Christianity: Apostasy and Cross-Cultural Interaction in Byzantine-Seljuk Relations', *Speculum* 86: 3 (July 2011), 599–601, and my critique in A. C. S. Peacock, 'The Seljuk Sultanate of Rūm and the Turkmen of the Byzantine Frontier, 1206–1279', *al-Masāq* 26 (2014), 267–87.

[10] Michel Balivet, *Romanie byzantine et pays de Rum turc: Histoire d'un espace d'imbrication greco-turque* (Istanbul: Isis Press, 1994).

[11] Charles Melville, 'Anatolia under the Mongols', in Kate Fleet (ed.), *The Cambridge History of Turkey*, vol. 1, *Byzantium to Turkey, 1071–1453* (Cambridge: Cambridge University Press, 2009), 52.

[12] Pancaroğlu, 'Caves, Borderlands and Configurations'.

[13] For some examples see, for instance, C. Edmund Bosworth, 'The City of Tarsus and the Arab–Byzantine Frontiers in Early and Middle ʿAbbāsid Times', *Oriens* 33 (1992), 274–5.

contingent of the Abbasid military, they did not constitute the bulk of the Muslim volunteers who flocked to the frontier to participate in jihad against Byzantium. Ibn Ḥawqal's famous description of Tarsūs in the tenth century, for example, tells us that the volunteers (*murābiṭūn*) came from not just the cities of Khurasan, Sijistan and Kirman in the east, but also the Hijaz, Syria, Yemen, Egypt and the Maghrib.[14]

In this chapter, I will address the nature of the Islamic–Byzantine frontier in the post-Abbasid period but before the Ottomans. My aim is less to describe the military structures of the frontier – which were probably negligible – but rather consider how it was perceived from the Seljuq point of view.[15] Did the Seljuqs, as Ibn Saʿīd, Wittek and more recent scholars seem to suggest, see themselves as heirs of the Abbasids, upholding a tradition of frontier warfare against Byzantium that stretched back to the seventh century? What role did the Byzantine frontier play in the mental worlds of the educated populations of places such as Konya, the Seljuq capital, who have bequeathed us most of the texts on which this study will be based? To address these questions, I will focus on the thirteenth century. This is a period of relative stability on the frontier between Byzantium and the Muslims but is also the earliest period to be adequately attested in the Arabic and Persian sources from Anatolia, which barely exist for the first century of Turkish domination. The thirteenth century also represents the zenith of the territorial extent of the Seljuq state in Anatolia, although after their defeat at Köse Dağ in 1243, the sultanate survived only as a vassal of the Mongols until its final disappearance in 1307.

The Seljuq Frontier World from the Euphrates to the Maeander

The most obvious discontinuity between Abbasid and Seljuq times was the shift in the location of the principal frontier zone, which, in the wake of the Turkish invasions, had moved some five hundred miles to the west, to a line

[14] Ibid., 282; Ibn Ḥawqal, *Kitāb al-Masālik wa'l-Mamālik*, ed. M. J. de Goeje (Leiden: Brill, 1873), 123.

[15] For studies of the frontier and Seljuq–Byzantine relations in this period see Peacock, 'The Seljuk Sultanate of Rūm and the Turkmen'; Dimitri Korobeinikov, *Byzantium and the Turks in the Thirteenth Century* (Oxford: Oxford University Press, 2014).

along the Maeander river that then extended north to the Dorylaion/Eskişehir region. This frontier remained relatively stable from the Seljuq victory over the Byzantines at Myriokephalon in 1176 to the end of the thirteenth century, when the rise of the Ottomans meant Byzantine territory came under renewed pressure. This was not, however, the Seljuqs' sole frontier with Christendom. On the Mediterranean coast, Byzantium maintained a foothold in Antalya until 1207, and the inhabitants evidently profoundly resented Seljuq rule, launching a major rebellion in 1216. Further east, the Armenian Kingdom of Cilicia occupied the littoral and mountainous interior until 1375, and despite the efforts of modern Turkish scholars to depict the Kingdom as accepting Seljuk vassalage, this seems far from the truth.[16] Indeed, in the early thirteenth century Cilicia was on occasion able to threaten the heartland of the Seljuk state in central Anatolia.[17] To the north, along the Black Sea, the state of the Grand Komnenoi of Trebizond dominated the littoral as far west as Sinop, which the Seljuqs captured in 1214. Although its conquest was proudly proclaimed in in a *fatḥnāma* sent to the caliph in Baghdad,[18] the Muslim frontier seems subsequently to have remained broadly static in this region until well into the fourteenth century. In the north east, the Seljuqs confronted the Georgians; after the Seljuqs' dramatic defeat at the Battle of Basiani in 1202, they seem to have made little attempt to expand eastwards, and the Seljuq principality of Erzurum was effectively a Georgian protectorate; indeed, in the first decade of the thirteenth century the Georgians were able to expand south as far as Lake Van.[19] Finally, we should not omit the Seljuq frontier with

[16] Sara Nur Yıldız, 'Reconceptualizing the Seljuk–Cilician Frontier: Armenians, Latins and Turks in Conflict and Alliance during the Early Thirteenth Century', in Florin Curta (ed.), *Borders, Barriers, and Ethnogenesis: Frontiers in Late Antiquity and the Middle Ages* (Turnhout: Brepols, 2005), 191–220.

[17] A. C. S. Peacock, 'An Interfaith Polemic of Medieval Anatolia: Qāḍī Burhān al-Dīn al-Anawī on the Armenians and their Heresies', in A. C. S. Peacock, Bruno De Nicola and Sara Nur Yıldız (eds), *Islam and Christianity in Medieval Anatolia* (Farnham: Ashgate, 2015), 246.

[18] Ibn Bībī, *al-Awāmir al-ʿAlāʾiyya fiʾl-Umūr al-ʿAlāʾiyya*, ed. Zhaleh Motahiddin (Tehran, 2011), 153–7.

[19] A. C. S. Peacock, 'Georgia and the Anatolian Turks in the 12th and 13th Centuries', *Anatolian Studies* 56 (2006), 127–46.

other Muslim states. After the absorption of the other Turkish principalities in Anatolia in the twelfth to early thirteenth century – the Danishmendids, Saltukids and Mengücekids – the Seljuq border with the Ayyubids in southeast Anatolia constituted the Seljuqs' major security problem. Each side adopted an aggressive attitude toward the other, with Seljuq attempts to advance on Aleppo countered by Ayyubid pushes as far north as Akhlat.[20] With the advent of Mongol rule, these problems were only exacerbated, as Anatolia constituted the frontline between the Ilkhanid Mongol rulers and the Ayyubids' successors the Mamluks, who were the Mongols' great enemies.

To do justice to the complexities of all these frontier regions is beyond the scope of this chapter. I will therefore concentrate on the westernmost frontier, where the Seljuqs confronted Byzantium in the form of the Lascarid state, although I will occasionally adduce relevant evidence from elsewhere. In what follows, it is important to remember that if the Byzantine–Islamic frontier seems somewhat poorly attested in this period, this is probably because it was always the inter-Muslim frontier with Syria that constituted a much graver concern to the Seljuqs, while for the first half of the thirteenth century the rump Byzantine state of Nicaea under the Lascarid emperors was preoccupied with the Latin occupation. Since the Fourth Crusade in 1204, Frankish forces had occupied Constantinople, and by the second decade of the thirteenth century they controlled a significant portion of western Anatolia, impeding communications between the north and south of the Lascarids' domains, representing a much more critical security threat than the Turks.[21] Similarly, the prestige of the Seljuq sultanate of Rūm was sustained not by victories over Byzantium but by hegemony over the Jazira, with its patchwork of Artuqid buffer states constantly shifting their loyalties between the Seljuqs and Ayyubids, and its Ayyubid princes who might be forced to accept Seljuq suzerainty. As Sara Nur Yıldız has put it, 'military and diplomatic gains against the Ayyubids in the Jazira was the Seljuq elites'

[20] For details, see Önder Kaya, *Selahaddin Sonrası Dönemde Anadolu'da Eyyubiler* (Istanbul: Yeditepe, 2007); also R. Stephen Humphries, *From Saladin to the Mongols: The Ayyubids of Damascus, 1193–1260* (Albany: State University of New York Press, 1977), 127–31, 214–27.

[21] Dimiter Angelov, *The Byzantine Hellene: The Life of Emperor Theodore Laskaris and Byzantium in the Thirteenth Century* (Cambridge: Cambridge University Press, 2019), 30–1, 39, 53–4.

most assured way of gaining power, wealth and fame'.[22] Moreover, the southeastern frontier presented a major security threat in the form of the Bābā'ī rebellion of 1240 which originated in the region, drawing its support from local Turkmen and Khwarazmian soldiers stationed there to follow a self-proclaimed prophet, Bābā Rasūl.[23]

The main targets of Seljuq campaigns clearly demonstrate that it was to the southeast frontier that thirteenth century sultans devoted their attention rather than the west. On deposition from the throne by his brother Sulaymānshāh in 1196, Ghiyāth al-Dīn Kaykhusraw I's first act was to seek help from the east, visiting Cilician Armenia, Elbistan, Malatya and Diyarbakır;[24] only when this failed did he look for Byzantine aid, finding refuge in Constantinople. Sultan ʿIzz al-Dīn Kaykāʾūs I (1211–19), who made a peace agreement with the Lascarids,[25] personally led forays against Sinop, Cilicia and Syria.[26] Indeed, the latter campaign, which ended in disaster, was an unprovoked attack that aimed explicitly at annexing Syrian territory.[27] In the heyday of the Seljuq state, ʿAlāʾ al-Dīn Kayqubād I (1219–37) launched campaigns in every direction except Byzantium. His reign started with the capture of Alanya, commanded by the sultan himself, which was followed by campaigns on the Euphrates frontier, capturing the old Abbasid fortification of Kahta and bringing to heel the rebellious Artuqids of Diyarbakır. He then adopted a more pacific policy towards the Ayyubids, seeking to forge

22 Sara Nur Yıldız, 'The Rise and Fall of a Tyrant in Seljuk Anatolia: Saʿd al-Din Köpek's Reign of Terror, 1237–8', in Robert Hillenbrand, A. C. S. Peacock and Firuza Abdullaeva (eds), *Ferdowsi, the Mongols and the History of Iran: Art, Literature and Culture from Early Islam to Qajar Persia. Studies in Honour of Charles Melville* (London: I. B. Tauris, 2013), 97; for Ayyubid submission to the Seljuqs, see ibid., 98.

23 For a recent discussion of this revolt, see A. C. S. Peacock, *Islam, Literature and Society in Mongol Anatolia* (Cambridge: Cambridge University Press, 2019), 241–8.

24 Ibn Bībī, *al-Awāmir al-ʿAlāʾiyya*, 40–8.

25 Ibid., 129–30. This also suited the Lascarids who wished to concentrate on retaking Constantinople; see Osman Turan, *Selçuklular Zamanında Türkiye: Siyâsi Tarih Alp Arslan'dan Osman Gazi'ye (1071–1328)* (Istanbul: Ötüken, 1971), 299–300. Nonetheless, it was interrupted by raiding, for shortly afterwards Ibn Bībī mentions that the sultan's senior amirs, Ḥusām al-Dīn Chūpān and Sayf al-Dīn Amīr Qizil had despatched a detachment (*fawj*) to raid the land of Rum (*ghazw-i bilād-i Rūm*).

26 Ibn Bībī, *al-Awāmir al-ʿAlāʾiyya*, 158–92.

27 Ibid., 177.

marriage links with the dynasty.[28] Nonetheless, ʿAlāʾ al-Dīn was obliged in person to come to Malatya, the main base for operations in the south, in response to clashes with the Ayyubids over the Artuqid buffer state of Kharberd (Harput).[29] Campaigns under ʿAlāʾ al-Dīn reached into the east of Anatolia too, and even to the Crimea; but of operations on the frontier with the Lascarids the sources are almost entirely silent.[30] A similar pattern obtained under ʿAlāʾ al-Dīn's successors. During the minority of Ghiyāth al-Dīn Kaykhusraw II (1237–46), the strongman Köpek, who was effective ruler of the sultanate during the years 1237–8, sought to establish his legitimacy by leading campaigns against the Ayyubids, seizing Sumaysat.[31] After Köpek's fall, Ghiyāth al-Dīn continued operations in the region, capturing Diyarbakır,[32] and suppressing the Bābāʾī rebellion which originated in the region.

With the advent of Mongol rule after Köse Dağ, the frontier character of the Euphrates basin was maintained. The Mamluk sultanate of Syria and Egypt faced their Mongol opponents from their fortresses of al-Bīra and al-Raḥba,[33] the latter being an Abbasid *thaghr* foundation which was closely associated with jihad and the cult of Baṭṭāl Ghāzī.[34] It was over the Taurus

[28] Ibid., 272ff, 348ff.

[29] Ibid., 391ff.

[30] An exception are the border clashes related in the 1220s by Syrian chronicles and Greek hagiographic materials; but it is striking that they do not make it into either the mainstream Byzantine or Seljuq historiographical traditions. See John Langdon, *Byzantium's Last Imperial Offensive in Asia Minor: the documentary evidence for and hagiographical lore about John III Ducas Vatatzes's crusade against the Turks, 1222 or 1225 to 1231* (New Rochelle, NY: A. D. Caratzas, 1992); these campaigns would have thus followed Vatatzes' campaigns against the Latins in Asia Minor in 1223–4, which met with limited success, see Angelov, *The Byzantine Hellene*, 58–9.

[31] Yıldız, 'The Rise and Fall of a Tyrant', 98.

[32] Ibn Bībī, *al-Awāmir al-ʿAlāʾiyya*, 435–40.

[33] Reuven Amitai-Preiss, *Mongols and Mamluks, The Mamluk–Ilkhanid War, 1260–1281* (Cambridge: Cambridge University Press, 1995), 202.

[34] Ernst Honigmann and Thierry Bianquis, 'al-Raḥba', *The Encyclopaedia of Islam, New Edition* (Leiden: Brill, 1995), 8: 393–6; Asa Eger, *The Islamic–Byzantine Frontier: Interaction and Exchange among Muslim and Christian Communities* (London: I. B. Tauris, 2017), 153, 212, 222, 234, 269; on its jihad associations, see ʿAlī b. Abī Bakr al-Harawī, *A Lonely Wayfarer's Guide to Pilgrimage*, trans. Josef Meri (Princeton, NJ: Darwin Press, 2004), 166–9.

mountains that in 1276 the armies of the Mamluk sultan Baybars marched to lay waste to Kayseri, one of the principal towns of the Mongols' vassal, the Seljuq state, just as those of the caliphs and Ḥamdānids regularly had done on their annual raids.[35] Contemporaries were themselves conscious of the parallels. The Mamluk chronicler of Baybars' Anatolian campaign, Ibn ʿAbd al-Ẓāhir, pointedly remarks that 'the life of this hero [Baybars] is better than the tale of that Baṭṭāl'.[36] Describing the Mamluk advance, he notes how the army reached Ḥadath al-Ḥamrāʾ, the famous frontier fort of Abbasid times, in his day known by its Turkish name Göynük ('Burned'). He remarks that 'we saw what Sayf al-Dawla b. Ḥamdān had built there while spears clashed against one another and the wave of fate battered each other' and cites al-Mutanabbī's famous ode on the Ḥamdānid–Byzantine battle at Ḥadath, *ʿalā qadr ahl al-ʿazm taʾtī al-ʿazāʾim*.[37] Through such historical and literary allusions, Ibn ʿAbd al-Ẓāhir sought to establish Baybars' place as a worthy successor to earlier generations of warriors against Byzantium.

If the military installations of the Euphrates frontier remained in use, the organisation of the Maeander valley frontier with Byzantium in the west bore no resemblance to the Abbasid *thughūr*. To start with, there was a striking lack of military infrastructure in the Maeander region. Consider, for instance, the core of the frontier region around Denizli, an area which changed hands several times over the late twelfth and thirteenth centuries, and where the Byzantines fortified the classical city of Hierapolis precisely in response to the threat.[38] Yet the only installation erected by the Seljuqs was a solitary caravanserai, which

[35] Amitai-Preiss, *Mongols and Mamluks*, 157–78.

[36] Ibn ʿAbd al-Ẓāhir is quoted in al-Qalqashandī, *Ṣubḥ al-Aʿshā fī Ṣināʿat al-Inshāʾ* (Cairo, 1919), 14: 108, reprinted in Faruk Sümer, *Yabanlu Pazarı: Selçuklular Devrinde Milletlerarası Büyük Bir Fuar* (Ankara: Türk Dünyası Araştırmaları Vakfı, 1985).

[37] Ibid., 111.

[38] Two useful recent studies of the region are Dimitri Korobeinikov, 'The Byzantine–Seljuk Border in Times of Trouble: Laodikeia in 1174–1204', in Alicia Simpson (ed.), *Byzantium 1180–1204: 'The Sad Quarter of a Century'?* (Athens: National Hellenic Research Foundation, 2015), 49–81; Dimitri Korobeinikov, 'The Formation of the Turkish Principalities in the Boundary Zone: From the Emirate of Denizli to the Beylik of Menteshe (1256–1302)', in Adnan Çevik and Murat Keçiş (eds), *Menteşeoğulları Tarihi* (Ankara: Türk Tarih Kurumu, 2016), 65–76. See also the study by Peter Thonemann, *The Maeander Valley: A Historical Geography from Antiquity to Byzantium* (Cambridge: Cambridge University Press, 2011).

can hardly have fulfilled the function of the *ribāṭs* that were the hallmark of the Abbasid *thughūr*. There is no archaeological or literary evidence of any significant Seljuq investment in walls, defences or other fortifications in Denizli or anywhere near it. The nearest important military installation that does crop up in our texts was the remote castle of Uluborlu, some fifty miles away high in the mountains, which was primarily used as a maximum-security prison for high-ranking Seljuq political prisoners.[39] Moreover, this absence of archaeological evidence is matched by the silence of our Seljuq texts, which tells us almost nothing of the military or political organisation of the frontier regions. Indeed, it is curious how little Seljuq chronicles and other literary texts tell us about even major cross-border clashes, sometimes completely ignoring clashes with Byzantium, such as the campaigns of John Vatatzes of the 1220s.[40] In fact, our major Islamic sources for clashes on the Byzantine–Seljuq border are not the Anatolian Persian texts, but an Arabic chronicle from Syria.[41]

While we have many accounts of Seljuq sultans doing battle, only in one instance does the Byzantine frontier feature prominently; even in famous clashes like Myriokephalon – barely attested in Muslim sources – there is no evidence that the Seljuq sultan was present. The only significant exception is an account of Ghiyāth al-Dīn Kaykhusraw I's campaign that led to the sultan's death at the Battle of Alaşehir/Philadelphia in 1211; yet even this occurs only in our major Persian chronicle of Seljuq Anatolia, Ibn Bībī's *al-Awāmir al-ʿAlāʾiyya*, composed probably after 1277.[42] Ibn Bībī states that the sultan issued firmans summoning troops to participate in a holy war (*jihād wa ghazā*), which is justified with reference to Qurʾan 2: 6 'Oh prophet wage war on the infidel and hypocrites and punish them.' Ibn Bībī indicates the existence of spies (*jāsūsān*) on the Byzantine side who informed the Lascarid ruler of the Seljuq army's approach, enabling him to summon from the 'tribes and clans and rulers of the land and inhabitants of the islands' (*qabāyil wa ʿashāyir wa ḥukkām-i bilād wa sukkān-i jazāyir*) a great army of 'Rūmīs, Alamān, Qipchaqs and Alans as well as Franks'.[43] In Ibn Bībī's

39 For the archaeological evidence, see Peacock, 'The Seljuq Sultanate of Rum and the Turkmen', 278, 280–1.

40 On this, see Langdon, *Byzantium's Last Imperial Offensive in Asia Minor*.

41 See Korobeinikov, *Byzantium and the Turks*, 156–9.

42 Ibn Bībī, *al-Awāmir al-ʿAlāʾiyya*, 102–10.

43 Ibn Bībī, *al-Awāmir al-ʿAlāʾiyya*, 106.

account, then, it is the Lascarid army that is depicted as reliant on the nomadic levies modern scholarship often associates with the Seljuqs, and this certainly has some factual basis as we do know that the Lascarids settled Qipchaq mercenaries in frontier areas.[44] Yet it must be said Ibn Bībī's description of the fighting is largely rhetorical and abstract, decorated with Arabic and Persian verse, such as quotations from Imru' al-Qays's famous *muʿallaqa*,[45] and gives us no real impression of the organisation of the frontier.

Despite the trauma of the death of Ghiyāth al-Dīn Kaykhusraw in battle, thereafter being commemorated in inscriptions as *al-sulṭān al-shahīd*, 'the martyred sultan', other sultans continued to lead their men into battle. Yet none did so on the western frontier. Why then, unlike his predecessors and successors, did Ghiyāth al-Dīn Kaykhusraw I personally lead a jihad on the Byzantine frontier? It is important to remember that, during his exile after being ousted by Rukn al-Dīn Sulaymanshāh, Ghiyāth al-Dīn had been forced to take refuge in Constantinople.[46] On Rukn al-Dīn's death, he had been briefly replaced by his infant son Qilij Arslān III, supported by a group of *amīrs*. Another group, however, led by the sons of the Danishmendid Yaghibasān, sent for Ghiyāth al-Dīn to return from exile. This met with considerable opposition from the people of Konya, and Ghiyāth al-Dīn was obliged to besiege the town. One of the leading figures in the opposition was the Qāḍī al-Tirmidhī, whom Ibn Bībī likens to the famous jurist and theologian Abū Layth al-Samarqandī. The Qāḍī had issued a fatwa stating that, 'Sultan Ghiyāth al-Dīn is unfit to be sultan on account of having made an alliance with the infidel and infringing the proscriptions of sharia while in their lands.'[47] This allegation may well have had some force, for Greek sources indicate that during his stay in Constantinople, Ghiyāth al-Dīn was baptised and adopted by the emperor Alexios III, and married the daughter of Manuel Mavrozomes, a high-ranking aristocrat.[48]

[44] Dimitri Korobeinikov, 'The Cumans in Paphlagonia', *Journal of Black Sea Studies* 18 (2015), 37–8; Angelov, *The Byzantine Hellene*, 51.

[45] Ibn Bībī, *al-Awāmir al-ʿAlāʾiyya*, 107.

[46] On his stay in Constantinople, see Beihammer, 'Defection', 640–2.

[47] Ibn Bībī, *al-Awāmir al-ʿAlāʾiyya*, 94–5.

[48] Beihammer, 'Defection', 640.

On seizing Konya, Ghiyāth al-Dīn had the Qāḍī killed. Ibn Bībī represents the Qāḍī's execution as an enormous crime that incurred God's wrath upon the sultan. For three years the gardens and farms of Konya did not bear fruit, and were destroyed by unexpected snows and cold snap, until finally the sultan admitted his mistake and did penance by recompensing the Qāḍī's relatives.[49] Although not explicitly stated in the text, it seems highly likely that Ghiyāth al-Dīn's jihad against Philadelphia was designed to assert his credentials as a good Islamic ruler and remove the stain of both his exile in Constantinople and his murder of Qāḍī al-Tirmidhī. No other Seljuq ruler had the same desperate need to counter allegations of his partiality to things Byzantine, so none other bothered himself with campaigning on the Byzantine frontier, a zone of minor importance when seen from Konya.

The Concept of the Frontier and its Place in Seljuq Anatolia

To understand how medieval Muslims conceptualised their frontier it is useful to examine what terms they used to describe it. Discontinuity with Abbasid practice is very clear here. Only rarely is the term *thaghr* or *thughūr* used in literary or historical texts to describe the frontier, and when it is, it does not seem to have any technical meaning beyond denoting a vague frontier area in general; it certainly does not imply any kind of network of fortifications as we find on the Abbasid *thughūr*.[50] The only consistent use of this term in the thirteenth century was in the honorific titles that were bestowed on towns. Thus Denizli is described as *dār al-thaghr*, as are Antalya and Samsun.[51] Nonetheless, the scholarly consensus is that by the thirteenth century, the Islamic–Byzantine frontier region was denoted by the Turkish term *ūj*, meaning point or extremity, which has even been claimed to be a synonym for *thaghr* (although the literal meaning of the latter is 'mouth' or 'opening').[52] Indeed the venerable *Encyclopaedia of*

[49] Ibn Bībī, *al-Awāmir al-ʿAlāʾiyya*, 95.

[50] For example, Ibn Bībī, *al-Awāmir al-ʿAlāʾiyya*, 619: *sadd-i thughūr-i ūj*; ibid., 637, the Mongol governor Samaghar is described as *ḥākim-i mamālik wa ḥāfiẓ-i thughūr-i rūm*.

[51] Turan, *Selçuklular Zamanında Türkiye*, 687–8.

[52] Korobeinikov, 'The Byzantine–Seljuk Border in Times of Trouble', 58.

Islam includes an article by Elizabeth Zachariadou which is devoted to discussing the *ūj* in Wittekian terms.[53]

The term '*wilāyat-i ūj*' or 'province of the *ūj*' is also found and Claude Cahen believed this denoted the special administrative arrangements for the frontier region.[54] The evidence for such special arrangements beyond the existence of this phrase is non-existent, however. Although we have a number of collections of archival documents from Seljuq and Mongol Anatolia such as the *Taqārīr al-Manāṣib*, which include numerous decrees of appointments for officials ranging from castle chatelains to viziers to poet laureate, none of these documents so much as alludes to the frontier, let alone gives us any sense of such special administrative arrangements for it.[55]

One rare piece of evidence we have for any kind of arrangements for the administration of the *ūj* comes from the chronicler Ibn Bībī, discussing the aftermath of the Seljuq conquest of the Danishmendid territories in the late twelfth century. The sons of the Danishmendid ruler Yaghibasān were made 'commanders of the *ūj* provinces' and 'all the amīrs and commanders of those regions followed their policy and their banner'.[56] The *ūj* played a major role in supplying the Seljuqs with soldiers; Ibn Bībī repeatedly refers to *ūjī* soldiers in the dynasty's service.[57] Moreover, these soldiers were not simply some ragtag nomadic army but could be mustered by written decree. Before the campaign against Kalonoros (Alanya), sultan ʿAlāʾ al-Dīn Kayqubād I

> ordered that firmāns be written to the regions of the *ūj* (*aṭrāf-i ūj*) to summon the armies. Immediately the court secretaries (*munshiyān-i bārgāh*) scattered their amber-like breaths upon the camphor of paper . . . They affixed the imperial signature (*tawqīʿ-i humāyūn*) and sent them by the hand of the guarding slave-soldiers (*ghulāmān-i yatāq*) to be entrusted to a messenger.[58]

53 Elizabeth Zachariadou, 'Udj', *Encyclopaedia of Islam, New Edition* (Leiden: Brill, 2000), 10: 777, and see my comments in Peacock, 'The Seljuq Sultanate of Rum and the Turkmen', 271–3.

54 Claude Cahen, *La Turquie pré-ottomane* (Istanbul: IFEA, 1988), 206.

55 The text of the *Taqārīr al-Manāṣib* is published in Osman Turan, *Türkiye Selçukluları Hakkında Resmi Vesikalar* (Ankara: Türk Tarih Kurumu, 1988).

56 Ibn Bībī, *al-Awāmir al-ʿAlāʾiyya*, 77, 80.

57 Ibid., 390, 408, 457, 461.

58 Ibid., 228.

On another occasion, the *ṣāḥib-dīwān* Shams al-Dīn is depicted as sending robes of honour and money to 'Kastamonu, Simre, Sinop and the regions of the *ūj*'.[59] Evidently these *ūj* regions were thus at least in this period subject to central control, and had in some form structures of government which would allow royal orders to be authenticated and communicated to the *ūj* soldiery.[60] If later in the thirteenth century the *ūj* became known as a hotbed of rebellion, this was doubtless closely connected to Turkmen resentment of Mongol rule as well as the breakdown in structures of authority that followed the Seljuq defeat at Köse Dağ.

The *ūj* regions then were integrated into the Seljuq state to some degree; but where were they? A careful examination of our medieval Anatolian texts suggests that *ūj* did not in fact refer to the Islamic–Byzantine frontier, or certainly not invariably.[61] The term is often coupled with the Turkmen (*turkī*, *atrāk*).[62] Rather than being racially mixed areas, as described by Zachariadou and Wittek, they were predominantly Turkish-populated areas, and thus, as in the passage by Ibn Saʿīd cited at the beginning of this essay, *ūj* can refer to a people, not a place. It is clear these *ūj* Turks were largely nomadic, and the *ūj* regions were often located far from the Islamic–Byzantine frontier. For example, the historian Aqsarāʾī (writing around 1323) tells us that the official Muʿīn al-Dīn Ṭughrāʾī, travelling from Konya to Kastamonu 'passed through the *ūj* where the Turks [i.e. the Turkmen] ambushed him'; he finally reached safety in Seferihisar, which was somewhere between Aksaray and Niğde.[63] In other words, the *ūj* here is right in the physical centre of the Seljuq state, in the heart of central Anatolia, nowhere near any frontier. On another occasion, in response to a Turkmen revolt, the Mongol-appointed

[59] Ibid., 604.

[60] Ibid., 180: 'farmānī bi umarā-yi ūj kih lashkarhā-yi maʿhūd bā Turkmān-i kamāndār wa sawārān-i bisyār bih khidmat-i paykar-i humāyūn daʿwat kunad'.

[61] I here supplement some of the conclusions I have reached in previous publications with additional evidence. See A. C. S. Peacock, 'Court and Nomadic Life in Saljuq Anatolia', in David Durand-Guédy (ed.), *Turko-Mongol Rulers, Cities and City Life* (Leiden: Brill, 2013), 199–205; Peacock, 'The Seljuq Sultanate of Rum and the Turkmen', 269, 274.

[62] For example, Ibn Bībī, *al-Awāmir al-ʿAlāʾiyya*, 604, 619.

[63] Aqsarāʾī, *Musāmarat al-Akhbār*, ed. Osman Turan (Ankara: Türk Tarih Kurumu, 1944), 249; for Seferihisar's location, see ibid., 125, 254.

ruler of Anatolia, the Pervane Muʿīn al-Dīn Muḥammad Beg, 'set out for the region of the *ūj* (*bi-jānib-i ūj*), which is the origin of revolt, and the region of Kastamonu'. This passage seems to locate the *ūj* somewhere in the Kastamonu-Çankırı region, Çankırı being specifically mentioned as the Pervane's first target.[64] Aqsarāʾī repeatedly refers to the *ūj* as the 'base of the revolt of rebels' (*ūj kih mustaqarr-i khurūj-i khawārij ast*),[65] but it often seems to denote the Kastamonu area, where we know there was strong Turkmen opposition to Mongol rule.[66] Although Aqsarāʾī refers to the coastal plain around Antalya as an *ūj* region when dealing with the thirteenth century, it is only described as such after its incorporation into the Seljuq state in view of its nomadic population.[67] On occasion, areas such as Denizli are included in the *ūj*, but by virtue of their substantial Turkmen population (as also noted by Ibn Saʿīd) rather than their frontier nature: one description by Ibn Bībī of an *ūj* rebellion suggests the latter was centred on 'Zalifre (Safranbolu), Honaz, Ladhiq (Denizli), Simre, Sinop, Samsun and Bafra'.[68] In other words, while the Islamic–Byzantine frontier region is suggested by the references to Honaz and Denizli, the other locations mentioned are deep in Paphlagonia, far from the border.

If, then, the term *ūj* did not mean the Islamic–Byzantine frontier but rather Turkmen areas that had been in many ways integrated into the Seljuq state, how was the frontier area referred to? For the most part there are few specific references to frontiers in texts. For example, when a doctor who has left a collection of his correspondence was sent by the ruler of Sinop to treat patients in the neighbouring non-Muslim lands, he simply referred to having been to the *dār al-kufr* ('abode of unbelief'; that part of the world

64 Aqsarāʾī, *Musāmarat al-Akhbār*, 247.

65 See also Aqsarāʾī, *Musāmarat al-Akhbār*, 203–4.

66 For example, Aqsarāʾī, *Musāmarat al-Akhbār*, 170; cf. Ibn Bībī, *al-Awāmir al-ʿAlāʾiyya*, 604, 635; for Turkmen revolts against the Mongols in the Kastamonu area, see Korobeinikov, *Byzantium and the Turks*, 274–81.

67 See, for example, Aqsarāʾī, *Musāmarat al-Akhbār*, 66, 71, 89, and the discussion in Peacock, 'Court and Nomadic Life', 201.

68 Ibn Bībī, *al-Awāmir al-ʿAlāʾiyya*, 619. Further on the Turkmen population in the Denizli region, see Peacock, 'The Seljuq Sultanate of Rum and the Turkmen'; Korobeinikov, 'The Byzantine–Seljuk Border in Times of Trouble'.

not yet ruled by Islamic law); there is no mention made of a border.[69] On the other hand some texts do indeed occasionally make reference to terms such as *ḥudūd* (borders) and *tukhūm* (limits, borderlines), and indeed the Greek loanword *sīnūr*, which is adopted into Anatolian Persian (and from which the modern Turkish word for frontier, *sınır* derives).[70] Yet none of these seems to designate any kind of special administrative region, or even really a distinct zone. On the Jaziran frontier it seems certain groups, above all the Khwarazmians, were employed as 'guardians of the frontier', and there is one fragment of evidence to suggest that Turkmen played the same role in the frontier districts around Sinop.[71]

If the frontier did not have, as far as we can tell, any special administrative status or indeed any significant military infrastructure, some evidence suggests that in some instances, built structures served to mark these *ḥudūd* or *tukhum* between the *dār al-Islām* and *dār al-kufr*. Ibn Saʿīd's comments about the function of the Baṭṭāl Ghāzī grave as marking the frontier (*ḥudūd*) are backed up by the thirteenth-century pilgrim al-Harawī, who comments that, 'The tomb of Abū Muḥammad al-Baṭṭāl is atop a hill at the boundaries of that land.'[72] The shrine of this Muslim warrior thus served to demarcate the boundaries of the Muslim world and the *dār al-ḥarb*. The shrine, at modern Seyitgazi, still stands. Although its present form largely dates to the Ottoman period, there is evidence it served as the burial place of Sultan ʿAlāʾ al-Dīn Kayqubād's mother.[73] However, in addition to such symbolic structures there were also practical ones. Recent archaeological work has also found that at

[69] Istanbul, Süleymaniye Yazma Eserler Kütüphanesi, MS Fatih 5604; see the summary in Turan, *Türkiye Selçukluları Hakkında Resmi Vesikalar*, 159–66, and the discussion of the correspondence in Bruno De Nicola, 'Letters from Mongol Anatolia: Professional, Political and Intellectual Connections among Members of a Persianised Elite', *Iran* 56 (2018), 77–90.

[70] For *sīnūr* see, for example, Aḥmad of Niğde, *al-Walad al-Shafiq*, ed. Ali Ertuğrul (Ankara: Türk Tarih Kurumu, 2015), 2: 350; *Divanı Sultan Veled*, ed. Feridun Nafiz Uzluk (Istanbul: Uzluk Basımevi, 1941), 226.

[71] Ibn Bībī, *al-Awāmir al-ʿAlāʾiyya*, 430–1, 625.

[72] Al-Harawī, *A Lonely Wayfarer's Guide to Pilgrimage*, 15.

[73] For a study of the shrine, see Zeynep Yürekli, *Architecture and Hagiography in the Ottoman Empire: The Politics of Bektashi Shrines in the Classical Age* (Farnham: Ashgate, 2012).

the bottom of the hill where the shrine stands was a caravanserai, probably constructed in the 1220s.[74]

Similarly, the shrine of the Cave of the Seven Sleepers at Elbistan, in the old Abbasid *thaghr* and near the Seljuq border with the Ayyubids, was patronised by the Seljuqs. This patronage may have been intended to assert the Seljuq claim to these frontier areas, to integrate these areas into the Seljuq state, and indeed to profit from them economically by the pilgrim traffic.[75] Elbistan in the late twelfth and early thirteenth century was ruled directly by a Seljuq prince, Mughīth al-Dīn Ṭughrilshāh, who held it as his *iqṭāʿ*, which may also explain Seljuq activity in the area.[76] Later, the shrine of the Seven Sleepers and nearby tomb of Diocletian was granted to the Mengücekid ruler Muẓaffar al-Dīn in compensation for his appanage of Kughūniya (Şebinkarahisar) which was annexed by ʿAlāʾ al-Dīn Kayqubād in 1228. It is testimony to the success of integration of this frontier region into the Seljuq state that it was considered safe enough to grant to an erstwhile rival.[77]

The construction of caravanserais, as can be observed at Seyitgazi, Elbistan, and Denizli, may be seen as part of the same strategy of integration, and we should bear in mind such caravanserais probably had a political purpose, acting as outposts of central government, centres for tax collection, and custom posts rather than purely as trade emporia.[78] Quite possibly they were also intended to keep a central government eye on local potentates like Mughīth al-Dīn. The heyday of caravanserai construction is the first half of the thirteenth century, suggesting an effort to bind these frontier areas into the Seljuq state, linking them with its central Anatolian heartland.[79] This picture of economic integration is

[74] Excavations were recently undertaken by Eskişehir Museum and apparently have not yet been published. I thank Scott Redford for this information.

[75] Pancaroğlu, 'Caves, Borderlands and Configurations', 275–9.

[76] Ibn Bībī, *al-Awāmir al-ʿAlāʾiyya*, 41: Mughīth al-Dīn Ṭughrilshāh, who had been allotted the territory of Elbistan as *iqṭāʿ* by Qilij Arslan, surrenders it to the deposed Ghiyāth al-Dīn Kaykhusraw I, but the latter then immediately granted it back to Mughīth al-Dīn.

[77] Ibn Bībī, *al-Awāmir al-ʿAlāʾiyya*, 329–30.

[78] Peacock, 'The Seljuq Sultanate of Rum and the Turkmen', 278, with further references.

[79] For an impression of caravanserai construction, see the classic work by Kurt Erdmann, *Das anatolische Karavansaray des 13. Jahrhunderts* (Berlin: Verlag Gebr. Mann, 1961–76); this may usefully be supplemented by Hakkı Acun (ed.), *Anadolu Selçuklu Dönemi Kervansarayları* (Ankara: T. C. Kültür ve Turizm Yayınları, 2007).

also supported by the evidence of *waqfiyyas*,[80] which show how revenue from properties in frontier locations such as Eskişehir would go to support foundations in Kırşehir in Central Anatolia.[81] Thus, while there is no evidence of any special administrative arrangements for frontier areas, which do not even seem to have been designated with a specific name, as argued above, there was evidently an effort to incorporate them into the Seljuq state in some form.

Frontier Warfare in Seljuq Literary Texts

The Arab–Byzantine frontier was the inspiration for literary works on both sides, from the Greek epic *Digenes Akrites* to the heroic stories of Baṭṭāl Ghāzī. The circulation of such tales in thirteenth- and fourteenth-century Anatolia is sometimes taken for granted on the basis of Ibn Saʿīd's references to the stories of Baṭṭāl Ghāzī in 'books of entertainment', and the existence of a later Turkish epic cycle, but the latter can be securely dated only to the fifteenth century. For sure, the references in al-Harawī to the cult of Baṭṭāl Ghāzī and the evidence of patronage of the tomb by Seljuq sultans do support the idea that this holy warrior's cult remained important. Yet while we do have evidence of Arabic manuscripts of the legend of Baṭṭāl being read elsewhere in the Middle East in this period,[82] there is no firm evidence to date of their written circulation in Seljuq Anatolia in the form of manuscripts or even references in Anatolian literary texts. One possible exception is the Turkish epic entitled *Danişmendname*, which draws substantially on legends of Abbasid times, including those of Baṭṭāl Ghāzī himself, and which has also come to us in a fifteenth-century version. The text traces its origins to the Seljuq period, purportedly having been recited before Sultan ʿIzz al-Dīn Kaykāʾūs II, while a sixteenth-century Ottoman source dates the work's composition to 642/1244, and states it was originally written in Persian.[83] Yet caution is

[80] List or register of inalienable religious charitable foundations under Islamic law.

[81] Judith Pfeiffer, 'Protecting Private Property vs. Negotiating Political Authority: Nur al-Din b. Jaja and his endowments in thirteenth century Anatolia', in Robert Hillenbrand, A. C. S. Peacock and Firuza Abdullaeva (eds), *Ferdowsi, the Mongols and the History of Iran: Art, Literature and Culture from Early Islam to Qajar Persia* (London: I. B. Tauris, 2013), 147–65.

[82] Konrad Hirschler, *The Written Word in the Medieval Arabic Lands: A Social and Cultural History of Reading Practices* (Edinburgh: Edinburgh University Press, 2012), 167–9.

[83] For discussion, see Peacock, *Islam, Literature and Society*, 153–4.

required here too. It was a common feature of Turkish texts to claim earlier antecedents, to bestow on themselves an air of authority. In reality, we know almost nothing of popular literature before the fourteenth century, and very little that can be said with certainty before the middle of it; yet the one reference we do have to the circulation of popular epics, from the 1330s, refers not to Baṭṭāl but to the stories of ʿAlī b. Abī Ṭālib and the Prophet's heroic uncle Ḥamza.[84] Of course, these two figures are also generally represented in popular texts as Muslim heroes battling the forces of unbelief, so such tales, which of course were widespread across the Muslim world, might have had an especial resonance in a frontier region. Yet it seems, on the basis of our present evidence, that the frontier did not leave much trace in the literary production of Seljuq Anatolia.

We are on slightly firmer ground with apocalyptic texts, of which we have two major extant examples from Seljuq Anatolia, a *malḥama* and a treatise on the Mahdi. The *malḥama* is a type of prognosticatory and apocalyptic text associated with the Prophet Daniel that predicts not just the weather and agriculture, but also wars, in particular frontier wars. Such works are known in both the Christian and Muslim tradition. The tenth-century Ottonian envoy to Constantinople, Liudprand of Cremona, left an intriguing account of how these texts were used by both Christian and Muslim communities to predict frontier strife and victory. Liudprand introduces his discussion of these books to explain why the Byzantine emperor Nicephorus II Phocas set out on a campaign against Syria:

> The Greeks and Saracens have certain writings which they call The Visions of Daniel; I should call them the Sibylline Books. In them is found written how many years each emperor shall live; what crisis will occur during his reign; whether he shall have peace or war and whether fortune will smile upon the Saracens. According to these prophecies the Assyrians [i.e. Muslims] in the time of the present emperor Nicephorus will not be able to resist the Greeks. After his death an emperor will rise worse than he . . . and more unwarlike; in whose time the Assyrians shall so prevail that they will bring under their rule all the country as far as Chalcedon, which is not far from Constantinople.

[84] Ibid., 207–8.

> Both peoples pay serious heed to these dates; and so now for one and the same reason the Greeks are pressing vigorously forward and the Saracens in despair offer no resistance, awaiting the time when they will attack and the Greeks in turn not resist.[85]

A number of *malḥamas* have survived, and David Cook has remarked that these texts represent a genre of apocalyptic literature specifically associated with the conquest of Constantinople.[86] They are thus obviously of interest from the point of view of identifying ways in which frontier fighting permeated consciousness more generally, although rather few Muslim *malḥamas* have been studied; an Arabic one has been published by Fodor, who suggested it was composed among the Christian communities of the Tur ʿAbdin in the late tenth to early eleventh centuries.[87] It is evident that such texts also circulated in Anatolia in our period. Ibn Bībī also tells of a Seljuq court *munajjim*, Athīr al-Dīn, active in the mid-thirteenth century, who was also a specialist in the prophecies of Daniel.[88] We also have a Persian one composed by the court physician and astrologer, Ḥubaysh-i Tiflīsī, who served the Seljuq sultan Qilij Arslān II (1156–92); the latter, incidentally, had an especially keen interest in the occult, like many members of the dynasty.[89] Although most of the *malḥama* texts that I have seen survive only in much later copies, raising questions about their date and attribution, we do have one significant medieval copy of Tiflīsī's Persian *Malḥamat-i Dāniyāl*, which

[85] Liudprand of Cremona, *Relatio de legatione Constantinopolitana (The Embassy to Constantinople)*, in *The Works of Liudprand of Cremona*, trans. F. A. Wright (London: Routledge, 1930), 233–77, here 257–8 (c. 39). In general, on these Daniel-related works, see Lorenzo Ditommaso, *The Book of Daniel and the Apocryphal Daniel Literature* (Leiden: Brill, 2005).

[86] David Cook, *Studies in Muslim Apocalyptic* (Princeton, NJ: Darwin Press, 2002), 23.

[87] Alexander Fodor, 'Malhamat Daniyal', in Gyula Káldy-Nagy (ed.), *The Muslim East: Studies in Honour of Julius Germanus* (Budapest: Loránd Eötvös University, 1974), 85–159.

[88] Ibn Bībī, *al-Awāmir al-ʿAlāʾiyya*, 523.

[89] Peacock, *Islam, Literature and Society*, 218–19; A. C. S. Peacock, 'A Seljuq Occult Text and its World: MS Paris persan 174', in S. Canby *et al.* (eds), *The Seljuqs and their Successors* (Edinburgh: Edinburgh University Press, 2020), 163–79. On Ḥubaysh-i Tiflīsī, see Tahsin Yazıcı, 'Ḥobayš b. Ebrāhim b. Moḥammad Teflisi', *Encyclopaedia Iranica*, https://iranicaonline.org/articles/hobays-b-ebrahim-b-mohammad-teflisi (last accessed 18 February 2022).

was copied under Mongol rule. Unlike most later manuscripts bearing the title, this one explicitly attributes the work to Tiflīsī, who tells us that it was composed after he had completed his *Qānūn al-Adab*, an Arabic–Persian dictionary dedicated to Qilij Arslān. It was based on Arabic books which it abridged, the *Kitāb Dāniyāl* and a work by Jaʿfar al-Ṣādiq, who is often associated with occult knowledge.[90]

The *Malḥamat-i Dāniyāl* is preserved in a *safīna*[91] now held in Çorum Hasan Paşa Manuscripts Library as MS 3028 on fol. 26b–72b; the manuscript containing a number of other Persian occult texts, including a *Jāmaspnāma*,[92] and a poem on medicine.[93] The copying date of the *Malḥamat* is given as Rabīʿ I 712/July 1312, by a scribe named Aḥmad b. ʿUthmān b. Abīʾl-Fakhr Muḥammad al-Qārūdī (?). Although no place is given, the medical poem is dated the same year, is evidently written in the same hand, and was copied in Akhlat.[94] We are then fairly safe in assuming it is likely the *Malḥamat* was copied in the same place. The enduring popularity of the work is suggested by a reader's note dated AH 944/1537–8.

The *Malḥamat* is divided into two chapters, the first dealing with prognostication based on the Romans' month, and the second based on the position of the moon in the zodiac, that is, the old Arab system. These discuss the signification of a month beginning on a particular day. Signs such as comets, earthquakes and eclipses are also discussed. As we might expect from Liudprand, wars with the Byzantines (Rūm) do feature prominently, although far from exclusively, among the events prognosticated, albeit in quite general terms. For example, under January, if a comet is seen, 'it signifies the power of kings, but for a brief period; disturbances and bloodshed in the west, and the enmity and hostility of kings towards Rūm, and the death

90 Ḥubaysh-i Tiflīsī, *Malḥamat-i Dāniyāl*, Çorum Hasan Paşa Yazma Eser Kütüphanesi, MS 3028, fol. 29b.

91 Literally, 'ship' or 'vessel' in Arabic. In connection with manuscripts, it denotes a style of book whose cover is elongated, because when opened, it (fancifully) resembles a long vessel.

92 Literally, 'Book of Jāmasp'. He was a legendary Persian scientist and vizier, said to have been a vizier of King Vishtasb c. 500 BC.

93 I will publish a fuller description of the manuscript elsewhere.

94 Çorum Hasan Paşa Yazma Eserler Kütüphanesi, MS 3028, fol. 12.

of many fish and fowl in this year'.[95] An eclipse of the moon in February, however, means 'much war between the army of Islam and the infidel'.[96] When a comet appears in Adhar, this means 'the death of the Caesar of Rūm or the death of a king in the west'.[97]

There are some suggestions that the text has been updated to fit Tiflīsī's own times: Rūm features under the signs of a rainbow in September in what may be a reference to the Fourth Crusade:

> If in the east they see it, it signifies that there will be war, enmity and bloodshed in the province of Fars, and some wise men [say] there will be war and enmity between the king of the west and the Caesar of Rūm, and in the end the king of the west will be victorious and many people of Rūm will be destroyed.[98]

There are also signs of adaptation in reaction to Muslim–Christian conflict during the Crusades. One passage discussing the significance of redness in the sky says that 'If redness is seen in the west, there will be bloodshed, strife and war between the army of Islam and the Franks in the west, and in the end the army of Islam will be victorious.'[99] However, it must be said that the references to wars with the Rūm form only a fairly minor part of Tiflīsī's *malḥama*, and certainly do not support the idea that this was a central feature of the genre. The geographical scope of Tiflīsī's *malḥama* stretches across the Muslim world, mentioning locations as remote as Zanzibar, and Rūm does not seem to be singled out for much specific attention.

Wars against the Christians also feature in the *Risāla fī Amr al-Mahdī*, attributed to the famous disciple of Ibn ʿArabī, Ṣadr al-Dīn al-Qunawī, and composed around 1266.[100] This is a common theme in the apocalyptic literature more generally, and should not be considered something unique to

95 Ḥubaysh-i Tiflīsī, *Malḥamat-i Dāniyāl*, fol. 41a.
96 Ibid., fol. 41a.
97 Ibid., fol. 44a.
98 Ibid., fol. 60a.
99 Ibid., fol. 56a.
100 See the discussion of this text in Peacock, *Islam, Literature and Society*, 226–9.

Anatolia. Indeed, it is perhaps striking that despite the border with Byzantium, only one such apocalyptic work from Seljuq Anatolia has come down to us. The *Risāla* states that the Mahdi

> will conquer Constantinople the Great with the saying of *allāhu akbar* and invoking the name of God, not with marching and mangonels. Constantinople the Great is the Roman city which the believers will surround in the presence of the Mahdi, proclaiming *allāhu akbar* all together in one go, at which a third of the walls will fall; they will say it a second time, at which the second third will fall; and a third time, at which the remaining third of the walls will fall.[101]

Yet despite the work's Anatolian provenance, the great Muslim–Christian battle at the end of time (*al-malḥama al-ʿuẓmā*) is located in Marj ʿAkka (Acre),[102] not anywhere in Anatolia, while the Mahdi himself comes from Salé in the Maghrib and will establish his seat in Damascus.

Both the *Risāla* and Tiflīsī's *Malḥamat-i Dāniyāl* reveal that proximity to Byzantium did not in fact significantly influence the thought world of Muslim intellectuals; in both instances these apocalyptic texts draw on much more general Muslim traditions in which battles with the Byzantines played a part. However, in neither case were such aspects emphasised in local Anatolian works. It is noteworthy, perhaps, that our sole extant medieval copy of Tiflīsī's *malḥama* was probably copied in Akhlat, far to the east of the Byzantine frontier.

Conclusion

Our texts do from time to time allude to frontier fighting as jihad or *ghazw*, holy war, as does, on occasion, the contemporary epigraphic record.[103] Yet this

101 Ṣadr al-Dīn al-Qunawī, *Risāla fī Amr al-Mahdī*, Istanbul, Süleymaniye Yazma Eserler Kütüphanesi, MS Ayasofya 4849, fol. 171a.

102 Ibid., fol. 175a.

103 See note 25 above, and Scott Redford and Gary Leiser, *Victory Inscribed: The Seljuk Fetihname on the Citadel Walls of Antalya, Turkey* (Antalya, 2008), 109; for other examples from Anatolia, see for example, Oya Pancaroğlu, 'The House of Mengüjek in Divriği: Constructions of Dynastic Identity in the Late Twelfth Century', in A. C. S. Peacock and Sara Nur Yıldız (eds), *The Seljuks of Anatolia: Court and Society in the Medieval Middle East* (London: I. B. Tauris, 2013), 45–53.

seems to have been a general rhetorical strategy rather than translating into concrete action on the part of the sultans, except under Ghiyāth al-Dīn Kaykhusraw I, whose unique personal circumstances impelled him to follow a different policy. On the whole, though, the evidence presented above suggests that, contrary to expectations, at least from the beginning of the thirteenth century, the Islamic–Byzantine frontier was of limited importance to the Islamic side. The relative lack of military activity on the Seljuq–Byzantine frontier is indicative of the fact that the Seljuqs stood to gain little from battling Byzantium over the Anatolian countryside, while the Byzantines remained preoccupied with the much greater prize of recapturing Constantinople, and after this was achieved in 1261, re-establishing authority in the Balkans. Although border clashes in Anatolia certainly happened, they did not form part of a coherent strategy; they are perhaps likely to have been incited largely by nomadic marauding and were certainly not worth commemorating in chronicles. Despite this perhaps rather underwhelming conclusion, it is I think still one worth making, for it allows us to reassess the nature of the Seljuq state while moving away from the Wittekian clichés that still dominate.

The Seljuqs and the elite of Konya did not envisage themselves as inhabiting the remote frontier province that modern scholarship has. On the contrary, they saw themselves as a major Islamic power, whose prestige was to be enhanced by asserting suzerainty over the Muslim-ruled lands of the Jazira and even Syria, and this is clearly reflected not just in the record of the sultans' campaigns but in the textual record that has survived. Manuscripts from Seljuq Anatolia indicate an interest in integrating the sultanate's history with that of earlier Islamic dynasties of the Middle East. Despite the fact that we have no chronicles of the Seljuqs of Anatolia from before Ibn Bībī's work, composed around 1278, other historical works certainly were read in Konya. The best known is Rāwandī's *Rāḥat al-Ṣudūr*, a Persian history-cum-compendium of useful knowledge, dedicated to Sultan Ghiyāth al-Dīn Kaykhusraw in 1210, which was intended to acculturate the Rūm Seljuqs in the ways of their Great Seljuq relatives whom Rāwandī had served.[104] In addition, a host of lesser-known manuscripts attest the Seljuqs elite's enduring fascination

[104] On this, see Sara Nur Yıldız, 'A Nadīm for the Sultan: Rāwandī and the Anatolian Seljuqs', in Peacock and Yıldız (eds), *The Seljuks of Anatolia*, 91–111.

with the recent history of the Islamic Middle East. Recently a complete copy has come to light of ʿImād al-Dīn al-Iṣfahānī's *Nuṣrat al-fatra*, dedicated to the history of the Great Seljuqs, which was made in Konya in 662/1263;[105] similarly historical works by Ibn al-Jawzī and Ibn al-Athīr were read and copied in Seljuq Anatolia.[106] The existence of such works suggests that despite the lack of an indigenous historiographical tradition, the Seljuqs were keenly aware of the broader Islamic culture and history of the region of which they aspired to be a part, indeed the dominant element, as suggested by their Syrian campaigns. This conception of Muslim Anatolia's place in the world was shared by Muslim intellectuals of Konya such as Ḥubaysh-i Tiflīsī and Ṣadr al-Dīn al-Qunawī. They drew on a wide range of Maghribi and Mashriqi sources to compose works which reflected in places the general Muslim interest in battle with Rūm and the fall of Constantinople, but certainly did not emphasise them. Byzantium was wholly peripheral to this world view. The lack of interest in fighting Byzantium is reflected in the broader textual culture of Seljuq Anatolia, with a lack of jihad treatises, such as we find from Syria in Crusader times.[107]

In the end, then, Wittek may not have been so wrong in seeing continuities between the Abbasid frontier on the Euphrates and that of Seljuq times. His mistake was to assume it was relocated to the west, where the actual dividing line between the Christian and Islamic worlds lay. Yet in reality, it was the Euphrates frontier that remained the Seljuqs' overwhelming strategic concern, reflecting their self-image as a Middle Eastern dynasty that was the true successor to the Great Seljuq sultanate and thus by right overlords of the Artuqids and Ayyubids. Ironically, this preoccupation of the Seljuqs precisely emulated the strategic concerns of their Byzantine predecessors. Yet it was not until the rise of Ottoman power in the fourteenth century that the Islamic frontier with Byzantium would again assume major political importance.

105 Medina, Maktabat Hikmat ʿArif, MS no. 6425/1, described in Muḥammad b. Muḥammad al-ʿImād al-Kātib al-Iṣfahānī, *Nuṣrat al-fatra wa-ʿuṣrat al-fiṭra*, ed. ʿIṣām Muṣṭafā ʿUqla (London, 2019), 1: 91–3.

106 Peacock, *Islam, Literature and Society*, 178.

107 See, for example, Suleiman Mourad and James Lindsay, *The Intensification and Reorientation of Sunni Jihad Ideology in the Crusader Period: Ibn ʿAsakir (1105–1176) of Damascus and his Age; with an edition and translation of Ibn ʿAsakir's* The Forty Hadiths for Inciting Jihad (Leiden: Brill, 2013).

SELECTED BIBLIOGRAPHY

Chapter 1

Andrae, Tor, *In the Garden of Myrtles: Studies in Early Islamic Mysticism*, trans. Birgitte Sharpe (Albany: State University of New York Press, 1987).

al-Anṭākī, Yaḥyā b. Saʿīd b. Yaḥyā *Taʾrīkh al-Anṭākī, al-maʿrūf bi-ṣilat taʾrīkh Awtīkhā* (Tripoli: Jarrūs Press, 1999).

Bonner, Michael, *Aristocratic Violence and Holy War: Studies in the Jihad and the Arab-Byzantine Frontier* (New Haven: American Oriental Society, 1996).

Bosworth, C. E., 'Byzantium and the Syrian frontier in the early Abbasid period', reprinted in C. E. Bosworth, *The Arabs, Byzantium, and Iran: Studies in Early Islamic History and Culture* (London: Routledge, 2016), article XII.

Bosworth, C. E., 'The City of Tarsus and the Arab-Byzantine Frontiers in Early and Middle ʿAbbāsid Times', *Oriens* 33 (1992), 268–86.

Bosworth, C. E., 'The Political and Dynastic History of the Iranian World (A.D. 1000–1217)', in J. A. Boyle (ed.), *The Cambridge History of Iran. Volume 5: The Seljuq and Mongol Periods* (Cambridge: Cambridge University Press, 1968), 1–202.

Cahen, Claude, *La Turquie pré-ottomane* (Istanbul: Institut Français des Études Anatoliennes, 1988).

Crone, Patricia, *God's Rule: Government and Islam, Six Centuries of Medieval Islamic Political Thought* (New York: Columbia University Press, 2004).

Drocourt, Nicolas, and Sebastian Kolditz, *A Companion to Byzantium and the West, 900–1204* (Leiden: Brill, 2021).

Eger, Asa, *The Islamic–Byzantine Frontier: Interaction and Exchange Among Muslim and Christian Communities* (New York: I. B. Tauris, 2015).

Haldon, John Frederick, and Hugh Kennedy, 'The Arab–Byzantine Frontier in the Eighth and Ninth Centuries: Military Organization and Society in the Borderlands', *Zbornik radova Vizantološkog instituta* 19 (1980), 79–116.

Hartmann, Angelika, *an-Nāṣir li-Dīn Allāh (1180–1225)* (Berlin: De Gruyter, 1975).

Hillenbrand, Carole, *The Crusades: Islamic Perspectives* (Edinburgh: University of Edinburgh Press, 1999).

Hillenbrand, Carole, *Turkish Myth and Muslim Symbol: The Battle of Manzikert* (Edinburgh: Edinburgh University Press, 2007).

Ibn al-Jawzī, Abū'l-Faraj ʿAbd al-Raḥmān, *Ṣifat al-ṣafwa*, ed. A. Bin ʿAlī (Cairo: Dār al-Ḥadīth, 1421/2000).

Ibn al-Mubarak, ʿAbdallāh, *Kitāb al-Jihād* (Beirut: Sharikat Abnāʾ Sharīf al-Anṣārī, 1409/1988).

Ibn al-Mulaqqin, Sirāj al-Dīn Abū Ḥafṣ ʿUmar, *Ṭabaqāt al-awliyāʾ*, ed. Muṣṭafā ʿAtā (Beirut: Dār al-Kutub al-ʿIlmiyya, 1988).

Ibn al-Munādī, Abū'l-Ḥusayn Aḥmad b. Jaʿfar, *Malāḥim*, ed. ʿAbd al-Karīm al-ʿUqaylī (Qumm: Dār al-Sīra, 1418/1998).

Khalīfa b. Khayyāṭ al-ʿUṣfurī, *Taʾrīkh Khalīfa b. Khayyāṭ*, ed. Muṣṭafā Fawwāz *et al.* (Beirut: Dār al-Fikr, 1415/1995).

Köhler, Michael, *Alliances and Treaties between Frankish and Muslim Rulers in the Middle East: Cross-cultural Diplomacy in the Period of the Crusades*, trans. P. Holt, rev. K. Hirschler (Leiden: Brill, 2013).

Korobeinikov, D. A., 'Raiders and Neighbours: The Turks (1040–1304)', in Jonathan Shepherd (ed.), *The Cambridge History of the Byzantine Empire, c. 500–1492* (Cambridge: Cambridge University Press, 2009), 692–728.

Lilie, Ralph-Johannes, *Byzantium and the Crusader States 1096–1204*, trans. J. C. Morris and Jean Ridings (Oxford: The Clarendon Press, 1993).

Lilie, Ralph-Johannes, 'Die Schlacht von Myriokephalon (1176): Auswirkungen auf das byzantinische Reich im ausgehenden 12. Jahrhundert', *Revue des études Byzantines* 35 (1977), 257–75.

Livne-Kafri, Ofer, 'Jerusalem in Early Islam: The Eschatological Aspect', *Arabica* 53: 3 (2006), 382–403.

al-Marwazī, Nuʿaym b. Ḥammād b. Muʿawiya b. al-Hārith al-Khuzāʿī, *al-Fitan* (Beirut: Dār al-Kutub al-ʿIlmiyya, 1418/1997).

Morton, Nicholas, *The Crusader States and Their Neighbours: A Military History, 1099–1187* (Oxford: Oxford University Press, 2020).

al-Samʿanī, ʿAbd al-Karīm b. Muḥammad, *Kitāb al-ansāb*, ed. ʿAbd al-Qādir ʿAṭā (Beirut: Dār al-Kutub al-ʿIlmiyya, 1419/1998).

Shoemaker, Stephen, *The Apocalypse of Empire: Imperial Eschatology in Late Antiquity and Early Islam* (Philadelphia: University of Pennsylvania Press, 2019).

al-Sijistānī, Abū Dā'ūd Sulaymān b. al-Ash'ath, *Kitāb al-Sunan: Sunan Abī Dā'ūd*, ed. Muḥammad 'Awāmma (Beirut: Mu'assasat al-Rayyān, 1998).

Taeschner, Franz, 'Die Islamischen Futuwwabünde: Das Problem ihrer Entsteihung und die Grundlinien ihrer Geschichte', *Zeitschrift der Deitschen Morgenländischen Gesellschaft* 87 (1933), 6–49.

Taeschner, Franz, 'Das Futuwwa-Rittertums des islamischen Mittelalters', *Beiträge zur Arabistik, Semitistik und Islamwissenschaften*, ed. R. Hartmann and H. Scheel (Leipzig: Harrassowitz Verlag, 1944), 340–85.

al-Ṭarsusī, Abū 'Amr 'Uthmān b. 'Abdallāh, *Siyar al-thughūr* (fragment), in Iḥsān 'Abbās (ed.), *Shadharāt min kutub mafqūda fi'l-ta'rikh* (Beirut: Dār al-Gharb al-Islāmī, 1408/1988), 37–48.

al-Tawḥīdī, Abū Ḥayyān, *al-Baṣā'ir wa'l-dhakhṣ'ir*, ed. Wadād al-Qāḍī (Beirut: Dār Ṣadr, 1988).

Tor, D. G., 'God's Cleric: Fuḍayl b. 'Iyāḍ and the Transition from Caliphal to Prophetic Sunna', in Behnam Sadeghi, Asad Q. Ahmed, Adam Silverstein and Robert Hoyland (eds), *Islamic Cultures, Islamic Contexts: Essays in Honor of Professor Patricia Crone* (Leiden: Brill, 2014), 195–228.

Tor, D. G., 'The Political Revival of the 'Abbāsid Caliphate: Al-Muqtafī and the Seljuqs', *Journal of the American Oriental Society* 137: 2 (2017), 301–14.

Tor, D. G., 'Privatized Jihad and Public Order in the Pre-Saljūq Period: The Role of the *Mutaṭṭawwi'a*', *Iranian Studies* 38: 4 (2005), 555–73.

Tor, D. G., *Violent Order: Religious Warfare, Chivalry, and the 'Ayyar Phenomenon in the Medieval Islamic World*, Istanbuler Texte und Studien der Deutschen Morgenländischen Gesellschaft, Band 11 (Würzburg: Ergon Verlag, 2007).

Treadgold, Warren, *The Byzantine Revival 780–842* (Stanford: Stanford University Press, 1988).

Turan, Osman, *Selçuklular Târihi ve Türk-Islâm Mediniyeti* (Ankara: Ötüken, 2004).

Chapter 2

Ahrweiler, Hélène, 'L'Asie Mineure et les invasions arabes (VIIe–IXe siècles)', *Revue historique* 227 (1962), 1–32.

Ahrweiler, Hélène, 'La frontière et les frontières de Byzance en Orient', in Mihai Berza and Eugen Stănescu (eds), *Actes du XIVe congrès international des études byzantines, Bucarest, 6–12 Septembre, 1971* (Bucarest: Editura Academiei Republicii Socialiste Romania, 1974), 209–30.

Beihammer, Alexander Daniel, *Byzantium and the Emergence of Muslim-Turkish Anatolia, ca. 1040–1130* (London: Birmingham Byzantine and Ottoman Studies, 2017).

Beihammer, Alexander, 'Defection across the Border of Islam and Christianity: Apostasy and Cross-Cultural Interaction in Byzantine-Seljuk Relations', *Speculum* 86 (2011), 597–651.

Bianquis, Thierry, *Damas et la Syrie sous la domination Fatimide (359–468/969–1076), essai d'interprétation de chroniques arabes médiévales*, 2 vols (Damascus: Institut Français de Damas, 1986–9).

Brandes, Wolfram, *Die Städte Kleinasiens im 7. und 8. Jahrhundert*, Berliner Byzantinistische Arbeiten 56 (Berlin: Akademie-Verlag, 1989).

Cahen, Claude, The Formation of Turkey, The Seljukid Sultanate of Rūm: Eleventh to Fourteenth Century, trans. and ed. Peter M. Holt (Harlow: Pearson Education, 2001).

Campagnolo-Pothitou, Maria, 'Les échanges de prisonniers entre Byzance et l'islam aux IXe et Xe siècles', *Journal of Oriental and African Studies* 7 (1995), pp. 1–56.

Canard, Marius, *Histoire de la dynastie des H'amdanides de Jazîra et de Syrie*, Publications de la Faculté des Lettres d'Alger, IIe Série, 21 (Paris: Presses Universitaires de France, 1952).

Cheynet, Jean-Claude, *Pouvoir et contestation à Byzance (963–1210)*, Byzantina Sorbonensia 9 (Paris: Publications de la Sorbonne, 1996).

Decker, Michael, 'Frontier Settlement and Economy in the Byzantine East', *Dumbarton Oaks Papers* 61 (2007), 217–67.

Dédéyan, Gérard, *Les arméniens entre grecs, musulmans et croisés: Études sure les pouvoirs arméniens dans le Proche-Orient méditerranéen (1068–1150)*, 2 vols (Lisbon: Fundação Calouste Gulbenkian, 2003).

Eger, Alexander Asa, The Islamic–Byzantine Frontier: Interaction and Exchange among Muslim and Christian Communities (London: I. B. Tauris, 2015).

Eger, Asa (ed.), *The Archaeology of Medieval Islamic Frontiers: From the Mediterranean to the Caspian Sea* (Louisville: University Press of Colorado, 2019).

Felix, Wolfgang, *Byzanz und die islamische Welt im frühen 11. Jahrhundert* (Vienna: Verlag der Österreichischen Akademie der Wissenschaften, 1981).

Haldon, John, '"Cappadocia will be given over to ruin and become a desert": Environmental evidence for historically-attested events in the 7th–10th centuries', in Klaus Belke, Ewald Kislinger, Andreas Külzer, Maria A. Stassinopoulou (eds), *Byzantina Mediterranea: Festschrift für Johannes Koder zum 65. Geburtstag* (Vienna: Böhlau Verlag, 2007), 215–30.

Haldon, John, *The Empire That Would Not Die: The Paradox of Eastern Roman Survival, 640–740* (Cambridge, MA: Harvard University Press, 2016).

Haldon, John, and Hugh Kennedy, 'The Arab–Byzantine Frontier in the Eighth and Ninth Centuries: Military Organisation and Society in the Borderlands', *Recueil des travaux de l'Institut d'études byzantines* 19 (1980), 79–116.

Haldon, John, *et al.*, 'The Climate and Environment of Byzantine Anatolia: Integrating Science, History, and Archaeology', *Journal of Interdisciplinary History* 45 (2014), 113–61.

Hild, Friedrich, and Marcell Restle, *Kappadokien (Kappadokia, Charsianon, Sebasteia und Lykandos)*, ÖADW, Denkschriften 149, Tabula Imperii Byzantini 2 (Vienna: Verlag der Österreichischen Akademie der Wissenschaften, 1981).

Holmes, Catherine, *Basil II and the Governance of Empire (976–1025)* (Oxford: Oxford University Press, 2005).

Honigmann, Ernst, Die Ostgrenze des byzantinischen Reiches von 363 bis 1071 nach griechischen, arabischen, syrischen und armenischen Quellen (Brussels: Librairie Orientale & Américaine, 1935).

Jankowiak, Marek, 'The First Arab Siege of Constantinople', *Travaux et Mémoires* 17 (2013), 237–320.

Kaegi, Walter E., *Byzantium and the Early Islamic Conquests* (Cambridge: Cambridge University Press, 1992).

Kennedy, Hugh, 'Byzantine–Arab Diplomacy in the Near East from the Islamic Conquests to the Mid-Eleventh Century', in Jonathan Shepard and Simon Franklin (eds), *Byzantine Diplomacy: Papers from the Twenty-fourth Spring Symposium of Byzantine Studies, Cambridge, March 1990* (Aldershot: Ashgate, 1992), 133–43.

Leveniotis, Georgios, *Η πολιτική κατάρρευση του Βυζαντίου στην Ανατολή, Το ανατολικό σύνορο και η κεντρική Μικρά Ασία κατά το β' ήμισυ του 11ου αι.*, 2 vols (Thessalonica: Byzantine Research Center, 2007).

Lilie, Ralf-Johannes, *Die byzantinische Reaktion auf die Ausbreitung der Araber, Studien zur Strukturwandlung des byzantinischen Staates im 7. und 8. Jhd.* (Munich: Institut für Byzantinistik und Neugriechische Philologie, 1976).

Niewöhner, Philipp (ed.), *The Archaeology of Byzantine Anatolia: From the End of Late Antiquity until the Coming of the Turks* (Oxford: Oxford University Press, 2017).

Oikononidès, Nicolas, 'L'organisation de la frontière orientale de Byzance aux Xe–XIe siècles et le Taktikon de L'Escorial', in Mihai Berza and Eugen Stănescu (eds), *Actes du XIVe congrès international des études byzantines, Bucarest, 6–12 Septembre, 1971* (Bucarest: Editura Academiei Republicii Socialiste Romania, 1974), 285–302.

Peacock, Andrew C. S., *Early Seljūq History, a New Interpretation* (London: Routledge, 2010).

Peacock, Andrew C. S., and Sara Nur Yıldız (eds), *The Seljuks of Anatolia: Court and Society in the Medieval Middle East* (London: I. B. Tauris, 2013).

Peacock, Andrew C. S., Bruno De Nicola, Sara Nur Yıldız (eds), *Islam and Christianity in Medieval Anatolia* (London: Routledge, 2015).

Ripper, Thomas, *Die Marwāniden von Diyār Bakr: Eine kurdische Dynastie im islamischen Mittelalter*, 2nd edn (Würzburg: Ergon, 2009).

Roche, Jason T., 'In the Wake of Mantzikert: The First Crusade and the Alexian Reconquest of Western Anatolia', *History* 94 (2009), 135–53.

Shukurov, Rustam, *The Byzantine Turks, 1204–1461*, The Medieval Mediterranean 105 (Leiden: Brill, 2016).

Todt, Klaus-Peter, *Dukat und griechisch-orthodoxes Patriarchat von Antiocheia in mittelbyzantinischer Zeit (969–1084)*, Mainzer Veröffentlichungen zur Byzantinistik 14 (Wiesbaden: Harrassowitz Verlag, 2018).

Turan, Osman, Selçuklular Zamanında Türkiye, Siyasî Tarih Alp Arslan'dan Osman Gâzi'ye (1071–1318), 18th edn (Istanbul: Ötüken, 2004).

Vest, Bernd Andreas, *Geschichte der Stadt Melitene under der umliegenden Gebiete: Vom Vorabend der arabischen bis zum Abschluss der türkischen Eroberung (um 600–1124)*, 3 vols (Hamburg: Verlag Dr. Kovač, 2007).

Vryonis, Speros, The Decline of Medieval Hellenism in Asia Minor and the Process of Islamization from the Eleventh through the Fifteenth Century (Berkeley: University of California Press, 1971).

Wittek, Paul, The Rise of the Ottoman Empire: Studies in the History of Turkey, Thirteenth–Fifteenth Centuries, ed. Colin Heywood with an Introduction and Afterword (Oxford: Routledge, 2012).

Chapter 3

Al-Balādhurī, Aḥmad b. Yaḥyā, *Futūḥ al-buldān*, ed. M. J. de Goeje (Leiden: Brill, 1866).

Bonner, Michael, 'The Naming of the Frontier: ʿAwāṣim, Thughūr and the Arab Geographers', *Bulletin of the School of Oriental and African Studies* 57 (1994), 17–24.

Eger, Asa, *The Islamic Byzantine Frontier* (London: I. B. Tauris, 2015).

Al-Ṭabarī, Abū Jaʿfar Muḥammad b. Jarīr, *Taʾrikh al-rusul waʾl-mulūk*, ed. M. J. de Goeje *et al.*, 3 parts (Leiden: Brill, 1879–1901).

Ibn Ḥawqal, Abūʾl-Qāṣsm al-Naṣībī, *Kitān ṣūrat al-arḍ*, ed. J. H. Kramers (Leiden: Brill, 1939).

Ibn Khurradādhbih, Abū'l-Qāsim 'Ubayd Allāh b. 'Abd Allāh, *Al-Masālik wa'l-mamālik*, ed. M. J. de Goeje (Leiden: Brill, 1889).

Qudāma b. Ja'far, *Kitāb al-kharāj*, ed. M. J. de Goeje (Leiden: Brill, 1889).

Al-Ya'qubī, Ibn Wādiḥ, *Ta'rīkh*, ed. M. T. Houtsma (Leiden: Brill, 1883).

Yāqūt al-Ḥamawī, *Mu'djam al-buldān* [*Jacut's Geographisches Wörterbuch*], I–VI, ed. F. Wüstenfeld (Leipzig, 1866–73/1924).

Chapter 4

Crone, Patricia, *The Nativist Prophets of Early Islamic Iran: Rural Revolt and Local Zoroastrianism* (New York: Cambridge University Press, 2012).

Eger, Asa, *The Islamic–Byzantine Frontier: Interaction and Exchange among Muslim and Christian Communities* (London: I. B. Tauris, 2015).

Garsoïan, N., and B. Hisard, 'Unité et diversité de la Caucasie médiévale (IV–XIth s.)', *Settimane di studio* 43 (1996), 275–367.

Hoyland, Robert G. (ed.), *From Albania to Arrān: The East Caucasus between Antiquity and Medieval Islam* (Piscataway: Gorgias Press, 2020).

Madelung, W., 'The Minor Dynasties of Northern Iran', in R. Frye (ed.), *The Cambridge History of Iran, Volume 4* (Cambridge: Cambridge University Press, 1975), 198–249.

Minorsky, Vladimir, 'Caucasica IV', *Bulletin of the School of Oriental and African Studies* 3 (1953), 504–29.

Preiser-Kapeller, Johannes, 'Central Peripheries. Empires and Elites across Byzantine and Muslim Frontiers in Comparison (700–900 CE)', in Wolfram Drews (ed.), *Die Interaktion von Herrschern und Eliten in imperialen Ordnungen des Mittelalters* (Berlin: De Gruyter, 2018), 91–113.

Shingiray, Irnia, *On the Path through the Shadow Empire: The Khazar Nomads at the Northwest Frontier of Iran and the Islamic Caliphate*. PhD thesis, Boston University, 2011.

Vacca, Alison, 'Conflict and Community in the Medieval Caucasus', *al-'Uṣūr al-Wusṭā* 25 (2017), 66–112.

Vacca, Alison, *Non-Muslim Provinces under Early Islam* (Cambridge: Cambridge University Press, 2017).

Chapter 5

Antoniadis-Bibicou, H., *Recherches sur les douanes à Byzance: L''octava', le 'kommerkion' et les commerciaires* (Paris: Librairie Armand Colin, 1963).

Curta, F., 'Linear Frontiers in the 9th Century: Bulgaria and Wessex', *Quaestiones Medii Aevi Novae* 16 (2011), 15–31.

Dagron, G., 'Byzance et la frontière: Idéologie et réalité', in O. Merisalo (ed.), *Frontiers in the Middle Ages* (Louvain-la-Neuve: Fédération Internationale des Instituts d'Études Médiévales, 2006), 303–18.

Durak, K., 'Traffic across the Cilician Frontier in the Ninth and Tenth Centuries: Movement of People between Byzantium and the Islamic Near East in the Early Middle Ages', in K. Frangoulis and E. Mpantaoui (eds), *Βυζάντιο και Αραβικός κόσμος: Συνάντηση Πολιτισμών* (Thessalonike: Aristotle University of Thessalonike, 2013), 141–54.

Eger, A. A., *The Islamic–Byzantine Frontier: Interaction and Exchange among Muslim and Christian Communities* (London: I. B. Tauris, 2015).

Gândilă, A., *Cultural Encounters on Byzantium's Northern Frontier, c.* AD *500–700: Coins, Artifacts and History* (Cambridge: Cambridge University Press, 2018).

Greatrex, G., 'Roman Frontiers and Foreign Policy in the East', in R. Alston and S. Lieu (eds), *Aspects of the Roman East: Papers in Honour of Professor Fergus Millar FBA* (Turnhout: Brepols, 2007), 103–73.

Holmes, C., 'Byzantium's Eastern Frontier in the Tenth and Eleventh Centuries', in D. Abulafia and N. Berend (eds), *Medieval Frontiers: Concepts and Practices* (Aldershot: Ashgate, 2002), 83–104.

Koutrakou, N., 'Diplomacy and Espionage: Their Role in Byzantine Foreign Relations, 8th–10th Centuries', *Graeco-Arabica* 6 (1995), 125–44.

Lee, A. D., *Information and Frontiers: Roman Foreign Relations in Late Antiquity* (Cambridge: Cambridge University Press, 1993).

Lilie, R.-J., 'The Byzantine–Arab Borderland from the Seventh to the Ninth Century', in F. Curta (ed.), *Borders, Barriers, and Ethnogenesis: Frontiers in Late Antiquity and the Middle Ages* (Turnhout: Brepols, 2005), 13–21.

Chapter 6

Primary sources

Abū ʿUbayd, Qāsim ibn Sallām, *The Book of Revenue (*Kitāb al-Amwāl*)*, trans. Imran Ahsan Khan Nyazee (Reading: Garnet, 2002).

Agapius, Maḥbūb ibn Qusṭanṭīn al-Manbijī = Vasiliev, A. A. (ed. and trans.), 'Kitab al-ʿUnvan (Histoire universelle, écrite par Agapius (Mahboub) de Menbidj), second partie, fasc. 2', *Patrologia Orientalis* 8 (1912), 399–547.

al-Balādhurī, Aḥmad ibn Yaḥyā, *Liber expugnationis regionum auctore Imámo Ahmed ibn Jahya ibn Djábir al-Beládsorí, quem e codice Leidensi et codice Musei Brittanici*, ed. M. J. de Goeje (Leiden: Brill, 1866).

Bar Hebraeus, Ibn al-ʿIbrī Abū ʾl-Faraj Ghrīghūriyūs, *Gregorii Barhebræi Chronicon Syriacum e codd. Mss. emendatum ac punctis vocalibus adnotationibusque locupletatum*, ed. Paul Bedjan (Paris: Maisonneuve, 1890).

Constantine Porphyrogenitus, *De administrando imperio*, ed. G. Y. Moravcsik, trans. R. J. H. Jenkins (Washington, DC: Dumbarton Oaks Center for Byzantine Studies, Trustees for Harvard University, 1967).

Chronicle of Zuqnīn = Chabot, J.-B. (ed.), *Chronincon anonymum Pseudo-Dionysianum vulgo dictum*, 4 vols (Louvain: L. Durbecq, 1949–89).

Chronicle of Zuqnīn = Harrak, Amir (trans.), *The Chronicle of Zuqnīn, Parts III and IV, A.D. 488–775* (Toronto: Pontifical Institute of Mediaeval Studies, 1999).

Eutychius, Yaḥyā ibn Saʿīd al-Anṭākī, *Annales*, 2 vols, eds L. Cheikho, B. Carra de Vaux and H. Zayyat (Louvain: Secrétariat du Corpus SCO, 1960–2).

Ibn al-ʿAdīm, Kamāl al-Dīn Abū ʾl-Qāsim ʿUmar ibn Aḥmad, *Bughyat al-ṭalab fī tārīkh ḥalab*, 11 vols, ed. Suhayl Zakkār (Damascus: no pub., 1988–9).

Ibn ʿAsākir, Thiqat al-Dīn Abū ʾl-Qāsim ʿAlī ibn Abī Muḥammad, *Tārīkh madīnat dimashq*, 80 vols, ed. ʿAlī Shīrī (Beirut: Dār al-Fikr lil-Ṭibāʿa wa-ʾl-Nashr wa-ʾl-Tawzīʿ, 1995–2000).

Ibn al-Athīr, Abū ʾl-Ḥasan ʿAlī ibn Muḥammad, *al-Kāmil fī ʾl-tārīkh*, 11 vols, ed. ʿUmar ʿAbd al-Salām Tadmurī (Beirut: Dār al-Kitāb al-ʿArabī, 1997).

Ibn al-Faqīh, Aḥmad ibn Muḥammad al-Hamadhānī, *Compendium libri Kitâb al-Boldân*, ed. M. J. de Goeje (Leiden: Brill, 1885).

Ibn al-Qilāʿī, Jibrāʾīl, *Zajaliyyāt jibrāʾīl ibn al-qilāʿī*, ed. Buṭrus al-Jumayyil (Beirut: Manshūrāt Dār Laḥd Khāṭir, 1982).

Ibn Zanjawayh, Abū Aḥmad Ḥumayd ibn Makhlad, *Kitāb al-amwāl*, 3 vols, ed. Shākir Dhīb Fayyāḍ (Riyad: Markaz al-Malik Fayṣal lil-Buḥūth wa-ʾl-Dirāsāt al-Islāmiyya, 1986).

Khalīfa ibn Khayyāṭ al-ʿUṣfurī, *Tārīkh khalīfa ibn khayyāṭ*, eds Muṣṭafā Najīb Fawwāz and Ḥikmat Kishlī Fawwāz (Beirut: Dār al-Kutub al-ʿIlmiyya, 1995).

al-Masʿūdī, Abū ʾl-Ḥasan ʿAlī ibn al-Ḥusayn, *Murūj al-dhahab wa-maʿādin al-jawhar (Les prairies d'or)*, 7 vols, ed. Charles Pellat (Beirut: Manshūrāt al-Jāmiʿa al-Lubnāniyya, 1966–79).

al-Muqaddasī, Shams al-Dīn Abū ʿAbdallāh Muḥammad ibn Aḥmad, *The Best Divisions for Knowledge of the Regions: A Translation of* Ahsan al-Taqasim fi Maʿrifat al-Aqalim, trans. Basil Anthony Collins with Muhammad Hamid al-Tai (Reading: Centre for Muslim Contribution to Civilization & Garnet Publishing Limited, 1994).

Michael the Great, *Chronique de Michel le Syrien: Patriarche jacobite d'Antioche (1166–1199)*, 4 vols, ed. and trans. J.-B. Chabot, 4 vols (Paris: Ernest Leroux, 1899–1910).

Nikephoros, Patriarch of Constantinople, *Short History*, ed. and trans. Cyril Mango (Washington, DC: Dumbarton Oaks Research Library and Collection, 1990).

Nuʿaym ibn Ḥammād al-Khuzāʿī al-Marwazī, *Kitāb al-fitan*, ed. Suhayl Zakkār (Beirut: Dār al-Fikr lil-Ṭibāʿa wa-ʾl-Nashr wa-ʾl-Tawzīʿ, 2003).

Nuʿaym ibn Ḥammād al-Khuzāʿī al-Marwazī, *'The Book of Tribulations': The Syrian Muslim Apocalyptic Tradition*, ed. and trans. David Cook (Edinburgh: Edinburgh University Press, 2017).

al-Shidyāq, Ṭannūs ibn Yūsuf, *Kitāb akhbār al-aʿyān fī jabal lubnān*, 2 vols, ed. Fuʾād Afrām al-Bustānī (Beirut: Manshūrāt al-Jāmiʿa al-Lubnāniyya, 1970).

al-Shihābī, Ḥaydar Aḥmad, *Kitāb tārīkh al-amīr ḥaydar aḥmad al-shihābī, Kitāb al-ghurar al-ḥisān fī tawārīkh ḥawādith al-azmān*, ed. Naʿūm Mughabghab (Cairo: Maṭbaʿat al-Salām, 1900).

al-Ṭabarī, Abū Jaʿfar Muḥammad ibn Jarīr, *Annales quos scripsit Abu Djafar Mohammed ibn Djarir at-Tabari cum aliis*, 15 vols in 3 pts, ed. M. J. de Goeje (Leiden: Brill, 1879–1901).

Theophanes Confessor, *Theophanis chronographia*, 2 vols, ed. Carolus de Boor (Leipzig: Teubner, 1883–5).

al-Yaʿqūbī, Abū ʾl-ʿAbbās Aḥmad ibn Abī Yaʿqūb, *Ibn Wādih qui dicitur al-Jaʿqubī Historiae*, 2 vols, ed. M. T. Houtsma (Leiden: Brill, 1883).

Yāqūt, Shihāb al-Dīn Abū ʿAbdallāh Yaʿqūb ibn ʿAbdallāh al-Ḥamawī, *Muʿjam al-buldān*, 5 vols, no ed. (Beirut: Dār Ṣādir, 1977).

Secondary sources

ʿAbbās, Iḥsān, *Tārīkh bilād al-shām fī ʾl-aṣr al-ʿabbāsī* (Amman: Manshūrāt Lajnat Tārīkh Bilād al-Shām – al-Jāmiʿa al-Urdunniyya – Jāmiʿat Yarmūk, 1992).

Cappel, Andrew J., 'The Byzantine Response to the 'Arab (10th–11th Centuries)', *Byzantinische Forschungen* 20 (1994), 113–32.

Chalhoub, Georges, *Recherches sur les Mardaïtes-Ǧarāǧima* (Kaslik: Université Saint-Esprit de Kaslik, 1999).

Cvetković, Miloš, 'The Settlement of the Mardaites and their Military-Administrative Position in the Themata of the West: A Chronology', *Zbornik radova Vizantološkog instituta* 54 (2017), 65–85.

Debié, Muriel, 'Christians in the Service of the Caliph: Through the Looking Glass of Communal Identities', in Antoine Borrut and Fred M. Donner (eds), *Christians and Others in the Umayyad State* (Chicago: Oriental Institute of the University of Chicago, 2016), 53–71.

El-Hāyek, Elias, 'Struggle for Survival: The Maronites of the Middle Ages', in Michael Gervers and Ramzi Jibran Bikhazi (eds), *Conversion and Continuity: Indigenous Christian Communities in Islamic Lands, Eighth to Fifteenth Centuries* (Toronto: Pontifical Institute of Mediaeval Studies, 1990), 407–21.

Haldon, John, *The Empire That Would Not Die: The Paradox of Eastern Roman Survival, 640–740* (Cambridge, MA: Harvard University Press, 2016).

Harris, William W., *Lebanon: A History, 600–2011* (New York: Oxford University Press, 2012).

Howard-Johnston, James, 'The Mardaites', in Tony Goodwin (ed.), *Arab–Byzantine Coins and History: Papers Presented at the 13th Seventh Century Syrian Numismatic Round Table Held at Corpus Christi College Oxford on 11th and 12th September 2011* (London: Archetype Publications, Ltd., 2012), 27–38.

Kurd ʿAlī, Muḥammad, *Kitāb khiṭaṭ al-shām*, 6 vols (Damascus: al-Maṭbaʿa al-Ḥadītha bi-Dimashq, 1925–8).

Levy-Rubin, Milka, *Non-Muslims in the Early Islamic Empire: From Surrender to Coexistence* (Cambridge: Cambridge University Press, 2011).

Moosa, Matti, 'Relation of the Maronites of Lebanon to the Mardaites and al-Jarājima', *Speculum* 44 (1969), 597–608.

Mpartikian, Chrats M., 'Hē lysē tou ainigmatos tōn Mardaïtōn', in Nia A. Stratos (ed.), *Byzantion: Aphierōma eton Andrea N. Strato*, 2 vols (Athens: no pub., 1986), here: ii, 17–39.

Ohta, Keiko, 'The Expansion of the Muslims and the Mountain Folk of Northern Syria: The Jarājima in the Umayyad Period', *Orient* 27 (1991), 74–94.

Ohta, Keiko, 'The Coptic Church and Coptic Communities in the Reign of al-Ma'mūn: A Study of the Social Context of the Bashmūric Revolt', *Annals of the Japan Association for Middle East Studies* 19 (2004), 87–116.

Sahner, Christian C., *Christian Martyrs under Islam: Religious Violence and the Making of the Muslim World* (Princeton, NJ: Princeton University Press, 2018).

Salibi, Kamal, *A House of Many Mansions: The History of Lebanon Reconsidered* (London: I. B. Tauris & Co., 1988).

Shaw, Brent D., 'Bandit Highlands and Lowland Peace: The Mountains of Isauria-Cilicia', *Journal of the Economic and Social History of the Orient* 33 (1990), 199–233, 237–70.

Woods, David, 'Corruption and Mistranslation: The Common Syriac Source on the Origins of the Mardaites', in Elizabeth Jeffreys (ed.), *Proceedings of the 21st International Congress of Byzantine Studies, 2006.* (Accessible online: http://www.

syriacstudies.com/AFSS/Syriac_Articles_in_English/Entries/2011/1/9_Corruption_and_Mistranslation__The_Common_Syriac_Source_on_the_Origin_of_the_Mardaites_David_Woods.html.)

Chapter 7

Allan, James W., *K. A. C. Creswell, A Short Account of Early Muslim Architecture. Revised and supplemented by James W. Allan* (Aldershot: Scolar Press, 1989).

Almagro, Martin, Luis Caballero, Juan Zozaya and Antonio Almagro, *Qusayr 'Amra: Residencia y Baños Omeyas en el Desierto de Jordania* (Madrid: Ministerio de Asuntos Exteriores, Dirección General de Relaciones Culturales; Junrta para la Protección de Monumentos y Bienes Culturales en el Exterior; Instituto Hispano-Árabe de Cultura, 1975).

Avni, Gideon, *The Byzantine–Islamic Transition in Palestine. An Archaeological Approach* (Oxford: Oxford University Press, 2014).

Bates, Michael L., 'The Coinage of Syria Under the Umayyads, 692–750 A.D.', in Muḥammad A. Bakhīt and Robert Schick (eds), *The History of Bilad al-Sham During the Umayyad Period, Fourth International Conference, 1987, Proceedings of the Third Symposium* ('Ammān: Bilad al-Sham History Committee, 1989), 195–228.

Behrens-Abouseif, Doris, 'The Lion-Gazelle Mosaic at Khirbat al-Mafjar', *Muqarnas* 14 (1997), 11–18.

Bettini, Sergio, 'Il Castello di Mschatta in Transgiordania nell' ambito dell' 'Arte di Potenza' tardoantica', in Sergio Bettini *et al.* (eds), *Anthemon. Scritti di archeologia e di antichità classiche in onore di Carlo Anti* (Florence: G. C. Sansoni, 1955), 321–66.

Claire, Andrée, and Marc Balty, *Pierres Chrétiennes de Syrie* (Paris: Éditions Eric Koehler, 1998).

Ettinghausen, Richard, *From Byzantium to Sasanian Iran and the Islamic World: Three Modes of Artistic Transference* (Leiden: Brill, 1972).

Flood, Finbarr B., and Gülru Necipoğlu (eds), *A Companion to Islamic Art and Architecture: Volume I. From the Prophet to the Mongols* (Hoboken, NJ: Wiley Blackwell, 2017).

Franz, Heinrich G., 'Die Stuckfenster im Qasr al-Hair al-Gharbi . . .', *Wissenschaftliche Annalen* 5 (1956), 465–83.

George, Alain, *The Umayyad Mosque of Damascus: Art, Faith and Empire in Early Islam* (London: Gingko, 2021).

Giudetti, Mattia, 'Sacred Spaces in Early Islam', in Flood and Necipoğlu, *Companion, I*, 130–50.

Grabar, Oleg, 'Ceremonial and Art at the Umayyad Court', PhD dissertation, Princeton University, 1954.

Grabar, Oleg, *The Dome of the Rock* (Cambridge, MA: Harvard University Press, 2006).

Hamilton, Robert W., *Khirbat al Mafjar: An Arabian Mansion in the Jordan Valley* (Oxford: Clarendon Press, 1959).

Hamilton, Robert W., 'Who built Khirbat al Mafjar?', *Levant* I (1969), 61–7.

Herzfeld, Ernst, 'Die Genesis der islamischen Kunst und das Mschatta-Problem', *Der Islam* I (1910), 27–63, 105–44 [for an English translation by Fritz Hillenbrand with assistance from Jonathan M. Bloom, see 'The Genesis of Islamic Art and the Mshatta Problem', in Jonathan M. Bloom (ed.), *Early Islamic Art and Architecture* (Aldershot: Variorum, 2002), 7–86].

Hillenbrand, Robert, 'Umayyad Woodwork in the Aqsa Mosque', in Johns, *Bayt al-Maqdis*, Part Two, 271–310.

Hillenbrand, Robert, 'Hishām's Balancing Act: The Case of Qaṣr al-Ḥair al-Gharbī', in Alain George and Andrew Marsham (eds), *Power, Patronage, and Memory in Early Islam. Perspectives on Umayyad Elites* (Oxford: Oxford University Press, 2018), 83–132.

Johns, Jeremy, *Bayt al-Maqdis: Jerusalem and Early Islam*, Oxford Studies in Islamic Art, IX, Part Two (Oxford: Oxford University Press, 1999).

Kendrick, Albert F., *Catalogue of Muhammadan Textiles of the Medieval Period* (London: HMSO, 1924).

Leal, Beatrice, ''Anjar: An Umayyad image of urbanism and its afterlife', in John Mitchell, John Moreland and Beatrice Leal (eds), *Encounters, Excavations and Argosies: Essays for Richard Hodges* (Oxford: Archaeopress, 2017), 172–89.

Levi, Doro, *Antioch Mosaic Pavements* I (Princeton, London and The Hague: Princeton University Press, Oxford University Press and Martinus Nijhoff, 1947).

Piccirillo, Michele, *The Mosaics of Jordan* ('Ammān: American Center of Oriental Research, 1993).

Raby, Julian, and Jeremy Johns (eds), *Bayt al-Maqdis: 'Abd al-Malik's Jerusalem. Part One*, Oxford Studies in Islamic Art IX (Oxford: Oxford University Press, 1992).

Sauvaget, Jean, 'Châteaux umayyades de Syrie: Contribution a l'étude de la colonisation arabe aux Ier et IIe siècles de l'hégire', *Revue des Études Islamiques* (1967), 1–52.

Schlumberger, Daniel, 'Deux fresques omeyyades', *Syria* XXV (1946–8/1–2), 86–102.

Schlumberger, Daniel, *Qasr el-Heir el Gharbi* (Paris: Librairie Orientale Paul Geuthner, 1986).

Talgam, Rina, *Mosaics of Faith. Floors of Pagans, Jews, Samaritans, Christians, and Muslims in the Holy Land* (Jerusalem and University Park, PA: Yad Ben-Zvi Press and The Pennsylvania State University Press, 2014).

Talgam, Rina, *The Stylistic Origins of Umayyad Sculpture and Architectural Decoration* (Wiesbaden: Harrassowitz Verlag, 2004).

Treadwell, Luke, 'The Formation of Religious and Caliphal Identity in the Umayyad Period: The Evidence of the Coinage', in Flood and Necipoğlu, *Companion, I*, 89–108.

Vibert-Guigue, Claude, and Ghazi Bisheh, *Les Peintures de Qusayr ʿAmra: Un bain omeyyade dans la* bâdiya *jordanienne* (Beirut: Institut Français du Proche-Orient, 2007).

Vogelsang-Eastwood, Gillian, 'Embroidered tiraz', in Gillian Vogelsang-Eastwood (ed.), *Encyclopedia of Embroidery from the Arab World* (London: Bloomsbury Academic, 2016), 140–50.

Volbach, W. Fritz, *Early Decorative Textiles*, trans. Yuri Gabriel (Feltham: Paul Hamlyn, 1969).

von Bothmer, Hans-Caspar Graf, 'Die Anfänge der Koranschreibung: Kodikologische und kunsthistorische Beobachtungen an den Koranfragmenten in Sanaa', in Hans-Caspar Graf von Bothmer, Karl-Heinz Ohlig und Gerd-Rüdiger Puin, 'Neue Wege der Koranforschung', *Magazin Forschung der Universität des Saarlandes* 1 (1999), 33–47.

Walker, John, *A catalogue of the Arab-Byzantine and post-reform Umaiyad coins* (London: Trustees of the British Museum, 1956).

Weber, Stefan, and Eva-Maria Troelenberg, 'Mschatta im Museum: Zur Geschichte eines bedeutenden Monuments frühislamischer Kunst', *Jahrbuch Preussischer Kulturbesitz* 46 (2010), 104–32.

Wellhausen, Julius, *The Arab Kingdom and its Fall*, trans. Margaret G. Weir (Beirut: Khayyats, 1963).

Williams, Elizabeth D., 'A Taste for Textiles: Designing Umayyad and ʿAbbāsid Interiors', in G. Bühl and E. D. Williams (eds), *Catalogue of the Textiles in the Dumbarton Oaks Byzantine Collection* (Washington, DC: Dumbarton Oaks, 2019), https://www.doaks.org/resources/textiles/essays/williams.

Chapter 8

Andriollo, Luisa, 'Aristocracy and literary production in the 10th century', in Aglae Pizzone (ed.), *The Author in Middle Byzantine Literature: Modes, Functions and Identities* (Berlin: De Gruyter, 2014), 119–38.

Andriollo, Luisa, *Constantinople et les provinces d'Asie Mineure, ixe–xie siècle: Administration impériale, sociétés locales et rôles de l'aristocratie* (Leuven: Peeters, 2017).

Andriollo, Luisa, 'Les Kourkouas (ɪxe–xɪe siècle)', *Studies in Byzantine Sigillography* 11 (2012), 57–87.

Bailey, Ryan, 'Arethas of Caesarea and the scholia on Philostratus' *Vita Apollonii* in *codex Laurentianus Pluteus* 69.33', *Byzantion* 86 (2016), 53–89.

Beaton, Roderick, and David Ricks (eds), *Digenes Akrites: New Approaches to Byzantine Heroic Poetry* (London: Routledge, 1993).

Caillet, Jean-Pierre, *et al.* (eds), *Des dieux civiques aux saints patrons (ive–viie siècle)* (Paris: Editions A&J Picard, 2015).

Eastmond, Anthony (ed.), *Eastern Approaches to Byzantium* (Aldershot: Ashgate, 2001).

Halkin, François, 'Saint Antoine le Jeune et Pétronas le vainqueur des Arabes en 863 (d'après un texte inédit)', *Analecta Bollandiana* 62 (1944), 187–225.

Kazhdan, Alexander, *A History of Byzantine Literature (850–1500)*, ed. C. Angelidi (Athens: National Hellenic Research Foundation, Institute for Byzantine Research, 2006).

Life of Antony the Younger, ed. Athanasios Papadopoulos-Kerameus, *Συλλογὴ παλαιστινιακῆς καὶ συριακῆς ἁγιολογίας* I, *Pravoslavnyi palestinskij sbornik* 19 (1907), 186–216.

The Life of Saint Basil the Younger, eds Denis F. Sullivan, A.-M. Talbot and S. McGrath (Washington, DC: Harvard University Press, 2014).

Magdalino, Paul, '*Digenes Akrites* and Byzantine Literature: The Twelfth Century Background to the Grottaferrata Version', in Roderick Beaton and David Ricks (eds), *Digenes Akrites: New Approaches to Byzantine Heroic Poetry* (London: Routledge, 1993), 1–14.

Métivier, Sophie, *Aristocratie et sainteté à Byzance (viiie-xie siècle)* (Brussels: Société des Bollandistes, 2019).

Métivier, Sophie, 'Peut-on parler d'une hagiographie aristocratique à Byzance (VIIIe-XIe siècle)?', in Antonio Rigo *et al.* (eds), *Byzantine Hagiography: Texts, Themes and Projects: Moscow, 12–14 November 2012* (Turnhout: Brepols, 2018), 179–99.

Rydén, Lennart, 'New Forms of Hagiography: Heroes and Saints', in *The 17th International Byzantine Congress: Major Papers* (New York: Aristide D. Caratzas Pub., 1986), 537–51.

Theophanes continuatus, ed. E. Bekker (Bonn, 1838).

Treadgold, Warren, *The Middle Byzantine Historians* (New York: Palgrave Macmillan, 2013).

Chapter 9

Primary sources

Bar Hebraeus, *The Chronography of Gregory Abu'l-Faraj 1225–1286*, trans. Ernest A. W. Budge (London: Oxford University Press, 1932).

Ibn al-Athīr, ʿIzz al-Dīn, *Al-Kāmil fīʾl-Tāʾrīkh*, ed. Carl J. Tornberg (repr. Beirut: Dār Bairūt, 1979).

Ibn al-Athīr, *Tāʾrīkh*, trans. Donald S. Richards as *The Annals of the Saljuq Turks: Selections from al-Kāmil fīʾl-Tāʾrīkh of ʿIzz al-Dīn Ibn al-Athīr* (London: RoutledgeCurzon, 2002).

Ibn al-Azraq, Aḥmad ibn Yūsuf ibn ʿAlī, *Tāʾrīkh Mayyāfāriqīn wa-Āmid*, ed. Badawī ʿAbd al-Laṭīf ʿAwad (Cairo: General Organisation for G.P.O.s, 1959).

Ibn Khallikān, Aḥmad b. Muḥammad Ibn Khallikān, *Kitāb Wafayāt al-Aʿyān*, trans. Baron William MacGuckin de Slane as *Ibn Khallikān's Biographical Dictionary*, 4 vols (repr. Beirut: Librairie du Liban, 1970).

Matthew of Edessa, *Parmutʾiwn*, trsnd. Édouard Dulaurier as *Chronique de Matthieu d'Edesse (962–1136) avec la Continuation de Grégoire le prêtre jusqu'en 1162 d'après trois manuscrits de la Bibliothèque Impériale de Paris* (Paris: A. Durand, 1858).

Michael Psellus, *Fourteen Byzantine Rulers: The Chronographia of Michael Psellus*, trans. Edgar R. A. Sewter (London: Penguin Books, 1966).

al-Muqaddasī, Shams al-Dīn Abū ʿAbdallāh Muḥammad b. Aḥmad, *Aḥsan al-taqāsīm fī maʿrifat al-aqālīm*, trans. Basil A. Collins as *The Best Divisions for Knowledge of the Regions* (Reading: Garnet Publishing, 2001).

Nāṣir-i Khusrau, *Nāṣer-e Khosraw's Book of Travels (Safarnāma)*, trans. Wheeler M. Thackston Jr (Albany, NY: Bibliotheca Persiana/State University of New York Press, 1986).

Secondary sources

Amedroz, Henry F., 'The Marwānid dynasty at Mayyāfāriqīn in the tenth and eleventh centuries A.D.', *Journal of the Royal Asiatic Society of Great Britain and Ireland* (1903), 123–54.

Beihammer, Alexander D., *Byzantium and the Emergence of Muslim–Turkish Anatolia, c.1040–1130* (Abingdon: Ashgate, 2017).

Blair, Sheila S., 'Decoration of city walls in the medieval Islamic world: The epigraphic message', in James D. Tracy (ed.), *City Walls: The Urban Enceinte in Global Perspective* (Cambridge: Cambridge University Press, 2000), 488–529.

Blaum, Paul A., 'A History of the Kurdish Marwānid Dynasty (983–1085), Part I', *Kurdish Studies: An International Journal* 5: 1–2 (1992), 54–68.

Blaum, Paul A., 'A History of the Kurdish Marwānid Dynasty (983–1085), Part II', *Kurdish Studies: An International Journal* 6: 1–2 (1993), 40–65.

Flury, Samuel, Islamische Schriftbänder. Amida – Diarbekr XI. Jahrhundert. Beilage zu den Jahresberichten des Gymnasiums, der Realschule und der Tochterschule in Basel. Schuljahr 1919/20 (Basel: Frobenius A.G., 1920).

Heidemann, Stefan, 'A new ruler of the Marwanid emirate in 401/1010 – and further considerations on the legitimizing power of regicide', *Aram* 9–10 (1997–8), 599–615.

Hillenbrand, Carole, 'Marwānids', *Encyclopaedia of Islam*², vi (Leiden: Brill, 1991), 626–7.

Hillenbrand, Carole, 'Mayyāfāriqīn', *Encyclopaedia of Islam*², vi (Leiden: Brill, 1991), 930–2.

Chapter 10

Βίος Ἀντωνίου τοῦ Νέου, e codice mutilo Atheniensi Suppl. 534, ed. Francois Halkin, 'Saint Antoine le Jeune et Pétronas le Vainqueur des Arabes en 863 (d'après un texte inédit)', *Analecta Bollandiana* 62 (1944), 187–225 (Greek text: 210–25) [= Francois Halkin, *Saints moines d'Orient* (London: Variorum Reprints, 1973), Nr. VIII].

al-Balâdhuri, *The Origins of the Islamic State being a translation from the Arabic accompanied with annotations, geographic and historic notes of the Kitâb futûḥ al-buldân of al-Imâm abu-l Abbâs Aḥmad ibn Jâbir al-Balâdhuri*, trans. Philip Khury Hitti (New York: Columbia University, 1916).

Beihammer, Alexander, 'Der harte Sturz des Bardas Skleros: Eine Fallstudie zu zwischenstaatlicher Kommunikation und Konfliktführung in der byzantinisch-arabischen Diplomatie des 10. Jahrhunderts', *Römisch Historische Mitteilungen* 45 (2003) 21–57.

Brandes, Wolfram, *Die Städte Kleinasiens im 7. und 8. Jahrhundert* (Berlin: Akademieverlag, 1989).

Brandes, Wolfram, *Finanzverwaltung in Krisenzeiten: Untersuchungen zur byzantinischen Administration im 6. – 9. Jahrhundert*, Forschungen zur byzantinischen Rechtsgeschichte 25 (Frankfurt: Löwenklau, 2002).

Codice diplomatico della repubblica di Genova dal 953 al 1163, ed. C. Imperiale di Sant' Angelo, vol. I. (Rome, 1936), vol. I–III (Rome, 1936, 1938, 1942).

Dölger, Franz, *Regesten der Kaiserurkunden des Oströmischen Reiches von 565–1453*, I. Teil, 2. Halbband: *Regesten von 867–1025*, zweite Auflage neu bearbeitet von Andreas E. Müller unter verantwortlicher Mitarbeit von Alexander Beihammer (München: C. H. Beck, 2003) (Corpus der griechischen Urkunden des Mittelalters und der neueren Zeit A/1,2).

Haldon, John Frederick, 'Military Service, Military Lands, and the Status of Soldiers: Current Problems and Interpretations', *Dumbarton Oaks Papers* 47 (1993), 1–67.

Haldon, John Frederick, 'Seventh-Century Continuities: the Ajnād and the "Thematic Myth"', in Averil Cameron (ed.), *The Byzantine and Islamic Near East, vol. 3:*

States, Resources, Armies, Studies in Late Antiquity and Early Islam 1 (Princeton, NJ: Darwin Press, 1995), 379–423.

Haldon, John Frederick, 'Theory and practice in tenth-century military administration: Chapters II, 44 and 45 of the *Book of Ceremonies*', *Travaux et Mémoires* 13 (2000), 201–352 (Greek text 203–35; Engl. trans. 202–34).

Ibn Šahrām, 'An Embassy from Baghdad to the Emperor Basil II', ed. H. F. Amedroz, *Journal of the Royal Asiatic Society* 46 (1914), 915–42.

Jouanno, Corinne, 'Digenis Akritis, the Two-Blood Border Lord', in Carolina Cupane and Bettina Krönung (eds), *Fictional Storytelling in the Medieval Eastern Mediterranean and Beyond* (Leiden: Brill, 2016), 260–84.

Kekaumenos, Strategikon, *Cecaumeni Strategicon et incerti scriptoris de officiis regiis libellus*, eds B. Wassiliewsky, V. Jernstedt (Petrograd, 1896). [New edition with Italian trans.: *Kekaumenos. Raccomandazioni e consigli di un galantuomo: Stratēgikon*, ed. and trans. Maria Dora Spadaro (Alessandria, 1998)]

Lemerle, Paul, 'L'histoire des Pauliciens d'Asie mineure d'après les sources grecques', *Travaux et Mémoires* 5 (1970), 1–144.

Lilie, Ralph-Johannes, *Die byzantinische Reaktion auf die Ausbreitung der Araber. Studien zur Strukturwandlung des byzantinischen Staates im 7. und 8. Jahrhundert*, Miscellanea Byzantina Monacensia 22 (München: Verlag des Byz. Instituts, 1976).

Lilie, Ralph-Johannes, *Handel und Politik zwischen dem Byzantinischen Reich und den italienischen Kommunen Venedig, Pisa und Genua in der Epoche der Komnenen und der Angeloi (1081–1204)* (Amsterdam: Hakkert, 1984). [Eine 2021 überarbeitete Fassung von diesem Werk ist online benutzbar unter Academia.edu.]

Lilie, Ralph-Johannes, 'Des Kaisers Macht und Ohnmacht: Zum Zerfall der Zentralgewalt in Byzanz vor dem vierten Kreuzzug', in Paul Speck and Ralph-Johannes Lilie, *Varia I*, Poikila Byzantina 4 (Bonn: Habelt, 1984), 9–120. [Eine 2021 überarbeitete Fassung von diesem Werk ist online benutzbar unter Academia.edu.]

Lilie, Ralph-Johannes, *Byzantium and the Crusader States 1096–1204*, trans. J. C. Morris and Jean E. Ridings (Oxford: Clarendon Press, 1993).

Lilie, Ralph-Johannes, 'Byzanz und der Islam: Konfrontation oder Koexistenz?', in Elisabeth Piltz (ed.), *Byzantium and Islam in Scandinavia*, Studies in Mediterranean Archaelogy 126 (Jonsered: P. Åströms Förlag, 1998), 13–26.

Lilie, Ralph-Johannes, 'The Byzantine–Arab Borderland from the 7th to the 9th Century', in Florin Curta (ed.), *Borders, Barriers, and Ethnogenesis. Frontiers in Late Antiquity and the Middle Ages* (Turnhout: Brepols, 2006), 13–21.

Lilie, Ralph-Johannes, *Einführung in die byzantinische Geschichte*, Urban Taschenbücher 617 (Stuttgart: Kohlhammer, 2007).

Partitio Terrarum Imperii Romaniae, ed. Antonio Carile, *Studi Veneziani* 7 (1965), 125–305.

Prosopographie der mittelbyzantinischen Zeit (= *PmbZ*). *Erste Abteilung (641–867)*, Friedhelm Winkelmanns and Ralph-Johannes Lilie *et al.*, 7 vols (Berlin: De Gruyter, 1998–2002); *Zweite Abteilung (867–1025)*, 9 vols (Berlin: De Gruyter, 2009–13). [Also available online at http://www.pom.bbaw.de/pmbz.]

Theophanes Continuatus, in *Theophanes Continuatus, Ioannes Cameniata, Symeon Magister, Georgius Monachus*, ex rec. I. Bekkeri (Bonn, 1838), 1–481.

Vryonis Jr, Speros, 'Nomadization and Islamization in Asia Minor', *Dumbarton Oaks Papers* 29 (1975), 41–71.

Vučetić, Martin Marko, 'Das Abkommen zwischen Kaiser Manuēl I. Komnēnos und Sultan Kiliç Arslan II. (1161/1162): Mechanismen zur Absicherung von Verträgen und ihr Scheitern', in Georg Jostkleigrewe and Gesa Wilangowsky (eds), *Der Bruch des Vertrages: Die Verbindlichkeit spätmittelalterlicher Diplomatie und ihre Grenzen*, Zeitschrift für Historische Forschung 55 (Berlin: Duncker & Humblot, 2018), 175–202.

Chapter 11

Āqsarā'ī, *Musāmarat al-Akhbār*, ed. Osman Turan (Ankara: Türk Tarih Kurumu, 1944).

Beihammer, Alexander D., 'Defection across the Border of Islam and Christianity: Apostasy and Cross-Cultural Interaction in Byzantine–Seljuk Relations', *Speculum* 86: 3 (July 2011), 597–651.

Bosworth, C. Edmund, 'The City of Tarsus and the Arab–Byzantine Frontiers in Early and Middle ʿAbbāsid Times', *Oriens* 33 (1992), 268–86.

Cahen, Claude, *Pre-Ottoman Turkey: A General Survey of the Material and Spiritual Culture and History c. 1071–1330* (New York: Taplinger, 1968).

Cahen, Claude, *La Turquie pré-ottomane* (Istanbul: IFEA, 1988).

Eger, Asa, *The Islamic–Byzantine Frontier: Interaction and Exchange Among Muslim and Christian Communities* (London: I. B. Tauris, 2017).

Ibn Bībī, *al-Awāmir al-ʿAlāʾiyya fiʾl-Umūr al-ʿAlāʾiyya*, ed. Zhaleh Motahiddin (Tehran, 2011).

Korobeinikov, Dimitri, *Byzantium and the Turks in the Thirteenth Century* (Oxford: Oxford University Press, 2014).

Korobeinikov, Dimitri, 'The Byzantine–Seljuk Border in Times of Trouble: Laodikeia in 1174–1204', in Alicia Simpson (ed.), *Byzantium 1180–1204: 'The Sad Quarter of a Century'?* (Athens: National Hellenic Research Foundation, 2015), 49–81.

Korobeinikov, Dimitri, 'The Formation of the Turkish Principalities in the Boundary Zone: From the Emirate of Denizli to the Beylik of Menteshe (1256–1302)', in Adnan Çevik and Murat Keçiş (eds), *Menteşeoğulları Tarihi* (Ankara: Türk Tarih Kurumu, 2016), 65–76.

Pancaroğlu, Oya, Çorum Haşan Caves, Borderlands and Configurations of Sacred Topography in Medieval Anatolia', *Mésogeios* 25–6 (2005), 249–81.

Peacock, A. C. S., 'The Seljuk Sultanate of Rūm and the Turkmen of the Byzantine Frontier, 1206–1279', *al-Masāq* 26 (2014), 267–87.

Peacock, A. C. S., *Islam, Literature and Society in Mongol Anatolia* (Cambridge: Cambridge University Press, 2019).

Turan, Osman, *Selçuklular Zamanında Türkiye: Siyâsi Tarih Alp Arslan'dan Osman Gazi'ye (1071–1328)* (Istanbul: Ötüken, 1971).

Wittek, Paul, *Das Fürstentum Mentesche: Studie zur Geschichte Westkleinasiens im 13.–15. Jh.* (Istanbul, 1934).

Wittek, Paul, 'Deux chapitres de l'histoire des Turcs de Roum', *Byzantion* 11 (1936), 285–319; Engl. trans. 'Two Chapters in the History of Rum', in Paul Wittek, *The Rise of the Ottoman Empire: Studies on the History of Turkey, thirteenth to fifteenth centuries*, ed. Colin Heywood (London: Routledge, 2015), 97–124.

Yıldız, Sara Nur, 'Reconceptualizing the Seljuk–Cilician Frontier: Armenians, Latins and Turks in Conflict and Alliance during the Early Thirteenth Century', in Florin Curta (ed.), *Borders, Barriers, and Ethnogenesis: Frontiers in Late Antiquity and the Middle Ages* (Turnhout: Brepols, 2005), 191–220.

Zachariadou, Elizabeth, 'Udj', *Encyclopaedia of Islam, 2nd edn* (*EI*^{2}), 12 vols, eds P. J. Bearman *et al.* (Leiden: E. J. Brill, 1960–2005).

INDEX

Abbasid caliphs, 30–1, 55, 147
  and the *'Awāṣim*, 71, 73, 75
  Caucasia, 87
  Christian resistance, 162, 163
  dissolution of power, 226
  Ibn Sa'īd's text on, 265–6
  jihad and, 37
  partisans of the Revolution, 161, 162
  policy of frontier consolidation, 53
  revolution, 750, 24, 87
  warfare and, 41
'Abd al-Malik, Caliph, 21, 84, 85, 137, 139–42, 144, 145
Abū 'Ubayda, 132
adaptation, Umayyad art, 181–94
administrative frontiers/organisation, 36, 37, 38, 58, 61, 277–80; *see also* *'Awāṣim*
agrarian economy, 50, 51–2
Ahrweiler, Hélène, 36, 38
akritai, 248, 263, 266
Akroinon, battle of, 54, 207, 208
'Alā' al-Dīn Kayqubād I, 272–3, 278
Aleppo, 13, 59–60, 63, 64, 115
  Romans treaty with emirate of, 111
  small dynasties, 227
al-Jurjūma, 139, 145
alliances *see* treaties and alliances, Arab–Byzantine
al-Muwaqqar, inscription on cistern, 196–9
Amanus, 131–2
Āmid, building works, 235, 236
Amorion, 45, 207
Anatolia, 13, 16, 19, 28, 271
  agrarian economy, 50, 51–2
  aristocracy, 218
  First Crusade, 66
  fortification works, 44–5
  Islamisation/Turkification of, 52–3, 268–9
  political fragmentation and cultural-religious diversity, 68

Anatolia (*cont.*)
Seljuk apocalyptic texts, 284–8
settlement patterns, 43–4
weather conditions, 49
western frontier, 67
Andriollo, Luisa, 213–14, 216, 218n
ʿAnjar, 174, 176, 177
Antalya, 270
Antioch, 13, 60, 61, 132
Antony the Younger, 221–2, 223–4, 257–8
apocalyptic works, Muslim, 20–1, 284–8
Aqsarāʾī, 279–80
Arab heroes, 208–9
Arab raids, and settlement patterns, 45–6
Arab–Byzantine coalitions and cross-border relations, 58
Arabic (language), 75, 98
Arabic sources, Syrian chronicle, 275
archaeological research, 42–3, 44, 45, 47–8
architecture and decoration *see* Umayyad art/architecture
Arethas, 217
Argyros, Eustathius, 210, 211
aristocracy, 58, 218, 260–4
agricultural estates, 51–2
Armenian, 65
Byzantine, 37, 65, 219, 252
Constantinople, 258–9
East-Anatolian origin, 224
and hagiography, 216, 218
Armenia/Armenians, 53, 61, 65–6, 80, 153, 157, 226, 253
allegiance switched to caliphate, 85
Christian pro-Byzantine coalition, 82–3
Inner and Outer, 94–5
and the Jarājima, 150
Armīniyya, 80
Arrān, 80, 83, 91, 92
ascetism (*zuhd*), 22
Asia Minor, 28, 37, 39, 60, 67, 253–4
Awāṣim, 71–7
Ayyubids, 271, 272–3
Azerbaijan, 80, 93

Bābak, 90, 97
Baghdad, 62, 76–7, 237; *see also* Abbasid caliphs
Bagratuni family, 85, 87, 95, 99
Bailey, Ryan, 217
Baʿlabakk, Great Temple, 186
Balādhurī, al-, 73–4, 131, 133, 148, 149
banditry, 139, 152, 156
Banū Aḥrār of Sanaa, 130, 134
Bardas Phokas, 252, 262
Bardas Skleros, 252, 262
Basil I, Emperor, 57, 248
Basil II, Emperor, 60, 62, 107–8, 119, 235, 251, 262
Basil Phokas *see* Phokades
Basil Skleros *see* Skleroi
Basil the Younger, 215, 220
Basileios Boioannes, 111
bath houses and halls, 177–8, 187–9, 193, 194–5, 201
Baṭṭāl Ghāzī, cult of, 266, 268, 273, 281, 283
Baybars, Mamluk sultan, 274

Bisson, Thomas, 31
Bonner, Michael, 37, 71–2, 75
Book of Ceremonies, 92, 93–4
Book of the Eparch, 116
border beyliks, 32
border guards, 118, 119–21
borders
  and 'fluid zones of interaction', 102–7
  as function of institutions, 122
  Romans understanding of, 102, 106–7
  as state artefacts, 107–22
Bughā, general, 90–1, 92
Bukhārī, al-, 20
Bulgarians, 109–10, 120, 121, 259–60
Buwayhids, 62
Būyids, 159, 236
Byzantine aristocracy, 37, 65, 252
Byzantine identity, 38
Byzantium/Byzantines
  Arab allies, 63–4
  art, 185
  and Caucasia, 79
  controlling border regions, 244–5
  early Muslim apocalyptic thought on, 19–21
  emperor at Mayyāfāriqīn, 237
  foreign trade, 117
  frontier communities, depictions of, 35–6
  generals. *see* heroes
  and the Jarājima, 125–6, 144, 157–60
  lack of control of the provinces, 260–4
  Lascarids, 275–6
  militarisation and expansion, 57–64, 255–6
  Muslim conquest of, 16, 17, 28, 32, 67
  population policy, 256, 257
  reconquista, 13–14, 34, 249
  and the Seljuks, 253, 256
  and Syria, 21, 159–60, 246
  theme organisation, 249–51
  trade policy, 259–60
  see also Christianity; Roman Empire; Seljuk Turks/dynasty; *individual names of emperors*

Caesarea, 44, 46
caliphate/caliphs, 18–19
  and Caucasia, 79–80, 85–6, 87
  death of Muʿāwiya, and civil war, 54
  and *futuwwa*, 29–31
  jihad and, 22
  and the pious ascetics, 23
  political collapse, 26
  weakness of, ninth–tenth centuries, 92, 95, 97
  see also individual names of caliphate/caliphs
Canard, Marius, 71, 155, 205
Cappadocia, 46–7, 51, 57, 66, 218, 252
caravanserais, 282
Caucasia
  and the caliphate, 79–80, 83, 85–6, 87
  Christian pro-Byzantine coalition, 82–3
  and local lords of, 88–96
  native elites and Muslim newcomers, 85, 87–8
  settlement patterns, 87–8
  as in-between zone, 98
Cave of the Seven Sleepers, 268, 282
Charpezikion, 250–1

chora, 48, 49
Christianity
ascetism, 23
Byzantine, 38
Caucasia, 80, 82–3, 98
Coptic uprisings, 162–3
Jarājima and, 129, 155–6, 157, 164
Syria and, 13, 160
see also Crusades
Chronicle of Zuqnīn, 163
Church of the Holy Sepulchre, 173, 174, 175
Cilicia, 47, 51, 261, 270
cities, provincial, 43–4; *see also* fortified cities and fortresses
climatic conditions/trends, 49
coalitions and cross-border relations (Byzantine–Arab), 58
Cobb, Paul, 161
coinage, 170, 179, 199
Constans, Emperor, 54
Constans II, Emperor, 83
Constantine Porphyrogenitus, 153–4
Constantine Porphyrogenitus, Emperor, 92–3
Constantine V, 247
Constantinople, 13, 24, 153, 276
access to, 244
apocalytic texts, 285
aristocracy, 258–9
and Cappadocia, 46
foreign trade, 114, 115, 116
Haghia Sophia, 185
hagiographers, 216–17, 218
Muslim conquest of (1453), 11, 17
peace treaty, 1000, 63
Cook, David, 20, 285
Council of Nicaea II, 787, 118
Creswell, K. A. C., 166–7, 189–90
Crusades, 16, 28–9, 31–2, 53, 66, 253
Cyprus, 13, 109–10, 140, 158

Dagron, Gilbert, 204–5
Damascus
Great Mosque of, 186–7, 189–90
Greater Syria, 169
Danishmendids, 278
Darband, 81, 86
Decker, Michael, 42, 45
decoration, monuments *see* Umayyad art/architecture
demographic patterns, 41, 43, 46, 50, 53
Denizli, 274–5, 277, 280, 282
Digenis Akritas (Byzantine epic), 35, 205–6, 219–20, 222, 248, 283
diplomacy, 56–7, 63, 64, 234–5
Diyār Bakr, 227, 237; *see also* Marwānids
Dome of the Rock, Jerusalem, 169, 172–3, 184–5, 186
Doukas, Constantine, 210, 215, 217
doukata, 60

economy, urban, 43–4
Eger, Asa, 37–8, 105–6
Egypt, 63, 73, 119, 158, 162–3, 236, 273
Elbistan, 282
elites, Caucasian, 88–96, 98–9
emirs, 219
emperors *see individual names of emperors*
Encyclopaedia of Islam, 71, 277–8

environmental-paleoclimatic research, 42, 49–50
epics, 204–5, 283–4; *see also* *Digenis Akritas* (Byzantine epic); hagiography
epigraphy, 170
Escorial Taktikon, 61
Euchaita, 44
Euphrates frontier, 273–4, 290; *see also* Abbasid caliphs
Eustathius Argyros, 211

Fatimids, 62–3, 64, 120; *see also* Egypt
feudalism *see futuwwa*
fiscal centralisation, and the *ʿAwāṣim*, 76–7
fiscal frontiers, 38
floor painting, Greater Syria, 190–2
'fluidity', 102–7, 123–4
fortified cities and fortresses, 44–5, 47, 245–6
  Roman, Syria, 181–4
  terminological variety, 48–9
  see also ʿAwāṣim
frontier communities, depictions of, 35
frontier fort, as model, 195–6; *see also* fortified cities and fortresses
frontiers, notions of, 38
futuwwa, 29–31

geographers, on the *ʿAwāṣim*, 73–6
Georgia/Georgians, 58, 60, 61, 62, 80, 84, 140, 226, 270
ghazawāt, 24
ghazw, 27
Ghiyāth al-Dīn Kaykhusraw I, 272–3, 275, 276–7

Grabar, Oleg, 167
Greatrex, Geoffrey, 101, 107
Grégoire, Henri, 204
Gregorios Dekapolites (saint), 121

Ḥadath al-Ḥamrāʾ, 274
hadith scholars, 22
Haghia Sophia, Constantinople, 185, 197, 199
hagiography, 215–16, 219–20, 222, 258
Ḥākim, al-, Caliph, 120
Haldon, John, 36, 43, 118, 121
Ḥamdānids of Aleppo, 59, 60
Hamilton, Robert W., 171
Ḥaram al-Sharīf, 174, 175
Harawī, al-, 281, 283
Hasanwayhids, 226, 227
heroes, 206–25
Hillenbrand, Carole, 28
Honigmann, Ernst, 35
horia, 107–8, 109
Howard-Johnston, James, 136
Hunger, Herbert, 34–5
hunting baths, 177, 178
hydraulic installations, 169

Ibn ʿAbd al-Ẓāhir, 274
Ibn al-ʿAdīm, 130
Ibn al-Athīr, 142
Ibn al-Azraq al-Fāriqī, 227–9, 231, 232, 235, 236–7, 240–1
Ibn al-Faqīh, 135
Ibn al-Mubārak, ʿAbdallāh, 20
Ibn al-Qilāʿī, 148–9
Ibn ʿAsākir, 139, 141, 146, 161
Ibn Bībī, 275–6, 277, 278, 280, 285

Ibn Ḥawqal, Abū'l-Qāṣsm al-Naṣībī, 26, 75, 94–5, 98, 269
Ibn Jahīr, 239, 242
Ibn Khurradādhbih, 74–5
ideological frontiers, 38
Ilyās, 149–50
imitation, Umayyad art, 172–81
inscriptions
on cistern, al-Muwaqqar, 196–9
Mayyāfāriqīn, 231
Āmid, 235
Iran *see* Persian Empire; Sasanian Empire
Iraq, 61
Isauria/Isaurians, 131–2
Ishkhānik, lord of Shakkī, 95, 96
Islam
and the Byzantine empire, 19–20
and conquest of Constantinople, 17
conversions to, 255
government, duty of, 17–18
proto-Sunni reformation of, 22–6, 27
see also caliphate/caliphs; Umayyad art/architecture

Jarājima
as Arab allies, 142, 144
Arab conquest and, 131–3
and the Byzantines, 157–60, 161, 164
displacement, 145
and the Marada, 151–3
origins, 127–31, 155–7
reigns of ʿAbd al-Malik and Justinian II, 137–42
revolt against financial abuse, 162
social composition of, 133–5
and 'Theodore', 146–7
and the Umayyads, 135–7
Jarrāḥ clan (Arabs), 63–4
Jerusalem, 13
Dome of the Rock, 172–3, 184–6
Holy Sepulchre, 173–4, 175
jihad, 18, 20, 25, 55, 60, 77
Abbasid–Byzantine frontier, 269
and Hārūn al-Rashīd, 72
Muslim military elites and, 37
privatising of, 22
and *thughūr*, 26–7
John of Dadai, 163–4
John Vatatzes, 275
Jurzān *see* Georgia/Georgians
Justinian II, Emperor, 84–5, 137, 139–40, 142

Kaldellis, Anthony, 52
Kamakha, 57
Kennedy, Hugh, 36, 96, 242
Khazars, 79, 84, 86, 88, 96–7, 98
Khirbat al-Mafjar, bath hall, 187–9, 193, 194–5, 201
Kiskisos, 47
Konya, 66, 67, 68, 276–7
Köpek, 273
Kourkouas, John, 93, 211–15, 219, 224
Kurds/Kurdish, dynasties, 63, 226–7, 229–30

landownership
and agrarian economy, 51–2
Roman imperial law, 111–12
Lascarids, 272, 273, 275–6

Lebanese chroniclers, 149
Lebanon, 153
Libya, hunting baths, 177, 178
literary sources
bias in, 41–2
interpretation of, 39–40
Liudprand of Cremona, 284–5
living conditions, borderland, 41–52
local powers, 88–96, 248–9, 255; *see also* aristocracy; *strategos*
Loulon, 48

Macedonian regime, 51, 58
Maghribī, Abū'l-Qāsim al-, 232, 239
Maghribī, Ibn Sa'īd, al-, 265–6, 281
malḥamas, 284–7
Manṣūr, al-, 153, 242
Manuel, 216, 217
manuscript production, Umayyad, 167
Manzikert, battle of, 16, 28, 52–3
Marada, 151–3
Mardaites, 125, 128, 131, 153–5
Maronite Church, 148
Maronites, 149, 151–2, 155
martyrs, Byzantine, 207–8
Marwān, Caliph, 180
Marwānids, 227–42
diplomacy and ceremony, 234–7
military and legitimising aspects, 231–4
other aspects, 238–42
Marzubān ibn Muḥammad ibn Musāfir al-Sallār, 94
Maslama ibn 'Abd al-Malik, 86, 134, 143, 145, 150
Mas'ūdī, 'Alī b. al-Ḥusayn, al-, 139, 208–9
Maymūn al-Jurjumānī, 143–4
Mayyāfāriqīn, 163–4, 229, 231–4, 236–8
Melias, 219
Melitene, 58, 61
Mesopotamia
Abbasid period, 163
Byzantine expansion, 53, 58, 59, 61, 64, 219, 225
local powers in, 264
military districts (*kleisourai*), 56–9
military organisation/society, 36, 38, 39–40, 43–5, 47–9; *see also* Byzantium/Byzantines; jihad
military saints, 208–9, 257–8; *see also* heroes; saints
military strongholds *see* fortified cities and fortresses
military treatise, on *Skirmishing*, 48
Mirdāsids of Aleppo, 64
Mokissos, 45, 46–7
monastic centres, 51–2
Mongols, 273–4
mosaic floors, 190, 201–2
Mshattā, palace, 186, 187, 195–6
Mu'āwiya, Caliph, 82, 83
Muḥammad b. Abī l-Sāj Dīwdād, 93
Mumahhid al-Dawla, 230, 231, 235–6
Muqaddasī, al-, 232
Mutanabbī, al-, 75
Mu'taṣim, al-, Caliph, 90, 249

Nāṣir, al- (Caliph), 29–31
Nāsir-i Khusrau, 233–4
Nasr al-Dawla, 229, 230, 232, 236–7, 238
death, 241–2
governance and defence, 238–9
overview, 241

Niewohner, Philipp, 45
Nikephoros II Phokas, Emperor (963–9), 48, 59
nomads, 227, 229
  Turkish, 66, 68, 240, 254, 256
  see also Khazars

Oikonomides, Nicolas, 61
Ottoman dynasty, 32, 270

paleoclimatic studies *see* environmental-paleoclimatic research
Palestine, 63, 133, 220, 221
papal envoys, and border control, 119–20
Paphlagonia, 218
Paulicians, 57, 248
  Persian Empire, 13, 79, 130, 226; *see also* Sasanian Empire
Persis, 93
Petronas, 221, 223, 224
Philostratus, 217
Phokades, 51, 52, 60
Phokas family, 252, 262
Podandos, 47
polis ('city'), 48–9
political frontiers, 38
pollen analysis, 49, 50–1
population policy, Byzantine, 247, 256, 257
prisoner exchanges, 47, 56–7
Psellus, Michael, 234

Qāḍī, 276–7
Qasr al-Ḥair al-Gharbī, 182, 184, 190–2, 193–4
Qinnasrīn, 73, 74–5
Qusair ʿAmra, 177–8

raiding, culture of, 265–6, 267; *see also* banditry; *ghazawāt*; jihad
Rashīd, Hārūn, al- (Caliph), 22, 55, 71–2, 73, 76–7, 88
Rawwād ibn al-Muthannā, al-, 88
Risāla fī Amr al-Mahdī, 287–8
Rodandos, 47, 251
Roman Empire/Romans
  and borders, 102, 106–7
  Christianity and, 12
  landownership and control, 56, 111–12
  on trade and exports, 114–18
  see also Byzantium/Byzantines; taxation
Roman triumphal arch, 187–8
Romanos IV Diogenes, Emperor, 66

Ṣadr al-Dīn al-Qunawī, 287
Sahl ibn Sunbāṭ, 89–91, 96, 97
saints, 118, 121–2, 208–9, 215, 220, 223, 257–8
Sājids, 94
Sasanian Empire, 12–13, 18–19, 78–9, 130, 160, 170
scholion, 217–18
Sebasteia, 44, 57
Seleucia, 56–7
Seljuk Turks/dynasty, 15–16, 39, 57, 60, 61–2, 65, 66, 67
  campaigns against the Ayyubids, 273
  chronicles on clashes with Byzantium, 275
  culture of raiding, 265–6, 267
  defeat of Byzantium, 16, 28, 253
  Diyār Bakr province, 242
  economic integration, 282–3

frontier warfare against Byzantium, 269
jihad and, 27–8
shrines and pilgrimages, 281–2
sources on Byzantine–Seljuq border clashes, 275
Sunnism and, 18n
see also Turkish military men
settlement patterns, 37–8, 43–4, 47, 76, 87–8; *see also* fortified cities and fortresses
Shaddādids, 63, 226
Shidyāq, Ṭannūs ibn Yūsuf, al-, 151–3
Shoemaker, Stephen, 20
sigillia (or *sphragides*), 121
silk, 180–1
Skleroi, 51, 52, 60
Skleros, Bardas, 107–8
Skylitzes, John, 48
slaves, 143–4, 156, 157
socio-economic structures, 36, 41–52, 67; *see also* settlement patterns
strategos, military, 249–51, 262
Sunnism, 18n
proto-Sunnism, 22–6, 27
Syria, 13, 275
and the Abbasids, 53
Byzantine expansion, 52, 225
Christians in, 53, 160
Crusaders in, 29
Fatimids and, 63
Islamic conquest of, 21, 246–7
Islamic–Byzantine borderlands, 13
Mamluk sultanate, 273
reigns of ʿAbd al-Malik and Justinian II, 137–42
Roman–Byzantine border control, 118, 119
Seljuks and, 15, 61, 272
see also Jarājima; Umayyad art/architecture

Ṭabarī, al-, 72, 75
tagmata, 257
taʾrīkh narratives, and the *ʿAwāṣim*, 72–3
Taron, 59, 61
Tarsus, 13, 26, 269
taxation, 74–5, 94
Caucasia, 87
Christian uprisings, 162
and the Jarājima, 150
Muslim conquerors, 133
Roman–Byzantine, 112, 113–14
Seljuk Turks/dynasty, 282–3
and the *thughūr*, 76
textiles, 167, 180–1
themes (provinces), 53–4, 56, 57, 59, 60–1, 249–51, 257
Theodore, 126, 145–50, 151, 153, 156, 161
Theodore Rshtuni, prince of Armenia, 82
Theodosioupolis, 44, 58, 59
Theophanes the Confessor, chronicle of, 53, 136, 140–1, 142, 146–7, 149, 156, 161, 207
Theophilos, 207, 215
thughūr, 26–7, 72, 75, 76
Tiflīs (modern Tblisi), 80
Tiflīsī, Ḥubaysh-i, 285–7
Timgad, Algeria, 176
Tirmidhī-al, *Qāḍī*, 276–7
trade networks, cross-border, 69, 114–19
trade policy, Byzantine, 259–60
Transcaucasia, 60, 61

transformation, Umayyad art, 194–200
Trapp, Erich, 219–20
travel permits, 119–22
Treadgold, Warren, 214
treaties and alliances, Arab–Byzantine, 58, 59, 60, 63, 111
685–6, 140, 142
716, 109, 121
816, 109, 121
Turco-Mongols, 28, 32
Turkish heroic tales, 35
Turkish military men, 88, 267, 268–9; *see also* Seljuk Turks/dynasty
Turkmen, 280–1
Ṭuwāna, battle of, 142–3, 144
Tyana, 46

ūj regions, administration of, 277–80
Umayyad art/architecture, 166–200
guiding principles, 171–96
historical context, 169–70
and the Mediterranean tradition, 170–1
Umayyad caliphate, 54, 72, 87, 143, 179
and the Jarājima, 125–6, 135–7, 142, 164
and the material culture of Greater Syria, 172

Vardanakert, battle of, 85
Vasiliev, Alexander A., 204
vassalages, 62, 82, 251
Vatatzes, John, 275
Venice, 117, 260
villas, Roman, 169, 182, 183
viziers, 232, 239
volunteers (*murābiṭūn*), Muslim, 269

*waqfiyya*s, 283
warfare
1030s, 64
and the ʿ*Awāṣim*, 72, 77
patterns of, 41
second Muslim civil war, 680–692, 83–4
supply needs, 66
see also Crusades; *specific names of battles*
Wittek, Paul, 266–9, 279, 290

Yaʿqūbī, Ibn Wāḍiḥ, al-, 73
Yāqūt al-Ḥamawī, 75, 142
Yemen, 87–8, 130, 135, 269

Zachariadou, Elizabeth, 278, 279